# THE NEW INDUSTRIAL REVOLUTION

PETER MARSH is former manufacturing editor for the *Financial Times*.

# THE NEW INDUSTRIAL REVOLUTION

CONSUMERS, GLOBALIZATION AND
THE END OF MASS PRODUCTION

## PETER MARSH

YALE UNIVERSITY PRESS
NEW HAVEN AND LONDON

For information about this and other Yale University Press publications, please contact:
U.S. Office: sales.press@yale.edu   www.yalebooks.com
Europe Office: sales @yaleup.co.uk   www.yalebooks.co.uk

Set in Minion Pro by IDSUK (Data Connection) Ltd
Printed in Great Britain by Hobbs the Printers Ltd, Totton, Hampshire

Library of Congress Cataloging-in-Publication Data

Marsh, Peter, 1952
   The new industrial revolution: consumers, globalization and the end of mass production / Peter Marsh.
      p. cm.
   ISBN 978-0-300-11777-6 (cl : alk. paper)
1. Industrialization—History—21st century.   2. Manufacturing industries—Technological innovations.   3. Consumption (Economics)—Social aspects.   4. Consumers' preferences.   5. Globalization—Economic aspects.   I. Title.
   HD2321.M237 2012
   338—dc23
                                                                    2012009769

A catalogue record for this book is available from the British Library.

ISBN 978–0–300–19723–5 (pbk)

10 9 8 7 6 5 4 3 2 1

# Contents

# Figures

# Preface

This book would have been impossible to write without the assistance of many people. Special thanks should be given to my former colleagues at the *Financial Times*, which I left in early 2013 after nearly 30 years. For much of my time there I wrote about industrial companies. The information I acquired in thousands of conversations in 30 countries furnished me with many anecdotes and experiences that provided the framework for the book. Without my work there, gaining access to these people would have been difficult, if not impossible.

Particular thanks are due to the four editors of the *Financial Times* during the time I worked there. Sir Geoffrey Owen, Sir Richard Lambert, Andrew Gowers and Lionel Barber have all been supportive. Thanks also to Arthur Goodhart, my literary agent while the book was being conceived and written. In the late 1990s I talked to Arthur about a work on global manufacturing. I felt a comprehensive book on this topic had yet to be written, yet deserved to be and that I was in a good position to try to do it. As the book went through many changes, Arthur was a great source of guidance. Showing huge faith in my ability to finish the book, plus patience at the many delays, was Robert Baldock of Yale University Press.

People in many companies and other organizations have provided me with what amounts to extended tutorials on different areas of manufacturing. I should give special mention to Giovanni Arvedi, Mike Baunton,

Daniel Collins, Eddie Davies, the late John Diebold, Wolfgang Eder, Sir Mike Gregory, Federico Mazzolari, Peter Marcus, Heinrich von Pierer, Hermann Simon, Martin Temple, the late Walter Stanners and Alan Wood.

My friend Peter Chatterton and my brother David Marsh have provided encouragement. Stephen Bayley, Bob Bischof, Steve Boorman, Andrew Cook, Gideon Franklin, Branko Moeys, Chris Rea and Hal Sirkin read all or part of the book and gave me useful feedback. On economic data I received much help from Prem Premakumar and Mark Killion at IHS Global Insight. For details of steel production going back to 1900, thanks to Steve Mackrell and Phil Hunt at the International Steel Statistics Bureau.

I gained useful guidance on economic trends throughout history from Bob Allen, Steve Broadberry, Kenneth Carlaw, Nick Crafts, Ruth Lea, Tim Leunig, Richard Lipsey, Joel Mokyr, Nathaniel Rosenberg, Bob Rowthorn, Andrew Sharpe, Eddy Szirmai and Tony Wrigley. Fridolin Krausmann was extremely helpful on data related to working out the environmental impact of manufacturing through its use of materials. Any errors and failures to draw the correct conclusions from both the past and present are down to me. Throughout this long project, I have gained much from the love and support of my wife Nikki and sons Christopher and Jonathan.

Peter Marsh, London, July 2013

# CHAPTER 1

# The growth machine

## In the beginning

> 'Gold is for the mistress – silver for the maid –
> Copper for the craftsman cunning at his trade.'
> 'Good!' said the Baron, sitting in his hall,
> 'But Iron – Cold Iron – is master of them all.'[1]

So wrote Rudyard Kipling, the celebrated English writer who – for much of his life – lived in the home of a seventeenth-century ironmaster. Kipling's words are as true today as they were when he was at the peak of his fame in the early 1900s and became the youngest ever person to receive the Nobel Prize for Literature. Since the beginning of civilization to 2011, the human race has created goods containing about 43 billion tonnes of iron.[2] Of this huge amount of metal, which has ended up in products from nuclear reactors to children's toys, almost half has been made since 1990. Most iron now used reaches its final form as steel, a tougher and stronger form of the metal containing traces of carbon.

Of the earth's mass of some 6,000 billion billion tonnes, about a third – so scientists estimate – is iron.[3] Most of it is too deeply buried to be accessible. Even so, there is enough iron available fairly close to the surface to keep the world's steel plants fed with raw materials for the next billion years, assuming 2011 rates of output.[4] Iron is almost always found as a compound. The most common are iron oxides, found in minerals such as hematite and magnetite. In these materials, iron and oxygen are linked in different combinations. To make iron from iron oxide requires a process called smelting. Smelting is what happens when minerals containing oxide-based ores are heated in a furnace with charcoal. In a chemical process called reduction, the charcoal combines with oxygen in the ore, producing carbon dioxide, and leaving the metal in a close to pure state.

Smelting has been known about for 5,000 years. It was originally useful in making copper and tin, the constituents of bronze. But it was a long time before anyone used smelting to make iron in large quantities. The reason for this lies in iron's chemical and physical characteristics. The temperature required for a smelting reaction is related to the melting point of the metal. Iron melts at 1,530 degrees centigrade, much higher than the equivalent temperature for copper or tin. Also, removing impurities, resulting from the presence in the ore of extraneous substances such as assorted clays and minerals, is more difficult in the case of iron than for other metals.

A breakthrough was made around 1200 BCE, probably either in or close to Mesopotamia – the name then for the region loosely centred on modern Iraq. Methods were devised to keep furnaces hot enough – probably at about 1,200 degrees centigrade – to make the iron smelting process work.[5] Furthermore, better processes were developed for separating out the impurities – called 'slag' – through pounding with a hammer. The developments were quickly replicated in many areas around the eastern Mediterranean. As iron became easier to make, more of it became available. This led to its price falling, by about 97 per cent in the 400 years to 1000 BCE.[6]

Steel was discovered at around the same time. It is a 'Goldilocks' material – the amount of carbon and other elements in the mix for a specific use has to be neither too much, nor too little, but just right. It was found that iron mixed with too little carbon gave a material that was quite soft, but could be shaped fairly easily. If the carbon concentration was too high, the metal was harder but brittle. In current terminology, iron with a small proportion of carbon (below 0.5 per cent) is called wrought iron.

When the amount of carbon is fairly high (above about 1.5 per cent), the result is pig (or cast) iron. Steel is not a single alloy but a range of variants on iron, with properties dependent on its chemistry. In steelworks today, adding small, specified quantities of elements such as vanadium, chromium and nickel is very important. Such switches in composition change the properties of the steel, for instance making it more corrosion-resistant, or better at conducting electricity. The period that started in around 1200 BCE is called the Iron Age. Historians generally regard it as having run its course after about 1,300 years. In truth, however, the Iron Age has never really ended.[7]

In early times, to define the composition of steel accurately was close to impossible. For all aspects of iron- and steel-making, progress was slow and empirical. However, for more than 1,000 years, one country – China – stood out as the leader in steel-making. China was well ahead in producing so-called blast furnaces – which employed bellows to blow in the air needed for smelting, using pistons driven by water power. The country knew how to build blast furnaces as early as 200 BCE, or 1,600 years ahead of Europe. For most of the Middle Ages, China's iron production was well ahead of Europe's, both in total output and on a per capita basis. But by the late seventeenth century, Britain was emerging as the place where the key events in iron- and steel-making would occur.[8]

## Forging ahead

At the centre of the changes was Sheffield, a city in northern England. It had the benefit of proximity to three sets of natural resources. The hills of the Pennines provided convenient sources of iron ore. The River Don flowing through the city provided a source of water power for blast furnaces. The city was also adjacent to large coalfields. Coal had by now replaced charcoal as the vital reducing agent for smelting.

Benjamin Huntsman was a locksmith and clockmaker, originally from Doncaster, who moved to Handsworth, a village near Sheffield, in 1740. He was initially less interested in making iron and steel than in using it in his products. But after becoming dissatisfied with the quality of the steel then available, he decided to try to find a new way to make the metal.[9]

Huntsman tackled the two critical issues that had confronted the iron-makers of Mesopotamia: increasing the temperature, and influencing the composition of an iron/carbon/slag mix.

Huntsman's advance was built around the design of special clay pots or crucibles capable of being heated to about 1,600 degrees centigrade without cracking or losing shape. A hot iron/carbon mixture, from a blast furnace, was poured into the crucible, together with small amounts of other materials – including some fragments of good-quality so-called blister steel. Impurities could be drained out through holes in the base of the crucible. The rate at which different substances were added or removed controlled the rate of formation of steel, and also its properties. Huntsman started using this 'crucible process' in about 1742. There were some drawbacks. The technology made steel in small quantities, suitable for such items as tools, cutlery and components for watches and clocks. It was a 'secondary' process: it relied on some small amounts of previously made blister steel if it was to work. Yet the procedure was repeatable: it followed a prescribed route that could be operated many times. Huntsman's was one of the first such techniques used in any industry. Even though it took more than a century for anyone to effect a real improvement on Huntsman's ideas by combining product quality with high speed, the technique pointed the way forward.

Huntsman's advance came when Britain had only a small share of world manufacturing. In 1750, the leader in global manufacturing was China, responsible for a third of output,[10] followed by India, with a quarter. The leading country in Europe was Russia, with 5 per cent of the world total, followed by France. The share for Britain and Ireland of 1.9 per cent resulted in a lowly tenth position in the league table.[11] But change was on the way.[12] In 1769, the Scottish engineer James Watt patented another 'big idea', not in materials but in providing power.[13] Improving on earlier designs, Watt invented a steam engine, useful both for pumping water from mines and for driving machinery. The steam engine is now regarded as one of the best examples of a 'general purpose technology':[14] a specific technology capable of extremely wide application, plus the ability to be improved on. The advent of Watt's engine fitted in with other key events that influenced industrial progress. 'About 1760, a wave of gadgets swept over England' was how one historian described the changes.[15] The manufacturing-related 'gadgets' included new machines for use in textiles and metals production.[16] Meanwhile, the advances in technology coincided with other changes more connected to society and economics. They included the first efforts to organize factories on a large scale; an increasing population, which was also healthier and better educated; the opening up of world trade; and the birth of joint stock companies that helped to encourage entrepreneurship.

As a result of these changes, between 1700 and 1890 the proportion of the British workforce employed in industry rose from 22 per cent to 43 per cent, while the comparable figure for agriculture declined from 56 per cent to 16 per cent.[17] In Britain and Ireland, manufacturing output per person rose eightfold between 1750 and 1860, four times as much as in France and Germany, and six times as much as in Italy and Russia. In China and India, manufacturing output per person fell. In 1800, Britain accounted for just over 4 per cent of world manufacturing production, making it the world's fourth biggest industrial power, behind China, India and Russia. But by 1860 it had become the largest in manufacturing output, accounting for almost 20 per cent of the world total, just ahead of China. The United States was in third place, with nearly 15 per cent.[18]

In Britain, manufacturing became part of the language. The word is derived from the Latin *manus* meaning 'hand', and *facio*, meaning 'to do'. While it was first recorded in around 1560, its use was rare. Shakespeare, who died in 1616, used neither 'manufacturing' nor 'factory' in any of his plays.[19] But from around 1800 the word became commonplace.[20] The seven decades of change from roughly 1780 to 1850 added up to the first age of manufacturing organized on a large scale, and was concentrated in Britain. It came to be known as the first industrial revolution, usually called *the* Industrial Revolution.[21] Of all the events that shaped the world in the final 500 years of the second millennium, the Industrial Revolution was the most important.

## Bridges to the future

Charles Babbage was a child of this period of change. Born in London in 1791, Babbage spent much of his childhood in Totnes, a small town in

Devon. After studying mathematics at Cambridge University, he became a fellow of the Royal Society at the age of 24. In a paper in 1822, Babbage described a calculating machine called a difference engine. The design of the machine involved several mechanical columns that could each move a series of wheels. Through a system of levers and gears, the wheels and columns could be manipulated so as to perform calculations. Babbage tried to build a working version of the machine but such was its complexity that he found the task beyond him.[22] Undaunted, he began the development of an even more advanced calculating machine that he called the analytical engine. Since the analytical engine was intended to be a 'universal computing device', capable of performing an extremely wide range of tasks depending on how it was programmed, the machine is often considered the forerunner of the modern computer. But like the difference engine, the analytical engine was not built in Babbage's lifetime. Both machines were too complicated for the engineering capabilities of the day. Babbage also found time to write one of the first treatises on manufacturing. In *On the Economy of Machinery and Manufactures*, published in 1832, he commented that behind every successful manufactured item was 'a series of failures, which have gradually led the way to excellence'.[23]

Sir Henry Bessemer would have agreed with this observation. But due to his greater practical skills, Bessemer was more likely than Babbage to make a success of theoretical ideas, by getting the engineering right. Born in a village near London in 1813, Bessemer followed the career of an inventor, working on novel printing systems, fraud-proof dies for stamping government documents, and processes to make high-value velvet for the textiles industry. He wrote of his approach: 'I had no fixed ideas, derived from long-established practice, to control and bias my mind, and did not suffer from the general belief that whatever is, is right.'[24]

Bessemer's biggest challenge came in the 1850s, the time of the Crimean War. He had been encouraged by Napoleon III, an ally of Britain at the time, to work on new types of cannon. Military engineers had found they could control the trajectory of shells more easily by 'spinning' them in the barrels of guns. But the spiralling motion of the projectiles added extra stresses, which were likely to make the gun shatter as it was fired. Iron needed replacing with a higher-strength material. Steel was the obvious choice. However, if it was to be used, Bessemer realized he would have to find an improved method of manufacturing the metal.[25]

Since Huntsman's day, Britain had become the world leader in steel-making. Out of the 70,000 tonnes made in 1850, Britain was responsible for 70 per cent, with Sheffield alone making half the global total.[26] Most of this steel was produced by a laborious process called 'puddling' – invented in 1768 by Henry Cort, a Hampshire ironmonger. This involved converting pig iron into wrought iron by removing carbon from a hot mix of metal, carbon and various impurities. It required a skilled, and strong, worker who had to continually stir the mixture with a metal rod. Then more carbon had to be added in the form of charcoal to create the correct form of steel alloy. Puddling was in a sense a side-step from the Huntsman technique. It was a way to make steel in larger quantities than the crucible method – albeit no more than about 30 kilograms at a time – but it had many shortcomings. As Bessemer wrote in his autobiography, 'at that date [the early 1850s] there was no steel suitable for structural purposes [capable of being made into large sections] . . . The process was long and costly.'[27]

Bessemer set out to make steel from pig iron in a single step. He did this by blowing cool air into the molten pig iron. The oxygen in the air mopped up some (but not all) of the carbon atoms present in the pig iron, by converting them into carbon dioxide, leaving behind steel. Because the reaction produced heat, the temperature rose as more air was blown in, so adding to the efficiency of the process. In 1856, Bessemer published the details in a paper given to the British Association. The new process used 'powerful machinery whereby a great deal of labour will be saved, and the [steelmaking] process [will] be greatly expedited'. He added that the Bessemer process would bring about a 'perfect revolution . . . in every iron-making district in the world'.[28]

In 1859, Bessemer chose Sheffield for the world's first steelworks based on 'converter' technology. The plant was a success. He licensed his ideas to metals entrepreneurs in both Britain and other countries. Bessemer's ideas were also improved on. The Siemens-Martin 'open hearth' process, introduced in 1865, led to closer control of the steel-making reactions, leading to a better-quality product.[29] Andrew Carnegie, the Scottish-born US industrialist, was among those influenced by Bessemer's thinking.

After emigrating to the US in 1848 when he was 13, Carnegie immediately gained work as a 'bobbin boy' – bringing raw material to the production line in a cotton works. After deciding to go into business for himself, Carnegie started manufacturing bridges, locomotives and rails, an activity that took him into steel-making. Having met Bessemer on a visit to England in 1868, Carnegie introduced Bessemer converter technology into the US soon afterwards. By 1899, his Pittsburgh-based Carnegie Steel was the biggest steel producer in the world, with an output in that year of 2.6 million tonnes.[30] (Two years later, Carnegie sold his company to J. P. Morgan for $400 million, creating US Steel, and making him the world's richest person.) Because Bessemer's technology, aided by complementary advances, made it possible to produce steel more quickly and easily, its price fell by 86 per cent in the 40 years to 1900. In 1900, world output of steel was 28.3 million tonnes, 400 times higher than half a century earlier.[31]

Global manufacturing production expanded considerably faster in the final 20 years of the nineteenth century, when the benefits of cheap steel were being fully felt, than in earlier periods. World industrial output climbed 67 per cent between 1880 and 1900, as compared to 42 per cent in the two decades prior to this, and just 22 per cent in the 1830–60 period. One consequence of the rate of global expansion was that the UK lost its position as the world's leading manufacturer. By 1900, the US took over, with nearly 24 per cent of world output, compared to the UK with 18.5 per cent, and Germany with 13.2 per cent.[32] Britain's role as the 'workshop of the world' had lasted for only 40 years. (By the end of the nineteenth century, the UK had also fallen from being the biggest steel-maker to number three, behind the US and Germany.)[33]

Among the factors behind the wider economic changes, one of the most important was cheap steel. It made possible new and improved products, from cars and farm equipment to steel-framed buildings. Machinery made from steel enabled higher output of other products such as chemicals, textiles and paper. In a final effect, use of all these products boosted growth in other, non-manufacturing parts of the economy, such as retailing, travel, banking and agriculture. In this way, cheap steel acted as a 'growth catalyst' for the world economy.[34]

## History's curve

The evolution of the steel industry is a specific example of a general rule of manufacturing: as experience in making a product increases, its cost goes down, while its quality (or sophistication) goes up. Another way to depict the rule is to talk about the 'experience' or 'learning' curve. As more affordable and better products become available, their impact on the rest of the economy becomes greater. While engineers tend to be most interested in how products are made, what really counts is how they are used.

Since the Industrial Revolution, there have been three similar eras. The 'transport revolution', which took place from approximately 1840 to 1890, is regarded as the second industrial revolution.[35] Overlapping slightly with the Industrial Revolution, the period was marked by new machines for transportation, including the steam-driven railway locomotive and the iron- or steel-hulled ship. The changes cut travel times both for people and for goods, boosting trade and the exchange of information. The key to their economic impact was not just their invention, but the fact that over time they improved, so generating more growth in the wider economy. Faster railway engines that broke down less often are an example. The products helped whole industries to expand, in both manufacturing and services.

The transport revolution was followed by – or merged with – the 'science revolution' which occurred between 1860 and 1930. Cheap steel was one product from this time. Others include the steam turbine, the electric motor and the internal combustion engine, together with a range of items made by new chemicals and materials industries, ranging from dyes to aluminium.[36] All these products appeared as a result of various bursts of innovation. But the processes that led to their availability did not end there. New knowledge was acquired which continued to have an impact on how the products were made, and influenced their characteristics.

Theodore Paul Wright, an engineer working at the Curtiss-Wright aircraft company in New York during the 1930s, was the first person to analyse in detail the relationship between production volumes, manufacturing capabilities and costs.[37] In 1936, Wright examined the impact on aircraft production of specific factors such as new designs, better materials and improved machining processes. The fact that more and better-quality aircraft could be built with improved production techniques was not surprising. What was more interesting was the finding that the best way to improve manufacturing capabilities was to increase output.[38]

As a result of more time spent doing something, technical prowess was more or less guaranteed to improve. Along the way costs would fall, while quality would rise. Wright discovered that every time aircraft output doubled, the costs of making a single unit declined 20 per cent. It was the first detailed evidence that the experience curve worked in real life. If manufacturers could make this work for a variety of other products, they could cut prices in line with costs, so outselling competitors and boosting market share and profitability. If at the same time product sophistication also increased, so much the better. Bruce Henderson, a US engineer and former Bible salesman, grasped the implications. In 1963, Henderson set up the Boston Consulting Group. He and his colleagues produced a range of studies showing that the experience curve worked for many industries apart from aircraft. 'It seems clear', Henderson wrote in 1972, 'that a large proportion of business success and failure [in manufacturing] can be explained simply in terms of experience curve effects.'[39]

Another person who understood the connections was Vannevar Bush. An electrical engineer and former maths teacher, Bush was in 1941 appointed the first director of the US's Office of Scientific Research and Development. In a 1945 paper describing the manufacture of radios, Bush illustrated how the experience curve worked.

Machines with interchangeable parts can now be constructed with great economy of effort . . . [A radio set] is made by the hundred million, tossed about in packages, plugged into sockets – and it works! Its gossamer parts, the precise location and alignment involved in its construction would have occupied a master craftsman of the guild for months; now it is built for thirty cents. The world has arrived at an age of cheap, complex devices of great reliability; and something is bound to come of it.[40]

## After Babbage

One of the projects financed by Bush's office was a computer development programme at the University of Pennsylvania's of Moore School of Electrical Engineering. Out of this emerged the Electronic Numerical Integrator Analyser and Computer (Eniac). It was created by John Mauchly and J. Presper Eckert, two of the school's top theoreticians. The Eniac – unveiled in 1946 – was the first general-purpose electronic computer, a modern version of Babbage's analytical engine. Mauchly and Eckert took more than two years to design and build the machine. The Eniac contained 17,468 thermionic valves or vacuum tubes, 70,000 resistors, 10,000 capacitors, 1,500 relays, 6,000 manual switches and 5 million soldered joints. It covered 167 square metres of floor space, weighed 30 tonnes and consumed 160 kilowatts of electricity. The machine was used primarily for military projects related to the 'cold war'. It worked out the trajectories of ballistic missiles, as well as calculations needed for the hydrogen bomb. In one second, the Eniac could perform 5,000 mathematical calculations, 1,000 times more than any previous machine.[41] In 2010 prices, the Eniac cost $6 million.[42]

While the building of Eniac was a breakthrough, an even bigger advance was soon to follow. Semiconductors are electronic devices in which many single components capable of acting as electric 'switches' are packed onto a small piece of material. The basic job of each component is either to let electricity through, or block it, with its exact behaviour governed by electronic instructions fed via a software program. By being either 'on' or 'off', the switch can handle the digital language of computer code. The reason these devices have their name is that they are built from materials such as silicon or germanium which can either behave as an insulator or a conductor as regards electricity flow – hence *semi*conductor.

In 1947, the world's first semiconductor device was invented. It was a particularly simple form of semiconductor called a transistor, equivalent to a single electrical 'switch' embedded in a piece of germanium. (Silicon became the preferred material for semiconductors a few years later.) Transistors became prime candidates to replace the valves used to perform calculations in early computers such as the Eniac. However, semiconductors were never going to be hugely useful if each contained just one component. What made them of greater interest was the integrated circuit: a semiconductor device capable of having more than one switch embedded in it. The world's first integrated circuit – a piece of germanium containing two circuits – was described in February 1959 in a patent filed by Jack Kilby of the US electronics company Texas Instruments.

Helped by the growing use of semiconductors, the number of computers in the US rose from 250 in 1955 to nearly 70,000 by 1968.[43] Transistors were still expensive. But as engineers learned how to squeeze more circuits on to a small 'chip' of material, the capabilities of semiconductors increased. Also, in step with extra expertise gained with greater experience, prices fell. This was illustrated by the unveiling in 1971 of the first microprocessor: a collection of circuits on a chip capable of performing like a fully fledged 'central processing unit' of a computer. Made by Intel, the first microprocessor – called the 4004 – contained 2,200 transistors. Weighted by the amount of computing power that it contained, the 4004 had a price 95 per cent lower than that of a comparable semiconductor chip of four years earlier.

Over the next 40 years, semiconductor companies spent tens of billions of dollars building ever more sophisticated factories, containing equipment capable of cramming more 'transistor equivalents' on to the same small area of silicon. In this effort, the semiconductor industry proved the veracity of 'Moore's law'.[44] In 1975, Gordon Moore, one of Intel's co-founders, predicted that the number of transistors per semiconductor would double every two years. He assumed costs would also fall at a corresponding rate. In 2010, an Intel X3370 microprocessor, containing 820 million transistors, sold for just over $300. The value of each transistor in the device was roughly 1/30,000th of a cent. In just over 60 years, the price of a transistor had fallen by a factor of 30 million. Moore's law has turned out to be largely correct, providing more evidence of the validity of the experience curve.

The huge reduction in prices of silicon-embedded electronic circuitry fuelled an explosion in the use of computers. This drove on the so-called 'computer revolution' that took place from 1950 to 2000, the fourth big period of change sparked by manufacturing. According to one estimate, in 1946 the world contained just 10 computers, counting machines roughly comparable to the Eniac. In 2010, the world contained about 2 billion computers, counting desktop and portable machines, plus other computing devices such as 'smart phones' and computerized switching systems that are part of telecommunications networks. On the basis of these numbers, the 'stock' of computers had risen by 200 million in less than 70 years. A standard personal computer in 2010 could handle 3 billion instructions a second, 600,000 more than the Eniac. It sold for about $650, or 1/17,000th of the price of the first machine of its type.

## The invitation

On Friday, 13 January 2006, Lakshmi Mittal held a small dinner party in London.[45] A steel industry entrepreneur and chief executive of Mittal Steel, Mittal was one of the world's wealthiest men. His main guest was Guy Dollé, chief executive of Luxembourg-based Arcelor. The setting was Mittal's neo-Palladian mansion in Kensington, which the Indian billionaire had bought in 2004 for £57 million from the motor racing magnate Bernie Ecclestone.

While industry rivals, Mittal and Dollé shared an all-consuming interest in the steel industry and the products it made possible. A former amateur footballer, the fiercely competitive Dollé had worked his way to the top of Arcelor in a smooth progression from engineering jobs to senior management.[46] Arcelor had resulted from the 2001 combination of three leading steel-makers based in France, Luxembourg and Spain, and was regarded as a jewel of European industry. Mittal grew up in Rajasthan in north-west India. For much of his early life, he lived in a house with bare concrete floors and no electricity. Mittal's first foray into the steel industry came in childhood. During breaks in the school holidays, he worked in a small steel plant run by his father in Calcutta. In the 1970s, Mittal set up a steelworks in Indonesia, using his father's money. Then came a series of acquisitions in countries including Trinidad and Tobago, Mexico, Kazakhstan and Romania.[47] In 2004, he announced the $4.5 billion purchase of International Steel Group, a US steel supplier. The deal made Mittal Steel the world's biggest steel-maker, inching ahead of Arcelor. To mark the occasion, Dollé sent him a note of congratulation.[48]

Over pre-dinner drinks, Mittal let slip what lay behind his invitation. He asked Dollé if he would agree to a merger between their two companies. That was how he put it anyway. What he meant was that he wanted to acquire Arcelor and integrate the two businesses, with Mittal firmly in control. 'If we linked up, we could accomplish many of the things that we both want, but we'd be on the same side,' Mittal said. 'Why don't we do it?' There was some logic to the idea. Uniting Mittal Steel with Arcelor would create a giant company with more than 300,000 employees, making steel on five continents. It would account for close to 10 per cent of global steel production, and have an annual output three times greater than its closest rival.[49]

Control over such a large part of the market would allow a merged company to dictate terms to customers, keeping prices and profits high. It would also be able to pool knowledge about the best steel-making techniques, and use its buying power to push down prices of raw materials when negotiating with suppliers of iron ore and coal. Mittal was especially keen to take over Arcelor's technologically advanced, albeit high-cost, factories in Western Europe. The plants had good relationships with many key customers, particularly in the car industry. There could be special benefits through linking these facilities with the units run by Mittal Steel in such places as Central Asia, Latin America and Eastern Europe. The two sets of plants had different attributes – the first operating at the top level of technology, the second making more basic kinds of steel with the help of low costs – and so could learn from each other. A combined company would be in a better position to fight the challenges facing the steel industry in the growing effort to reduce emissions of carbon dioxide – of which steel-making is one of the biggest producers – as part of broader moves to combat environmental threats. It would also have a potentially stronger role in carving out a leadership position in the 'emerging' regions of China, India and Brazil. But the words that Mittal might have conveyed to Dollé to express why a merger was a good idea went unsaid. The Frenchman quickly killed any discussion with a terse rejoinder: 'I'm not interested.' Dollé was keen to strengthen his company, but on his own terms, not Mittal's. He was not sure he could work jointly with Mittal. Dollé also suspected that fitting together two companies with such differing patterns of plants and corporate structure might lead to insoluble stresses.

The talk at the dinner moved on to less controversial topics, and the evening ended amicably enough. But two weeks later, Mittal – unmoved by Dollé's opposition – went public with his plan, unveiling an unsolicited $22.5 billion takeover offer for Arcelor. What followed was a bitter, five-month fight.[50] It was marked by relentless sparring between the two companies, political interventions by several European governments, plus a series of orchestrated moves by each company's investment banking teams to sway shareholders. Throughout the battle, Dollé kept up a barrage of invective against his rival, with Mittal generally trying to occupy the higher moral ground by insisting a merged company would be good for its workers and the communities where they lived, as well as shareholders. Ultimately, Mittal raised his bid to $33.6 billion, some 50 per cent above his original offer. Money talked, and on 25 June, with Dollé still opposing the deal, the Arcelor board accepted.[51]

## The shape of the future

Having fought the takeover with such ferocity, Dollé could hardly accept Mittal's offer of a job in the new company. Within a few days of the deal's conclusion, the Frenchman announced his retirement. Taking over at the helm of ArcelorMittal, as the merged company was called, Mittal now had the chance to reflect on what lay ahead. As president and main shareholder, he was in a strong position.

For all the talk about the world moving into a 'post-industrial' age, factories in the early twenty-first century are turning out considerably more goods than ever before. In 2010, manufacturing output was roughly one and a half times higher than in 1990, 57 times above what it had been in 1900, and 200 times in excess of the output in 1800 (see Figure 1). Between 1800 and 2010, world manufacturing output rose by an average of 2.6 per cent a year, as against the comparable 2 per cent annual increase in gross domestic product – measuring the productive effort of the entire global economy – over the same period. The average annual rate of growth of manufacturing output between 2000 and 2010 was 1.8 per cent, a figure

**Figure 1 World manufacturing output and GDP, 1800–2010**
(output measured as an index where 1800 = 100)

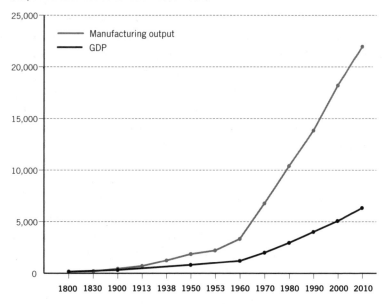

**Notes:** manufacturing output calculated in value-added; both sets of data use constant 2005 dollars.

**Sources:** P. Bairoch (as quoted in Paul Kennedy, *The Rise and Fall of the Great Powers*), IHS Global Insight, World Trade Organization, 2011 Annual Report (http://www.wto.org/english/res_e/statis_e/its2011_e/its11_appendix_e.pdf), UN data base, Maddison, *The World Economy Historical Statistics*, author's estimates.

that appears considerable, given the slump that much of the world's factory production suffered during the deep economic recession of 2008–9. Allowing for inflation, the selling price for steel in 2010 was 25 per cent lower than a century previously, following a period in which production had risen more than fortyfold.[52] This record indicates that the experience curve is working, at least for steel. All the signs are that this will continue for other products as well.

Across manufacturing, technology – the application of science to industry – is playing an ever bigger role. In the nineteenth and early twentieth centuries, changes in manufacturing had been driven by developments in a relatively small number of technologies, including steam power, metalworking, electricity generation and chemicals. In the twenty-first century, the number of technologies exerting an impact on manufacturing has expanded. The list now includes electronics, biotechnology, the internet and lasers, with many subdisciplines within these main areas. Meanwhile, the pace of change in these different fields is increasing, as a result of more scientists and engineers, and more money being directed by governments and companies to research and development. Also technology is being treated as a *system* of ideas in which advances in disparate fields are capable of being linked to create a wider variety of new products and processes, in fields from medical hardware to consumer electronics.

Another change concerns the general characteristics of products. In the past, manufacturers concentrated on making goods to meet a broad range of requirements, within the boundaries of keeping quality high and prices reasonably low. The idea of 'bespoke' manufacturing – creating different products to satisfy individual tastes – was regarded as being outside the province of most companies. Now, driven by the demands of consumers, plus shifts in technology that make it easier to accommodate their requirements, the idea of tailoring products to suit different needs is becoming more central.

What constitutes a successful manufacturer is also being redefined. Up to about 1990, production was considered by far the most important part of the work of a manufacturing business. Parcelling this out for other companies to take care of was rarely contemplated. But in the early years of the twenty-first century, the realization grew that making products is just one part of the 'value chain' of company operations. Others include design and development, and the way products are maintained or 'serviced' after installation. To be considered a great manufacturer, companies do not now need to make anything, even though they will almost certainly know a lot about what this entails. Increasingly, elements of the value chain are being left to a variety of businesses in different countries. The management of this mix is becoming a highly prized skill.

In many product areas, opportunities are opening up as a result of convergence of technological changes, globalization and the use of the internet as a marketing tool. These have provided the basis for new 'niche industries' – sectors that concentrate on narrow types of products, often aimed at small groups of customers around the world. The companies that supply goods in these niches are frequently barely known. Yet in many cases, they are expanding sales and profits quickly, and exerting an increasing influence on people's lives, even in ways that are largely invisible.

In a further broad trend, the concept of 'sustainable manufacturing' is becoming critical. Driven by concerns about global warming and materials depletion, the world has become more aware of the environmental damage caused by humankind's activities, many of them linked to manufacturing. As a result, there is more interest in making manufacturing processes less environmentally damaging, and creating new products that help to reduce use of materials and energy. From being considered a key cause of the world's environmental ills, production industries are increasingly viewed as part of the possible solution.

Meanwhile the most important locations for industrial production are broadening out. The list of 'manufacturing-capable' countries is now much longer than the limited number that had a role in the four industrial revolutions to date. In 2010, the proportion of world manufacturing that took place outside the conventionally defined 'developed' nations reached 41 per cent, compared with 27 per cent in 2000 and 24 per cent in 1990 (see Figure 2).[53] The list of 'emerging' economies is headed by China.[54] After staying on the sidelines of global manufacturing for 150 years, China started to catch up in the 1990s. The rate of growth was such that in 2010 China reclaimed the position of the world's biggest manufacturing country by output, overtaking the US which had been the number one for more than a century.[55] Other nations that for most of the twentieth century had only a minor impact on global industry also began to make their presence felt. Among such countries are India, Brazil, South Korea and Russia. Even with the increasing role of these fast-expanding economies, there remain many opportunities for companies located in the main developed countries. Many of these businesses are part of 'clusters' of enterprises that operate in the same industry and are based in the same small area. Even in a world of dispersed value chains in manufacturing there remains a place for companies that stress local linkages.

**Figure 2 Shares of world manufacturing since 1800**
**a) Showing the split between rich and poor countries**
(calculated as value-added in 2005 dollars.)

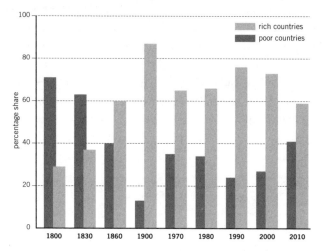

**Notes:** Rich countries are N. America, W. Europe, Japan, Australia. Poor countries are all those that are not rich. Japan is counted as "poor" until 1970; rich after 1970. Russia is counted as rich until this date; poor afterwards.

**b) For five leading nations**

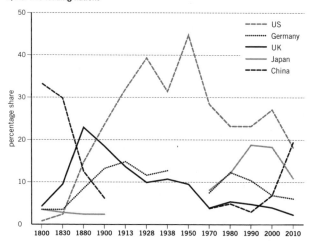

**Sources:** P. Bairoch, 'International Industrialisation Levels from 1750 to 1980'; IHS Global Insight, 'Global manufacturing output data 1980–2010'; UN, Stephen Broadberry, *The Productivity Race.*

These features – covering technology, choice, value chains, niches, the environment, the new manufacturing nations and clusters – are all important. But their biggest impact is in the way they are becoming increasingly intertwined. The results will be a mix of opportunities and threats. They will be apparent not only to powerful industrialists such as Mittal but to people running much smaller production businesses in virtually every sector. The resulting shifts will be felt by just about everyone. Picking apart what is likely to happen will not be easy. But of the magnitude of the changes there is little doubt. A new industrial revolution has begun.

# CHAPTER 2

# The power of technology

## Role play

In 1685, Louis XIV – the Sun King – granted permission to the Marquis Charles Henri Gaspard de Lénoncourt to construct an ironworks at Dillingen, a village near Saarlouis in what was then a corner of eastern France.[1] The plant produced raw iron together with finished products such as ovens and chimney plates – and also small amounts of steel, made in a labour-intensive refining process. Over the following century, the works gradually improved its technology, in particular with the introduction of better methods to specify the mix of iron and carbon in steel to improve quality.

In the late 1700s, new processes in the technology of 'steel rolling' were developed in Britain. These involved passing relatively thick sections of steel between rotating metal blocks to make thinner sheets, giving a wider range of applications. In 1804 the Dillingen mill became one of the first in continental Europe to use rolling on a commercial scale, for instance to make metal plates for shipbuilding. By the early twenty-first century Dillingen was part of Germany – following multiple changes of jurisdiction as this corner of Europe was swapped between Germany and France. The works were now run by Dillinger Hütte,[2] a company in which Arcelor had a 51 per cent stake, with smaller shareholdings owned by German investors. Building on its technological strengths of the previous 300 years, Dillinger Hütte was one of the biggest companies in the world making heavy steel plate for oil and gas pipelines, earth-moving equipment and bridges. One of its key strengths was its sophisticated rolling technology, used to make plate to tolerances of less than a millimetre.

When Lakshmi Mittal acquired Arcelor in 2006, his new business became, almost by accident, the majority owner of Dillinger Hütte. In the excitement of the bid battle, the steel magnate had given the Dillingen-based company little thought. But as Mittal got on with the job of making the merger work, he paid Dillinger Hütte more attention. If he could integrate it properly into ArcelorMittal, the Indian billionaire would have access to Dillinger Hütte's strengths in plate-making technology that could be useful in other parts of his business. The expertise would help to counter JFE and Nippon Steel – two large Japanese steel-makers which are also leaders in steel plate and strong competitors in new markets in Asia.

But there was a snag. To exert maximum influence over Dillinger Hütte, Mittal had to boost ArcelorMittal's stake to above 70 per cent. This followed from an obscure part of its constitution stipulating that a shareholder could take management control only if its stake reached this level. During 2007 and early 2008, Mittal held secret talks with the other large shareholder in Dillinger to see if it would sell some of its stake. The investor was a private trust with strong links to the federal state of Saarland where Dillinger Hütte is based. The Saarland politicians and business people who controlled the trust were extremely cool. Outright acquisition by ArcelorMittal would leave Dillinger playing a peripheral role in a sprawling global empire, its best technology used elsewhere. Mittal indicated he would pay at least $1 billion for the shares he needed. 'Of course ArcelorMittal would gain from this, but so would your company – it would become part of a much bigger business, providing a solid platform for growth,' he told the trust.[3]

But on this occasion Mittal's persuasive manner – and the promise of a lot of money – failed to carry the day. Late in 2008, Mittal abandoned the effort to take control of the company. As one of Mittal's aides commented: 'This was a battle that was not just about money.' The fight over Dillinger Hütte had essentially been about the control of technology. The outcome denied Mittal access to a prized stock of practical knowledge, and damaged his reputation for deal-making. In a wider sense, the affair illustrated the power of technology to influence manufacturing. Dillinger Hütte's history also underlines the idea that technology – in whatever product area – rarely stands still. While individual technologies are improved, they also combine with others to make existing products more useful, and to make new ones possible. In the new industrial revolution, there is more technology available, and the possibilities for using it are increasing.

## A switch in time

If you ask Eddie Davies how he became wealthy, he will hand you some small, circular pieces of metal, each the size of a Polo mint. Like the mint, they are roughly 1 centimetre in diameter, and have a hole in the middle. Where they differ is that they have a small 'tongue' protruding into the hole from the solid rim. In 2005, Davies made $160 million from the sale of the company that produces these metal objects.[4] Davies shares with Mittal a strong interest in football. While Davies owns Bolton Wanderers, a club with an illustrious pedigree that is one of the oldest members of the UK's premier league, Mittal is a large minority shareholder in Queens Park Rangers, a London club that won promotion to the premiership in 2011. Both men are also fascinated by metals technology. In the Englishman's case, the interest is reflected in his collection of Japanese cloisonné, a delicate form of enamelware. Less obviously attractive than Davies's prized enamel, the Polo-like metal pieces on which he has based his career each weigh only half a gram. Known as 'blades', they are vital parts of electric kettles. They act as 'fail-safe' devices to ensure kettles can be used without boiling dry and catching fire. Every day, an estimated 1 billion people use a kettle that contains one of Davies's blades. Strix, the company that makes them, is based on the Isle of Man, off the north-west coast of England.

In the 1970s, kettles were used predominantly for tea-making. But now someone is just as likely to buy a kettle – perhaps in China or Russia – to boil water to make soup or coffee as for a cup of tea. Two of every three of the 80 million kettles made in 2009 incorporated at least one control device made by Strix. Kettles are produced mainly from plastic rather than steel (the material favoured in the 1990s), which has made them more attractive, and cheaper. Helping further to reduce prices was the migration between the mid-1980s and 2010 of 85 per cent of the world's kettle production to China.

The blades in Strix's kettle controls are produced from layers of different metal alloys, built up in a 'sandwich' structure by being rolled together using versions of the machines operated by Dillinger Hütte. Strix goes to some lengths to protect its technical secrets. The alloys contain a range of metals, among them iron, copper, nickel and chromium. But the precise identity of the ingredients in the strips, and the combination in which they are formulated, are not disclosed in any of the 500 patents Strix has published on kettle controls. Neither are these details divulged to anyone other than trusted partners in its manufacturing processes. In 2009, Strix needed about 200 tonnes of strip, supplied by Kanthal, a Swedish company, and others around Europe. The strip is shipped to a small Strix factory in Ramsey, on the Isle of Man. Here, the metal is converted into blades using special stamping machines. The blades are then sent to other Strix factories – the main one being in China – where they are assembled into control units that form part of kettles.

Strix has based its business not just on knowledge of materials. Control of movement plays a big part, as does management of energy. As different materials heat up, they expand at different rates. A layered arrangement of two metals is known as a 'bi-metallic' strip, while one with three layers is a 'tri-metallic' strip. In such a product, the interplay between the constituents in the sandwich will determine what happens to the piece of metal as a whole. By choosing specific types of metal that change their shape in particular ways when heated or cooled, Strix's engineers have devised a series of bi-metallic (and also tri-metallic) switches that behave as electrical switches.

In the manufacturing process, the blades are made slightly curved, so they are bulging outwards. But when the water in the kettle reaches boiling point at close to 100 degrees centigrade, the blade changes shape, so the curve faces inwards. This sudden 'snapping' action takes place in a matter of microseconds. The movement of about 2.5 millimetres pushes a small rod out of contact with the source of electrical power, breaking the supply and preventing the possibility of overheating. If the same energy capabilities of a Strix blade were to be distributed around the muscles of the human body, then the average person would become a super-strong weightlifter, capable of raising a 100-tonne truck.[5]

The ideas behind metals being used as a switch were devised by British clockmakers in the late eighteenth century. They used bi-metallic strips to form parts of clock springs. Different combinations of layers could be used to adjust for distortion temperature, to ensure clocks ran on time. The event that led to Strix's switch was the Second World War. It was the first major conflict to feature widespread use of aircraft. Electrically heated flying suits were needed to keep aircrew warm. Some form of simple mechanical control – a heat regulator or thermostat – was required to ensure the electricity warmed the suit to the right temperature and then cut out.[6]

In the early 1940s, Eric Taylor, a UK engineer, was working for Baxter, Woodhouse & Taylor, a clothing company in Manchester partly owned by his family. A keen glider pilot, Taylor created a bi-metallic switch to act as a non-electrical thermostat for flying suits. He persuaded his family company to incorporate the switches into the garments that it sold to the UK and US air forces, using the 'Windak' trade name. Once the war ended, Taylor founded Otter Controls, in Stockport near Manchester. He used his controls in items such as windscreen wipers, electric blankets, electricity generators – and kettles. When Eric Taylor died in 1972, his son John took control of the company. But he sparked a family row when in 1982 he quit Otter and set up Strix on the Isle of Man. John's defection left Otter (which by then had moved to Buxton in Derbyshire) controlled by other members of the Taylor family. The dispute led to fierce antipathy between the two companies, as both Strix and Otter battled for dominance in the kettles control business.

In 1984, John Taylor stepped aside from running Strix, recruiting Eddie Davies, a physics-trained engineer who was also a qualified accountant, to take over as chief executive.[7] While continuing to work at Strix, effectively as chief scientist, John Taylor invented a new form of tri-metallic strip that moved the company on from the two-layer systems his father had devised. In 1997, Strix set up the company's first overseas factory in China, in the southern city of Guangzhou. The move not only cut costs, but pushed

Strix's production much closer to its main customers in the kettle industry. By 2011, the company had most of its 850-strong workforce in China. It had about 200 staff on the Isle of Man, 85 of them in research and development, compared with 700 in 1997. As for Davies, his role in running Strix effectively ended in 2005 when he and Taylor sold the business for $550 million to a venture capital company.[8]

According to Paul Hussey, Strix's current chief executive, research and development, as well as blade production, are likely to stay on the Isle of Man for the foreseeable future. This is due partly to the high skills of its existing labour force. Also, says Hussey, the Isle of Man – far from the world's main industrial centres – is a better place to site sensitive technical processes than China, where control of intellectual property is notoriously difficult. Hussey admits to 'worries' about the possibility of the company's secrets leaking out if Strix moved its key centres for technology away from the island.[9]

## New dimensions

A 90-minute car journey to the east of São Paulo takes the visitor to a series of broad tree-lined avenues that connect up the São Jose dos Campos industrial complex. While it acts as the home for a number of other companies, the main business in the complex is Embraer, a Brazilian company that is the world's third largest maker of commercial aircraft. At the centre of the complex, where Embraer employs 12,000 people, is an installation of which the company is especially proud. Inside Embraer's 'virtual reality' room, visitors are asked to don special spectacles. Then, by watching a giant computer screen, they can inspect in three dimensions the inside and outside of a 'virtual' aeroplane. The room is used by engineers to simulate how new components or subassemblies can change the shape or performance of aircraft still in the planning stage.

Fabio Capela, a development engineer at Embraer, explains that without such simulation equipment, designing and building a modern aircraft would be close to impossible. He explains that an aircraft contains more than 200,000 unique parts. The figure excludes assembly components such as rivets and screws, but includes the parts inside large subassemblies such as engines. (An engine can contain 15,000 components.) 'Each part can be described in a line of computer code in our simulation system,' Capela says. 'Using this, we can experiment to a huge degree as to where all the parts can fit. We can improve the designs with much more freedom than if we were to do everything through drawings.'[10] The software also predicts what will happen to parts of aeroplanes once in use – for instance how heat flows through parts of the fuselage or engine turbines – and so helps in devising maintenance programmes.

The virtual reality equipment at Embraer is an example of computer-aided analysis[11] applied to manufacturing. Through this, design engineers can describe products before they are built, by conjuring up diagrams or pictures of them on computer screens in the three dimensions of the physical universe. By building in extra software that looks ahead to how products will behave, engineers can also enter a fourth dimension, time.

In 2010 the world's manufacturers spent about $1,200 billion on developing new products. An increasing amount of this work involves manipulation of data, using clever software programs. Sales of computer-aided analysis software in 2010 came to about $20 billion, or less than 2 per cent of the total development spending.[12] But without the software, the development expenditure would be a lot less useful. Charles Lang, a UK computer scientist who was a 1970s pioneer in turning ideas in computer-aided design and analysis into business, sums up: 'What used to be regarded as an esoteric technology has become mainstream. It means just about every kind of manufactured product, from toasters to missiles, can be made more reliable and efficient, take less time to develop, and have better functionality.'[13]

Computer-aided analysis in manufacturing is part of the explosion in information processing, triggered by developments in computing. The amount of stored information was insignificant until Johannes Gutenberg invented the printing press in the late fifteenth century. The device created a way to produce books and other documents on a large scale. It greatly increased people's ability to process and transfer information. Up to then, this could be done only by writing by hand, drawing pictures or talking. The advent of cheap computers in the late twentieth century changed the nature of information flow even more.

Now, the world's store of information (more than 99 per cent of this in electronic form) is doubling roughly every two years. In 2011, according to one study, the amount of information stored in digital devices of all kinds – counting all kinds of office and home computers, mobile phones and factory control systems – came to 1,800 exabytes (1,800 billion billion bytes).[14] This is roughly 14 million times the information stored in all the books ever written.[15]

A substantial part of this information store is related to the development or production of factory-made goods. Building Boeing's new 787 Dreamliner super-jumbo jet requires a mass of data, stored in computers run by the company or its suppliers. The information in the computer programs used to build it adds up to 16,000 gigabytes, roughly equivalent to a library of 20 million books.[16]

The first steps towards computer-aided analysis took place more than 600 years ago. Nicolas Oresme, a French logician and scholar who became Bishop of Lisieux in 1377, published several tracts that described mathematically the movement of the earth around the sun. Some 300 years later, the philosopher René Descartes developed these ideas so he could define the shapes of ordinary objects – such as pieces of metal – by reference to mathematical codes describing the position of points on their surface. Étienne-Jules Marey, a French physiologist, further refined this work in the nineteenth century through his invention of the spirograph. This was an instrument capable of translating the movements of machines or animals into a series of pictures, which could then be depicted as a sequence of numbers. All these ideas created the basis for the analytic geometry behind engineering drawing, and, when translated to a binary code, three-dimensional computer modelling.[17]

Following these advances, the birth of the first electronic computers in the 1940s and 1950s led to efforts to represent in the digital code the shapes of engineering products. Patrick Hanratty is considered the 'father' of computer-aided design. When working for General Electric in the 1950s, Hanratty developed some of the first software capable of translating information about shape and physical form into binary code. In the 1970s, Hanratty created a software program for computer-aided design called Adam.[18] The program was incorporated into software sold by

Computervision, a US company that was a pioneer in computer-aided design. One of the most widely used software design packages is Catia (short for Conception Assistée Tridimensionnelle Interactive) which is produced by Paris-based Dassault Systèmes. Programs made by Dassault are used by Strix to develop new kettle controls and by Embraer in its São Paulo control room.

One of the latest advances in computer-aided analysis is to add to the four dimensions – covering physical space and time – that the discipline currently works in. There is now the prospect of supplementing the technology with what amounts to a fifth dimension: a way of providing information about products before they are built that is channelled not through words or illustrations, but by touch or body movements. The aim of these ideas is to add more refinements to the software of computer-aided analysis equipment to make the modelling of products more lifelike.

Finding ways to process information in this way is part of the new science of 'haptics': the study of the sense of touch. A leader in this field is Reachin Technologies, a company in Stockholm. Reachin has built simulation systems incorporating 'data gloves', worn on the hands like any other form of glove. They incorporate special sensors that interact with computer equipment. The sensors can be used to gauge how new products will behave, via the sense of touch. Such technology can be used in the design of new products. Using a screen and three-dimensional image analysis, engineers can build up a picture of what a new car will look like, before any prototypes have been built. With the gloves, the wearer can get a feeling – literally – for what a car steering wheel would be like if it were to be built. Some of the first big commercial applications for haptics are likely to be in computer games. Makers of these products have already added new features so people in their living rooms can interact with them through means other than a keyboard or computer mouse.

Haptics could permit people to play the games by grasping a touch pad, feeling how warm it is, and then reacting accordingly. Under such a system, different grades of temperature could be used to depict whether the user is winning or losing a mock battle being played out on a screen. Other potential applications are in the controls of excavators. Operators could derive information about the characteristics of the rock their machines are digging into by the tactile sense of 'hardness' or 'softness' transmitted through a joystick. As a result of this knowledge of the rock, they could alter the way they move the excavator bucket, applying more pressure for hard rock than for soft material. For haptics to develop into useful tools would require new techniques in the three-dimensional software used in current applications of computer-aided analysis. It would also require novel types of sensor devices, incorporating heating elements and vibratory devices to provide the equivalent senses of touch that people obtain through the nerve endings in their fingers.

'Body-to-computer' interaction is one of the themes behind products such as Nintendo's Wii or Microsoft's Kinect machines. These products receive information through wireless 'pointing devices' and small video cameras that can capture information from movement – such as someone waving a hand or jumping up and down. The computer has been 'taught' in advance to recognize changes in position of different parts of the body and interpret these in specific ways. There is a wide range of potential applications for computer control methods of this sort well beyond video games. Microsoft is exploring, with adaptations of its Kinect technology, an idea to enable surgeons performing intricate operations to call up computerized images of body organs using hand gestures. The same technology could permit new generations of 'hands-free' mobile devices or enable severely disabled people to control an array of gadgets by moving a finger or foot.

## Power trip

Energy is a basic requirement for life. On earth, all the energy used for every living organism or item of equipment comes – either directly or indirectly – from the sun. The planet's main stock of energy is in the form of fossil fuels, derived from decomposed plant matter laid down over millions of years. Energy locked inside coal, oil or gas has to be liberated in some way, and put into a form capable of being used. The way this is done is by machines, devised with the help of a series of increasingly advanced technologies.

Since early times, there have been four basic options for people when it comes to finding sources of energy. The first was a 'do-it-yourself' approach based on using the energy provided by the human body, where the basic source is food.[19] A person at rest is using energy at the rate of about 80 watts, similar to the energy requirement of an incandescent light bulb. A person doing heavy work is likely to generate energy at 8–10 times this rate. The watt is a basic unit of power, which is the rate of use, or generation, of energy. The best-known unit for measuring energy is the joule: 1 watt is 1 joule per second.[20] The watt is named after James Watt, the inventor of the most useful form of steam engine. In 2010, the energy required for all human activities, including that generated by people but excluding the output of animals, used in jobs in agriculture or for transport, was 536 exajoules or 536 billion billion ($10^{18}$) joules. Details of growth in the world's energy consumption are given in Figure 3.

Assuming people were able to organize themselves (or be organized) into large groups, human-based energy could be scaled up, for instance for big jobs such as building pyramids or medieval cathedrals. The second possibility was to employ animals to supplement human energy. The power available from a horse is about 500 watts, equivalent to six people of average physique working reasonably hard. Another source of energy was to harness the power from natural sources such as fast-moving rivers or strong winds. Watermills have existed since Roman times. In 200 CE, a Gallo-Roman settlement near Arles, in what is now France, had 16 water wheels.[21] They drove a series of corn mills, grinding 28 tonnes of wheat a day. According to the Domesday Book, eleventh-century Britain had 5,624 watermills.[22] Over the next few hundred years, windmills became widespread in Europe and elsewhere. Windmills were more adaptable than watermills. Many designs allowed them to swivel to align with whichever direction the wind was blowing, increasing their usefulness.[23] Watermills and windmills were used for jobs such as grinding corn or operating rudimentary machinery to blow the air into blast furnaces. But the amount of energy available from water- or wind-powered machinery was limited. A medieval watermill could supply no more than 1.5 kilowatts (1,500 watts). Even the biggest medieval windmill generated only about 7.5 kilowatts. A modern truck generates energy at a rate 35 times higher.

### Figure 3 Global energy use since early times

(In gigajoules (GJ) ($10^9$ joules) and picajoules (PJ) ($10^{15}$ joules))

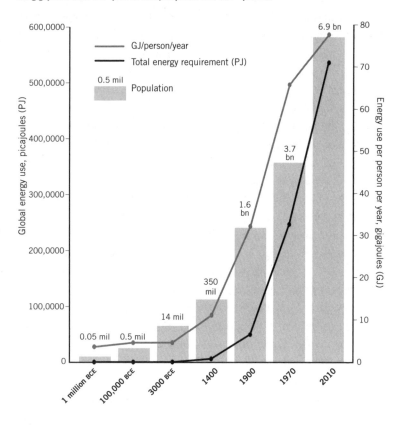

**Note:** The data for energy include energy produced by human muscle power, but exclude use of animals to meet human energy requirements, as in powering agricultural implements.

1 Exajoule (EJ) = 1,000 Petajoules (PJ)  = 1 million Terajoules (TJ) = 1 billion Gigajoules (GJ) = 1 billion billion joules

**Sources:** UN population database (http://esa.un.org/unpd/wpp/Excel-Data/population.htm); Energy Research Centre of the Netherlands (ECN); IEA, *World Energy Statistics 2011*, 2011, http://www.ecn.nl/home/David Christian, 'World History in Context'; Westra, http://openlearn.open.ac.uk/mod/oucontent/view.php?id=399545&section=1; Courtney, 'Historical Perspectives of Energy Consumption'; Maddison, Angus, *The World Economy: A Millennial Perspective*; Maddison, *The World Economy: Historical Statistics*.

What was lacking was a reliable and controllable power source, which could be scaled up. This is where the fourth option – tapping the energy stored inside fossil fuels – became important. In 1698, Thomas Savery of Totnes, in Devon, south-west England, published a patent describing how to raise a fluid such as water 'by the impellent force of fire'. Savery's device was the first steam engine, based on heating a supply of water in a boiler using coal. The steam passes into a series of cylinders. As the steam condenses inside each one to re-form water, it contracts, forming a partial vacuum. Assuming the cylinders are linked by pipes to the water that needs to be lifted, the atmospheric pressure acting on this water forces it into the unoccupied space. Savery's design provided one of the first workable ways to transfer energy from a fossil fuel into movement that could be used for a range of jobs.

In 1708, Thomas Newcomen, another Devon engineer, produced an improved engine that incorporated rods and other mechanisms that could drive machinery. In 1769, the Scottish inventor James Watt unveiled a still better machine that used energy more efficiently (less was wasted) than Newcomen's engines. Soon afterwards, the first large-scale factories started to appear in Britain. They contained many machines – for jobs such as spinning or weaving in the textiles industry – whose operation depended on rotary motion. With the help of a simple system of mechanical devices based around 'sun-and-planet' gears, the energy output from Watt's engines could be converted to a rotary form. As a result, Watt's engines became the prime power source for the factories that featured in the first industrial revolution. By 1870, steam engines used in Britain and based on the inventor's design produced an output of 3 gigawatts (3 billion watts) – equivalent to the work of 6 million horses. In 1890, steam engines produced almost 80 per cent of the energy requirements for US factories, superseding waterpower which up to the 1850s had remained the main energy source.[24]

## Rotary club

In the modern world, an enormous number of mechanisms rely on rotary motion. Inside cars are hundreds of largely hidden rotary devices (including gears, motors and drive systems) without which the vehicle would not function. Much the same is true of machine tools, refrigerator compressors and the circular saw. Equipment for providing energy – not just modern windmills (now called windpower machines) but most electricity generators – relies on rotary motion. The reason for wheels' ubiquity is, partly, their usefulness, and partly their efficient use of energy. When a wheel spins, it transfers energy continuously along all the points on its surface. If rotating wheels can be linked – by axles, belts or gear teeth – they can channel energy over distances greater than the diameter of a single wheel. Contrast rotary movement to lateral or up-and-down movements, as seen in a sliding beam or a piston in a pump, where the motion goes one way and then another. Here, energy has to be consumed through continuous processes of acceleration, followed by deceleration. Lateral movement is always more wasteful of energy than the rotary form.

The first wheels appeared in Mesopotamia around 3,500 BCE. They were used initially as a way of shaping clay objects, as in the 'potter's wheel'. A few hundred years afterwards, wheels found use in transportation, in rudimentary chariots. The wheel made its first documented appearance in Europe in 1000 BCE. The first wheels in Britain are recorded in 500 BCE, for use in carts drawn by horses or oxen. In medieval Europe, wheels (or rotary devices) appeared in many mechanisms, including ploughs, clocks and pulleys.[25] All required gradual improvements in the production of spokes, rims and axles. The need for these innovations triggered changes in other technologies, such as metals production, cutting systems and metrology. The historian Lewis Mumford notes: 'The technical advance that characterises specifically the modern age is that from ... [lateral movement] ... to rotary motions.'[26]

Wheels stimulated the birth of an 'enabling technology' important for many machines: the industrial bearing. Most wheels and rotating devices require bearings of some sort. Their job is to occupy the space between a wheel's shaft and axle, and connect the two smoothly, minimizing frictional losses. Jakob Leupold, a German mechanical pioneer of the eighteenth century who influenced James Watt, called friction 'the great robber' of energy.[27] Early forms of bearing were simple metal or wooden liners. In the first century CE, one such liner, made of wood, featured inside a ship used by the Roman emperor Caligula. Its purpose was to ensure that a dining table used on board could swivel satisfactorily, so as not to lead to too much disruption for diners during heavy swells. Around 1500, Leonardo da Vinci produced designs for industrial bearings, using metal balls and rollers. But the metallurgists of Leonardo's day were unable to make metal tough and hard enough to create bearings that would work as he had intended. It took advances in steel-making techniques in the nineteenth century to produce new forms of tough metals that could act as the main components in ball or roller bearings.

The nineteenth-century enthusiasm for bicycling helped stimulate technical advances. Ernst Sachs, who was born in 1867 in Koblenz, was an avid early cyclist, keen on racing. After an accident cut short his cycling career, Sachs moved to Schweinfurt – a town to the east of Frankfurt am Main – to take a job as a mechanic. A year later, Sachs teamed up with Karl Fichtel to form a new company – Schweinfurter Präzisions-Kugellagerwerke Fichtel & Sachs – to make ball bearings for bicycles, using the new steel-making technologies.

The company became a world force in bearing technologies, diversifying into other areas such as vehicle components, before being taken over by the German industrial group Mannesmann in 1987 and then by ZF, another large German company, in 2001. Schweinfurt continues to be an important centre for ZF Sachs, as the company is now called. The town is home to several other bearings production businesses, among them the German subsidiary of SKF, a Swedish industrial group founded in 1879 that is the world's biggest maker of bearings.

In 1885, Gottlieb Daimler produced the first internal combustion engine, a system to create reciprocating movement that could then be translated into rotation via a crankshaft. The internal combustion engine stimulated the birth of the automotive industry and – among other things – generated a big demand for the bearings for the rotary devices that cars contain. In 2010 the bearings industry had sales of about $30 billion, with the biggest companies including SKF along with INA of Germany, Japan's NTN and Timken of the US. A philosophy shared by all these businesses is to improve technology, by linking advances in disciplines including electronic control, wear resistance and chemical lubricants, so as to make bearings that cost less, last longer and work better.

## Spin doctors

In 1831, the English scientist Michael Faraday discovered electromagnetism. By means of this, electricity could be generated by rotating a coil through a magnetic field. The same principle could work in reverse. Rotary motion could be produced by pushing current through a coil under similar conditions. This idea led to the electric motor, devised in 1834 by Thomas Davenport, a US engineer-cum-blacksmith. The German engineer Wernher von Siemens founded the Siemens electrical goods company in Berlin in 1847. In 1866 he advanced Faraday's theories by inventing the dynamo. It used self-powering 'electromagnets', rather than permanent magnets, to create the magnetic fields required for electricity generation. The dynamo permitted electricity to be produced in large amounts, and at relatively low cost. Von Siemens later proclaimed that electricity would 'produce a complete revolution' in the conditions in which people worked.[28]

Von Siemens's ideas required energy to be put in a rotary form – to permit the turning action required to create electricity under the electromagnetic principle. Some efforts were made to use steam engines. But they were too inefficient, and noisy, for this job. To find something suitable, engineers reverted to old ideas – but ones capable of improvement. The key person here was Sir Charles Parsons, a UK engineer who had worked on ships' engines and rocket-powered torpedoes. In 1884, he published a patent for a steam turbine. It used the same basic mechanism as the watermill – a fluid pushing up against a wheel to create rotation. Parsons's turbine was based on steam directed against angled blades set into a wheel. The machines used energy from coal to heat up water to create the steam, and were the first systems to produce electricity in a reliable way. In 1889, he set up C. A. Parsons & Co. in Newcastle-upon-Tyne to manufacture turbines and sell them around the world.[29]

The power output of Parsons's first turbines provided little more energy than a vintage windmill of the 1500s. Nonetheless, he started to persuade entrepreneurs to install them. The world's first commercial power plant based on steam turbines was set up in 1890, also in Newcastle.[30] It produced power using a pair of 75 kilowatt turbines. After this, with more companies around the world building their own versions of turbines, progress was rapid. After electricity started to become available reliably and in reasonably large quantities, it quickly found uses in driving many classes of man-made products, from light bulbs to industrial machines.[31] By the time Parsons died in 1931, individual steam turbines based on his original ideas were each producing 70 megawatts (70 million watts) of power, almost 10,000 times greater than his first machines. Electricity went from providing 5 per cent of the power requirement for US manufacturing in 1900, to 70 per cent by 1950. New ways to produce electricity in a cheap, convenient and plentiful form are among the pervasive 'general purpose technologies' that have had a big impact on the world.

The most advanced modern equivalents of Parsons's steam turbines are machines called gas turbines. Instead of steam, they use a fast-flowing stream of hot gas, formed from the burning of natural gas, to turn a wheel so as to generate electricity. The constituents of the hot gas are largely air, carbon dioxide, steam and other products of the combustion reaction. Since the energy-carrying capacity of the hot gas is greater than for steam alone, gas turbines offer higher efficiencies than their steam equivalents. Gas turbines are now the most popular form of electricity generator based on fossil fuel. Developments in gas turbines for power generation were triggered by work in the 1920s by Sir Frank Whittle, a UK engineer who in 1930 brought out a patent for the jet engine for air travel. The jet engine is a form of gas turbine (powered by kerosene or a similar fuel) for propulsion. Whittle's basic design is at the heart of all the jet engines produced by the world's three biggest makers of these products: General Electric and Pratt & Whitney of the US and Britain's Rolls-Royce.

The first gas-turbine electricity plant was built in Neuchâtel, Switzerland, in 1939, by Brown Boveri, a Swiss engineering company that half a century later was to merge with Asea of Sweden to form ABB, now one of the world's biggest electrical engineering groups. The unit had an output of 4 megawatts and an operating efficiency – the ratio of the amount of energy coming out of the system in the form of electricity to the amount going in, in the form of natural gas – of 18 per cent.[32] In contrast, gas turbines sold in 2010 were much bigger and more efficient.[33] The big four makers of gas turbines include General Electric, Siemens, France's Alstom and Mitsubishi Heavy Industries of Japan. Their latest machines have an output of 300 megawatts and an efficiency of about 60 per cent.[34] The difference in size and efficiency of the machines shows up in prices. Between 1900 and 2000, US residential electricity prices fell by approximately 94 per cent, adjusted for inflation in the economy as a whole over the period.[35] In the 50 years to 2000, the costs of transporting a person a set distance on an aircraft dropped by a similar amount, with improvements in engine technology being a big factor.[36]

These changes would not have taken place without big advances in technology. New steel alloys used in the blades and combustion chambers of turbines allow the machines to run at higher temperatures, without the metal parts deforming. As a result, more of the hot gases can be passed through in a given time, increasing the system's energy output. Better chemical coatings on the turbine blades allow them to handle the high temperatures without becoming damaged through wear. Some of the most important parts of modern turbines include the small nozzles that feed natural gas into the combustion chamber before it is burnt. More accurate machine tools, and better programming methods for computer-aided design, allow the components in the nozzles to be shaped to tighter tolerances, enabling combustion to work more effectively. Computerized modelling techniques to simulate how turbines will function when in use have also had an impact. They have allowed engineers to devise better procedures for operating the machines to provide as much energy as possible while minimizing wear and tear. They have also been able to come up with better routines for maintaining the equipment, for instance by replacing parts. All these disparate areas of technology have required systematic improvement, with successive generations of new ideas built on what has gone before.

## Manufacturing's glue

One person who comes close to being a twenty-first-century successor to a Davenport or a Whittle is Shigenobu Nagamori, a Japanese engineer who is chief executive of Nidec, a company based in Kyoto. Along with Siemens and ABB, Nidec is one of the three biggest makers of electric motors. Nagamori was brought up in a tiny three-roomed house in Kyoto with his parents and six brothers and sisters. He then became an electrical engineer, starting Nidec in 1973. Standing out from the conventional 'consensus culture' in Japan, Nagamori proclaims his ambitions to be the 'number one' in everything he does. On a commercial aircraft or a train, he insists on being given the best seat.

Nagamori says that his company's engineers are continually investigating new uses for Nidec's motors – which end up in products from the Apple iPod to the controls for windscreen wipers for cars. 'We are interested in everything that spins and moves. Fifty years ago, what we call the "rice" of industry – the most mainstream product that drives everything else – was steel and 25 years ago it was semiconductors. But today it's the electric motor.'[37] Half the world's electricity demand comes from motors. In 2010 the world contained about 200 billion of these devices, making the motor population roughly 30 times bigger than the human one.[38] Nagamori is highly ambitious and likes to think long term. By 2030 – when he will be 86 – he wants his company to have annual sales of $100 billion (10 times more than in 2010) and 1 million employees.[39]

Nidec is by far the largest maker of specialist low-energy motors that operate under electronic control. A motor of this sort uses digital 'intelligence' to match the requirements of the job it is required to do with its operating characteristics. As a result, power is supplied only when it is needed. Typically, an electronic motor of this description uses a third less energy than a conventional motor. Nagamori says that motors of this sort can play a big part in helping to cut the world's energy bill through reducing electricity use.

Most of the world's electricity is created through the combustion of fossil fuels, as happens in steam and gas turbines. Since burning of fossil fuels leads to emissions of carbon dioxide, electricity generation is one of the biggest factors behind the growing concentrations in the atmosphere of this gas – the main culprit, so scientists believe, for global warming. So if the electricity used in motors can be reduced, this will have a big effect in reducing the impact of climate change. 'If you cut the energy used by motors by 1 per cent, you'd save in one year the equivalent of Thailand's entire electricity demand,' Nagamori says.

Nidec's research and development team, based in a series of centres in Japan, comprises a mix of experts in technologies from semiconductors and power engineering to materials processing and materials cutting. The improvements they are pursuing cover many of the technologies being investigated by global manufacturers – most of which can be categorized as advances concerning materials processing, management of energy and movement, and analysis of information. In some senses, nothing much has changed. Paying attention to these four areas of technology has occupied scientists and engineers for the past 300 years. But this underlines the point that most 'new' ideas in technology have evolved from products and processes that have existed for a long time. Even a product such as the laser – hailed as a breakthrough when it appeared in 1960 – had its roots in optics theory and materials processing that had been under study for almost a century. Professor Nathaniel Rosenberg, an authority on technological change, has observed that most of the money spent by companies and governments on research and development is devoted to 'making small improvements on technologies that already exist'.[40]

It follows, therefore, that the greater the 'stock' of technology in the world, the more of a basis there is for new ideas to emerge. However technology is measured, two things can be said with certainty – the amount of it is increasing, and the rate at which new concepts and applications are emerging is also going up. The number of people working in industry and trying to develop variants on existing technologies is increasing. Many of them are based in nations such as China and India that as recently as the 1990s played very little part in the global effort to devise new manufacturing ideas.

To add to this 'push' factor related to the amount of technology is a 'pull' element that concerns the needs of businesses. Technology has become more important to their overall strategies. Competition in industry has increased. This is a result of the opening up of the world through globalization, and the emergence of the internet as a mechanism to generate ideas and transfer information. The greater competition is causing more companies to search for new product and process ideas to replace or supplement existing ones.

Often, companies are replacing existing stocks of products more quickly, a trend evident in the shorter 'life cycles' of items from mobile telephones to detergents. In other instances, businesses are broadening their products to move into fields that for them are new. In these efforts, companies often feel technological advances are crucial. One example is Unilever, the big consumer goods company, which has introduced new products such as water purifiers and laser-based skin treatment systems. The moves have required the company to develop – either internally or with collaborators – a range of novel technologies in fields including membrane-based filtration and semiconductor lasers.

Many new products are characterized by a mix of technologies with few obvious links. For instance, companies in the medical device industry are developing products that bring together software, biotechnology and electrical engineering. These companies, including General Electric and Siemens, are devising new diagnostic tools that use a mix of these ideas to give doctors new methods of determining illness and monitoring the treatments to combat them.

Also, as companies evolve they realize their products and processes will work better if they treat technology as a 'systemic' resource – built up from knowledge in dozens of areas – rather than as a collection of individual ideas. A good example concerns the automation equipment used to run factory processes, made by companies such as ABB or Emerson. The machines are at the heart of hundreds of different types of manufacturing operations, in factories making everything from microchips to cement. To ensure the equipment operates at the highest level, the companies producing these systems have to understand many technologies. The list includes software, steel processing, precision cutting, hydraulics, semiconductors, fluid dynamics and three-dimensional modelling. If they can knit together such know-how, the companies concerned are more likely to succeed commercially. Technology is the glue behind much of manufacturing. In the new industrial revolution, the prizes for developing new ideas, collaborating with partners and applying the results in new products will be greater than ever before.

# CHAPTER 3

# The spice of life

## Glazing ahead

According to the Roman historian Pliny, glass was discovered by accident around 5000 BCE. In Pliny's account, Phoenician sailors, resting on a sandy beach in Syria, lit a fire to cook their food. To support their cooking pots, they used part of their cargo, which included blocks of soda (sodium carbonate), a common chemical used as a form of soap and for cooking. Once the fire was established, the soda melted, and became mixed with sand (silicon dioxide). The viscous liquid that resulted later cooled into a trans-lucent, solid state: the first man-made glass. While most solids have mole-cules arranged in a set structure, in glass they are positioned in a disordered way, allowing for the possibility of many different forms. Of all the materials known to humankind, glass lends itself to variation particularly well.[1]

People later learned how to make glass by design. The most prominent early glass-making civilizations were in the eastern Mediterranean, notably in Egypt, around 1450 BCE. Glassworkers used the material to create drinking cups, figurines, jewellery and furniture inlays. The techniques relied on skilled, expensive labour. The high cost of most glass products put them out of reach of all but the wealthy.

Between the first century BCE and the fifth century CE, Rome ruled a giant empire that at its height stretched from the Atlantic Ocean to the

Persian Gulf. The Romans discovered glass-blowing: the use of long tubes to propel air into molten glass. It gave glass workers new means to make novel shapes, textures and colours. The technique helped to formalize glass-making procedures, making skills easier to transfer and reducing costs. Glass objects remained 'high-end' items, with earthenware invariably a lot cheaper. However, glass-blowing meant the material started to edge away from being the preserve of the rich, and to become more a part of everyday life.[2]

By the thirteenth century Venice had become the world's leading centre in glass technology, making items from mirrors to church windows. In 1291, the city's rulers ordered its glass-makers to relocate from the crowded central area to Murano, a nearby island with more space. There, risks that industrial accidents would cause fires were reduced. In an effort to ensure Venice kept its technical lead, the glassworkers were banned from leaving Murano, under pain of death.[3] In spite of this, some moved away, taking vital know-how with them. The dispersal of skilled artisans helped the development of new centres of glass-making in the rest of Italy, as well as in countries such as Britain, France and the Netherlands.

One of the beneficiaries of this process of 'technology transfer' is Bisazza, a company based in Vicenza, 60 kilometres from Venice. On the front wall of its factory is a giant picture of a rose, made from thousands of small glass fragments. Employing 850 people, Bisazza is one of the world's leading makers of glass mosaics. Renato Bisazza, an engineer, started the business in 1956. His first employees were mainly former glassworkers from Murano.

Bisazza makes its products from a 'menu' of 400 small glass tiles. Each tile is differentiated by colour or texture. The different types of tile are made from mixtures of up to 200 chemicals, formulated in processes unique to the company. In 2009, Bisazza sold 3,000 mosaics, 90 per cent being 'one-off' products tailored to the customer's requirements. The rest came from standard designs which involve only a small amount of modification to fit in with what the customer wants.

Renato's son Piero, an intense individual with a love of American literature, is now the company's chief executive. 'We have to use technology and be creative. We cannot offer the same products as everyone else.'[4] Using engineering principles to provide choice and creativity, within constraints imposed by cost and affordability, is at the heart of modern manufacturing. Frequently, this manifests itself through using standardized processes of design and manufacturing to create 'customized' products – items aimed at meeting the specific needs of purchasers but at an acceptable cost. How companies provide affordable choice will be a key feature of the new industrial revolution.

## Out of the shipyard

In 1958, J. K. Galbraith noted that industrial progress was not just a matter of economics. It could also be measured by the degree to which products deviate from standardized designs to satisfy the full range of human requirements. 'So long as the consumer adds new products – seeks variety rather than quantity – he may, like a museum, accumulate without diminishing the urgency of his wants.'[5]

People's desire for cheap variation is readily apparent. Take the different types of yoghurt in supermarkets, the huge variety of clothes in different retailers and the explosion in TV channels and internet sites. In manufacturing, affordable choice has taken a long time to evolve. It has passed through four distinct stages, and is now in a fifth. The different stages have always been based on a balance between two approaches – customization and standardization – and whether goods are made in small or large amounts.

The first of these phases was 'low-volume customization'. The period coincided with early glass-making. It involved the first rudimentary processes to make products from other materials such as wood, clay and metals. For the sake of simplicity, this era can be said to have started with the beginning of the Iron Age. It lasted for nearly 3,000 years, until roughly 1500 CE.

During the time of low-volume customization, everything was made on a customized – or one-off – basis. Even with semi-formalized techniques such as glass-blowing, procedures were slow and expensive. Standardized designs, bringing with them significant cost reductions, were difficult, if not impossible, to achieve. Items made with these materials included ornaments, pots and pans, and weapons such as arrow heads and swords. They were rarely required in large volumes. But even when they were, people had little option other than to produce each item separately, treating each as different, even if the goal was to make them all the same.

As to how manufacturing evolved from this era, Venice again has a central role. In the heart of the city, a few minutes' stroll from the Piazza San Marco, are two massive towers, guarded by a pair of large stone lions. They mark the entrance to the Venice Arsenal.[6] Founded in 1104, the Venice Arsenal was one of the world's first large naval production yards. It derives its name from the Arabic *darsina*, meaning 'workshop'. Later, 'arsenal' was lent to military workshops generally. The word was appropriated by Arsenal Football Club, formed in 1886 by members of Royal Arsenal, a large dockyard in Woolwich, south-east London.

The Venice Arsenal is now used mainly for exhibitions. But in 1500, with 16,000 workers, it was close to the height of its capabilities. The yard made firearms as well as large wooden-hulled ships, with the latter often produced extremely fast, perhaps one every two days.

The focus on speed was one of the reasons why the Arsenal was the first organization to adopt a new kind of production system based around 'interchangeable' parts. Interchangeable parts were vital to the start of the second phase of manufacturing processes: 'low-volume standardization'. The period enabled production workers to start making their goods on more of a repeatable, consistent basis. Starting in 1500 in the Venice shipyard, the era continued for 400 years. In interchangeable parts production, groups of components are divided into families. Inside each family, parts are identical. Components made in this way are easier to assemble into a product than parts made in a non-standard fashion. Parts of this kind also lend themselves – at least in theory – to use in production systems, permitting a lot of variation.

A brick is an everyday example of an interchangeable part. Builders can construct houses easily because they know that each brick they use (within a defined family of bricks) is the same. Bricks in different families of shape and size are straightforward to make. Brick producers have an interest in introducing standards for 'interchange-ability', enabling virtually all brick producers to follow the same set of rules. Many other types of interchangeable part – from nuts and bolts to car components – follow similar rules to ensure compatibility. Other systems of interchangeable part are, however, unique to individual companies. Bisazza has its menu of 400 types of glass tiles, which no other producer has the ability, or necessarily the interest, to replicate.

The Venice Arsenal switched to the new process not just on the grounds of boosting efficiency. Customer requirements also played a part. The more closely components adhered to standardized formats, the more likely the design of the complete ship would also fit a common pattern. The more the ships were essentially the same, the easier they were to maintain, such as through refits, and also to operate. Changes in technology were another factor. More accurate procedures for fashioning components such as beams, nails and metal pinions helped the standardization process.

Interchangeable parts production – linked to low-volume standardization – was a key factor behind the Arsenal's relatively brief period of industrial leadership. From 1500, it retained its dominant position in European shipbuilding for only about a century. Shipbuilders in other countries such as Britain and the Netherlands caught up, and Venice's rulers lost their eagerness to try out new ideas. In 1797 Venice was occupied by Napoleon, and the shipyard's decline became terminal.

## On the block

The logic behind interchangeable parts was fairly clear, and so were its benefits. But from the time of Venice's espousal of the technique it took nearly 300 years for developments to move on significantly. Interchangeable parts required some of the production improvements that followed from the first industrial revolution – such as advances in precision engineering and metals cutting – to reach a more mature phase.

Some of the early ideas in the first industrial revolution had an immediate impact in the US. Eli Whitney was born in Massachusetts in 1765, 11 years before the country's declaration of independence. He became a school teacher, before settling in Georgia. In 1793, Whitney designed a new kind of cotton gin. A cotton gin is a machine for separating cotton seed from the rest of the plant. It is based on rotary mechanisms that push raw cotton through a series of wire screens. Whitney based his equipment on 'kits' of interchangeable components that he was able to make with the help of new, more precise metals production techniques. Through such routes, he was able to make gins in a more systematic way, cut their costs and win more business. Later, Whitney applied the concept to other products, including guns, sewing machines and agricultural equipment.[7]

At about the same time, Henry Maudslay was in the early stage of his engineering career.[8] Maudslay's father was a joiner from Bolton – an important centre during the early days of organized industry. Before Henry was born, the family moved to London. In 1783, at the age of 12, Maudslay started his first job, at the Woolwich Arsenal. During six years there, Maudslay learned many of the technical skills that were to help when he started his own engineering business, in 1797. Two years after this, in 1799, Maudslay was introduced to another prominent engineer, to discuss projects of mutual interest. Marc Isambard Brunel was the father of Isambard Kingdom Brunel. Marc was born in France but emigrated to the US, where he became the chief engineer of the city of New York. His jobs there included designing various commercial buildings, a shipyard and a factory for making cannon. Ever restless, he moved to Britain in 1799. Of the various possibilities he discussed with Maudslay, the most exciting involved the Royal Navy, then in the throes of a big shipbuilding programme. The Navy needed to make 100,000 pulley blocks a year for use in rigging. At the time, all these items were made by hand. The Navy was keen to reduce its dependence on skilled labour and cut costs. Brunel's management skills, together with Maudslay's talents as a machine maker, provided the answer.

In 1806, they installed in a Portsmouth dockyard a series of steam-powered machines that made the parts for pulley blocks in a standardized way. With 45 of these machines, the blocks could be made at the rate of 130,000 a year. The process was quicker than the old manual methods, and made the items more accurately. The workforce was cut from 110 to 10 men, reducing costs dramatically. As a result of this and other achievements, in 1841 Brunel was knighted by Queen Victoria– although not before serving a term in a debtors' prison.

Thanks to the efforts of Brunel, Maudslay and others who followed them, interchangeable – or standardized – parts became an element of the lexicon of manufacturing. They were an essential feature of the big capital goods industries of the nineteenth century, including textile machines, cutting tools and steam engines. The principle of standard designs and patterns was also important in some of the new consumer sectors that expanded quickly, such as clothing. In terms of the total output of goods from such industries, production volumes remained fairly low – certainly relative to modern times.

Even as late as the 1890s, by no means all sectors followed the principles of low-volume standardization. During the late nineteenth century, the first cars were created from parts that were non-standardized and non-interchangeable. In many areas of manufacturing, there was little urgent need to make parts (and also complete products) according to standardized processes. Introducing the necessary procedures normally involved considerable costs, in the shape of new investments in machine tools and design. These could seldom be justified unless the savings from standardization were also high. For this to happen, products needed to be made in large volumes – something that would happen only when demand climbed substantially higher than was the case in most industries during the nineteenth century. The era of low-volume standardization required the emergence of 'mass markets' before it evolved into something new and more powerful.

## As long as it's black

Car production became the first 'mass production' industry. But initially it was an artisan operation, built around the craft skills of previous centuries. In the early days of car-making, groups of two or three men made the vehicles by hand, using components made to order by other companies. But as demand built up, the industry was forced to change. The notion of creating machines to make products in larger volumes, as well as more cheaply, became increasingly attractive. Henry Ford was the catalyst. Born in 1863 in rural Michigan, Ford became an apprentice engineer before starting a job in a lighting company. Having created his own self-propelled vehicle powered by a petrol engine – which he called the Quadricycle – in 1903 he set up Ford Motor Company.[9]

In 1908, the entrepreneur unveiled his design for the Model T – also known as the 'Tin Lizzie'. The vehicle was reasonably priced and reliable. It was also relatively simple to operate and maintain. In 1910, Ford Motor Company built the world's first mass production plant, in Highland Park, a suburb of Detroit. The factory used the system of interchangeable parts, introduced for making standard products but in large numbers. It was the start of 'high-volume standardization' – the third key stage for manufacturing processes. The period lasted from 1900 to 1980.

Between 1908 and 1927, Ford manufactured 14.7 million Model Ts in Highland Park and other factories. Annual production built up to a peak in 1923, when it reached 2 million.[10] Given that at the start of the century, cars had been regarded as no more than technological curiosities, the figures were astounding. With the higher output, and helped by the processes used to manufacture the products, the price of the Model T dropped from $850 in 1909 to $690 in 1912, and less than half this a decade later.[11]

The cars were characterized not only by quality – but also by the inflexibility of their design. They were manufactured according to Henry Ford's adage: 'The customer can have a car in any colour as long as it's black.'[12] The lack of variability did not, however, seem to matter. The Model T was one of the best-selling manufactured products of the age.

Ford's factories – in keeping with the general concept of high-volume standardization – were based on moving production lines. The lines moved cars in varying stages of completion past stationary workers, who fitted components to a basic vehicle body or shell to assemble the complete product. The process required heavy use of machine tools and other new production systems. Under the system, manual 'craft' work was minimized. Large numbers of unskilled workers operated specific tools on the line, in a pre-set manner.[13] Their productivity was extremely high. In 1914, the company accounted for about 50 per cent of the US car market. But because of its high output per employee, Ford employed only about 15 per cent of the industry's workforce.[14] Impressive productivity helped the company to push down prices, enabling it to move further ahead of competitors. Later, Ford's mass production concepts spread to other car manufacturers, and to other businesses, from furniture to electrical goods. High-volume standardization was the foremost manufacturing technology for virtually the whole of the twentieth century.

Everyone agreed the system was enormously effective – even so, some commentators started to speculate on what might replace it. High-volume standardization used a system of interchangeable parts but was inherently inflexible. It lent itself to making products that were the same, but worked far less well with products that were different. In 1952, John Diebold published his book *Automation*. He noted that most of the factories of the era depended on 'inflexible production machinery' that was 'useless' in efforts to make goods in relatively short production runs where designs were changed frequently.[15]

The possibilities were spelt out even more clearly in *Management: Tasks, Responsibilities, Practices*, a 1973 book by Peter Drucker. It explained how mass production might evolve, becoming 'flexible' rather than 'inflexible'. According to Drucker, flexible mass production would be able to 'turn out a very large variety of truly different products, and yet have a totally standardized process of production'. The key was to approach manufacturing differently:

> The specific technique for applying the principle of flexible mass production is the systematic analysis of products to find the pattern that underlies their apparent diversity. Then this pattern can be organized so that the minimum number of standardized [interchangeable] parts will make possible the assembly of the maximum number of products. The burden of diversity, in other words, is taken out of manufacturing and shifted to assembly.[16]

He forecast: 'Flexible mass production . . . will increasingly become the mass-production system of tomorrow.'[17]

## Tinker, tailor

Drucker's term of flexible mass production means the same as 'high-volume customization'. This is the name given to the process that features in the fourth phase of manufacturing. It started in 1980, a few years after Drucker published his book. High-volume customization is also some-times referred to as 'lean production', or 'mass customization'. *The Machine That Changed the World*, a book about the automotive industry, concen-trates on lean production, a term coined in 1988 by Massachusetts Institute of Technology researcher John Krafcik.[18] In the book, Jim Womack and his fellow authors define lean production as combining 'the advantages of craft production and [inflexible] mass production, while avoiding the high cost of the former and rigidity of the latter'. Lean production, they say, employs 'teams of multi-skilled workers at all levels of the organization and [uses] highly flexible, increasingly automated machines to produce volumes of products in enormous variety'.[19]

A key concept is to eliminate waste in terms of unnecessary stocks of spare parts or complete products. Instead of having buffer supplies of components throughout the process, parts 'flow' through the system – either by automated transfer mechanisms or (more commonly) through people moving the components around.[20] They arrive at specific produc-tion stages precisely when they are needed. As a result there is a much more direct link between what the customer wants and what is being made. Both the execution of orders, and requirements for variation, can be handled more readily. To make this philosophy work, new systems of control were needed, built up around the powerful, cheap computers that appeared from the 1980s onwards – and which started to feature increas-ingly in factories, for instance as part of new 'computer numerically controlled' (CNC) machine tools.

The principles of the new type of manufacturing process were first applied, as with high-volume standardization, to the car. There were plenty of challenges. A car is a complicated machine. A modern vehicle contains 30,000 parts. These have to be fitted together to form 1,000 or so key subassemblies – such as engines, transmissions, steering mechanisms and so on – before the final assembly stages. To use such a large number of components to make a range of vehicle types is a lot harder than to do the same when creating just one model. The company that did most to establish the principles of high-volume customization was Toyota, now the world's biggest car-maker.

Sakichi Toyoda, Toyota's founder, was the son of a carpenter. He was born in 1867, four years after Ford. With a deep interest in engineering, he was continually playing around with new ideas, and had a tenacious streak. In 1887, Toyoda started an engineering business in Nagoya to exploit some of his ideas, particularly in the field of textile machines.[21]

After running, not particularly successfully, a small weaving plant near Tokyo, Toyoda returned to inventing. In 1896 he established a Nagoya company, Toyoda Loom Works, one of several textiles-related enterprises with which the engineer was associated. Among Toyoda's inventions when running this business was an automatic 'fail-safe' device that would stop a loom automatically should a fault occur, such as a thread breaking. This led Toyoda to create a design for a 'mistake-proof' loom containing other similar systems for assisting control. All of them indicated his interest in devising new 'feedback' mechanisms by which information from the outside world could be fed automatically to the control of machines. The system of feedback helped them to operate with less human intervention. Such advances meant one person could operate several machines at the same time, rather than just one, helping efficiency. The mix of automation and worker involvement that featured in the new loom illustrated Toyoda's interest in *jidoka*, or 'automation with a human touch'.[22]

In 1907, Toyoda realized that while he had plenty of good ideas for new machines, he lacked the most up-to-date know-how in production methodology. For this, Toyoda turned to the US. He recruited Charles Francis, an American engineer who had settled in Japan. Francis had previously worked at the Pratt & Whitney machine tool company in Connecticut. He introduced to Toyoda's factory the methodology behind interchangeable parts, a set of ideas that had at that time not been properly assimilated in Japan. Francis also encouraged his Japanese employer to install the machine tools and gauges needed to make the ideas work. As a result, Toyoda's operations became more efficient and its products improved. From 1926, Toyoda's textile machine interests were consolidated under a new company, Toyoda Automatic Loom Works.

With many of his previous companies, Toyoda had been only a minority shareholder. On this occasion, however, he had complete control. The new freedom enabled Toyoda to start the action necessary to exploit new business opportunities. He despatched his son Kiichiro to the US and Europe to investigate the emerging automotive industry. After starting a division of his loom company to build prototype cars and engines, in 1937 Sakichi Toyoda established a separate company to concentrate on this business. He put his son in charge, and made Eiji Toyoda, a cousin of Kiichiro, head of manufacturing. Sakichi thought about employing his family name in the title of the new enterprise. But in Japanese, Toyoda means 'abundant rice field', which Sakichi thought inappropriate for a company selling cars to ordinary people. He wanted a neutral name, and plumped for one that has no meaning in the Japanese language. In this way, Toyota Motor Corporation was born.

In 1950, with Toyota still in a learning phase, Eiji Toyoda went to the US for three months to visit car plants. In that year, 8 million cars were made globally. Of these, more than 6 million were produced in the US. Just 16,000 came from factories in Japan. Toyoda arranged a tour of Ford's giant Rouge factory near Detroit. Built in 1927, it was a bigger and improved version of the Highland Park plant, and dedicated like that one to high-volume standardization. Designed by Albert Kahn, the plant had 93 buildings, 150 kilometres of rail tracks, 43 kilometres of conveyors, 53,000 machine tools and 75,000 employees.[23] In 1950, it had a maximum output of 7,000 vehicles a day. This was more than twice as many as Toyota had made in all the 13 years it had so far existed.

Eiji Toyoda could hardly fail to be impressed. But he also noticed that a lot of the production effort was wasteful. Instead of being shipped directly to dealers, cars remained in stockyards until orders emerged. If customers failed to materialize, Ford had to sell the stock at a discount. In most stages of production, buffer supplies of components, or partly built cars, were required to provide material for the next sequence of manufacturing. These features required extra management effort to handle the buffer stocks, plus generous amounts of plant space. They also pushed up inventory costs. Moreover, the system was attuned to making cars predominantly to the same design. Eiji reasoned that the Ford system would be truly effective only when making a limited range of cars in extremely high volumes, and where demand for different types of product barely changed.

In all other circumstances, its inherent weaknesses would be exposed. He decided even a scaled-down version of the Ford system would not be right for Japan, where demand for cars was much lower than in the US and where the requirements for variety were greater.

## Shopping around

In 1956, it was the turn of Taiichi Ohno, Toyota's chief production engineer, to make a US trip. He visited not just car plants but supermarkets. Such places were substantially bigger, and stacked with more food and other goods, than their counterparts in Japan. Inside these temples to consumer choice, Ohno was said to have 'marvelled at the way customers chose exactly what they wanted, and in the quantities that they wanted'.[24] He also admired how the supermarkets 'supplied merchandise in a simple, efficient and timely manner'. The logic behind supermarkets became part of the way that Toyota planned its own version of high-volume customization or flexible mass production – for which it has its own name, the Toyota Production System. Such has been Toyota's impact that the Toyota Production System is now regarded by many engineers as the main process for combining mass production with customization.

Toyota's system evolved through a series of stages. It reached a state of reasonable sophistication by 1980. Its central element is how it links supply and demand, and builds in requirements for variation. The way this works features both automated methods to send data between different stages of production, and the use of human operators to intervene directly in the different stages of manufacturing. Similar 'information pathways' can be built into the links between Toyota factories and those run by its suppliers, to ensure that the transfer of both information and parts and materials flows smoothly.

As Toyota introduced its new thinking, its ideas were helped by a new approach to reducing manufacturing defects. This focused on encouraging workers to correct problems on the production line while they were happening, rather than waiting for someone else to attend to defects at the end of the production line. The approach goes back to the principles of *jidoka*: a mix of automated techniques and human operation.

In promoting this style of working, Toyota's engineers drew on concepts established by another key influence, W. Edwards Deming, a US manufacturing expert and 'quality guru'. During the 1950s, Deming gave a series of lectures to Japanese business audiences. His ideas about using statistical tools to measure quality, while following this up with concise methods to get to the heart of problems and rectify them, were particularly well received by top Toyota executives. One of Deming's central tenets was that automation was rarely the complete answer to companies' problems, and that better methods to train people and motivate them were often at the heart of what was needed. Shoichiro Toyoda, Kiichiro's son, succeeded his father and grandfather by becoming Toyota president in 1982. In a speech in 1991, Shoichiro Toyoda paid tribute to the US quality expert: 'There is not a day I don't think about what Dr Deming meant to us.'[25]

In the early 1970s, as Japan's automotive industry became larger and more powerful, the rest of the world began to pay attention to Toyota's progress. From producing 7 per cent of the world's cars in 1967, Japan's share doubled over the next four years, while during the same period the US's share fell from 41 per cent to 33 per cent. By the 1980s, the concepts behind the Toyota Production System had been adopted by other Japanese vehicle-makers, notably Nissan and Honda, and then spread further afield. While Toyota engineers had unashamedly adopted ideas from US experts, adapting them where they saw fit, it became fashionable in the 1980s for groups of US and European engineers to undertake 'study tours' of Japanese plants to learn about the new manufacturing methods. In just over 30 years, Japan had progressed from student to teacher. The process of dissemination of ideas has continued. Talk to virtually any large car manufacturer, as well as many other non-automotive businesses, and it will turn out the company follows production principles very close to Toyota's. Probably the crowning couple of years for the company came in 2007 and 2008 when Toyota's sales hit extremely high levels. In 2008 it made 9.2 million cars, trucks and buses, bringing its production above that of General Motors for the first time.[26] As a result, Toyota in that year became the world's biggest automotive maker by volume, the first time for 77 years that General Motors had not had this accolade.[27]

Subsequently, the Japanese company's fortunes waned somewhat as a result of a series of commercial and financial setbacks.[28] Even so, Toyota's reputation as having triggered an important trend among manufacturers remained solid enough. In 2010, Toyota made 8.6 million cars, buses and trucks, almost twice the figure of 15 years earlier. More than half its 2010 output came from plants outside Japan, compared to 27 per cent in 1995.[29] By providing a common set of procedures that could be replicated globally, the Toyota Production System made it easier for the company to set up factories in countries where it might otherwise have struggled to establish a foothold. The system is capable of producing a broad range of vehicles, measured in terms of both the number of model types and also of the number of permutations within each model. A basic model of car can be varied enormously, by switching between key components such as engines and drive systems, giving it different ancillary features in the area of audio equipment or, at the most basic level, changing its colour. On the basis of estimates related to the degree of potential permutation it seems likely that across the company's total model range, in the course of a year's output of vehicles a maximum of only about five would share the same product features. This indicates that out of the 8.6 million units made by the company, there were about 1.7 million variants.[30] The way in which Toyota makes its cars to such a large degree of variety is shared by most big car-makers, together with an increasing number of production companies in other areas of goods.

## Toolkits for variation

The fifth stage in the evolution of manufacturing processes is 'mass personalization'. The concept pushes the idea of variation a step further than in high-volume customization. High-volume customization – of which the Toyota Production System is the best-known example – is aimed at creating products according to a range of customer tastes and requirements. However, the process is rarely used to make products so special that they are unique. The difference between high-volume custom-ization and mass personalization is one of nuance. It would be unusual, for instance, for an individual Toyota model to be made for the sole benefit of just one customer. Under mass personalization, this could happen fairly easily. Mass personalization has many overlapping characteristics with high-volume customization, with the features of the latter taken to more extreme lengths. The era of mass personalization started in 2000. It is continuing alongside the earlier period of high-volume customization, which has yet to run its course. The production processes that feature in the new industrial revolution will feature a mix of both types of manufacturing system, with the second starting to dominate as the period of change picks up speed.[31]

The global leader in mass personalization manufacturing is Paris-based Essilor, the world's biggest maker of spectacle lenses. In 2010, Essilor made 320 million lenses, roughly a quarter of world demand. Of the total made by the French company, roughly 100 million were unique. The customers for this part of the company's output are 400,000 opticians in 100 countries. The large number of Essilor's products subject to mass personalization follows from most spectacle lenses prescribed by opticians having to be made to order. This is to suit the requirements of the individuals whose eyesight needs correcting. The other 220 million lenses made by Essilor in 2010 were made to standard designs, and sold to individuals with a wide range of relatively mild sight disorders (such as different degrees of long-sightedness) through retail outlets.

To enable it to handle mass personalization,[32] Essilor organizes its production in two steps. The first involves manufacture of moulded plastic 'blanks' – small pieces of plastic. The blanks are made in 14 'mass production' plants spread globally. They are produced in a large variety of shapes, sizes and chemical compositions. Depending on the combination of these factors, Essilor makes its blanks in about 400,000 different types. The wide range of blanks is Essilor's own system of interchangeable parts. It creates the menu of possibilities to choose from when taking personalization a step further. This is what happens in a second stage of manufacturing, which takes place in 330 small laboratories. The centres are close to the opticians that are Essilor's main customers, and are mainly based in Europe and North America. Essilor's second phase of manufacturing involves machine-based cutting operations together with the addition of thin coatings of chemicals to influence optical properties. A key to the process is a network of 20,000 computers in Essilor facilities around the world. The machines store information about patients' prescriptions, and convert this to instructions used by production equipment in Essilor's laboratories. Xavier Fontanet – who stepped down as the company's chairman in 2012 – is the Essilor executive who has done most to develop mass personalization. 'One of our strengths is that we have to be good at handling complexity. You could just as easily describe Essilor as an information company rather than a manufacturer.' According to Fontanet, the data are fundamental to organizing the 100 or so process steps necessary for the conversion of the blanks to the specific lenses for customers, often in a matter of hours to meet the demand for speed.[33]

Mass personalization encompasses production steps that involve a mix of automated and manual processes. Often, as in Essilor's case, it involves building up a range of basic product types – analogous to the French company's lens blanks – that are tailored to suit the needs of customers. A business that operates in this way is Left Foot Company of Finland, which uses its own system of mass personalization to make tailored shoes. Stannah is a UK business that is a world leader in stairlifts for elderly people. It uses a related set of manufacturing principles to make many of its products as unique items. They need to be made like this since they have to fit individual staircases, many of which have unique specifications. Mass personalization shares many characteristics with the procedures in use in 'low-volume customization' – the first general method of manufacturing that was in use prior to 1500. The difference, however, is that the procedures today involve some automated procedures to cut costs and increase precision in a way that could barely have been contemplated by the manufacturing workers of 500 years ago.

One way to provide a guide as to how much individual companies have promoted the concept of variability is to establish their 'variation quotients'. The variation quotient for any manufacturer is its average revenue per product variant. As a general rule, the lower the figure, the further the company has gone in building into its production operations the ability to cater for customer requirements. The notion of variation quotients provides a useful guide but should not be used to measure the amount of variation in the products of extremely small companies – with annual revenues of perhaps just a few thousand dollars – where the low sales figure may give a a distorted view of product variation. For instance, a company with annual sales of just $100 and one product type might under the calculations established here be considered to have a variation quotient of $100. However, the small size of the company in this case makes the calculation inappropriate. With sales in 2010 of $4 billion, and approximately 120 million types of product,[34] Essilor's variation quotient is about $33. The equivalent number for Left Foot Company is $90. Metsec, a British maker of structural steel beams for the building industry, which like these companies sets out to sell across a wide range of product types to meet different customers' needs, has a variation quotient of $400. Zehnder, which is based in Switzerland and makes central-heating radiators, has a quotient somewhat higher at $2,000.

Such low numbers for the variation quotient are far from the norm. For the UK tractor factory in Basildon, Essex, of US-based CNH, the world's second biggest maker of agricultural machines, the variation quotient is $93,000.[35] For Toyota, the figure is $200,000; BASF, the German chemicals group, has a variation quotient of $500,000, while the comparable number for Inditex, the Spanish clothing manufacturer, is $300,000. For products such as chemicals or clothing – where one type of molecule or item such as a pair of trousers can be replicated many times – the high variation quotients for the manufacturers concerned give a realistic view of the variation capabilities of the business. But in the case of the large number of companies that make complex machines comprising many parts, the relatively high variation quotients that sometimes occur for these businesses may provide an understated view of the amount of variation involved in their products. For tractor or car makers such as CNH or Toyota, their products may sell for tens of thousands of dollars but contain thousands, sometimes tens of thousands, of parts made by suppliers, most of which can vary by large amounts. Variation is therefore more of a norm in manufacturing than the relatively high figures that emerge from the calculations for some machine makers may suggest. A survey of 150 companies' products conducted by the author – together with adjustments based on the need to weight the figures towards companies making components rather than those producing machinery and other complex assemblies – suggests that an average figure for the whole of manufacturing is about $3,000.[36] The combined annual sales of the world's manufacturers in 2010 were about $30,000 billion. A rough calculation therefore suggests that the number of manufactured variants – unique product types – that emerged from the world's factories in 2010 is about 10 billion.[37]

## Standard deviation

Surveys of the amount of variation in factories 50 or even 10 years ago do not exist. But anecdotal evidence suggests that the degree of diversity is increasing, sometimes rapidly. The changes are driven by the accelerating requirements for new, improved, or just different products, both from industrial customers and consumers. It is also happening because it *can* happen. For variation in factories to be economic at relatively low cost requires flexible production systems that are now widely available. Such toolkits for variation – mostly based on the Toyota Production System, with some important concepts also established by other companies, such as Essilor – are much more prevalent in the early twenty-first century than even 10 years earlier.

The moves in this direction will become more marked. One factor behind the changes relates to technology. Machining and other processing operations can now be controlled so as to make even sophisticated parts in small batches, sometimes just one component at a time. An example concerns 'rapid prototyping' or 'additive manufacturing' machines. The equipment makes complex pieces of plastic or metal in processes controlled by computer programs. The machines work using a variety of procedures, such as through building up a piece of solid plastic in a layer-by-layer approach through 'curing' (solidifying) liquid plastic resin using lasers. Stratasys, a US company, is selling a version of these machines that it calls '3D printers', sold for making parts for goods from cars to furniture. The technology's development has been helped by its declining cost. In 2010, Stratasys sold its machines for $15,000, compared to the $700,000 they cost 15 years earlier. Also helpful is that machines of this type can be used in conjunction with new computer-aided design techniques, distributed to remote locations by the internet, which make it easier to produce unique designs.[38] Production machines that can be programmed quickly to create new, tailored products can be used to make a large range of goods, from children's toys used in promotional drives to packaging materials needed for 'one-off' product campaigns to mark events such as a football World Cup. By around 2040, many observers expect 3D printing to become a mainstream part of manufacturing, making parts for many products from jet engines to cars, and with particular relevance for products where customization to fit personal or physiological needs is important. Such items could include medical implants, hearing aids, lighting systems and specialized furniture.[39] When 3D printing techniques become an everyday part of manufacturing, mass personalization will truly have come of age.

The demands of the marketplace add another element. As competition increases, one way for companies to differentiate themselves is to offer more variation, at lower cost. In the case of products where customization options will become more important, high-cost countries are likely to play a more prominent role. As a result of the shift in global manufacturing towards emerging economies, manufacturers in many high-cost nations have had to cut costs, while their output has declined. But the trend towards greater customization will be helpful to many manufacturing businesses in high-cost nations. In tailored manufacturing, companies will invariably need to respond quickly to demands for customers for product changes. This will require more of the production steps for customization or personalization to be undertaken close to the customer. Many of the consumers at whom customized goods are targeted are likely to live in the rich nations. This will increase the likelihood of more product tailoring to be done in these parts of the world. Furthermore, many of the key technologies that will be important in providing such customization are complex, involving a mix of automation with craft skills. Up to now, development of technologies of this sort has been largely the preserve of engineers located in the main industrialized nations. Assuming the rich countries can keep their lead in these areas, they should continue to play the biggest role in the essential engineering developments required for flexible automation. The jobs that result from these trends will to some degree compensate for some of the jobs lost in manufacturing since the 1990s.

There will be some limits to the extent of the changes. Not all manufacturing will move in the direction of making goods in a diverse way, based around flexible but automated techniques such as high-volume customization. There will always be a need to make products using customized procedures but built around one-off components, and made in small volumes. Essentially, this describes the age-old craft-based manufacturing methods of low-volume customization in the pre-1500 era. Items made in this way are often extraordinarily attractive, as well as expensive. Examples include top-of-the-range watches, custom-built cars and elaborate pieces of decorative ironwork for buildings. As long as customers are happy to pay the high prices invariably charged for such items, making them in non-standardized ways will continue to be attractive.

Some items – especially some types of consumer goods – will resist the trend towards customization. This will be on the grounds that the customer for these goods has no desire to see the product 'tweaked' to reflect his or her own personal tastes. In many instances, the customer's preferences go in the opposite direction. Examples include electronic gadgetry such as mobile phones or music players. One of the attractions of the Apple iPhone or iPad is that it is distinctive and recognizable. Every consumer who buys such a product does so at least partly to share the experience of others with the same product. In these cases, Apple might find it pointless to attempt to build in product options.

However, sectors and products that fail to follow the trend towards product diversity will be in the minority. Even industries that for virtually all their history have made goods in long production runs, without much variation, are affected by the trends. Most steel companies make and sell hundreds of grades of steel. They are increasingly focusing on making these available to customers in a greater range of variants, to fit in with their exact requirements. Ashok Aggarwal, head of rolling technology at JSW, an Indian steel company, illustrates what is happening. Pointing to an array of instruments that control production at the company's large steelworks near Bangalore, Aggarwal explains:

> A decade ago we used to say to customers we can give you steel in about
> 20 different shapes, and this would be the end of the conversation. But

now, we can have a discussion that is a lot more interactive. Because of the more flexible way we control the [steel-making] process, we say to customers: 'What would you like?' and then we make it for them.[40]

In 1785, the English poet William Cowper wrote: 'Variety's the very spice of life, That gives it all its flavour.'[41] As the new industrial revolution gathers pace, the ability to provide this variety – within boundaries of cost, and with the customer exerting an ever bigger influence – will increasingly become a defining feature.

# CHAPTER 4

# Free association

## Thin air

Poole on England's rural southern coast boasts a balmy climate and a scenic natural harbour. A less well-known fact about this small town is that it is an important centre in the global electronics industry. Separated by a 20-minute taxi ride are the headquarters of two companies – Westwind and Air Bearings – that are the world's biggest producers of devices called air-bearing spindles, or 'air spindles'. An air spindle is a small electric motor, whose shaft rotates on what is called an air bearing. An air bearing is essentially a thin film of compressed air. A typical air-bearing spindle sells for $500 upwards. Made out of about 100 metal parts packed into a steel tube, it is roughly the shape of a half-used roll of kitchen tissue. The devices hardly look very impressive. Yet without air spindles, the world's electronics industry would find it practically impossible to function in its current form.

The development and use of air spindles are linked to two key trends in electronics: greater miniaturization and improved production efficiencies. Air spindles play a part in a widespread manufacturing process in the electronics industry: the production of printed circuit boards. Printed circuit boards feature in virtually every item of electronic equipment. They are pieces of plastic that act as the base for components such as microchips and capacitors. Since the 1990s, devices such as mobile phones and portable computers have shrunk enormously. At the same time, their capability to process information has risen. This has required ever smaller boards, each holding larger numbers of tiny but more powerful electronic components.

All printed circuit boards contain tiny holes – sometimes thousands of them. The holes in circuit boards act as conduits for ultra-thin strands of metal that provide electrical connections between pairs of components. The more holes in the board, and the smaller they are, the more components can be fitted into a small space. Also, the faster the drilling machines making the holes, the less time it takes to make the complete board, helping to reduce production costs. Where air-bearing spindles enter the story concerns their use in the drilling machines. In an air spindle, the air molecules supporting the shaft of the motor replace the conventional metal balls or rollers used in most kinds of industrial bearing. When the shaft turns in an air spindle, it does so supported not on pieces of steel but on gas molecules. As a result, energy losses due to friction are reduced practically to zero. This enables the motor to rotate at up to 5,000 times a second, 30 times faster than a jet engine, with a barely perceptible degree of lateral movement, or 'wobble'. The holes have a diameter of as little as 40 micrometres – or 40 millionths of a metre, equivalent to half the width of a human hair.

Without air spindles, the drilling machines used in the printed circuit board industry would be unable to make holes of such dimensions to the required accuracy. They would also work much more slowly. There would be a corresponding impact on the whole of the electronics industry. It would still be possible to make the wide range of electronic gadgets on which the world depends, but they would become bulkier, less powerful and more expensive. In 2010, Westwind and Air Bearings accounted for about 80 per cent of the $100 million worth of air spindles sold to the world's makers of drilling machines for printed circuit boards.[1] While Westwind has another plant in China besides the one in Poole, Air Bearings operates just one factory. Both businesses have their main research and development operations in Poole. Both can trace their histories to one man: Nigel Allen, an engineer who also practised dentistry.[2] He set up Westwind in 1963, after having experimented with air bearings in an effort to improve dentists' drills. Air Bearings was started 30 years later by one of Allen's former colleagues.[3] While Westwind is now owned by GSI, a US technology group, Air Bearings is part of Hitachi, the Japanese electronics giant.

Westwind and Air Bearings are a critical part of the 'value chain' for the electronics industry. The value chain for any product encompasses all the activities that contribute to its creation.[4] Companies involved in a value chain function as part of a pyramid. Those in the bottom layers, like Westwind and Air Bearings, provide products and services to support businesses higher up. At each level, the manufacturer adds value to whatever input of materials and technology it starts with. With each company in the chain responsible for specific components or production processes, the effect of each participant can be felt by all the other players through a sequence of often highly complicated interactions.

As a result of changes in technology, easier communications and a bigger role in manufacturing for many more countries, the way value chains can operate is immensely variable. The value chain for one product can involve hundreds of companies and individuals spread globally. The important businesses in a value chain for a specific set of products can sometimes be widely dispersed. Equally, they may be concentrated in one country, or even one small district. Such is the range of possibilities that forming part of manufacturing value chains offers opportunities for many companies around the world. The opportunities will increase as the new industrial revolution progresses.

## Pea source

In the Hans Christian Andersen story 'The princess and the pea',[5] a young woman is given a test: if her skin is sensitive enough to feel a pea, even though it is buried below a pile of mattresses and eiderdowns, then she must be a real princess. In the story, the impact of the pea indeed comes through, and the woman finds sleeping in her improvised bed impossible due to the bruising. Her prize for suffering this degree of discomfort is to be married off to a handsome prince.

In a manufacturing value chain, the sequence of interactions between many adjacent elements plays a similar role to the way the pea is felt through the layers of bedding. The impact of components and companies at the bottom of the chain can have a considerable influence on the way the complete chain works. In the case of air spindles, the Poole businesses sell them to makers of drilling machines such as the German companies Schmoll and Lenz, Tong-Tai and Takisawa of Taiwan and Han's Laser, based in China. The drilling machines in turn are provided to large makers of printed circuit boards, including Meiko and Ibiden of Japan and Tripod and Unimicron of Taiwan. The boards are then passed to the producers of electronic equipment, perhaps through several more layers of suppliers, before ending up embedded in the kinds of products bought by consumers. If something happens to disrupt the manufacturing process for air spindles – the equivalent of the pea in the story – then the supply of the consumer products with which everyone is familiar will be impeded.

The name given to the way the parts of the value chain are linked up is 'interconnected manufacturing'. The elements behind interconnected manufacturing are not new. The most obvious set of influences on a manufacturer comes from its purchases of components from outside suppliers. This has been part of the way industry operates for hundreds of years. Interconnected manufacturing also involves the relationships between different parts of the same company. Many large companies started splitting their activities between several sites, sometimes separated by long distances, as long ago as the 1930s. The concept of the value chain has been recognized for at least 20 years. In *The Competitive Advantage of Nations*, Michael Porter noted: 'A firm is more than the sum of its activities. A firm's value chain is an interdependent system or network of activities, connected by linkages.' Porter pointed out that the way the linkages are managed 'can be a decisive source of competitive advantage'.[6]

But what has altered since 1990 when Porter's book was published – and will change even more in the coming years – is the nature of the connections. As the new industrial revolution proceeds, the connections will become denser, more complex and more susceptible to sudden shifts in technology or market forces. The fragmentation of activities will become greater, as more businesses in different countries find they can participate.

The number of countries with an opportunity to play a part will rise, as technology continues to flow from the 'rich' to the 'poor' parts of the world. Power over decision-making will be shared more evenly between managers in a variety of countries, rather than being concentrated in the high-cost, industrialized nations. What might seem an inconsequential part of the complete chain of steps can have unexpectedly big repercussions. Management of value chains is an increasingly sought-after skill. About 2 million people around the world in both big and small companies do this job.

The full extent of interconnected manufacturing began to have an impact around 2000, about the time the new industrial revolution began. Full interconnected manufacturing is the fourth stage in the way the connections important to production industries have evolved. The first such phase was from 1850 to 1930. Manufacturers selling goods around the world did so mainly through overseas marketing offices. At this stage, such companies – even the biggest ones – rarely bothered to build their own plants in foreign countries. The companies reasoned that the markets they were selling into could be catered for by exports. Siemens is an example. Founded in 1847 in Berlin, the electrical goods pioneer had an international perspective from the start. It set up marketing offices in Russia and the UK as early as the 1850s, to help in selling goods such as telephone cables.

Ford Motor Company started its first non-US marketing operation, in London, in 1909. Neither Siemens nor Ford found it necessary to set up overseas plants in their early years. Frequently, companies made most of the components for their finished goods in their own factories, often in one giant works that also took care of final assembly. Where parts suppliers were used, they were usually located in the company's home country, in many instances in the same town or region as the headquarters.

But as the pace of industrial development quickened in the twentieth century, companies began to see the logic of basing their manufacturing in a wider range of countries where they wanted to sell their products. Often it was easier to sell directly into a country from a local plant, which could double up as a sales and marketing headquarters. Familiarity with the way products were made could sometimes help directly with sales – such as through sales staff having a deeper knowledge of the technical aspects of how the product works. A factory close to the customer in a specific country could often do the necessary job of adapting a standard product meant for global use to fit in with local requirements – such as to comply with national as opposed to international electrical or safety standards.

A manufacturing unit located in a country where goods were being sold meant any restrictive tariffs on imports could be avoided. Also, companies could improve their standing with foreign governments by providing jobs in local factories. The resulting political kudos was useful in industries such as military equipment or pharmaceuticals, which relied on orders from state-owned bodies.

For all these reasons, towards the end of the first phase of interconnected manufacturing, there was a limited amount of overseas plant building. Ford was ahead of the trend. Immediately after the First World War, it established several production operations in Europe. In the early 1920s, it was responsible for 40 per cent of all the cars made in the UK. But its European factories were far from full-fledged manufacturing units. They were largely assembly operations, relying on parts shipped mainly from Ford units in Detroit.

From around 1930, in the second phase of interconnected manufacturing, companies embarked on a much broader and more extensive series of manufacturing ventures outside their home nations. Ford's first big integrated plant outside North America was a large works on reclaimed marshland by the River Thames in Dagenham, east London.[7] Dubbed the 'Detroit of Europe', the works cost £5 million when built – equivalent to $400 million in 2010 money. About the same time, Ford established another big European plant, in Cologne. General Motors, Ford's US rival,[8] acted similarly by building factories in Europe. Other US businesses that followed a related strategy by moving into Europe included the electrical products group General Electric, the Caterpillar construction machinery company, and Dupont, the chemicals maker.

For many years, most overseas plants were largely independent of manufacturers' main factories back home. There was little coordination, at least on a day-to-day basis, between the companies' foreign plants and their domestic operations. The list of countries where the factories were located was relatively short. Nearly all were industrialized nations. The markets where the goods would be sold were also mainly in the 'developed' part of the world. Outside the main industrialized nations, expertise in manufacturing processes, as in all aspects of technology, was fairly low. So it would not have been possible to set up factories in the world's 'developing' regions such as Asia and South America, whatever the potential attraction of low costs, without unacceptably compromising quality.

The third stage in the development of the production connections started in the early 1980s. Due to economic expansion, there was an acceleration in plant building on a global basis. Companies could appreciate the advantages of constructing factories in the 'emerging' countries whose economies were showing signs of rapid growth. By doing this, the companies could both gain the benefits of lower costs and give themselves a better chance of selling products and services in these regions, as incomes and demand rose. As these plants became more established, their ability to handle new technologies and processes increased, leading to better-quality products.

Total global foreign direct investment – covering money put into business operations across borders for all economic activity – increased from $50 billion in 1980 to $1,900 billion in 2007. However, as a result of the world economic slowdown the total fell to $1,400 billion in 2010. Of the total figure in 2010, about 40 per cent was linked to manufacturing projects.[9] Much of this money financed new factories and distribution networks. The increased investments were helped by a reduction in trade barriers, easier travel and communications, plus a continuation of the long-term trend pushing down shipping costs.[10] A big stimulus was provided by the collapse of communism in Russia and other Eastern European countries, and government deregulation in nations such as India. Also important was the loosening of restrictions governing Western company activity and investment in China. These reforms were welcomed by foreign companies that saw the country as a promising place in which to expand.

## Hybrid thinking

One of the driving forces behind the latest phase in interconnected manufacturing has been convergence. Technology and quality standards in different parts of the world have become more similar. The number of 'manufacturing-capable' countries has increased, opening up the opportunities for value chains to become more dispersed. But convergence has its limits. Discrepancies between people's disposable incomes, and the mixes of goods and services they spend their money on, are still fairly wide. The divisions are particularly large between countries in the rich and poor regions. It is the continuing divergence in incomes and wages in different parts of the world – as well as the differences that remain in technology and engineering capabilities – that help to explain how many value chains take shape.

Of these differentiating features, wage rates are the most important. For a typical product made in a country with relatively high wages, labour expenses account for 10–25 per cent of manufacturing costs. As a result of lower wage rates elsewhere, the cost of making an item in an emerging, low-cost economy may be 30–50 per cent of the comparable amount in Western Europe, the US or Japan.[11] Such discrepancies go a long way to explaining the shift in the past 20 years of more manufacturing to low-cost nations such as China, Thailand, India or Brazil. When manufacturing moves in this way from a high-cost to a low-cost region, it is often described as an example of 'outsourcing' or 'offshoring'.

But when contemplating such moves, production managers normally need to consider more than just manufacturing costs. Often, a well-run plant in a traditional industrialized nation, even with its higher wages, can offer better quality and productivity than a comparable unit elsewhere. It might also be more adept at key technological processes, concerning, for instance, making design changes to suit specific customers. Kasra Ferdows, a professor at Georgetown University, suggests manufacturing networks should provide the best possible 'trade-off' between costs, quality, technological competence and flexibility. It follows that businesses with their main markets in high-cost nations, which make products in high volumes with relatively few design changes between production runs, are the most likely to opt for a strategy based around low-cost outsourcing. For products that need to be customized – with design changes to make the item suit different purchasers – outsourcing of this sort often does not work.[12]

In many industries, taking account of all the variables in making different types of goods, it makes sense to opt for a compromise in how manufacturing is organized. Production functions are split in a sensible way between high-cost and low-cost parts of the world. The name given to efforts to combine the aspects of running plants in both rich and poor nations is 'hybrid' or 'hybridized' manufacturing.[13] A key requirement is for companies to understand the contributions that managers from a range of countries can make to specific challenges, and mix them in the most appropriate way. According to Jay Swaminathan, a supply chain expert at the University of North Carolina, the companies that will do best in operating global value chains will be those with 'open attitudes' and 'an interest in trying to learn from others'.[14] The way information can flow in a hybridized factory network is likely also to be more varied than before, with a stronger role for the emerging economies. Navi Radjou, an industry specialist at Judge Business School at the University of Cambridge, observes: 'Once business solutions flowed only from west to east. Now they are flowing from east to west as well.'[15]

The two-plant system run by Westwind in the UK and China illustrates how hybridization can work. Under the Westwind strategy, the Poole factory focuses on more sophisticated, hard-to-make air bearing spindles. It leaves Suzhou to handle the manufacture of higher-volume but less costly devices. While the number of devices made by the UK facility is lower, the spindles produced there sell for higher prices. Steve Webb, chief executive of Westwind, says he manages the two centres 'as though they are one factory' but with different production lines for the different types of air bearing.[16] The ability to provide customers with a range of products with many levels of sophistication, and with prices that reflect this disparity, makes the company more competitive, Webb believes.

Further ahead, however, the Suzhou plant seems likely to expand faster than its UK counterpart. Not only does it have the benefit of lower costs, but it is closer to the most important electronics factories – in China – where Westwind spindles are used. As China's manufacturing workforce becomes more experienced, so Westwind's Suzhou employees seem likely to start matching the technological standards of their UK counterparts. This will probably give the company more opportunity to make spindles of greater technical sophistication in the Suzhou plant, rather than to continue to allocate most of this work to Poole.

Lakshmi Mittal is an advocate of hybrid manufacturing. One of the ArcelorMittal chief executive's strong beliefs is in the benefits of combining ideas from different steel plants around the world – in both high-cost and low-cost countries – and applying the results. One long-term possibility that could result from such logic is to use plants in low-cost nations as sources of cheap, semi-finished steel for shipping to high-value plants. There, the unfinished steel could be converted into sophisticated products such as corrosion-resistant exterior panels for the automotive industry, and sold to local customers. To ensure ideas from both sets of plants can be shared as widely as possible, ArcelorMittal has split the basic procedures behind steel-making into about 10 key processes – such as blast furnace operation or techniques for making cast sheets thinner – which are common to many of the company's 50 major plants. Individuals from these units meet regularly to assess how to improve their own operations with good ideas from other facilities. Bill Scotting, an ArcelorMittal manager who has played a key part in the company's 'knowledge management' programme, says the sharing of ideas has created 'a ripple effect' that has led to general improvements in a range of procedures that have helped the company's profitability.[17]

Another person keen on the hybrid style for manufacturing is Ratan Tata, another Indian industrialist.[18] Tata is the veteran chairman of Tata, India's biggest industrial group. In 2007, he authorized the $13.1 billion acquisition by Tata Steel of the Anglo-Dutch Corus steel company. The deal was driven by much the same logic as that behind the bringing together of the high-cost and low-cost plants in the Mittal Steel/Arcelor transaction. The key units in the transaction were a series of steel facilities formerly run in Europe by Corus – mainly in the UK, with a big plant at IJmuiden near Amsterdam – and a highly efficient operation run by Tata Steel in Jamshedpur in eastern India.

A year after the Corus acquisition, Ratan Tata followed up with a still bolder move which extended the concepts of hybridization into the car industry. The $2.3 billion purchase of Jaguar Land Rover (JLR) brought two of Britain's best-known car brands under the ownership of Tata

Motors, the Tata group's automotive arm. A long-time automotive enthusiast, Tata was particularly keen to bring together the contrasting engineering skills of the UK and Indian parts of the business. JLR has particular strengths in engine and transmission technology. It is ahead of many other companies in exploring ideas for small 'micro-turbine' engines that use ideas borrowed from jet engines to provide greater thrust. Meanwhile the Indian part of the group has special expertise in lightweight materials based on novel forms of steel or carbon fibre-reinforced plastic. Such materials saw use in Tata Motor's pioneering Nano car, launched in India in 2008, and one of the cheapest and smallest vehicles yet created. Use of such low-weight substances is likely to be increasingly important in efforts by many car-makers to cut the weight of their vehicles and as a result reduce fuel consumption – thereby lowering the output of carbon dioxide, a key part of the effort to combat global warming.[19]

To run Tata Motors in its hybridized form, Ratan Tata recruited Carl-Peter Forster, a German automotive manager, as Tata Motors' chief executive. In 2011, Forster announced a five-year, $7.5 billion plan under which JLR will design and produce a series of new cars, with the work taking place in tandem with related developments in India. Forster is enthusiastic about what he believes are the benefits of his group's 'twin track' approach. 'We have a combination of a low-cost base and a rapidly growing market in India, and a strong technological position in Britain. That gives us a lot of advantages which we can build on.'[20]

## Plant openings

Komatsu has its own special approach to interconnected manufacturing. The Japanese company is the world's second biggest maker of construction machines. It is keen, up to a point, on a key idea behind hybridized manufacturing: sharing power along the value chain. But at Komatsu, industrial democracy runs only so far. Managers at the company have instituted a form of hybridized manufacturing in which there is little doubt about who is in charge. In 2010, Japan was responsible for about 20 per cent of Komatsu's sales, but 40 per cent of production. The discrepancy illustrates the company's insistence that its Japan-based plants are ahead of all the others in terms of technical capability and productivity – in spite of Japan's relatively high costs.

Komatsu makes a point of keeping in Japan its most important factories. These make high-value subsystems and components such as diesel engines and hydraulic mechanisms. The most telling illustration of this 'Japan first' mentality is that all Komatsu's engines are made in one Japanese plant, in Oyama, 100 kilometres north of Tokyo. Komatsu has formulated a manufacturing strategy in which hybridization is combined with the principle of 'mother' plants. These act as the lead units in devising new technologies or production processes for particular types of construction machine, such as wheeled loaders or excavators. Secondary – or 'child' – factories elsewhere put the ideas into operation under the guidance of engineers from the mother plants. Of Komatsu's nine mother plants, four are in Japan. Underlining the point that, in Komatsu's eyes, any convergence in operating standards between its plants in high-cost and low-cost nations still has some way to go, all the other mother plants are in high-cost parts of the world – two in Germany, and one each in the US, Italy and Sweden.

Hiyoyuki Ogawa is the manager of one of Komatsu's mother plants – a factory in Hitachinaka near Tokyo. Ogawa's factory is Komatsu's lead unit for making large mining trucks. Part of his responsibility is to supervise operations at two secondary units run by Komatsu in India and Indonesia, which make dump trucks in lower volumes than in Hitachinaka. 'When we develop new ideas [in technology or production] in Japan, a short time later we will aim to introduce the same thinking into our overseas factories also.'[21] But as Ogawa explains, Komatsu always ensures its mother factories are ahead of the others. While its engineers are communicating new thinking to other plants, others are working on more advanced concepts that will be passed to the rest of the plant network later. In this way, so the company thinks, it will be hard for Japan ever to lose its technical lead. As for the extent of Komatsu's focus on Japan, Kunio Noji, Komatsu's chief executive, believes this is justified by the country's standards of engineering excellence, which he feels are unlikely to be surpassed in the foreseeable future. Speaking in 2010, he ruled out any imminent move to build a new Komatsu engine plant anywhere else – and certainly not in

China, which is where demand for construction equipment is moving ahead faster than anywhere else.[22]

Notwithstanding Komatsu's approach, it would be a mistake to think that in hybridized manufacturing factories in China and other low-cost countries are always given a subsidiary role. In some instances, the companies concerned have invested in special processes or technologies, so that plants in low-cost nations can make, perhaps against expectations, high-quality items to be sold at high prices. In other cases, these countries can be the source of good ideas that are useful for managers and engineers in other parts of the company.

The German kitchen appliance supplier BSH operates one of its most advanced plants in Wuxi, China. It is the company's sole site worldwide for making sophisticated washer-dryers that sell for roughly $1,000. In 2010 Nokia of Finland, the world's biggest maker of mobile phones, operated 11 plants, designated as being for either 'low-value' or 'high-value' products. Of the six categorized as low value, all are in what are normally regarded as low-cost locations, including Hungary, India, Brazil, Mexico, Romania and Dongguan in China. But another Nokia unit in China – in Beijing – is grouped among the company's high-value plants. The factory is regarded by Nokia managers as having the expertise and equipment necessary to make relatively sophisticated devices, along with comparable units in Finland, Sweden, Britain and South Korea.[23]

Luxembourg-based Element Six, the world's biggest maker of artificial diamonds, which is part-owned by De Beers, has set up a form of hybridized manufacturing which involves a strategy to learn from China. In 2006 it started a plant in Suzhou to copy the techniques of Chinese rivals in making artificial diamond – which is produced through compressing graphite under high pressure. Christian Hultner, Element Six's chief executive at the time, remarked in 2008:

Most manufacturers are concerned about the Chinese taking their ideas; we decided to do things the other way round. [In the Suzhou plant] we used Chinese management, Chinese workers and Chinese machines. We put into this plant not an iota of technology [from outside China]. But we succeeded in finding out a lot about the Chinese way of organizing manufacturing in this field, which has been highly useful in the rest of our worldwide production operations.[24]

In keeping with trying to learn from contrasting approaches in different parts of the world, some companies based in industrialized nations have made an effort to move more top managers away from their head offices and in particular into the emerging economies. The companies hope these people will be in a better position to discover new thinking from these parts of the world, and where appropriate put it into practice elsewhere. The approach is in contrast to the way most companies have been run in the past. The conventional strategy has been to give managers in a company's head office, normally in the US, Europe or Japan, the lead role in areas such as product design, marketing and manufacturing processes. The ideas they devised were then largely imposed on the rest of their companies' global network.

Eaton is a US industrial goods company that has changed its structure in tune with globalization. In 2000, 80 per cent of Eaton's sales came from the US. America was also where most of its workers, and nearly all its top managers, were based. Over the next 10 years, the company became a lot more global. In 2010, less than half its revenues came from the US, which employed a similar proportion of the total workforce. Having recognized the degree to which its operations have changed, the company has altered its management structure to suit. In 2010, the majority of its most senior executives with operational responsibilities were based abroad, with two each in China and Switzerland and one in Brazil, as against four in the US. 'You cannot have an agile international company where all the decisions are made by the [company] head office,' says Sandy Cutler, Eaton's chief executive.[25]

Other companies have devolved at least some parts of their decision-making away from head offices. One of the first companies moving in this direction was Volvo, the Swedish industrial group. In 1998, it designated South Korea as the head office of its hydraulic excavator division. It argued that this country rather than Sweden was best placed to take the lead in this aspect of the company's operations. This was on the grounds of South Korea's leading role in hydraulics technology, plus the many customers in

Asia for excavators. PerkinElmer, a US maker of scientific instruments, has followed a similar philosophy. In 2008, it stationed Daniel Marshak, its chief scientist, in China, as a way to learn as much as possible about the country's technical capabilities. In 2010, General Electric based its head of global operations – with responsibility for all the activities of the group outside the US – in Hong Kong rather than Brussels. M&W Zander, a German industrial and services company, which is the world's biggest provider of 'clean rooms' for semiconductor manufacturing, has its head office for this technology in Singapore. Springs Global, a US/Brazilian textile maker, has a chief executive based in São Paulo, with most of its key operations elsewhere in Brazil.

## Taking aim

Fitting into the broad trend of the increased fragmentation of the value chain is the key area of research and development. The proportion of such work that multinationals do outside the main industrialized countries is rising fast. In 2010 Siemens had 12 per cent of its 30,000 R&D workers in Asia, up from 7 per cent five years earlier. About 100 American companies have Chinese research and development centres, while roughly 50 have similar operations in India. In India, companies including Philips are working on new products in areas such as lighting and medical equipment. The Dutch company knows that if such goods are to sell in reasonably high volumes in India, their prices will need to be considerably less than is the case in a typical Western country. Such pressures will influence its India-based engineers and scientists when developing these items. If these people can create the necessary low-cost processes for creating products of this sort, still keeping them high in terms of quality, it might be possible to use the same or slightly modified products in Philips's sales operations in high-cost countries also. In this way, the company would find a new way to tackle the constant challenge of devising routes to cut costs, while maintaining acceptable standards of quality and reliability.

Siemens has already generated some successes through a similar programme. The German industrial conglomerate set its India-based engineers to work when the company established that a form of 'interventional' X-ray machine – the kind used in operating theatres – was too expensive for India and other emerging markets. A team at its corporate technology centre in Goa concentrated on the camera at the scanner's heart and developed a local replacement costing only about $500, compared with the original's $2,000. 'The new camera is not a cheap copy of a Western model,' says Vishnu Swaminathan, head of the embedded hardware system programme at Siemens's India technology group. 'We redesigned everything from scratch with a view to cutting costs while meeting the specific needs of local doctors.'[26] While Siemens's research efforts with this hardware will be applied initially in India, they will also almost certainly find use in the company's more traditional markets in Europe and the US.

Such patterns mark a break with the past. Development and design of manufactured goods was usually done close to, if not at, the place where the items were made. This partly reflected the costs and difficulties of transporting components and finished goods over long distances, plus wariness by most companies of the technical skills of engineers and scientists in low-cost nations. Another factor that acted against separating these functions was the general lack of suitable telecommunications networks for transferring design data over long distances. However, it is now becoming increasingly common to see companies that are based in high-cost nations separate design from production as part of a deliberate business strategy.

The principles of making a distinction between production and design in manufacturing were first formulated in the early nineteenth century. As part of this, the jobs were sometimes separated out to different entities, even if they were still in the same country. The trendsetters were American gun-makers and designers. Gun production was among the industries that benefited from the moves in this period towards standardized parts manufacturing.

In 1798 Eli Whitney, the inventor of the cotton gin, started an armoury in New Haven, Connecticut. Following his death in 1825, his son, Eli Whitney Jr, took it over. The plant started making guns not just according to the Whitneys' own designs. It also started working for US gun companies that had decided they would rather concentrate on design and development, as opposed to the physical aspects of manufacturing. An example of one such arrangement involved a deal between the younger Whitney and Samuel Colt. Under this venture, Colt produced the design for new types of revolver and other weapons, and Whitney's workers made them for him. It was the start of what is now called 'contract manufacturing' – a form of outsourcing.

A similar pattern was replicated by another gun pioneer, John Moses Browning. His contribution, however, was to make outsourcing international. In 1879, at the age of 24, Browning started a business in Ogden, Utah, to make weapons. A lifelong Mormon, Browning published 100 patents covering different aspects of guns. But he was always much more interested in design than in production. In 1883, he linked up with Winchester Repeating Arms of New Haven, a company established by Oliver Winchester, which produced Browning's products under contract. By 1902, the two men had fallen out, and Browning switched partners. He agreed a deal with Fabrique Nationale d'Armes de Guerre, a Belgian gunmaker based in Herstal, near Liège in Belgium. FN Herstal, as the company is now called, had been started in 1889 by a consortium of Belgian engineers. Its first contract was making 150,000 rifles for the Belgian army, using a design by Mauser, a German company. After completing this job, Herstal was eager to use its production expertise in other collaborative ventures. Browning spent a lot of time in Belgium, setting up home there before his death in 1926. Herstal's connection with Browning helped it to become a successful global manufacturer. Along the way, it started its own design operations. In 1977, FN Herstal acquired Browning Arms Company, John Moses Browning's old company, so gaining the full rights to use its former partner's name. It is now among the world's top five gun manufacturers. Without its early foray into a pioneering form of contract manufacturing, the company might not have progressed this far.

The separation of physical production from design is now fairly common among many manufacturers based in high-cost nations. In many instances, physical production and design are both kept within the company. However, the former is 'offshored' to a low-cost country to save money, while the design continues to be based in the country where the company's headquarters are located. This approach is in effect another variant on hybridized manufacturing. It is a strategy that has been put into effect – with evident success – by Dyson, the UK domestic appliance company.

The business was started in 1993 by James (now Sir James) Dyson.[27] The company became known for a key technological breakthrough: the design of the first 'bagless' vacuum cleaner, a principle later copied by many other much bigger manufacturers. In 2002, Dyson announced he was shifting virtually all his company's manufacturing to a new plant in Malaysia, to benefit from what he said was a better network of suppliers than was available in Britain, as well as lower labour costs.

The switch in strategy led to 590 job losses in Malmesbury, the town near Bristol where Dyson is based. It caused an outcry among trade union representatives and other commentators who argued that by pulling out of production in the UK, the company was turning its back on its home nation, and that the local economy would suffer as a result. However, Dyson argued that the better cost structure for manufacturing in Malaysia – coupled with excellent opportunities for organizing research and development in Britain – would lead to a stronger company.

Dyson explained 18 months later:

> We could not even source plastics from Britain. We were having to go to Germany especially for products such as cable rewinds and metal tubes and we found the suppliers there were very bad. In Malaysia a lot of the components we need are made within a 10 mile radius of our factory. It's like Birmingham was 30 years ago.[28]

According to Dyson in this interview, the shift of production to Asia cut the company's manufacturing costs by 75 per cent, and gave it 'a chance of survival' through a new strategy built around increasing research and development spending.

From the perspective of late 2011, Dyson's approach seems to have paid off. Rather than run down the Malmesbury site, Dyson built it up as an engineering centre. Its staff devised new ideas for products such as electric motors and domestic cooling fans – which the company put into production in its low-cost Malaysia-based factory and supply network. Dyson has consistently expanded, gaining a large share of the market for vacuum cleaners in the US and Japan. In 2011, the company also announced an entry into the field of high-tech floor heaters, using a new product based on the research in Wiltshire. Dyson's electric heater uses the same 'air movement' technology that features in its bladeless fans, and employs ideas borrowed from jet engines and turbochargers. After the redundancies in 2002, Dyson's employment in Malmesbury was 1,000, and then it grew to 1,400 by late 2011, including an engineering corps of 550. In 2011, worldwide the company had 3,400 staff, which it aims to expand to 4,000 by 2014. According to Dyson, the splitting of the company's functions between Britain and Malaysia – together with other linkages with suppliers mainly in Malaysia and nearby – provides a combination that in the globalized conditions of the twenty-first century makes economic sense.[29]

## On track

A more radical manifestation of a similar approach is for the company concerned to go a stage further than Dyson and become a 'design-only' or 'factory-less' goods producer. Under this strategy, the business stops making goods in its own factories altogether, and subcontracts this job to others, normally in a low-cost country. Going down this route involves a certain amount of semantic distortion. The company concerned is still properly described as a manufacturer, since it holds legal title to products, and designs and sells them. However, in the purest sense it no longer makes things. It then becomes possible to be regarded as a superb manufacturer – without any plants.

Phil Knight and Bill Bowerman have had a big impact on setting the pattern for design-only manufacturers. Knight and Bowerman are the founders of Nike, the world's biggest producer of sports shoes and clothing. Knight was a running enthusiast, and enrolled at the University of Oregon in Portland in 1955. There, he became friendly with Bowerman, an athletics coach. After graduation, Knight went to Stanford University to study for an MBA. He wrote a paper entitled 'Can Japanese sports shoes do to German sports shoes what Japanese cameras did to German cameras?' The paper discussed the possibility of using Japanese factories to make good-quality sports shoes that had been designed in the US. In the 1960s, Japanese factories had much lower costs than counterparts in Western Europe and the US, due to substantially lower wages.[30]

When the pair started Nike in 1964, Knight's MBA analysis became the blueprint for its operations. Bowerman's role was to design the company's first shoes, which were comfortable and hard-wearing, while also reducing muscle and foot strain. From the start, Nike did virtually no manufacturing in its own plants. Instead, it concentrated on product development and marketing. Initially, it contracted out production to Onitsuka, a Japanese sports shoe manufacturer. Then it gradually built up a network of other factories around the world. Bowerman died in 1999, but Knight remained as chief executive until 2004, when he moved to chairman.

In 2010, the Nike company had 34,000 employees, of whom 5,800 were in its head office in Beaverton, a suburb of Portland in Oregon. Most of Nike's staff work in design, sales, marketing and administration, and also in the company's extensive chain of shops around the world. The company does an extremely limited amount of production at its own facilities, mainly early development versions of new shoes or garments, or special components such as advanced foams for foot support. The rest of Nike's production is contracted out to 700 factories run by other manufacturers under contract. The plants are in 33 countries – with China, Thailand, Vietnam, Indonesia and India accounting for almost half the total – and employ 800,000 people. In 2010, factory-less goods producers were recognized officially as playing a key role in the US economy. To reflect these businesses' economic contribution, US government statisticians began reorganizing the way data describing US output are collated to take into account the role of such enterprises in manufacturing as a whole.

In factory-less goods production, the relationships between the design only company and its suppliers become even more important than is the case with businesses that retain at least some amount of physical manufacturing. Daniel Corsten, a professor at IE Business School in Madrid, says the interactions in such operations illustrate two key points about how value chains are organized. First, it is essential for businesses to consider their supply networks not just as opportunities to reduce costs, but also as ways to introduce new ideas in technology that can lead to benefits in terms of product design. 'Companies that organise networks of suppliers should consider them not just as sources of cost reduction but as sources of innovation.' Second, in the effort to make supply chains as simple as possible, companies should not be too fearful, in cases where simplicity is inappropriate, about making their operations complex. Corsten believes it is important to remember the 'law of complexity', coined in 1956 by the British psychiatrist and cyberneticist William Ross Ashby. According to this law, complicated technologies and products require complex supply systems if they are to be successful. 'It is pointless companies trying to design out complexity from what they do if this will make their products less useful,' says Corsten. 'What they need to do is to learn how to manage complicated supply relationships as expertly as possible.'

Considering the handling of these interactions, the Madrid professor makes the distinction between suppliers operating on an 'open standard' basis and those that are 'closed standard'. In the former, applying to sectors such as trucks and aircraft, suppliers are left to devise many of the most important innovations, in areas such as braking systems for road vehicles and hydraulic actuators for aircraft undercarriages. They share out ideas fairly freely with a number of suppliers in these industries, all of which have much the same opportunity to benefit from them. In closed-standard interactions, the suppliers impose tighter controls over the flow of ideas, and are commonly locked into closer relationships with specific clients. Correspondingly, the customer – which might be a producer of a factory-less good – is likely to be freer in providing its own design infor-mation to a supplier in a closed-standard network than to one involving open standards.[31]

## Open or closed

The computer industry is built largely around open-standard supply rela-tionships. Some of the key companies in this industry are businesses involved in what are called electronics manufacturing services (EMS) – outsourcing operations specifically for the electronics industry. Leading EMS companies include Hon Hai (also known as Foxconn) and Quanta of Taiwan, Singapore-based Flextronics and Sanmina-SCI of the US. With most of their plants in China and other low-cost countries, the EMS companies act as vital hubs in the supply chain for the industry, making products such as computers or games players on behalf of large branded goods suppliers such as Sony or Dell.

Most of the supplier/customer relationships that are important in electronics are open standard. A supplier that has devised a novel way to make circuit boards, or to put components on them, is generally free to use the same technology in selling goods and services to all the companies in its supply network. In the air bearings business, the relationships of Westwind and Air Bearings with their customers are again based on open-standard linkages. Cisco is an example of a branded goods maker in electronics that has virtually no manufacturing of its own. Instead it relies on networks of suppliers based on open-standard connections. The US company is the world's biggest producer of internet routing equipment – the electronic hubs that ensure the worldwide web works. Cisco employs 20,000 engineers to design its products and about 2,000 'supply chain professionals' – people who manage the linkages between the various businesses in the Cisco value chain.

In semiconductors, it is becoming less common to find companies that run their own plants. To build a new chip plant can cost $6 billion. Unless it turns out its products in very high volumes, it is rarely economic for a semiconductor company to choose to operate its own factories. Instead, many businesses in this sector have switched to the 'fabless' (fabrication-less) model. In this, they concentrate on their own activities in design, and leave the production to 'semiconductor foundries' – manufacturing specialists such as Taiwan Semiconductor Manufacturing Company (TSMC). Most fabless companies rely on their suppliers for innovative process technologies – for instance new ways to shrink the dimensions of circuitry to enable more components to be packed into a small space – in what is a series of open-standard interactions. A company that follows this approach is Qualcomm, a San Diego business that specializes in semiconductors for mobile phones and employs 17,500 people, substantial numbers of whom work in design and development, with virtually no one in a classical 'production' job. One business that as a competitor to TSMC is a key player in the open-standard chip foundry sector – and also displays some of the characteristics of hybridized manufacturing – is Abu Dhabi-based Globalfoundries. The company has an unusually widely spread network of plants for this industry, with operations in Germany, Singapore and New York State. It thinks this mix of facilities will provide the best service to the network of fabless chip concerns around the world that it wants to turn into key customers.

However, there are also many examples of companies for which closed-standard relationships are important. One such business is Einhell, a consumer products company based in Landau, near Munich. It started out in the 1970s as a conventional manufacturer, with virtually all its design and production operations in Germany. In the early 2000s, arguing that its German factories were too expensive, Einhell decided to leave manufacturing to others. It shut its German plants, switching instead to a network of more than 70 subcontractors in China to which it entrusted production of the items it sells – which include power drills, hedge trimmers and portable generators. Einhell's design and development operations have, however, stayed in Germany, where it employs about 30 people doing these jobs. One of their roles is to keep abreast of the latest trends in factory processes, as well as to work out what kinds of domestic products German consumers are most likely to find appealing. Einhell also has a technical staff of about 80 in an office in Shanghai. These people liaise with subcontractors in China to ensure they are capable of replicating as faithfully as possible the designs being created in Landau. The relationships are built around closed interactions. It is in Einhell's interests if as many as possible of the technologies that it employs in products contain innovative ideas from suppliers that are not widely shared with others. Jan Teichert, Einhell's chief financial officer, says that even if the company does not involve itself with manufacturing directly, it has to be highly knowledgeable about the manufacturing processes entailed, plus the know-how that its suppliers are turning into products on Einhell's behalf. 'To operate in this way [with production and design separated], you have to be extremely serious about the design function. But you also have to be very close to what's going on in the factories, even if you do not operate them.'[32]

In cases of big jumps in technology or manufacturing processes, a design-only manufacturer that relies on closed-standard interactions can gain considerable benefits. Apple is one company that has operated closed-standard relationships successfully. Apple follows the route of many other US electronics groups in contracting out virtually all its manufacturing to other companies, mainly based in China. The connections are supervised by about 1,000 supply chain experts at Apple's headquarters in Cupertino, California.

The company's biggest-selling products include its iPhone launched in 2007, and the iPad computer tablet announced three years later. The screens in these products incorporate special 'touch-sensitive' technology that enables users to control the device – such as zooming in or out of an illustration – by moving one or more fingers through a range of positions on the screen. The system uses a mixture of optical and electrical sensors based on ideas originally devised by Fingerworks, a US company with which Apple had a special supply agreement – an example of a closed-system arrangement – prior to Apple buying the smaller business in 2002. In other similar interactions, Apple has worked closely with two electronics companies based in South Korea – Samsung and LG – to improve the quality of the iPad's display screen. Through these relationships, the screen has been made easier to view in sunlight, by providing sharper pictures.

Similar examples of closed-system arrangements involving Apple have included its links with other suppliers that have been responsible for innovations in fields such as novel processing chips and graphics software. They have also extended to its relations with companies that supply devices called accelerometers. Accelerometers adjust for movement and help to align the display screen in portable devices with the way the user is holding it to make it easier to view. The closed nature of many of these links had enabled Apple to keep some at least of the innovations for which companies in its value chain are responsible from spreading to other businesses in electronics. This way of operating, so Apple thinks, has helped it to maintain a competitive lead on many rivals making similar products.

Closed-standard procedures can also have their disadvantages. If a product or technology in a closed-standard process suffers an unexpected failure, then the negative consequences for the customers is magnified, since it is only this company, and none of its rivals, that experiences the ensuing negative fall-out. Toyota's safety scares in 2009 and 2010 were linked to faulty components probably from small suppliers with which Toyota had a closed relationship.[33] In 2010 something similar happened when one of Rolls-Royce's engines blew up in a Qantas jet in mid-air. The incident forced an emergency landing and many months of concern for Rolls-Royce while it traced the source of the problem to a defect in a small pipe, made either internally or by one of its suppliers.[34] In both cases, the faulty components were made as part of a closed-standard supply chain. Had Toyota and Rolls-Royce used open-standard thinking in these instances, they would have been forced to share any innovatory aspects to the design of the components with competitors. But almost certainly, problems with the design would have shown up sooner, due to more businesses having an opportunity to test the parts. As a result, the two companies would have been spared the consequences of what were for them near-catastrophic series of events.

## The write stuff

If design is a key part of interconnected manufacturing, the supply of materials plays a big role too. This is appreciated by Count Anton Wolfang von Faber-Castell, chief executive of Faber-Castell, one of Europe's oldest industrial companies. Founded in 1761, Faber-Castell is one of the world's biggest makers of pencils, a product invented more than four centuries ago. In spite of the growth in digital information, there seems little danger of pencils going out of fashion. In 2010, about 20 billion pencils were made, half of them in China. Faber-Castell produced about a tenth of the total. Von Faber-Castell says good design has played a part in ensuring his company's longevity. But he also points to Faber-Castell's procurement of materials, involving supply chains that stretch around the world, while also featuring important partners in Germany. 'Graphite, clay and wood – these are the most important materials for us. The nature of these materials – and who we buy them from – is essential to what we do.'[35]

The company's oldest factory is in Stein, near Nuremburg, where Faber-Castell was set up by Kaspar Castell, a cabinetmaker. It has 13 other plants, including sites in Brazil, India, China and Indonesia.[36] The key ingredient in a pencil is graphite, the material used to impart letters and illustration onto a page. Graphite is a form of carbon that constitutes so-called 'pencil lead'.[37] In Faber-Castell's early days, graphite from the Lake District in north-west England was considered the best material. Then in 1856, the company switched supply, after buying a graphite mine in remote Siberia. In 1914, Faber-Castell turned to a source of graphite that was a lot closer to Stein. It formed a partnership with Graphit Kropfmühl, a German mining company that initially dug graphite from deposits in Passau. The relationship between the two companies is still in place, even if most of the graphite for Faber-Castell's pencils comes from mines that Graphit Kropfmühl has started in China, Sri Lanka and Zimbabwe.

Purchased in a powdered form, graphite for pencil production has to be mixed with small quantities of special clay to provide 'writeability' and resilience. Faber-Castell buys its clay from a mine in Klingenberg am Main, a town some 200 kilometres from Stein. The producer of the mineral is Tonwerk der Stadt Klingenberg, a company owned by the town's municipal authority. 'To make a top-quality pencil, you need top-quality clay,' asserts von Faber-Castell. 'So for the very best pencils, you have to use clay from the mine at Klingenberg. We have tested other clays but found them to be inferior.'

If the Count shows enthusiasm for forms of graphite and clay that he considers right for his company, he sounds positively evangelical when it comes to wood. It is the wood in pencils that provides the essential 'feel' that distinguishes one brand from another, he avers. 'If you don't get the wood right, it's hard to sell pencils.' To provide material for its large pencil factory in Brazil, the company goes to the lengths of growing its own pine trees, at a 100 square kilometre plantation in the central state of Minas Gerais. For the high-quality, expensive pencils that the company continues to make in Stein, Faber-Castell uses incense cedar, a specialist form of wood grown in California and Oregon, which is then shipped to Tianjin in China for processing, before making its final journey to Stein.[38] Von Faber-Castell says that in all its supply chain arrangements it must be willing to alter the details of its relationships and to take into account availability of new materials or shifting patterns of demand. Even a company as old as his business has to be ready to try out new ideas.

Faber-Castell has had a longer track record than most companies in adapting to changes in the business environment, and altering its strategies to suit. However, Faber-Castell – in the company of many other manufacturers – recognizes that it is now on the cusp of a new period of change. The pressures and opportunities to alter what it does are likely to be still greater than in the past. The opening up of global communications, advances in technology and the relative convergence in the manufacturing capabilities of much of the world are all increasing the possible variants in the way value chains are organized, for pencils and much else.

There are tremendous opportunities for companies to gain competitive advantages from adapting to these shifts and exploiting them. However, the most successful forms of interconnected manufacturing are also likely to involve some recognition of the potential for disruption. This can happen, for instance, if a supplier or technology provider in one part of a chain suddenly finds it is unable to fulfil its responsibilities. The problems of this sort that can occur were illustrated in the earthquake and tsunami disaster in northern Japan in 2011. The catastrophe affected a range of industries globally that relied on supply from Japanese companies of specialized components.[39] The hardest-hit industries were in the automotive, construction equipment and electronics sectors – all sectors where Japanese businesses have strong competitive leads. The episode showed that placing too much reliance on specific businesses in a small region – especially when the region is prone to natural disasters as is the case of much of earthquake-prone Japan – can sometimes lead to difficulties for companies that base their strategies on global value chains. When the region concerned is important for many companies' supply routes, the potential problems are magnified. The Japanese disaster of 2011 made many companies reappraise how they organize their supply chains and as a result build more redundancy into overall planning so that if – for some reason – a key supplier is put out of action then others may be able to step in as replacements.

While flexibility is required to take account of potential disasters, businesses also need to be alive to the possibilities of altering their value chain arrangements to take account of new opportunities. Switches in approach can take place, for instance, if a supplier in a specific part of the world devises a new technological answer to a recurring problem, or finds it can master a specific challenge related to costs. Companies will need to be reasonably quick to take account of such changes, without wanting to be so keen to move to new partners that they jeopardize long-running relationships. While big companies will exert the biggest influences on the way value chains evolve, there will also be many opportunities for small businesses, particularly if they possess new components or products that are advanced versions of others that already exist or tackle old problems in a fresh way.

Value chains involve key linkages – some organized in a simple way, others much more complex – between businesses around the world. The associations that take place need to be properly structured and reasonably solid, yet not so rigid that the companies involved lack the freedom to be able to alter some of their elements.[40] 'Free association' is a good term to describe the salient characteristics of the most successful forms of value chain. As the new industrial revolution progresses, companies with the organizational verve and technological credentials to make free association work for them will have a good base from which to move ahead of their competitors.

# CHAPTER 5

# Niche thinking

## Innovation window

In 2010, Panasonic, the Japanese electronics company, unveiled a giant 152-inch flat-screen television. With a screen bigger than a king-size mattress, it was still thin enough to hang on a wall. A few years earlier, such a product would have been hard to imagine. But television technology has changed. Products built around bulbous cathode-ray tubes (CRTs) are rapidly disappearing, and being replaced by sleek products just a few inches thick. Nearly all the thin screens use liquid-crystal displays (LCDs), based on small 'pixel elements' formed from specialized chemicals. Flat screens have also almost completely replaced CRTs in the displays used in desktop computers. The same technology is used in mobile phone and portable computer displays. Without LCD technology, the products would either not exist or would be much bulkier and harder to use.

The key component in LCD screens is a form of extremely pure, thin glass that has been under development since the 1960s. However, it was only from around 2000, with the sales of the first LCD televisions, that this form of glass became important as a product. In a flat display, the glass forms the outer two layers of a 'sandwich' arrangement of materials. In between is a thin film of liquid-crystal chemicals, whose colours can be modified by electrical signals. In 2010, sales of the televisions, computers, games players, industrial control systems and related products that use LCD glass came to about $1,000 billion – almost 100 times greater than the value of the glass.[1]

Making and selling LCD glass is an 'industry niche'.[2] The product requires sophisticated technology and forms part of a narrow market with few competitors – but a market capable of a lot of growth and one where the applications are not limited by geography. LCD glass shares another characteristic with many niche products in that it is barely known about. Most – although by no means all – niche sectors involve products sold not to consumers but to engineers. A large percentage of the world's inhabitants spend a great part of their lives staring at LCD glass in their living rooms. In spite of this, precisely what LCD glass consists of is a matter of zero importance to most people. The company responsible for making 60–65 per cent of the world's LCD glass – providing it with a rich source of profits – is Corning, a US materials and technology business started in 1851.

The number of niche industries has never been counted but almost certainly runs to thousands. Examples of niches can be found in virtually every broad product area, from machinery to textiles. Most countries with strong manufacturing industries have dozens if not hundreds of businesses – such as Corning – that specialize in these narrow fields. The influence of 'sliver' or 'micro' sectors, already important, is set to increase. Advances in technology, particularly the way different technical disciplines can be fused with each other, are creating opportunities for more niches. Companies with a strong record of dominance in one niche are often in a good position to perform equally well in new slivers. Meanwhile, their products and components frequently help the growth of businesses in other areas of manufacturing, sometimes also involving micro-sectors. Niche manufacturing will both be helped by the new industrial revolution and shape its progress.

## The rise of Eagle

The companies that focus on niches are often relatively small businesses in industries dominated by big ones. In the television and computer sectors, Corning – although a sizeable business in its own right – is a lot smaller than most of the consumer electronics and computer makers it sells to. Often, the area of technology that is the key to leadership is hard to master. This provides a substantial barrier to new companies entering the sector. A company intent on progressing in a niche field frequently seeks a difficult technology out of choice. Jonney Shih, chief executive of Asustek, a Taiwanese electronics company, believes sliver businesses should 'look for blue oceans' and avoid 'red oceans'.[3] According to this terminology, blue oceans are areas of technology few people know much about, and which are ripe for exploitation. Red oceans are the competitive fields, often populated by very big companies with the muscle to crowd out smaller businesses, even those with promising new ideas.

Jim Collins, a US business commentator, points out that many niche companies can be categorized as 'plough horses', not 'show horses'.[4] They get on with running their businesses, rather than spend a lot of time telling the world about their exploits. Hermann Simon, a German management consultant, has coined the term 'hidden champion' to describe such enterprises.[5] He says that in many cases the narrowness of the markets favoured by niche companies is matched by the 'depth' of their products. By this he means that businesses of this kind normally produce many different families of products within a tight sector. They can also sell services that address the 'complete solution' of a problem within a specific market.

Niche sectors rarely add up to sales of products and services of more than $1 billion a year, and some can be a lot smaller. The LCD glass sector is at the upper end of what would normally be considered niche. In 2010, the combined revenues of all the players in the LCD glass business came to about $12 billion. As for sliver companies, most have annual sales of no more than about $2 billion, with only a handful having revenues of more than a few hundred million dollars. For a company specializing in micro-businesses, Corning is a relatively large player, with sales in 2010 of $6.6 billion. LCD glass is Corning's biggest-selling product, sold under the Eagle brand.[6]

Corning's founder was Amory Houghton, a businessman born in 1812. Houghton spent his early career in construction, trading and real estate. But then, following a conversation with an itinerant UK glass craftsman, Houghton became enthusiastic about glass. In 1851, he bought a stake in

Bay State Glass, a glass producer based in Somerville, Massachusetts. In 1868, Houghton moved the company to Corning, a small town in western New York State, after which the business took on its current name.[7] The town of Corning remains an isolated, sleepy place, surrounded by rolling hills and a long way from the world's main industrial centres.

Instead of focusing on conventional areas of glass-making such as bottles and windows, from early on Corning tried to find new areas of application in industrial fields. In 1879, under the control of Amory Houghton's two sons, Amory Jr and Charles, the company devised an automated way to make the thin glass shapes needed for the first light bulbs, invented around the same time by Thomas Edison, the founder of General Electric. In 1908, by which time light-bulb glass was providing Corning with half its revenues, the company became one of the first in the US to set up a large research laboratory. Arthur Day, a scientist and Corning director, set out the company's interest in becoming a 'knowledge-based' organization. 'I wish to anticipate the fact that needs are constantly changing . . . The best equipment with which to meet these changes is a little broader knowledge than that your contemporaries happen to possess.'[8] The philosophy was in tune with that articulated in 2007 by James Flaws, Corning's chief financial officer. 'We [Corning] deliberately focus on difficult areas [of technology]. We feel we are not very good at dealing with non-difficult things.'[9]

These preoccupations showed up in the products Corning focused on. In 1912, it invented special shatter-free glass for railway signal lanterns. In 1934, Franklin Hyde, one of Corning's chemists, created a new form of silicon-based material called silicone – a kind of plasticized glass – that had huge applications in fields as diverse as industrial sealants and breast implants. Shortly after the Second World War, the company devised a high-speed process for making the glass tubes used in the first CRT televisions. It also played a big part in the development of optical fibre, the thin strands of glass that have replaced copper wires in many long-distance telecommunications networks.

Corning's invention of LCD glass can be traced to 1959, when its researchers devised a process called fusion overflow. Molten glass is heated to 1,600 degrees centigrade and channelled into a special trough so that it flows over the sides. As the glass drips down, it falls as a thin sheet, surrounded only by air. As a result, contamination is much lower than in orthodox glass-making. The process provided a route to making glass of high purity, with an extremely smooth surface. However, the possibilities of using this new type of glass in industry seemed slim. In the 1960s, the company tried to use fusion as a basis for making new and improved windshields for cars but the results were disappointing and the product never went on the market.

In 1973, liquid crystals for use in electronic displays, based on chemicals called cyano-biphenyls, were invented in Britain. The breakthrough came from a collaboration led by the University of Hull, researchers at BDH, a UK company, and the Royal Signals and Radar Establishment, part of the Ministry of Defence. The technology found use in the displays for the first hand-held electronic calculators, made by Japanese companies such as Sharp and Casio. Electronic watches were another early application. The tiny displays used in all these products were based on ordinary glass made in processes similar to those used for window sheets.

In 1982, Corning opened a research laboratory near Tokyo. It marked, in part, an effort to move closer to the Japanese consumer electronics industry that was acquiring a reputation for innovation. Corning talked to Japanese businesses such as Sharp, Panasonic and Sony about new technologies they were keen to see developed. One topic of discussion concerned LCD displays. The companies wanted to scale up LCD technology so it could be used in large displays for computer screens and televisions. Ordinary glass sheet was of little use in these products. Because of the lack of purity and the surface defects in glass of this type, large screens made from it had a picture resolution that was extremely poor. Corning's engineers thought fusion glass might provide the answer. The company sold small amounts of the glass to its Japanese customers to test out how well it worked. However, progress during the 1980s and 1990s was slow. The market for flat-screen displays seemed very small. Most customers were reasonably happy with the CRT units they had already. The need for change seemed less than obvious. Also fusion glass was expensive. So using it for the new flat screens that LCD would make possible – especially for extremely large versions suitable for televisions

– still seemed to show little promise. But struck by the possibilities for saving space that LCD technology offered, and with the cramped nature of many Japanese homes and offices of particular relevance, the electronics companies persisted with their interest. Corning responded by continuing with its development of fusion glass. It was keen to adapt it to meet the needs of its potential Japanese customers, and also to bring down costs.

The biggest changes in quality and usefulness of the glass took place between 2000 and 2010. Over this period, Corning spent $4 billion on building new fusion glass factories, mainly in Japan, Taiwan and South Korea. It also invested $1 billion on research and development, much of this going into new ways to make the material in bigger sheets, as a result cutting its cost. Over the same time, Corning's main customers in the television industry expanded to include several Taiwanese and Korean businesses. The companies became more adept at making LCD technology work in television displays. For instance, they formulated improved methods to control the pixel elements in the displays, using novel software techniques, aided by advances in electronics components.

The combined effort by Corning and its customers paid off with a huge rise in sales of LCD televisions. In 2002, fewer than 1 million LCD sets were sold. This figure accounted for less than 1 per cent of sales in 2002 of televisions of all kinds, the remaining units being mainly based on CRT technology. By 2010, demand for LCD televisions had soared some 200 times to 190 million, or 77 per cent of all the televisions sold in that year. By 2014, according to Corning's projections, sales of LCD televisions will climb to 300 million, or 95 per cent of the likely sales of televisions of all kinds. The remaining 5 per cent will be almost entirely based on plasma display technology, with sales of CRT units by then having fallen practically to zero.[10]

In 2002, a 42-inch LCD television sold for about $10,000. Four years after this, the price had dropped to $1,000. By 2010, the figure had fallen by another half. In 2011, it was possible to buy a 42-inch television for comfortably below $450. Between 2000 and 2010, sales of LCD glass climbed by a factor of 17. In 2010, the amount of LCD glass sold to the electronics industry would, if laid out in sheets, have filled a space measuring 50 kilometres by 50 kilometres – enough to pave all of Manhattan nearly 50 times. LCD televisions have been one of the most popular consumer products of the early twenty-first century. They would never have been developed without the micro-sector of LCD glass.

## Slivers' shapers

There are many more niche businesses – and sliver sectors in which they can compete – in manufacturing than in services. In a 2009 sample of 2,000 niche businesses, 90 per were predominantly manufacturers.[11] Of these companies, four out of every five made industrial rather than consumer products. The other 10 per cent in the survey were largely service businesses. There are two main reasons why niches lend themselves more readily to manufacturing than to services. One of them concerns the characteristics of goods, while the other is to do with the way products and services are sold. Capitalizing on new ideas in technology, supported by inventive approaches in marketing, it is not too difficult to devise a new product sector that stands out from other businesses. Doing the equivalent with services is harder. Most services are almost by definition extremely variable. A hairdresser can, for instance, cut someone's hair in a multitude of different ways. So the opportunities for fragmentation of services into small, separate fields that are readily distinguishable are a lot fewer.

Once a sliver sector has been defined, setting up and operating a viable business is easier in manufacturing than in services. In any niche, the number of customers is, almost by definition, fairly small. The size of the potential market in a single country is therefore normally not enough to provide a micro-company with the revenues it needs to cover its costs. This is why most niches require an international clientele if they are to prosper. Products are relatively easy to ship between countries, with the help of a relatively small number of sales and marketing people either in the home nation or abroad. Doing the equivalent with services is more difficult. Most services – such as selling insurance or doing repair work – require large numbers of people operating close to where the service is being sold. Paying for the sizeable employee base needed to sell services on a global basis is frequently beyond the capabilities of the predominantly small to medium-sized companies that feature in micro-sectors.

Many companies associated with niche fields have, like Corning, long histories, with a culture oriented towards innovation. Tokyo-based Japan Steel Works (JSW) is the world's biggest company making large steel components for the pressure vessels used in nuclear power stations. It uses some of the basic steel-making techniques practised by the producers of Japanese samurai swords in the fifteenth century. Capitalizing on some of this history, JSW was formed in 1907 as a maker of large steel castings mainly for heavy artillery. Initially, it had an alliance with two big Sheffield-based steel businesses, Sir W. G. Armstrong & Company and Vickers, Sons & Maxim. The UK companies allowed JSW to use some of their techniques in metals processing. In exchange, JSW put work their way in Japan. Buoyed by its extensive history in metals processing, JSW moved into the nuclear field at the end of the 1990s. Over the next decade it spent about $1 billion building up its position in this technology with a mix of capital investments and research programmes. In 2010, JSW accounted for 80 per cent of the $300 million global sales of the specialized components that constitute its main niche.

Other companies specializing in micro-sectors are more recent. In 1965, Dave Willis started Whitford, a small chemicals business based near Philadelphia, with the help of $100,000 borrowed from his father. He has built this up to become one of the world's two biggest producers of non-stick coatings used in applications from cookware to oil drilling equipment. Behind this success has been a dogged persistence, based around developing ever more specialized systems of coatings, based on chemicals called fluoropolymers. At the last count, Whitford had 2,200 product formulas for its specialized coatings, and supplied 2,500 companies. Willis says a patient approach has been essential. '[I've] slowly amassed a lot of knowledge and then applied it.'[12] Britain's most accomplished niche manufacturer is Renishaw, a business based near Bristol which was started in 1973 by David (now Sir David) McMurtry, an unassuming former aerospace engineer who is the author of more than 200 patents. The Renishaw chairman and chief executive's motto is: 'Always keep ahead of others in the game.'[13] By this he means pour money into research and development to maintain the company's leadership in the narrow area of high-tech probes for machine tools – precision devices that ensure tools cut metal to the correct dimensions in industries from aerospace to lawnmowers. In 2010, Renishaw was responsible for about 60 per cent of a global business worth $250 million a year.

Close ties to customers is another frequent characteristic for niche businesses. Pietro Carnaghi, a company in Italy, is the world's biggest maker of vertical machining lathes. Carnaghi makes giant machines for shaping large circular metal parts, such as components of gas turbines or aircraft fuselages. Its customers include giant businesses including Boeing and Siemens. The main driving force behind the company has been Flavio Radice, its managing director since 1973, who is married to the grand-daughter of the company's founder. Radice says a small niche supplier should try to make itself indispensable to the large businesses that are usually its most important customers. 'For our customers these [our products] are strategic . . . tools. They can perform operations on metal that cannot be done in any other way.'[14]

There is little argument about which country is the world capital for niche businesses. Germany has large numbers of privately owned engineering companies – many of them part of the *Mittelstand* group of mid-sized family businesses that are a key part of the German economy. Many are leaders in highly specialized niches. There is some evidence that Germany – together with the two other important German-speaking nations, Austria and Switzerland – account for more than half all the sliver businesses so far identified.[15] Their track record is for the most part impressive. According to Simon's research, the average German sliver company grew in sales by more than 100 per cent during the decade to 2009, in the process generating 1 million jobs both in Germany and abroad.[16]

Much of Germany's success in micro-industries can be explained by history. For centuries, the country has had a strong association with engineering and technology. The craft guilds that evolved in the country in medieval times were built around leadership in skills linked to fields such as metalworking and textiles. Some of these skills are still in evidence, in a suitably modified form. Edward Krubasik, a leading commentator on German industry who is a former board member at Siemens, observes: 'Germany has used the technology base it established in medieval times as a platform for success in the twenty-first century.'[17]

Another favourable factor may have been the political system prevalent in Germany until the late nineteenth century. Until then, most of Germany had existed as a series of small, independent states. The notion of a strong, centralized government setting out policies for the country as a whole came to Germany a lot later than, for instance, France and Britain. There is a case for arguing that Germany's political system of small, self-determining fiefdoms helped to breed groups of entrepreneurs keen to succeed on an independent basis with little help from the state or anyone else. With the additional strong interest in the country in technology, the mindsets of many people interested in business tended to push them towards the engineering-based niches in which many German companies excel. Lorenz Raith, who spent 20 years at the Schaeffler industrial bearings maker, a leading example of a German hidden champion, points to the 'down-to-earth orientation of the pioneer generation' – the people who either started many niche leaders in the 1940s or 1950s or had to revive older businesses in the unpromising conditions in Germany after the Second World War.[18] 'These managers had hardly any capital for expansion and had to make intense efforts to increase productivity through new ideas, as well as building up positions in world markets,' says Raith.[19]

Berthold Leibinger is a German industrialist who heads one of the best examples in the country of a sliver company. Leibinger is typical of the people commonly found running such businesses in Germany: obsessed by technology, unafraid of hard work and eager to see their companies develop over several generations. He describes his own preoccupations with engineering: 'To talk about a new product, even to draw sketches, discuss and propose solutions, this is fascinating.'[20] Leibinger's own story is illustrative. The son of a dealer in oriental art, Leibinger ignored his father's advice not to venture into engineering and took up an engineering apprenticeship in 1950 at a company called Trumpf. Trumpf was a small family business based near Stuttgart, which was started in 1923 as a maker of small metal shafts used in dental drills and printing machines. In 1973, after completing a period of university training as an engineer and rising up the management hierarchy at Trumpf, Leibinger acquired enough money to buy out the previous owners to take control. His goal was to move Trumpf into a more specialized field where it could compete on a global basis.

In 1979, Leibinger saw the chance to build up strength in precision cutting machines using lasers, then relatively novel devices. After touring the US seeking laser suppliers, he found no product whose technical specifications matched what he wanted. So Leibinger set up a design group to make specific lasers expressly built for cutting metal. He assembled a team of physicists who 'understand the shop floor'.[21] It was a bold effort for a company that had had some success in mechanical engineering, but whose core skills did not include the optics technology that laser developers require. But the move turned out a success. All the lasers used in Trumpf's cutting machines are now made by its own laser division. This part of the company has developed into one of the world's biggest makers of lasers, selling the devices to outsiders as well as meeting Trumpf's internal needs. However, Trumpf is mainly known for its top position in its own specialized industry niche. In 2010 the company accounted for 30 per cent of the $3 billion global sales of laser cutting machines. The equipment has become a vital tool for businesses cutting sheet metal, for making into products from traffic lights to furniture.

## Growth drive

The way niche companies move into new fields can vary enormously. However, there is nearly always a common theme. They invariably evolve into a novel sector that has a connection – in terms of either technology or customers – with an industry that they know about already. Germany has many examples of long-established sliver specialists which have shown such progressions. Many of the German hidden champions have been owned by the same families for centuries. The stable ownership pattern has in many cases encouraged the businesses to focus on discrete sectors where they have built up strengths over a long time. This can provide a platform for moving into a new but related sector. Even if the efforts to move into new businesses are normally fairly cautious, the search for novelty, and interest in new thinking, is a vital part of these companies' business approach. Leibinger comments: 'It's never enough to do something [new] once; you've got to do new things over and again.'[22] The German entrepreneur's own company has shown how sliver companies can evolve. In the 1990s, Leibinger recognized that specialized areas of medical technology represented a promising growth area. Helped by its knowledge of optics technology, Trumpf started the development of special light sources used in hospital operating theatres. It is now among the world leaders in this industry. For good measure it is in a strong position also in a further sector that is related to this lighting niche: the design and production of hospital operating tables.

Other German niche companies – some of them extremely old, but all of them highly interested in applying new ideas – have followed a similar pattern. Achenbach Buschhütten, the world's biggest maker of rolling machines for aluminium production, can trace its roots to 1452, when three brothers set up a metals foundry near Siegen, near Essen, specializing in iron and steel. When the company started, both rolling technology and aluminium manufacturing were inventions that were hundreds of years into the future. But moving into a field that encompassed both was a logical development for a business that had always focused on metals know-how. Another example of a hidden champion is Leoni, which was started near Nuremburg in 1596 by Anthoni Fournier, a Frenchman. The company originally made gold and silver threads for embroidery. In the twentieth century, Leoni moved into a field that in concept was not too dissimilar. Capitalizing on its ability to create complex patterns from long strands of metal, the company started making wiring harnesses – assemblies of cables that form the 'backbone' of most types of modern equipment powered by electricity. Leoni is now one of the biggest companies in the world, making cable assemblies for cars, with sales in 2010 of $3.5 billion and plants and sales offices in 34 countries. J. D. Neuhaus, formed in 1745, has evolved from its initial occupation of making small hand-operated jacks for use by carters to become one of the biggest makers of specialized lifting hoists.

Progressions of a similar nature have been followed in some other German companies that were established in more recent years. Weckerle was started by Peter Weckerle in 1965 as one of the world's first makers of automatic machines for moulding lipsticks. In the 1990s, the company used this expertise to turn itself into the world's biggest supplier of equipment for producing a range of 'stick-based' consumer products, from cosmetics pencils to 'glue sticks'. While it had to find new customers for its broader range of products, it had the advantage of the technical know-how involved in specialized moulding that it had amassed some years earlier. Another German illustration is Bartec, set up in 1975 by Reinhold Barlian as a producer of safety switches for petrol pumps. Barlian soon realized he could use his company's know-how in safety-related engineering to extend its reach. It is now the world leader in safety-critical control technology used in industries including oil and gas, chemical and mining. It has 10 factories worldwide and 28 sales offices in Europe, America and Asia.

Sometimes the 'edging out' into new fields can be especially imaginative. Vitronic was started in 1984 by Norbert Stein. It made camera-based systems to record the movement of goods on production lines using computerized image processing. In the 1990s, it started edging out into new fields away from engineering but which remained based on 'machine vision' software. It found it could adapt its technology to make 'whole body scanners' that recorded people's size and shape, enabling them to be fitted for suits and dresses much more quickly than with conventional processes based around measuring tape. A still more inspired move by Stein was to modify his company's camera technology so the devices could record details about cars and trucks travelling along highways, using images either from gantries above the road or from satellites. The company is now a global leader in the niche of supplying sensor systems for the traffic management projects becoming more popular in many towns and cities.

Often, the micro-sector companies need a special source of advice or new ideas that will help them shift into a new area. A business that moved into a niche with the assistance of technology from another company – from Germany – was Fandstan, a UK engineering group. The company was started in 1979 by Lord Tanlaw, a UK peer with a family background in business and a special interest in manufacturing. Fandstan initially opted to specialize in a number of fairly narrow areas of technology, many of them linked to the railway industry, among them the production of the pantographs seen in many types of electric trains that pick up current from wires above the track. In the 1980s the company became interested in aluminium/steel composite rails. The technology for welding the two metals in a 'seamless' combination had been invented in the 1970s by Alusingen, a German company. The products used the electrical properties of aluminium to make rails with a better conductivity than steel on its own. However, the steel in the composite system provided the strength needed to make the rail suitable for use on a track.

Fandstan bought samples of the Alusingen product and tested it.'We liked what we saw [of the Alusingen rail] but felt sure that the technology behind it could be improved,' recalls Michael Bostelmann, Fandstan's chief executive.[23] The UK company accordingly devised a new type of welding machine that created an improved join between the two metals in the rail, and was straightforward to operate. 'As far as I know we have a world lead [on welding machines of this sort] and are keen to protect the technology as best we can,' says Bostelmann. Composite rail of this sort is more expensive than conventional steel rail. It is used in specialized applications such as city-based metro systems where high current-carrying capacity is required. In 2010, Fandstan accounted for 60 per cent of the world sales of these products of about $100 million.

Disco is a Japanese company that started in 1937, close to the big naval shipyards in Hiroshima. Initially it concentrated on grinding and cutting wheels for use in fabricating the steel sheet used in marine construction. It later adapted its machinery skills to start producing cutting machines and tools for jobs in precision engineering, such as making small parts for electricity meters. When the semiconductor industry started to become important in the 1970s, Disco saw the chance of becoming a big force in this sector. It turned its attention to designing special machines, like its grinding mechanisms based on rotational motion, for slicing the large circular pieces of silicon called wafers into individual microchips. In semiconductor manufacturing, these wafers have to be cut extremely accurately – and fast – in one of the final stages of production.

Due to the precision required for the cutting, low-friction air bearings – as opposed to conventional metal bearings – were required to act as the housings for the motors in the machines. In finding out about air bearings, Disco was helped by its collaboration in the late 1970s with Loadpoint, a UK company that was then a leader in these products. Disco bought air bearings from Loadpoint for fitting into its early versions of wafer cutters.

The Japanese company went on to design and produce air bearings expressly made for its machines, arguing it could do this job better than anyone else. It is now self-sufficient in the technology and among the world leaders in air bearing devices – even though it does not sell them to any other company. Disco's strength in this field has helped it to become by far the world's biggest maker of wafer cutting machines, accounting in 2010 for approximately three-quarters of a world market of $700 million.[24]

Most businesses that will be niche leaders in the next few decades are – almost certainly – already established. However, there are also some promising examples of relatively new niche companies that are exploiting new ideas. Switzerland-based Micro Mobility, a leading maker of small scooters for children, was started in 1996 by Wim Oubouter, a former banker. Haystack Dryers was founded in 2000 in the UK and has become one of the world's leading manufacturers of body dryers. Body dryers are novel machines that behave like super-sized versions of hair dryers to remove moisture from the clothes or body after people have got out of a swimming pool or been soaked with water in an amusement park. In 2002, Steve Billington, an engineer, started Mercia International, a UK business that dominates the field of 'snap-on' fittings for hydraulics pipes in coal mining. The same year saw the start of Belrobotics, a world leader in self-guiding lawnmowers, set up in Belgium by Michael Coenraets. In 2003, the Swedish designer Stefan Ytterborn formed Poc, the world's biggest maker of ski helmets. The underlying characteristic behind all these companies is their interest in applying the latest technical thinking to meet a need for products that is global, and is not being catered for by existing technologies or industries.

## Multi-micro companies

In 1805, Napoleon Bonaparte granted Jean-Jacques Daniel Dony a conces-sion to the Vieille-Montagne mine near Liège. The mine was one of Europe's most important locations for digging from the ground zinc oxide – the most obvious starting material for zinc metal. Dony was a canon at Saint-Pierre Collegiate Church in Liège, now part of Belgium and for centuries a centre for the metals industry. Like many clerics of the time, he had established a parallel career in a non-religious field, in his case chemistry. Dony had discovered how to turn zinc oxide into zinc, then seeing a surge in demand as the industrialization of Europe got under way.

After setting up his own company, Dony used the technology of rolling – then becoming established in iron-making – to turn his zinc into final products. Among the items he made in this way were bathtubs, one of which he presented to Napoleon. In 1813, he sold his stake in the company, six years later dying in poverty. But Dony's company lived on. In 1837 it formed the basis of what was called the Société Anonyme des Mines et Fonderies de Zinc de la Vieille-Montagne, the oldest predecessor business in what is now known as Umicore, a metals and minerals company based in Brussels.[25]

Virtually all Umicore's products are in global slivers. All have connections with metals refining and knowledge of materials that, in many cases, have their roots in developments that go back to Dony's day. The sectors include materials for batteries and specialist solar cells for space satellites. One of the company's biggest divisions is automotive catalysts, complex products based on metals including platinum, palladium and ruthenium. Automotive catalysts are fitted to cars' exhausts to clean up emissions. World sales of automotive catalysts in 2010 came to about $3 billion. It is a business with only three significant suppliers: Johnson Matthey of the UK, Germany's BASF, and Umicore. Umicore is also an important supplier in a field with total sales of just a few million dollars a year: making and selling specialist platinum linings for certain kinds of chemical processes. One of its customers for these products is Corning. In most of the company's fusion tanks used to make LCD glass, the linings are made of platinum, supplied by Umicore.

Umicore's operations underline how, frequently, a company may compete in many niche fields simultaneously. If it can operate in one such sliver, then it often finds it has the administrative and engineering skills to manage several. Another example of a 'multi-micro' business is Heraeus. The company was started in 1851 when Wilhelm Carl Heraeus, a chemist, took over his father's pharmacy in Hanau, Germany. Like Umicore, Heraeus was keen to find new ways to process platinum, which at that time was difficult to make in a pure form but had many potential applications, for instance in jewellery. The reason why platinum processing was difficult was because it melts at such a high temperature – around 1,700 degrees centigrade. Managing such high temperatures – necessary for most forms of platinum refining – was then extremely difficult for most metals businesses. Having learned how to operate chemical and physical reactions at temperatures this high, Heraeus later in the nineteenth century and in the early part of the twentieth century turned its attention to other metals that also required special processing technologies. 'When you are in this kind of field [platinum], you become curious about a lot of other metals with similar properties,' Horst Heidsieck, a former Heraeus chief executive, explains.[26] The specialism the company built up in high-temperature refining procedures led it into processing metals such as gold, silver, osmium and rhodium. It later used these metals in bonding wires for microchips and special coatings for computer disks – fields where Heraeus is now a leader.

Halma is a British multi-niche company that started out managing tea plantations in Ceylon. It was set up in 1894, as the Nahalma Tea Estate Company, changing its name in 1973. A year earlier, David Barber had joined the company as chief executive, a post he held for 22 years. Combining aggressive business instincts with a cerebral nature, Barber set out a strategy of transforming the company into a high-value engineering group, focusing on niche sectors. To put the strategy into effect, Halma subsequently bought 100 companies over a 30-year period. Most of these were leaders in narrow fields, including sensors for spotting fires or for use in health diagnosis systems, devices that monitor food or water quality, safety sensors for elevators and specialized locks to deny unauthorized people access to installations such as oil platforms. The aim in most of the businesses that Halma entered was to build a market share in the niche of at least 50 per cent, so Barber explained in an interview in 2003. Always, his main interest was identifying and then acquiring 'intellectual assets – technology, application and market knowledge'.[27] In 2010, Halma had 36 business units that operate globally. It sells 1,000 different types of product, split between three broad areas – infrastructure sensors for buildings, health and analysis equipment, and industrial safety devices. The products sell for between $20 and $2,000, and are bought by 10,000 different customers – which are almost always other companies, rather than consumers. Halma's growth has been helped by the general trend in manufacturing for product prices to fall, or at least to rise by smaller amounts than in other parts of the economy. As Barber pointed out in 2003:

> As we grow our own sales along with the markets . . . our own R&D [has an impact] on product selling prices. In some cases, when this reduces the complexity and size of, for instance, electronic components, and then is also coupled with big productivity increases and low-cost overseas procurement, it can lead to very substantial price reductions for customers and large increases in unit volume for us.

## Building on niches

If Halma's businesses are a collection of niches, so are those of US-based Caterpillar. The company is the world's biggest maker of earth-moving machines such as bulldozers, wheel loaders and excavators. In 2010, world sales of construction machines came to about $100 billion. The construction machinery business is vital to infrastructure development the world over. Without equipment such as excavators, bulldozers and cranes, projects from dams to airports would never be built – or would be developed at an impossibly slow speed. The business of construction machines can be considered a collection of about 50 individual sectors. They encompass businesses selling relatively well-known types of machine – such as large excavators or wheel loaders – to much smaller and more specialized fields. Among the latter are the subdivisions of the construction machine business selling road pavers for highway construction, mini-excavators for doing jobs in small spaces such as digging trenches, and giant mining trucks that are each the size of a four-storey house.

Many of these smaller niches are highly specialized, and feature among the main suppliers of fairly small companies that operate on a global basis. Some examples of these niche producers are the German companies Wirtgen and Putzmeister,[28] which specialize in asphalt pavers and concrete pumps respectively; Skyjack and Besser, both of the US, which make aerial access platforms and concrete moulding machines; UK-based ALE, which supplies heavy-lift machines for installations such as oil rigs; and Austria's Palfinger, which produces small truck-based cranes lifting relatively light loads. While Caterpillar is considered by most people a large company, with sales in 2010 of $42 billion and 104,000 employees, it can also be considered a collection of smaller businesses each operating in a fairly narrow area.

Caterpillar can trace its origins to two Californian manufacturers of some of the world's earliest engine-powered tractors. The first of these, Holt Brothers, was formed in 1863, initially as a wood trader. It was run by four brothers, led by Benjamin Holt. Holt Brothers moved into 'wheel crawlers', steam-powered agricultural machines that used tank-like tracks to travel over rough terrain. The second company was C. L. Best Tractor, set up in the 1880s by Daniel Best. In 1925 Holt Brothers and C. L. Best Tractor merged to form Caterpillar. During the 1930s, Caterpillar moved its headquarters from California to the quiet Illinois town of Peoria.[29]

To build its leading position in its various micro-markets, Caterpillar has not only directed a lot of research and development effort into devising new machines, but has had to become knowledgeable about the manufacture of specific components vital to the different niches in which it operates. Such components – made either by Caterpillar or by suppliers with which it has a close relationship – often constitute a separate micro-industry. Niche industries are frequently built up from, and rely for their success on, other niches.

High-power diesel engines constitute one such example. Diesel engines are a field in which Caterpillar is itself a world leader. It makes the engines for its own use and also sells them to outside customers. A second niche area on which Caterpillar relies – but where it has no in-house production – concerns specialist steel plate. The metal forms the tough, corrosion-resistant buckets which its machines use to shovel or pick up earth. In this field, Caterpillar relies on close relationships with suppliers. Steel plate of the specifications useful in the construction equipment industry comprises a business with sales in 2010 of about $1 billion. The main suppliers include Germany's Dillinger Hütte and SSAB of Sweden.

Hydraulic pumps comprise a further sector that is vital both for Caterpillar and for virtually all the other companies making different classes of construction equipment.[30] Hydraulic devices push a fluid such as oil through thin tubes to transmit power. They are particularly good at producing large forces, subject to close control, in a small space. The human heart is an example of a hydraulic pump: its job is to push blood around the body to provide nutrients to cells. In an excavator or similar mechanism, a hydraulic drive system (based around a pump) is required to provide the power to lift earth or demolish buildings. The drive system has to be closely controlled, so that the excavator works efficiently, without using energy when it is not needed, and also to protect the safety of operators and other people nearby.

The ideas behind hydraulic pumps were devised by the seventeenth-century French mathematician Blaise Pascal. Pascal discovered that liquids do not compress in the same way as a gas such as air. Instead, if pressure is applied to a point in the liquid, all the other parts of the liquid will transmit this pressure equally, in all directions. Using this principle, liquid under pressure in a narrow tube can be directed into a wider area, such as a cylinder with a piston inside. In this way, a force is produced that is much greater than that initially applied. Nearly 150 years after Pascal, Joseph Bramah, a London-based engineer, was the next person to contribute to hydraulics technology. Bramah had already established his credentials with designs for mechanical locks and water closets. In 1795, he published a patent for a hydraulic press. It used high-pressure water to drive a piston, and operated in a similar way to a modern hydraulic pump.[31]

Bramah's pump relied on an ingenious 'self-tightening' leather collar that enclosed the sides of the piston. The collar stopped water leaking out, so preventing a fall in the pressure of the complete unit that would have damaged its effectiveness. The inventor of this part of the system was the UK engineer Henry Maudslay. Between leaving his first job at London's Royal Arsenal in 1789, and setting up his own business in 1797, Maudslay was employed as an assistant in Bramah's London engineering company.[32]

Hydraulic systems based on pumps were introduced in excavator machinery in the 1940s and 1950s. It soon became clear that in terms of power, capability and ease of control, they were much more useful than previous excavator designs that used cables (driven by petrol or steam engines) to control the machines' moving parts. Outside a few specialized applications, cable-driven excavators quickly became little more than museum pieces.

Producing specialized hydraulic pumps (and associated components such as hydraulic cylinders) for excavators and other construction machines is a 'sliver' business with sales estimated in 2010 at about $7 billion a year. The biggest companies include KYB, Kawasaki Heavy Industries, Nabtesco and Komatsu of Japan, Bosch of Germany and the US-based Eaton, Sauer-Danfoss and Parker-Hannifin. Powered by a diesel engine, modern pumps work at pressures up to 1,000 times greater than that of the atmosphere. The hydraulic units drive the 'arms' of the excavator that do the work of shifting building debris or rock. An 85-tonne excavator made by Caterpillar (and costing $1.5 million) incorporates an arm weighing 10 tonnes. Many arms of this sort are powerful enough to dig foundations on a building site, while also sufficiently sensitive to be capable of cracking a hard-boiled egg and leaving it fit to be eaten for breakfast.[33]

In other instances of the way that many micro-industries are built on the basis of other niches, Nikon and Canon of Japan and ASML of the Netherlands are the three leaders in another sliver: machines called wafer steppers. Wafer steppers are used in semiconductor engineering to 'print' extremely thin lines on silicon, to mark the positions of tiny transistors. The wafer stepper makers require specialist high-power lasers for their systems, and the lasers are made by another small group of niche businesses led by Cymer of the US and Japan's Gigaphoton. Inside the lasers are high-precision lenses made by businesses such as SLS Optics, based on the Isle of Man. In turn, companies such as SLS rely on other sliver businesses. They include Heraeus, and Schott, another German company, both of which make the pure pieces of glass blanks used as raw materials for precision optics devices. Another illustration of the tendency for slivers to require other slivers for key materials or components involves Maxwell Technologies. The US company is the world leader in the niche of supercapacitors, devices that store large amounts of energy, used, for instance, in electric cars. A key producer of materials on which the company relies is Kuraray, a Japanese chemical producer. This is the world's biggest maker of the specially treated 'activated' carbon that is a vital component for such capacitors, and part of another micro-industry. These are all instances of niche businesses which help others to achieve success. It is virtually impossible to say which niches will be important in the next few decades. But it can be stated with certainty that more niches will become apparent. As this happens, more opportunities will arise for both big and small businesses.

## A global view

To establish a strong and lasting position in a sliver nearly always means having a global view. Through such a strategy, the company can reach the maximum number of customers in what is often a limited product range. From a defensive viewpoint, it can use this global position as a shield against competition. A strong German niche business that puts into practice this approach is Klingelnberg, a company with its biggest operations in Germany but which is based in Zurich. Klingelnberg, which started in 1863, is a leader in gear-cutting machines, used in many areas of engineering. Diether Klingelnberg, the company's supervisory board chairman, attributes the company's success to its single-mindedness in building up market share in countries outside Germany. By 2010, it had sales offices or distributor arrangements in 39 countries. 'You have to specify the market [niche] very, very precisely . . . Then we invest a lot, hire people and build up the market share quickly through growth.' Klingelnberg says opportunities for selling have multiplied in the past 10 years, as a result of globalization. 'The market [for gear cutting] has become much bigger: it is much easier for us to sell in China, Russia or India now.'[34]

Yamazaki Mazak of Japan, the world's biggest maker of machine tools, illustrates how a company can build a competitive advantage in a niche and then maintain it over a long period. Devised by Henry Maudslay and others in the eighteenth century, machine tools are cutting systems for shaping parts from metal, plastic and wood. They are the workhorses of manufacturing, required for just about every industry, from toys to telephones. Most of the components made by machine tools are never seen by consumers, even though they are used inside other products that may be familiar. Maudslay's machines required human operators. Since the 1960s, with the advent of automated methods of manufacturing, machine tools have become subject to increasingly sophisticated computer controls. Reflecting this, today's machine tools rely on skills in information technology as much as those in metal cutting. Computer-aided analysis is used to devise the shapes of the parts to be made. The tools do intricate jobs under the supervision of computer programs, turning out parts accurately and at great speed. The power and sophistication of machine tools have increased immensely in the past 100 years, leading to big productivity improvements in the industries that use them. Technological advances in machine tools are one reason for the increased usefulness and lower price of manufactured products.

Global sales of machine tools in 2010 came to about $70 billion. The industry can be split into 500 separate slivers, depending on the way the machines operate and their main applications. Individual niches for machine tools include many kinds of lathe, machining centres, and boring, drilling and gear-cutting equipment. The family-owned Yamazaki – based near Nagoya – had sales in 2009 of about $2 billion, with roughly 80 per cent of this coming from outside Japan. Rather like Caterpillar, Yamazaki can be regarded as a 'multi-micro' company making a collection of different types of niche products within a broad sector.

Yamazaki was started in 1919 by Sadakichi Yamazaki, who as a teenager gained early expertise in engineering by working in a shipyard, mirroring Maudslay's experience.[35] Yamazaki's international expansion started with Teruyuki Yamazaki, Sadakichi's son, who took over as company president in 1958. Teruyuki says that from early in his career he had a 'dream' to 'produce equipment of similar high standards' to that of the world's top machine tool companies, almost all of them based in the US or Western Europe.

In 1974, Yamazaki opened its first non-Japanese factory, in Kentucky, close to what was then the heart of the US's machine tool industry. In 1987, it established a factory in Worcester, in the UK's industrial Midlands. Since then, the company has opened more plants in Singapore and China. In addition to the factories, the company has technical centres to provide engineering support for customers in more than 20 countries, including

Brazil, India, Thailand, Denmark and New Zealand. About a quarter of the company's 6,200 worldwide staff work in areas such as after-sales service and application engineering, in an effort to ensure that once Yamazaki wins customers, they are kept happy. Yamazaki's website reflects its global approach, providing information in 13 languages, including Danish, Hungarian, Portuguese and Thai.[36]

Other niche companies also use the internet as a key part of their marketing operations. Hilti is a company based in Lichtenstein which is a world leader in industrial tools. It has 1,000 families of products ranging from screws to drilling machines. With 200,000 customers, the company has a different part of its website for every one of the 148 countries where it operates.[37] Woodward, a US company that specializes in electronic control systems for diesel and aircraft engines, goes even further. Its website gives information about 800 organizations, including its own subsidiaries as well as external service companies, that sell and maintain its products in 215 countries.[38] Tente Rollen, a German company which is one of the world's biggest makers of casters, has an internet site which uses 35 languages, including Persian, Latvian and Croatian.[39] Even keener to communicate is Blum, an Austrian hinge manufacturer, whose website works in 40 languages.[40] If the worldwide web had never been invented, the barriers to becoming successful for many niche players would have been much higher. Lennart Evrell, the former chief executive of Munters, a Swedish company which is the world's largest producer of dehumidifying equipment, observed in 2000: 'Using the internet we [Munters] can sell to 100 customers using the same resources that we previously needed to sell to five.'[41]

## The service dimension

Munters was established in 1955 by Carl Munters, a scientist who had invented a way of extracting moisture from air using a special 'desiccant wheel'. Heavily protected by patents, the product provided a good base for the company's expansion into a range of industries that needed to control humidity, from poultry farming to semiconductor manufacture. But in the 1980s, its patent protection began to taper off. This resulted in rivals boosting their share of the market for dehumidifying machines. Munters therefore began to cast around for a new source of revenues. In 1985, it set up a service division. The company targeted customers with water-damaged buildings who wanted to renovate them after floods or fires. Among the company's early clients was Queen Elizabeth of England. After Windsor Castle suffered a blaze in 1992, the structure was badly affected by the large volumes of water needed to control the fire. Munters' employees were a key part of the restoration team. In 2009, services accounted for two-fifths of Munters' sales of $915 million, and almost half its 4,000 worldwide workforce.[42]

The example of Munters illustrates how manufacturing companies in many fields increasingly gain a large percentage of their sales by offering services. This is the case for businesses in large market sectors as well as in niches. A good example of the first type of company is Rolls-Royce. Out of the UK aero-engine company's 2010 sales of $18 billion, roughly half came from service revenues. The payments were gained from operations such as engine maintenance, and 'remote diagnosis' in which the company's engineers monitor how their products are performing while they are in flight. For many micro-industry companies, the specialized nature of what they do provides a good base for adding services to support the sale of products. Following a change of ownership in 2001, Munters' service operation is now run independently of its manufacturing arm, with the two sets of activities controlled by two separate companies. It is more common, however, for niche manufacturers to add a service offering to its mainstream business, without trying to differentiate between what is manufacturing and what is service. When a customer is sold a product, it makes only one payment to cover both the manufacturing and service elements embedded within the item. An example of a company that operates in this way is Zumtobel. Based in Austria, Zumtobel is among the world's biggest producers of customized lighting systems used in office blocks, factories and sports stadiums. Of its sales in 2009 of $1.4 billion, roughly 20 per cent came from what amount to service payments but are not spelt out as such in any customer contract. The 'payments' are made as part of the total contract price, covering not just parts and engineering installations but the provision of design ideas and consultancy. Of the company's 7,500 employees, about a third work in service-related activities (including sales), where they spend most of their time liaising with customers. Andreas Ludwig, Zumtobel's former chief executive, believes that the service side of its business is a source of competitive advantage, acting as a barrier to other businesses attempting to encroach into its market.[43]

Combining service and manufacturing is a big part of a niche segment of the steel business: making and selling specialist seamless pipe for oil and gas drilling. Pipe of this type has to be tough and strong enough to withstand high pressures, while coping with the corrosive effects of oil and other fluids passing through it. In some cases, the pipe can sell for $25,000 a tonne, or 50 times more than standard steel. This part of the steel business adds up to a niche with annual sales of about $10 billion. The three biggest companies in the industry are Buenos Aires-based Tenaris, Vallourec of France and TMK of Russia. All of them have to make their products in small volumes, to comply with requirements of an oil industry customer that might want pieces of specially made pipe for a specific job. Paolo Rocca, chief executive of Tenaris, says his 22,000 staff have to have the 'mindset of a service company as much as that of a manufacturer'.[44] About a quarter of the company's sales come from service-related work.

Touch Bionics, a UK company that is the world leader in making artificial hands for people who have suffered extreme injuries or have been affected by genetic disorders, works in a similar way. Its headquarters near Edinburgh incorporates a small factory for making its products. Another part of the building – just as important to how the company operates – is a 'customer service area'. Here therapists and counsellors meet people receiving new body parts and discuss both the design of the products and how best a person being fitted with a new bionic hand can use it.

Artificial hands that are advanced enough to operate in a way similar to real human hands are a striking example of a niche for the twenty-first century. It would be far-fetched, however, to pretend that the opportunities for niches have only just been invented. Global slivers are an example of a phenomenon that has existed for hundreds of years. However, as the world becomes more complex and more dependent on technology, new niches will become apparent, offering opportunities for a wide range of companies. Companies in high-cost countries with a strong record in technology development have up to now had the most success in micro sectors. There is every indication that this record will continue, in spite of the growing prominence since the end of the 1990s of businesses located in fast-expanding economies such as China and India.

The successful enterprises in niches in the next 30 years will include many companies that already exist. Just as people who can speak more than one language are normally in a better position than others to learn new ones, so it will be relatively easy for companies adept at managing sliver sectors to move into emerging fields that are similar. In many cases, the companies that are already experienced in the world of slivers will themselves devise the shape of the new industries. Niche companies will be among the success stories as the new industrial revolution takes hold.

# CHAPTER 6

# The environmental imperative

## The reckoning

Football supporters are not normally regarded as being ecological warriors. But a few months before the 2010 World Cup kicked off in South Africa, lovers of the game were given the chance to do their bit – albeit in a modest fashion – for the environment. The US company Nike – the world's biggest maker of sporting goods – unveiled a special range of 1.5 million football shirts made from 3 million plastic drinks bottles that would otherwise have been thrown away. The initiative saved the company from having to buy 250 tonnes of polyester from chemical suppliers. Some of Nike's new shirts were handed to the nine World Cup teams that it sponsors, with most of them going on sale to the teams' supporters. While the promotion was to some degree a marketing gimmick, it also had a serious aim – to demonstrate the links between factory production and the health of the planet.

Most polyester used in clothing is made from chemicals derived from fossil fuels that have to be removed from the earth and processed, using large amounts of energy. Being based on recycled polyethylene terephthalate (PET), a form of polyester widely used in drinks bottles, the environmental impact of Nike's limited new range of sportswear was considerably less than if the shirts had been made from virgin materials. The project was designed to draw attention to how reuse of materials can help to tackle environmental challenges. In 2010, drinks manufacturers required for their products some 500 billion bottles containing 16 million tonnes of PET. Such plastic bottles usually have a 'lifetime' of just a few weeks. After use, only about a fifth of the bottles made in 2010 were recycled into new products such as clothing or furniture parts, with the rest being largely discarded on to landfill sites.[1]

In 2010, the world's manufacturers made products containing about 15.3 billion tonnes of solid matter. This consisted of 4.4 billion tonnes of metals and minerals, including 1 billion tonnes of iron; 4.2 billion tonnes of biomass, including wood and other plants; 3.7 billion tonnes of fossil fuels; and 3 billion tonnes of limestone and other materials used in construction-related products such as cement or bricks. Manufacturing processes account for just under a quarter of total materials consumption, the rest being used in areas such as construction, mining and food production.[2]

Removing the materials from the earth, or, in the case of biomass, growing it, requires large quantities of energy. More energy is used during the factory processes needed to turn the materials into products. When the products are sold to consumers or industrial customers, another sequence of energy consumption is often triggered. Many types of product – for instance, electricity generation equipment, cars and domestic appliances – require energy to make them work. To dispose of products after use frequently takes even more energy. In 2010, taking into account all these factors, making and using manufactured products accounted for roughly 90 per cent of the world's energy consumption. Producing and consuming energy – most of which is derived from fossil fuels – invariably leads to emissions of carbon dioxide, the main gas associated with global warming. It follows that manufactured products are also responsible for a large share – again probably about 90 per cent – of emissions of this gas if both the production and use phases of these items are taken into account. In 2010, carbon dioxide emissions from man-made sources came to about 39 billion tonnes,[3] of which 13.4 billion tonnes were due to manufacturing processes. However, of the roughly 25 billion tonnes of the gas emitted as a result of operations not directly involved with manufacturing, about

20 billion tonnes entered the atmosphere due to processes that required manufactured products, such as vehicle transport using petrol-driven engines or generation of electricity based on gas or steam turbines. Figure 4 provides a more detailed breakdown of the sources of man-made dioxide in 2010.[4]

**Figure 4 World carbon dioxide emissions, 2010**

((billion tonnes) by process)

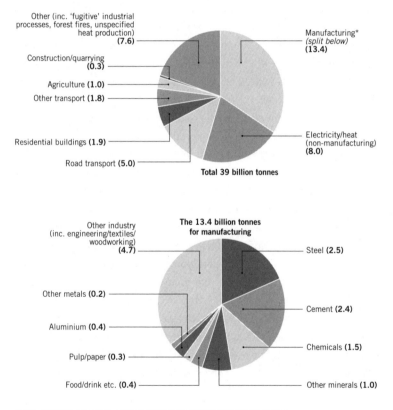

Other (inc. 'fugitive' industrial processes, forest fires, unspecified heat production) **(7.6)**

Construction/quarrying **(0.3)**

Agriculture **(1.0)**

Other transport **(1.8)**

Residential buildings **(1.9)**

Road transport **(5.0)**

Manufacturing* *(split below)* **(13.4)**

Electricity/heat (non-manufacturing) **(8.0)**

**Total 39 billion tonnes**

**The 13.4 billion tonnes for manufacturing**

Other industry (inc. engineering/textiles/woodworking) **(4.7)**

Other metals **(0.2)**

Aluminium **(0.4)**

Pulp/paper **(0.3)**

Food/drink etc. **(0.4)**

Steel **(2.5)**

Cement **(2.4)**

Chemicals **(1.5)**

Other minerals **(1.0)**

**Notes:** * includes $CO_2$ produced in electricity/heat consumed in manufacturing.

**Source:** International Energy Agency, Netherlands environment agency. World Steel Association, European Chemical Industry Council, author's estimates. (The charts first appeared in *FT*, 30 December 2011.)

Other unwanted by-products from industrial processes include large amounts of nitrogen oxides, sulphur oxides and particulate matter that are released into the air. Many such products, including many organic chemicals and metals, work their way into the earth and water supplies as a result of manufacturing processes. Some may cause long-term harm to human health, or damage the ecosystems on which wildlife relies. The disposal of manufactured goods invariably leads to further environmental burdens.

Most forms of plastic are likely to stay intact for centuries before degrading into natural products. The amount of plastic either in use or made in past processes and still existing comes to about 30 billion tonnes – enough to fill a cavity 2 kilometres deep and covering Greater London. According to the World Wildlife Fund, humanity's 'ecological footprint', representing the scale of its consumption of the earth's resources, doubled over the 40 years to 2007. The point was then reached, according to the Fund's calculations, where consumption was 50 per cent higher than a 'sustainable' treatment of the earth's resources would allow.[5]

No matter how useful man-made products are, there is nearly always a price to pay. A key feature of the first industrial revolution – and the three big periods of industrial change that followed – was the profligate manner in which manufacturers used natural materials and released harmful man-made substances into the environment.

In the new industrial revolution, the approach will be different. It will be built around stewarding resources and minimizing ecological disturbances. It will involve the development of new processes and products designed to tackle some of the most pressing environmental challenges – such as reducing carbon dioxide linked to energy generation. There seems a good chance that the new industrial revolution will trigger an unprecedented sequence of events: a world in which economic expansion continues, but with manufacturing for the first time reducing environmental pressures rather than adding to them.

## God's work

An example of 'heavy industry' in ancient times was Wadi Faynan in Jordan, 120 kilometres north of the modern Red Sea port of Aqaba. Part of the Roman Empire in the first century CE, the site used smelting processes to make large amounts of copper and lead. Toxic dust and other residues from the plant leaked out into the local surroundings, so much so that some of the effects are still evident.[6] The extent of the pollution could hardly have failed to stir resentment locally. But historians have failed to find much evidence of concerns in early times about the ecological effects of industrial operations. For a long time, it was generally understood that the earth, and everything in it, was open for exploitation by humankind in whatever way seemed most appropriate. The Bible set the tone: 'And God blessed them, and God said unto them, "Be fruitful, and multiply, and replenish the earth, and subdue it: and have dominion over the fish of the sea, and over the fowl of the air, and over every living thing that moveth upon the earth." '[7]

In poetry, and other expressions of the arts, there was the occasional reminder of the foolishness of valuing material wealth higher than nature. In about 700 CE, Li Bai, the Chinese poet, opined:

Everlasting as the heaven and the earth
Yet roomful of gold and jade shall not last
Hundred years of wealth amounts to what?[8]

The first real indications of concerns about the impact of economic growth on the environment came with the Industrial Revolution in late eighteenth-century and nineteenth-century England. In 1813 William Wordsworth contemplated some of the newly industrialized regions of northern England, and issued this lament:

With you I grieve, when on the darker side
Of this great change I look; and there behold
Such outrage done to nature as compels
The indignant power to justify herself.[9]

Around the same time, Thomas Malthus, a British clergyman, warned of the dangers of population growth putting potentially catastrophic strains on the earth's resources. John Ruskin drew a distinction between material well-being and the negative impact of overconsumption. He invented a new word for this, 'illth', to signify the antithesis of what he considered true wealth.[10] In 1835 Alexis de Tocqueville, in *Journeys to England and Ireland*, wrote about a district of Manchester:

> The land is given over to industry's use. . . . The fetid, muddy waters, stained with a thousand colours by the factories they pass, of one of the streams . . . wander slowly round this refuge of poverty . . . Often from the top of their steep banks one sees an attempt at a road opening out through the debris of earth, and the foundations of some houses or the recent ruin of others. It is the Styx of this new Hades. Look up and around this place you will see the huge palaces of industry. You will hear the noise of furnaces, the whistle of steam. These vast structures keep air and light out of the human habitations which they dominate; they envelop them in perpetual fog; here is the slave, there the master; there the wealth of some, here the poverty of most; there the organised effort of thousands produce, to the profit of one man, what society has not yet learnt to give.[11]

Aldo Leopold, a US ecologist, was one of the first people to popularize the link between economic growth, materials use and environmental damage. In 1932 he wrote:

> When I submit these thoughts to a printing press, I am helping cut down the woods. When I pour cream in my coffee, I am helping to drain a marsh for cows to graze, and to exterminate the birds of Brazil. When I go birding or hunting in my Ford, I am devastating an oil field, and re-electing an imperialist to get me rubber.[12]

A key concern in later decades was what many took to be the 'threat' of the chemicals industry – a business that had barely existed before the twentieth century. Rachel Carson, in *Silent Spring*, published in 1962, voiced anxieties that the build-up in the environment of toxic chemicals might be leading to massive health problems. In the book, she focused on products such as pesticides and plastic additives which were supposed to be helping mankind but which were, so Carson set out to show, slowly poisoning it. In 1972, the Club of Rome, a group of environmental thinkers and politicians, published a report entitled *The Limits to Growth*. It sold 12 million copies and ignited debate about how economic expansion could be managed within ecological restraints. The British historian Arnold Toynbee warned in 1976: 'Man is the first species of living being . . . that has acquired the power to wreck the biosphere and, in wrecking it, to liquidate himself.'[13]

Toynbee's words took on new urgency when – also in 1976 – an explosion occurred in a small chemical plant in the district of Seveso close to Milan. A cloud of a highly toxic chemical called TCDD affected the densely populated area around the site. It killed thousands of wild animals and is thought to have exposed about 37,000 people to potential danger. The affair triggered a massive tightening in legislation, at least in developed countries, to ward off similar events. Seveso was followed soon afterwards by an accident that was many times more serious. In 1984, in Bhopal, India, methyl isocyanate gas leaking from a chemical plant run by the US company Union Carbide caused at least 3,000 deaths, and huge suffering among many others whose health was permanently damaged.

Since then, fears about global warming, triggered by a build-up in the atmosphere of carbon dioxide and other 'greenhouse' gases, have added to awareness about environmental issues. Emissions of carbon dioxide related to man-made activities, linked mainly to combustion of carbon-containing fossil fuels, rose from 2.5 billion tonnes in 1890 to 9 billion tonnes in 1950. Since then, they have risen more than fourfold. A number of high-level scientific reports have warned of growing dangers to the planet, such as widespread flooding due to partial melting of the earth's icecaps, should carbon dioxide emissions fail to fall from the 430 parts per million recorded in 2008. A strong point of view in the scientific community is that unless the world sets a path on achieving a cut in carbon dioxide emissions to as little as 5–10 billion tonnes by 2050, humankind will be heading for disaster.[14]

## A new consciousness

Amory Lovins, chairman and chief scientist of the Rocky Mountain Institute, a research group in Colorado, has followed changes in businesses' environmental strategies since the 1970s. 'There's been a remarkable shift in attitudes by companies [from the end of the 1990s] in their approach to environmental thinking. What started off as defensive lip-service to environmental concerns has turned into a genuine and profound interest in making changes.'[15]

Nike's 2010 project related to PET bottles was one such example. It was followed a year later by an announcement from PepsiCo. The US food and drinks company announced it had developed a process to make a new form of drinks container also made from PET, and looking and feeling like conventional bottles. However, in this case the PET molecules are assembled neither from oil and gas nor reprocessed plastic, but from vegetable matter and food waste. PepsiCo said that, depending on technical trials, it could start making its 'bio-bottles', using switchgrass, pine bark and corn husks, from 2012. Later, the company could use other 'renewable' starting materials such as orange peel or oat hulls. Coca-Cola has a similar initiative in which parts of its drinks bottles are based on chemicals from biological sources. In a few years, according to the company's plans, most of its plastic drinks containers could be made completely from such biologically based materials.

Adidas and Puma, two big German companies that are competitors to Nike, are trying to set out a new ecology-oriented strategy for manufacturing. They are working with suppliers to orchestrate a switch to growing cotton in new ways so as to reduce water consumption and land use. In some cases, growing cotton in a 'sustainable' manner can cut water consumption by half, while also requiring the use of only 40 per cent of the land area, compared to conventional techniques. In 2011, Puma became one of the first manufacturers to publish what it believed was the true cost of carbon dioxide emissions associated with its manufacturing processes. The company approached this issue unusually thoroughly. It commissioned researchers to examine the complete value chain involved in its manufacturing. The study went so far, for instance, as to calculate the carbon dioxide emissions associated with rearing the cattle from whose hides the leather used in Puma's footwear is made. The company concluded that the total drain on the earth's resources due to its emissions in 2010 of 717,000 tonnes of carbon dioxide was \$66 million, or \$93 a tonne, a figure well above previous estimates. Jochen Zeitz, Puma's chairman, said publication of the data was a useful step to 'providing transparent benchmarks' about emissions of carbon dioxide to promote consciousness about trying to cut this back. 'The current economic model that originated . . . in the [first] industrial revolution must be changed and evolve into a new business paradigm: one that works with nature and not against it . . . we must account for the cost to nature of doing our business.'[16]

Henkel, another German company that is a big supplier of industrial chemicals, has introduced new families of adhesives and coatings (for instance to protect goods from corrosion) that have a less obtrusive environmental impact than existing materials. It is working with a range of companies, in sectors such as automotive, construction and general engineering, to find applications for them. The Japanese car-maker Nissan and its French affiliate Renault are investing $4 billion into the development of a novel electric car powered by batteries, rather than petroleum. Producers of electric motors such as Emerson and Siemens are devising new forms of motors controlled by digital devices that use 20–30 per cent less energy than previous generations.

Electrolux, a big Swedish maker of household appliances, acknowledges that 75 per cent of energy use and carbon emissions associated with its products are linked to their 'use phase', with only a small part coming from manufacturing. It has introduced a new family of vacuum cleaners – made mainly from recycled plastic – which use half as much energy as conventional devices. Illustrating that many consumers are interested in working out the environmental impact of the goods that they buy, a number of consumer groups now supply this information, by providing the 'carbon footprint' of products from shampoos to baby wipes. One of the best established of these information sources is GoodGuide, founded in 2007 by Dara O'Rourke, a professor of environmental and labour policy at the University of California at Berkeley. The guide ranks 100,000 consumer items according to a scoring system based on an assessment of the products' environmental impact.[17]

Desso is a Netherlands-based carpet manufacturer that has changed many of the materials in its products to make them more environmentally benign. For instance, it has replaced the PVC plastic commonly used as a backing fabric with another polymer-based product called Ecobase that is easy to recycle and uses less energy. Stef Kranendijk, Desso's chief executive, points to the link between the 'ecological rating' of Desso's carpets and their acceptance in the marketplace. 'The more we make our products more sustainable, the better our customers like it,' he says.[18] An example of a new company started to meet an environmental objective is San Francisco-based Method. It was established in 2000 by Adam Lowry, a climate scientist, and Eric Ryan, a marketing expert. Method has worked out the formulations for new generations of cleaning fluids with a lower environmental footprint than conventional chemicals. Lowry says that sustainability is mainly a 'design problem'. It is about making sure the ingredients in products are right from an environmental point of view, without compromising quality. While committed to reducing the environmental impact of manufacturing, Lowry shies away from trying to target Method's products only at those consumers interested in 'sustainable' issues. 'Our goal is not to sell products that are known mainly for having a small impact on the environment. What I am really interested in is making goods that work better than anything else on the market – but which do so by adhering to principles of sustainability.'[19]

In a novel twist on the broad issue of recycling, RockTron, a British company, has devised a method of turning virtually valueless waste materials into valuable and environmentally benign 'eco-minerals' that can be used in sectors from aerospace to toy-making. It has raised more than $50 million to fund a process that uses fly ash – a largely useless by-product of burning coal in power stations – to produce tiny glass spheres that can be used as filler in a range of structural parts. The world contains about 6 billion tonnes of fly ash mainly stored close to power stations. As well as being unsightly, these huge stockpiles are also a health hazard. In RockTron's process, which it wants to install in a series of materials reclamation plants around the world, the fly ash would be converted into industrial fillers. Such fillers commonly cost several hundred pounds per tonne and their production – taking into account mining as well as subsequent processing – requires large amounts of energy as well as new sources of materials. Tens of millions of tonnes of conventional fillers are used annually in the manufacture of goods such as tyres, cables, flooring, medical appliances and white goods. 'We think we've invented the twenty-first-century equivalent of alchemy – and one that can provide useful materials while also tacking an immense environmental problem,' says John Watt, Rocktron's co-founder.[20]

Blue Coat, a US maker of internet routers – devices to handle data traffic – has reorganized its worldwide supply chain to cut out unnecessary production steps. As a result, the company has reduced the carbon emissions linked to transport of its components and finished goods around the world. It has also made it easier to recycle the materials in its products into new items once the products' lives are over. David Cox, Blue Coat's vice president for operations, points out the overlap between the principles of environmental management and conventional business practices. Many ideas aimed at making companies' operations more sustainable fit in with normal commercial objectives. In Blue Coat's case, between 2008 and 2010 it cut its overall 'carbon footprint' by 8 per cent, while also reducing costs by $3.3 million annually. 'When businesses start trying to make their activities more sustainable, they often think this will be expensive, but that it will be worth doing because "green" is good,' says Cox. 'When they discover that by removing waste and becoming more efficient they are increasing rather than reducing their chances to make money, they find this rather exciting.'[21]

## Cradle rocks

In 2011, Maersk Line, the operator of the world's biggest fleet of container ships, announced an order for 10 new vessels that will be larger than anything yet afloat. The Danish company's Triple-E ships will be 400 metres long, each capable of carrying up to 300,000 tonnes of cargo. The boats will have their own 'environmental passports' describing exactly what they are made of. Of each vessel's unloaded weight of 60,000 tonnes, about 98 per cent will consist of five types of steel. The rest will comprise hundreds of different grades of other materials, consisting of metals, plastic, wood, minerals and chemicals. The documentation will outline how the materials in the ships were made, together with assembly methods, while also cataloguing the effects on the environment of all the manufacturing steps. The effort should provide clues as to new fabrication methods that will have less of an impact. It will also provide guidelines as to how the substances in the boats can be reused once the vessels – which should be in service around 2014 – have reached the end of their lives.

Maersk has worked on this project with the Environmental Protection Encouragement Agency (EPEA), a consultancy in Hamburg which promotes 'cradle to cradle' manufacturing.[22] EPEA was set up in 1987 by Michael Braungart, its director. An evangelical German chemist, Braungart is one of the world's leading thinkers on the links between materials, product design and manufacturing, and how science and engineering can be applied to meet environmental challenges. Cradle to cradle is based around specifying materials used in new products so as to minimize energy use and exposure to toxicity, while building in opportunities for reuse. It denotes an alternative to the more familiar 'cradle to grave' progression for manufacturing. While cradle to grave is a linear process, cradle to cradle is circular. In the former, once the use phase for products is over, they reach a 'dead end'. The materials either enter a landfill site or have to be subjected to a final technical procedure, which can be expensive, to render them harmless from an environmental perspective, but also useless. Relying on cradle to grave processes is unintelligent and unimaginative, Braungart believes. Far better, he says, to engineer the supply-use–disposal chain for manufacturing to increase the chances of 'life after death' for the products. 'Waste is food,' he says.[23]

Many of Braungart's ideas can be traced to Walter Stahel, a Swiss architect and engineer. In 1976, Stahel was the co-author of a report for the European Commission on the 'loop economy'.[24] Stahel defined this as involving both a continual recycling of materials between old and new products, and an emphasis on repair and resale of items that were surplus to the requirements of their original owners but which were useful to others. In 1982, Stahel set up the Product Life Institute, a consultancy in Geneva, as a way to develop these ideas.

In a further paper in 1987, Stahel focused on a key aspect of a loop economy. Assuming that such a circular system of materials flow can be made to work effectively, the source materials in such a system are, by definition, both easy to find and fairly cheap. Due to these lower costs, companies that work this way might aspire to achieve better profits than their competitors in a classical 'throughput economy'. Stahel was the first to use 'cradle to cradle' as a term to define a production system for a loop economy. Braungart later appropriated the phrase – and the concept behind it – for his own use, something that Stahel seems relaxed about.[25]

Since 1995, Braungart has collaborated with Bill McDonough, a US architect with whom he runs a separate US-based consultancy. When working with companies, Braungart and McDonough start by analysing the materials they use in their current products. They then move on to designing new ones where the mix of materials is changed to fit in with cradle to cradle principles. Braungart's toolkit is a digital 'library' of information about 10,000 chemicals widely used in manufacturing. Much of this toolkit is based on work done by Braungart for Nike in the 1990s. Each substance in the library is graded according to factors such as its impact on the health of humans and other organisms, the energy associated with making it, and how much of it can be reused. Among the products now on sale that have been developed and manufactured according to Braungart's principles are new types of building materials made by Saint-Gobain of France, hair conditioners produced by the US's Procter & Gamble, and toilet paper from Van Houtum, a Dutch paper producer. Other companies which have used his ideas include Puma, Dow Chemical, the Dutch chemicals business DSM and Alcoa, the big US aluminium company.

Braungart provides an example of work he did with Philips to design a new hairdryer:

When we did the original design, it contained 500 ingredients, of which 460 met the EPEA criteria for being acceptable in this particular product, while 40 did not. We worked with the customer to replace as many as possible of the 40 with substances whose technical performance would be just as good, but whose rating from a cradle to cradle perspective would be higher.

Where possible, Braungart encourages companies to simplify their production processes. He wants them to reduce manufacturing steps and use fewer types of materials. For instance, he says it is possible to redesign a washing machine so that instead of containing up to 250 types of plastic, a typical number for such a product, it uses just six materials of this sort.

> Each [of the 250 types] is there to meet various criteria that its designers have formulated. But often the performance of the complete machine is no worse if fewer materials are used. Reducing the number is likely to reduce the overall environmental impact of the product, for instance by making it easier to make the substances capable of being recycled.[26]

However, the spreading out of supply chains and growth in outsourcing can sometimes lead to problems. 'A product assembled in Germany may be made from components produced in India and sub-components from China. The result is that companies often are unfamiliar with the material composition of their products, which may be wholly unsuitable for the purpose for which the products are intended.'[27] An example of this, Braungart believes, is that some children's toys contain plastic additives incorporated into parts during production steps whose details the toy-maker knows little about. The materials can cause allergies or other health problems when they leak out during use – without the manufacturer having any clue that the chemicals were present. Rigorously applied cradle-to-cradle manufacturing would avoid these difficulties by ensuring that all the steps in the supply chain were fully documented, so that all the key players in the manufacturing steps were aware of the details of every ingredient.

One of the best places to see cradle to cradle thinking at work – at least in embryo form – is in a series of 35 small chemical plants in Europe, mainly in the Netherlands, Belgium, France and Portugal. The plants' owner is Van Gansewinkel, a Dutch company that is one of Europe's biggest handlers of waste materials. If the company's vision becomes a reality, it will transform itself over the next 10 years into a 'closed loop materials producer'. It will become the principal actor in facilitating a continuous production of useful materials from waste. It would use the residues of existing industrial processes, or material such as carpet or paper that has reached the end of its useful life, and extract useful substances, from organic chemicals to metals and minerals. These would then be diverted to other companies to form the start of new industrial processes. Another company that follows similar thinking is Recellular, a Michigan company which claims to be the world's biggest recycler of mobile phones. In 2009, Recellular was responsible for reusing materials from 5 million phones so that they found new applications in other products. Braungart is upbeat about the possibilities, and puts chemistry at the centre of the new philosophy. 'Chemists are often gloomy because they feel they are to blame for the [environmental] excesses of manufacturing. But this is wrong. Chemists can use innovation to invent new generations of products, and new ways to make them. They are the key to the future.'[28]

## Material evidence

Besides Stahel, Friedrich Schmidt-Bleek is another environmental thinker whose work helped Braungart to formulate his own ideas. A German environmental chemist, Schmidt-Bleek was in 1993 among the founders of the Wuppertal Institute, a German environmental research group. In 1997 he set up another new organization, the Factor 10 Institute, based in Provence. Schmidt-Bleek believes the world needs to cut its materials use by at least a factor of 10 over the next 20–30 years, if it is to have a sustainable future. One of Schmidt-Bleek's contributions has been to popularize the idea of the 'overburden' or 'ecological rucksack' of products. The overburden is the amount of material that has to be moved or processed to make the item in question but which has no functional use.

In his book *The Fossil Makers*, Schmidt-Bleek wrote:

In order to extract one gram of platinum from a platinum mine, for example, we must displace and modify 300,000 grams of rock. Without platinum we would not have the catalytic converter in our automobiles. Two to three grams of platinum are found in one such catalytic converter, in addition to high-quality steels, ceramics and other materials. Thus, the *ecological rucksack* of the catalytic converter, i.e. the total amount of material translocated for the purpose of constructing it, amounts to about one metric ton of environment. This means in effect that the catalytic converter burdens the automobile with as much matter as the car itself weighs.

According to Schmidt-Bleek's calculations, many industrial products carry ecological rucksacks at least 30 times greater than their own weights. The need to move or process this large amount of material associated with the substance being used in industry – but which does not have any value by itself – adds enormously to the world's environmental strains, not least by pushing up energy use. Schmidt-Bleek concludes that 'a substantial part of our current energy problems [related to concerns about over-use of fossil fuels] could be reduced by dematerializing the economy'.[29]

Another area where Schmidt-Bleek has been influential is in promoting the concept of the 'embodied energy' and the 'embodied carbon dioxide' of common substances. These values are the amounts of energy needed to make a set amount of material, along with the carbon dioxide emissions associated with the material's manufacture. The figures provide a sense of the hidden environmental burden linked to specific substances. Most metals, plastics and man-made minerals have fairly high embodied energies, with similarly high carbon dioxide ratings. The corresponding figures for biomass and other products such as traditional building materials are generally much lower. That explains why the embodied energy of a steel-framed house is three times higher than that of a wooden house of a similar size. The embodied energy per tonne of an aircraft is five times higher than that of a car, due mainly to the former's high concentration of aluminium – a metal with a particularly high energy rating due to the power-hungry way in which it is made.

Work of this kind has led to 'life-cycle assessment', an area of study that started in earnest in the 1970s and where interest among manufacturers is increasing fast. In this analysis, details related to embodied energy and carbon dioxide emissions for the manufacture of specific products are put alongside what happens during their useful lives. Life-cycle assessments are now done for a wide range of products from snack foods to power plants. It has become particularly popular to work out carbon dioxide emissions associated with specific types of goods, taking into account production, use and disposal. The results give the 'carbon footprint' of the products.

The first full life cycle analysis of a manufactured product was done in 1969. Coca-Cola studied whether it would be better from an environmental perspective to use glass or plastic for drinks bottles. Because glass is a natural material, many people might have expected glass would be the better choice. However, based on a study of all the factors, Coca-Cola decided it should opt instead for plastic. The logic behind this was that the company could make its plastic bottles in its own factories, reducing the need for transport and the energy that these shipments would consume. The fact that plastic bottles are lighter than glass ones would add to the degree to which energy in transport is minimized. A calculation of carbon footprints using 2010 data shows that plastic bottles still retain a lead over glass in terms of the impact over the full life cycle.[30] However aluminium cans also score relatively well in terms of environmental impact, even given the high embedded energy of the metal, mainly because they are recycled more readily. In most developed countries such as the UK and US, half of all aluminium cans are put to new uses, compared to 20–30 per cent for glass and plastic packaging. But it would be wrong to think recycling is always better than using new materials. A 2010 study from the Stanford Research Institute in California pointed out that in cases of poorly designed recycling schemes – where transport costs are high and collection volumes are low – making products from raw materials can be a better environmental choice.[31]

A key part of the efforts to cut the carbon footprints of beverage packaging is to use computer-aided design and new manufacturing methods to reduce the weight of materials in both bottles and cans. In the 20 years to 2010, packaging manufacturers shaved 40 per cent off the weight of a standard PET bottle, while an aluminium can of a similar size is likely now to weigh only 10 grams, a quarter of the weight of the equivalent item (which then would have been made of steel) in 1983. In 2010, Coca-Cola made approximately 300 billion bottles and cans for all its types of drinks. For a wide range of reasons, linked to marketing and costs as well as environmental factors, 60 per cent of its packages were made from PET, with the rest split between glass, aluminium and steel.[32]

## Steel challenge

Marianne Ludwig is the proprietor of Tremont Scoops, an ice cream parlour in Cleveland, Ohio. Her shop is about a kilometre and a half from a big ArcelorMittal steel plant. Being so close to this large works – which in 2011 employed about 1,700 people – makes the area unattractive from an environmental point of view. Ludwig and other local residents have voiced complaints over the years about a number of issues linked to the plant such as dust, bad smells and sudden noises. The emissions from the site in 2010 included 19,700 tonnes of carbon monoxide, 1,464 tonnes of nitrogen oxides, 769 tonnes of sulphur dioxide, 579 tonnes of particulate matter, 82 tonnes of organic chemicals, together with an estimated 3.7 million tonnes of carbon dioxide. Other unwanted by-products included zinc, manganese, hydrochloric acid, lead, vanadium, chromium, copper, barium and cadmium, all of which can cause a number of health hazards.[33] 'My neighbours and I live in a world of grit,' says Ludwig. Her views are not dissimilar to many of those who live close to steel plants virtually everywhere. However, Ludwig, who has lived in the area since 1997, is philosophical. 'The air quality where I live is not the best I could hope for. On the other hand, the plant is open and employing people and a lot of people who live nearby are happy about this.'[34]

In many countries the environmental problems associated with steel plants – as with manufacturing generally – have diminished over time.[35] Eric Hauge, general manager of the Cleveland plant, says: 'ArcelorMittal recognizes that the steelmaking process has an impact on the environment. That said, we take our environmental performance seriously. We are working to continuously improve our environmental footprint – reducing energy use and emissions, minimizing waste through recycling and beneficial reuse initiatives, and partnering with the community on sustainability projects.'[36] Discussing the sector as a whole, the official view of ArcelorMittal officials, as summed up in the company's 2009 environmental report, is that facing up to the environmental consequences of steel production is 'one of the most intractable challenges the steel industry has to face.'[37]

To make 1 tonne of steel using the most popular blast furnace route requires 1.4 tonnes of iron ore, 770 kilograms of coal, 150 kilograms of limestone and 120 kilograms of recycled steel, along with smaller quantities of many other elements, including nickel, chromium and silicon.[38] Of the 1.4 billion tonnes of steel produced in 2010, two-thirds was made using the blast furnace process, in about 50 countries. The rest was made mainly through recycling scrap steel by remelting it in 'mini-mills' based on electric arc furnaces. This last process is a good example of the 'loop economy' in action. Most of the raw material for mini-mills is scrap steel. Reusing scrap in this way means steel-makers no longer have to inject a lot of energy into manufacturing processes to make new metal. Therefore the carbon dioxide emissions associated with mini-mills are much less than those which come with steel made by the blast furnace method. However, even mini-mills have a high environmental impact, from the large amount of power used for remelting. Counting all the processes used in steel-making, in 2010 the steel industry was responsible for roughly a quarter of the energy costs associated with making goods in the world's factories, with a similar share of the carbon dioxide emissions linked to factories. Output of carbon dioxide from steel plants in 2010 came to about 2.5 billion tonnes – some 6.4 per cent of the world's production of this gas due to man-made activities.[39]

The amount of carbon dioxide emitted by different steel plants varies according to the details of their processes, which to some degree depends on age. The more modern the facility, the more likely it is that its carbon dioxide per tonne of steel will be relatively low. The 2010 figures for blast furnace-based steel plants in Europe range from an average of about 2 tonnes in Europe to about 3 tonnes in countries such as China and India.[40] In the world's less developed regions, the technology to minimize emissions of carbon dioxide, along with other types of pollution, is normally less sophisticated than those in Western Europe, the US and Japan. Also, tougher legislation is in place in the rich nations to force businesses into adopting more rigorous environmental standards. In Europe, the regulations on carbon dioxide production from steel plants look set to become even tighter. Under new European Union rules intended to 'decarbonize' the European economy, a system of special benchmarks for carbon emissions from steel plants, along with those from all other industries, will enter into force from 2013. Most companies will be forced to reduce their emissions even more, or pay penalties in the form of expensive 'carbon credits'. Lakshmi Mittal has said that fitting in with the new regulations in Europe will be a 'tough challenge' for his company. He complains also about the lack of a 'level playing field' in environmental regulations affecting steel in different countries, since the carbon dioxide emissions regime affecting Europe is set to be significantly tighter than anywhere else. 'This will affect Europe's manufacturing competitiveness,' Mittal warned in 2010.[41]

On the same issue, Wolfgang Eder – chief executive of Voestalpine, Austria's biggest steel-maker – is no less vociferous. Eder argues that most steel plants in Europe have already reduced emissions to 'close to the scientific limit'. However, he is somewhat more relaxed than Mittal when it comes to the impact on his own company of tighter government rules for carbon dioxide emissions. This is largely on the grounds that Voestalpine's main plant in Linz is one of the leaders in Europe in terms of its environmental record. The average output of carbon dioxide produced by the unit in 2009 per tonne of steel was about 1.5 tonnes – well below most comparable steelworks. Behind this are a range of costly technical improvements introduced in the plant since the mid-1990s. Eder says that moving in this direction may have been expensive but brings business benefits. 'Reducing our environmental impact cuts out waste, helps us to make better products and ultimately leads to higher profits.'

Eder – like Mittal – is keen to point out that discussion about steel-making and its environmental challenges has to go beyond steel's manufacturing side. The 'use phase' is also important. 'Steel is thought of as being a contributor to environmental problems – but it can be part of the solution as well,' Eder observes.[42] Both ArcelorMittal and Voestalpine, along with several other steel-makers, have introduced new types of high-strength steel for cars. These are intended to reduce carbon dioxide emissions of vehicles generally – which in 2010 were responsible for approaching 12.8 per cent of global output of the gas (see Figure 4). Because substituting high-strength steel for conventional material in a car body cuts the overall body weight, the vehicle requires less fuel. As a result, carbon dioxide emissions in the use phase are reduced, possibly by about 2 per cent a year. Over the next few years, more car-makers are turning to high-strength steel of this sort as one way to make their vehicles perform in a 'greener' manner, and so cut the amount of carbon dioxide being pumped into the atmosphere by man-made objects.

Van Reenan, a South African manufacturer of truck parts, has used similar thinking in its product strategy. It is a large supplier of the big 'tipper bodies' that feature in the giant dump trucks used to transport earth and rock around quarries. The exposed parts in these vehicles have to withstand a lot of wear and tear, requiring steel grades that are as strong and abrasion-resistant as possible. Using a new kind of strong and hard steel made by the Swedish steel-maker SSAB, Van Reenan found it could engineer into its trucks a similar amount of body strength and toughness as previously, while cutting the overall weight of each truck by 8 tonnes. The result has been to increase the fuel economy of a vehicle fitted with the new parts by 10 per cent. This leads to a similar cut in carbon dioxide emissions, together with a reduction in the operating costs of each truck in a mining company's fleet of $100,000 a year.

Outside the automotive industry, there are other examples of steel's potential to reduce the impact of manufacturing on the environment in terms of how it is used. One instance concerns the steam and power turbines used to create electricity. The higher the pressures and temperatures at which these machines work, the more electricity can be delivered per unit of energy used to run them. As a result of the smaller amounts of fuel being burned, the emissions of carbon dioxide per unit of electricity that is created will go down. One way to achieve higher pressures and temperatures is to replace conventional steel in turbine components with tougher and more durable high-strength steel that can withstand extreme conditions more easily. General Electric, Alstom, Mitsubishi Heavy Industries and Siemens – the world's biggest makers of power station equipment – are among the leaders in using new steel grades in this way.

A study by the Boston Consulting Group provides some insights.[43] The research looked at Germany. It would be possible to cut the country's emissions of carbon dioxide by 74 million tonnes – or approximately a third of what Germany wants to achieve between 2007 and 2020 to meet climate change goals – through the use of high-strength steel in various parts of the economy. The applications include using the material in cars, trucks and power stations, and also wind turbines, electric motors and transformers. The extra carbon dioxide created by the production of the steel needed for the new applications would come to about 12 million tonnes a year by 2020. The annual savings in carbon dioxide emissions from using steel in this way would be six times higher than the additional environmental burden imposed at the manufacturing stage.

## Sand power

Production of solar cells – and using them to create electricity – looks set to become one of the fastest-growing high-technology industries of the early part of the twenty-first century. It will also mark a big step in the global effort to devise more sustainable ways to produce energy and at the same time drive economic growth. Solar (or photovoltaic) cells replicate one of nature's cleverest tricks: the conversion of power from the sun to other forms of energy in the chloroplast of plants. Solar cells use the special electronic properties of semiconductors such as silicon. Under certain conditions, silicon can be made to interact with photons of infrared radiation from sunlight to produce electricity. Solar cells are now among the most promising devices capable of using 'renewable' resources to create power on a large scale. Because burning carbon is no longer involved, energy can be generated without having to produce carbon dioxide at the same time. In 2010, only about 2 per cent of the world's electricity needs came from solar energy. But the sector is growing fast. In 2010, world solar cell production doubled compared to the previous year, to 20.5 gigawatts. The solar industry's revenues in the same year came to $82 billion, four times higher than in 2006. The International Energy Agency estimates that as a result of the changes now being considered in the world's energy mix, solar power could represent 20 to 25 per cent of global electricity production by 2050.

A key to the manufacturing side of the industry is making high-purity silicon, also called polysilicon: the form of semiconductor suitable for turning into solar cells. The starting point for making polysilicon is silicon dioxide, the main ingredient in sand. Turning this into silicon of the required purity requires specialist technology which is highly energy-intensive. Given efforts to use solar cells to create energy in an 'environmentally friendly' manner, finding ways to cut the power needed in making polysilicon is an important goal. In 1990, less than 1,000 tonnes of polysilicon was made. In 2003, output reached 7,000 tonnes. By 2010, production had increased to more than 100,000 tonnes, and some estimates suggest 1 million tonnes could be required by 2050. The world's biggest maker of this material is US-based Hemlock, owned by a consortium of US and Japanese groups, while others include Shin-Etsu of Japan and Renewable Energy Corporation of Norway.

However, Chinese companies are fast becoming a bigger force in this part of the value chain for the solar industry. China is already a substantial – perhaps even dominant – force in the area of solar cells. In 2010, four of the world's six biggest makers of solar cells were Chinese, with the top two positions taken by Suntech and JA Solar. Nearly two-thirds of global cell production came from either China or Taiwan. Now, Chinese companies have aspirations to figure among the top producers of the high-purity silicon on which the sector depends.

One of the fastest-expanding business in polysilicon supply is China-based Asia Silicon, based in Xining, in Qinghai province in northern China. At the end of 2008, it completed the construction of a $150 million plant capable of making 2,000 tonnes a year of polysilicon. By 2015, the company plans to have invested another $450 million to increase production to 10,000 tonnes a year. One of the keys to doing well in this specific business, says Wang Tihu, its chief executive and founder, is to keep control of costs, and in particular to reduce the amount of energy used to create polysilicon.[44] In 2011, China National Bluestar, a large state-owned chemicals producer, announced a bold move in this same direction. In one of the biggest acquisitions by a Chinese business of a foreign engineering group, Bluestar paid $2 billion to acquire Elkem, a Norwegian manufacturer of specialist materials with a particular interest in solar energy. Elkem's most valuable asset is probably a $600 million plant in Kristiansand that has the capacity to make up to 6,000 tonnes a year of polysilicon. The factory uses a special process, devised by Norwegian engineers in the early 1990s, that cuts the energy needed to make polysilicon by three-quarters. Under the deal, Bluestar, in which a minority shareholder is Blackstone, a leading New York investment group, is likely to continue to run the Kristiansand factory, while replicating some of the Norwegian technology in plants in China. In any new investments or collaborative projects either in China or elsewhere, Bluestar will use Blackstone's links to help find new sources of funds or partners.

The rise of the solar industry – and the involvement in Norway of powerful businesses with roots in China and on Wall Street – underlines the opportunities for companies in areas of manufacturing linked to the environmental challenge. China looks as though it is moving into a strong position in key areas of the solar industry. However, many areas of environmental technology – both in the solar field and outside – hold numerous possibilities for development of new products and processes. The technologies may be linked to improving existing manufacturing methods, or devising new products that tackle the big ecological challenges of the twenty-first century. In both these broad areas, there are big chances for companies in all regions – both in the emerging economies and in the mature, developed regions – to emerge as winners.

It is natural enough for people to worry that the products of manufacturing are contributing to the environmental problems that the world is struggling to counter. A truer depiction of the situation is not, however, that the world has too much manufacturing. It is that the world has too much of the wrong sort. There is too much manufacturing that increases the environmental pressures on the planet. In the new industrial revolution, the focus will switch away from turning out goods without much thought about the burdens being imposed on the planet's fragile ecosystems. In place will be a new environmental imperative which involves not one but two goals, both of which will be capable of being met. The next 30 years will show that it is possible to use manufacturing to continue to improve the material well-being of the world's population – while at the same time taking care of the environment so that the earth's future is safeguarded.

# CHAPTER 7

# China rising

## Walking outside

An advocate of all kinds of industrial expansion, Mao Zedong was especially keen on steel production, a business he considered vital to a nation's economic strength. Anshan, an industrial city in Liaoning province in north-east China, is a place that Mao would have liked to visit. The city boasts several freshwater pools fed by hot springs, where the Chinese leader could have indulged his love of swimming. But Anshan's pride is the sprawling flagship plant of Anshan Iron & Steel, a state-owned company that in 2010 produced 21 million tonnes of steel. Better known as Ansteel, the company was in 2010 the world's thirteenth biggest steel-maker by output.[1]

The chief executive of Ansteel is Zhang Xiaogang, an animated yet softly spoken engineer and a leading enthusiast for creating stronger links between Chinese industry and the rest of the world. In 2011, Zhang became chairman of the World Steel Association, a Brussels-based body representing the world's biggest steel companies. It was the first time any Chinese citizen had taken the reins of a large international business organization. In his own business, Zhang has articulated a strategy to turn Ansteel into a global company, with the help of collaborative efforts with other steel-makers. Zhang's ambitions illustrate how China's already sizeable influence on global manufacturing is set to grow.

In 2010, after a decade of rapid growth, helped by low labour costs and sizeable investments in production technology, China became the world's largest manufacturing country, taking over from the US. China accounted for almost 20 per cent of the world's manufacturing output in 2010, up from 7 per cent in 2000, and 3 per cent in 1990.[2] It is by far the biggest steel producer, supplying more than 600 million tonnes of the metal in 2010, or 44 per cent of global output.[3] It makes more cars, cement, computers, mobile phones, textiles and aluminium than any other nation. China is also the world's biggest energy user and goods exporter.[4]

China's rise has fed through to the rest of the world economy in several ways.[5] The vociferous demand by China-based manufacturers for raw materials such as iron has driven up mining investments in Australia, Brazil and parts of Africa. Imports into China of specialist components to feed its manufacturing industry – and of machinery that China cannot make itself – have boomed. These trends have helped a large number of industrial companies – especially in countries such as Germany and Japan with strong engineering sectors – that have seen China turn into a major market.

China's low-price goods, from televisions to gardening equipment, have been welcomed by millions of ordinary people. But the low prices have also helped industrial companies in developed regions that use cheap imported Chinese components and finished products to become more competitive. Often, the companies have capitalized on the cost advantages more directly, by starting their own plants in China.[6] In these instances, their motivation is sometimes to sell to the growing Chinese market, as well as to use the country as an export centre. Of China's 200 biggest exporters in 2009, 153 were companies containing a sizeable foreign stake.[7]

All these effects have benefited the shareholders and employees of many manufacturers in the world's rich countries. But there have been negative repercussions too. Spiralling Chinese exports of low-cost goods have made many makers of comparable products in high-cost regions uncompetitive, since they have been unable to reduce their costs to the same level. Large numbers have been forced out of business, with resulting heavy job losses. China's surging exports have contributed to trade imbalances, exacerbating political tensions, particularly with the US. Criticism has especially centred on the state ownership of many big Chinese industrial groups such as Ansteel. Their government links give them access to cheap loans and other sources of finance that are not available to private sector competitors, so some allege, in a way that provides unfair advantages.[8] Broader concerns about China's place in the world are also relevant. Some commentators worry about the impact of a Communist dictatorship that might, at some stage, want to exert its growing and extensive military power in a threatening way.[9]

There is one set of changes affecting industry that almost everyone agrees will have an increasing impact. *Zou chu qu* is a slogan in China that is gaining greater currency.[10] It means walk outside – or look beyond your own region. More top Chinese executives are, like Zhang, intent on setting up stronger links with other countries – not purely by exporting, but by agreeing joint ventures, or acquiring overseas assets which they then operate. Between 2005 and 2009, China's companies spent $145 billion on overseas acquisitions. In 2010 the figure was more than $50 billion, and the numbers look set to grow even more.[11] Many of these deals are likely to take place in manufacturing and engineering, as China attempts to complement its skills and experience in low-cost production with access to new technologies and markets. The deeper ties with overseas companies add to the sequence of interactions connecting China and other countries. The nature of these linkages, and the political backdrop to how they unfold, will be a key component of the new industrial revolution.

## A new ball game

Ansteel was started in Anshan in 1916, as a joint Japanese/Chinese industrial venture called Anshan Zhenzing Iron Ore Company. Japan had emerged as victor in the Russo-Japanese war in 1904–5, a conflict sparked by both powers' designs on the whole of the north-east China region – then known as Manchuria. The area has long enjoyed a reputation as an industrial powerhouse, since it enjoys plentiful sources of iron ore and coal, and has good access to ports. By 1949, when Mao took control of China following the country's bloody civil war, Ansteel was a long way ahead of virtually all China's other steel plants in technological capability.

Mao used the Anshan factory complex as an 'education centre' in steel-making for the whole country.

After joining Ansteel in 1974 as an engineer, Zhang worked his way up through management jobs. In 1994, fired by an ambition to explore America and improve his knowledge of English, Zhang was given a one-year US visa. He planned to take temporary leave to study engineering at the Massachusetts Institute of Technology. But at the last moment Zhang's bosses stopped him going, arguing that his work was too valuable. Zhang tried to hide his disappointment. He threw himself into learning English, reading as many books in this language as he could find. They included an autobiography of Andrew Carnegie, self-help management books by Jack Welch, and *War and Peace*. Given the job of Ansteel chief executive in 2004, Zhang has maintained his interest in foreign connections. He argues that to develop as a company Ansteel must increase its influence outside China. 'Participation in markets outside China is a way of testing our products and processes, to make sure they are up to the best levels of other countries.'[12] He thinks a good way to achieve this is through joint ventures with other steel-makers.

Zhang has a good relationship with several top international steel managers, including John Surma, chief executive of US Steel, and Ekkehard Schulz, the former chief executive of Germany's ThyssenKrupp. He gets on well with Lakshmi Mittal, describing the Indian industrialist as a 'good fellow' and someone whose approach to globalization he would like to emulate.[13] As for Mittal, he has sound reasons to seek a rapport with top figures in China's steel industry. The stronger are these relationships, the better placed he is to improve ArcelorMittal's presence in the country. So far, Mittal has formed just two production ventures in China, both fairly small. They consist of minority stakes, arranged in 2005 and 2007, in two second-tier Chinese steel-makers, Hunan Valin and China Oriental.

Mittal's goals for China have been held back by government policy. Beijing takes a strong line on preventing foreign businesses from gaining control of industries that it considers 'strategic'. Steel is placed in this category, along with car manufacturing, telecommunications and banking. In such businesses, overseas companies are allowed to take only minority stakes in Chinese enterprises. While many inward investors find this

'China for the Chinese' policy frustrating, most of them, Mittal included, are restrained in voicing their views, for fear of annoying the Chinese political hierarchy and upsetting what influence they have.[14] But for some years Mittal has been working quietly to extend his participation in Chinese steel-making. One way to do this would be to pursue collaboration with a big Chinese steel company.

In early 2008, at a meeting for top steel executives in Rome organized by the World Steel Association, Mittal saw his chance. After organizing a private discussion with Zhang, Mittal made a proposal. It was an echo of his conversation with Arcelor's Guy Dollé two years earlier. 'You have international aspirations and your company is highly respected,' Mittal told Zhang. 'Why don't we join forces?' The Indian billionaire wanted Zhang to agree to ArcelorMittal taking a 25 per cent share in Ansteel, in exchange for a sizeable cash injection. A stake of this size would make Mittal some way from being a majority partner, and might be a deal that Beijing could countenance.

To make his proposal more attractive, Mittal reverted to his interest in sport. He was aware that Zhang's company takes table tennis seriously, as do many businesses in China. Mittal offered to send some of India's top table tennis players to Ansteel to take part in exhibition matches and receive tuition in Chinese playing techniques. He thought he could arrange this through his political contacts in New Delhi. Later, in a reciprocal arrangement, the leading players from China could travel to India for the same purpose. The ping-pong diplomacy could, so Mittal thought, help to bring China and India together in a general way, and so reinforce his own plans for a special connection in the steel industry. While Zhang was unsure what to make of the table tennis initiative, he responded favourably to the idea of an ArcelorMittal connection. But he told Mittal that a 25 per cent stake was unrealistic. Zhang suggested instead a less ambitious tie-up, with the shareholding by Mittal's company limited to 2 per cent. Zhang also advanced an idea of his own. He was interested in a joint production venture outside China. 'It could be any time, any place.' But he left the details vague. Mittal interpreted Zhang's comments as a rejection. He was disappointed, but not particularly surprised. Soon after his meeting, Mittal dropped any ideas for a partnership with Ansteel.[15]

But for Zhang, the episode encouraged him to think more deeply about international expansion. In 2010, he announced his readiness to proceed with one such venture. Zhang said Ansteel would take a 17 per cent stake in a new $175 million steel plant to be built in Amory, Mississippi. It would mark the first time that a Chinese company had a role in operating a steel mill in the US. The majority partner was Steel Development, a US business in which John Correnti, a veteran US steel executive, is the main investor. The plant was due to make steel bar for the construction industry, a fairly undemanding part of the steel sector. However, the deal would enable Zhang's company to build up valuable experience in the US. It could, Zhang thought, be a prelude to other ventures, perhaps in Europe or Asia.

To Zhang's surprise, however, the proposed deal ran into a torrent of criticism. The negative sentiments reflected the feeling among many Western businesses – particularly in the US – that China was becoming too big and powerful. Criticism centred on the financial advantages that the state-backed Ansteel might enjoy, if it was permitted to gain a foothold in the US steel industry, over private sector rivals. Another complaint – shared not just by some companies but by many US politicians – concerns what they regard as the artificially low level of China's domestic currency compared to the dollar.[16] In the past decade, China has used the country's high savings to purchase vast foreign currency reserves, mainly in dollars.[17] The dollar purchases have pushed up its value, and as a consequence depressed the renminbi. China's critics say the actions in buying dollars have kept the Chinese currency at 20–30 per cent below its true market value, making it easier to export from China to other countries whose currencies are dollar-denominated, while making importing into China harder. Exacerbating these concerns, in 2010 the US's trade deficit with China hit a record $273 billion, a threefold rise on the figure in 2000. The currency mismatch, say some onlookers, helps the whole of China-based industry, and makes it easier for companies such as Ansteel to consider foreign expansions.

André Gerdau Johannpeter, chief executive of Gerdau, a Brazilian company with nearly 30 per cent of its production in the US, was one critic. 'I am concerned when a government owns a steel company and provides it with subsidies and other forms of help in such a way that it affects its competitive position with privately owned producers.'[18] Tom Danjczek, president of the Steel Manufacturers Association, a US trade group, also weighed in. He 'particularly objected' to Anshan's involvement in Correnti's project on the grounds that it benefited from 'easy access to government loans and an artificially low currency'.[19] Zhang played down the controversy. Arguing that the Mississippi plant would have only the most minor impact on the US steel business, he said the project's critics had 'nothing to worry about'. Zhang also dismissed the idea that Ansteel gained any help from having Beijing as its main shareholder. 'We [Ansteel] can borrow from banks [in China] not because we are state-owned but because we are successful and profitable.' As for the arguments about the alleged 'manipulation' of the renminbi, Zhang said he 'did not recognize' that this activity took place.[20]

## Lost ground

China's industrial rise – and its impact on the world – marks a return to the past. Until the early nineteenth century, China had been a global leader in many areas of industry for hundreds of years. Chinese metal-workers worked out how to make high-quality iron soon after the technology was invented in Mesopotamia. During the 300-year Ming dynasty, which ended in the mid-seventeenth century, China was responsible for a series of impressive technological breakthroughs. These included the invention of paper, clocks, ships' rudders, the compass, the cannon and the metal plough. Yet by the early eighteenth century, China's leadership had ebbed away. Countries in Europe, followed by the US, became the world's top industrial countries. 'The greatest enigma in the history of technology is the failure of China to sustain its technological supremacy,' Joel Mokyr has observed.[21] In *The Wealth and Poverty of Nations*, David Landes concluded that throughout its history China 'lacked institutions for finding and learning – schools, academies, learned societies, challenges and competitions'.[22] The relative absence of such social structures meant China was in a poor position to learn from other countries once they began to move ahead. When the first industrial revolution started in

Britain, China had no way of maintaining its previous position. For virtually all the 250 years from 1750, China was in technological and industrial decline.

When Mao gained power, he was determined that the country should catch up. However, the data for world steel-making in 1950 show how weak China's position had become. In that year China made 600,000 tonnes of steel – or 0.3 per cent of the global total of just under 190 million tonnes. In the same year, the US made 86 million tonnes, Britain 17 million tonnes, and Germany 12 million tonnes.[23] Mao's 'great leap forward' was a set of policies announced in 1957 to promote Chinese industrialization. Mao's goal was to turn the country from an agrarian society to a manufacturing giant. At the centre of the programme was the forced establishment of networks of agricultural communes to replace private farms. There were also heavy state-directed investments in industry. But the results were at best erratic, at worst disastrous. In the summer of 1958, Mao set China's steel target for the year by arbitrarily doubling the figure recorded for 1957 of 5.3 million tonnes. This led to a frenetic effort to put into operation roughly 5 million tonnes of new production – mainly from plants built from scratch – in less than six months. People from around the country, normally with minimal training, were encouraged to construct rudimentary steel mills on spare pieces of land. Some 30,000 people died in industrial accidents. The records suggest China made 8 million tonnes of steel in 1958 – not far off Mao's target. But much of this was of poor quality, and little better than useless.[24] The crash programme to build steel plants illustrated the farcical – and tragic – character of Mao's planned 'leap'. Up to 40 million people are thought to have died as a result of the reform efforts, many of them due to famine.

In 1978, two years after Mao himself died, Deng Xiaoping took over as China's leader. Deng initiated the political programmes that finally put the country on a sustainable path to growth. An arch-pragmatist, he stressed that China should set aside its communist principles by welcoming foreign involvement in the economy, even if this meant cooperating with some of the biggest exponents of global capitalism. While stressing that 'mechanical application of foreign experience will get us [China] nowhere', Deng stated that China should 'learn from foreign countries and draw on their experience'. He was particularly keen to draw lessons from Japan's rise as an industrial power, which involved a mixture of state direction and an unleashing of entrepreneurial forces. Deng's policies led to a huge volume of foreign investment. Since the late 1970s, some $1,000 billion has come into the country from foreign businesses, with much of this going towards factory investments.

One of the main places where Deng's ideas took effect was Shenzhen, a city in southern China. In 1979, Shenzhen's main industry was fishing. It was surrounded by rice fields and lacked even a bus service. But in that year, Deng selected Shenzhen to be one of China's first experimental centres in free-market capitalism, with a special focus on manufacturing. The town was designated a 'special economic zone', in which companies from abroad were encouraged to locate to set up new plants. 'Abroad' also meant Hong Kong, at that time cut off politically from China. Wilfred Yeung, an engineer born in Hong Kong, was among the first industrialists from the island to come to Shenzhen. Yeung was the chief executive of Ace Mold, an engineering company he had started in 1988. He set up his first small plant in Shenzhen in 1991. 'When we came to Shenzhen, there was very little here,' he recalls. 'There was no history of manufacturing. We found a small factory to rent and managed to recruit 25 people who had previously been farmers or builders. We installed 12 manual machines [machine tools] and trained the people to work them. We had only the vaguest hope that the venture would succeed.'[25]

Ace Mold is now one of tens of thousands of manufacturing businesses crammed into what is known as the Pearl River Delta, centred on Shenzhen and a series of other cities. The delta is now one of the world's leading regions for manufacturing. Gordon Styles, a British manufacturing engineer, emigrated to the delta in 2005. He set up Star Prototype, an engineering business, in Zhongshan. Describing China as the 'most powerful nation on earth' and a 'fantastic' location for a new business, Styles says that moving to the delta was 'like coming home'.[26]

A key moment was in 1996 when China overtook Japan to become the world's largest steel-maker. Figure 5 indicates how China has since 1900 slowly caught up with – and then overtaken by a long way – other leading countries in steel production. In 2009, it took from the US the role of the

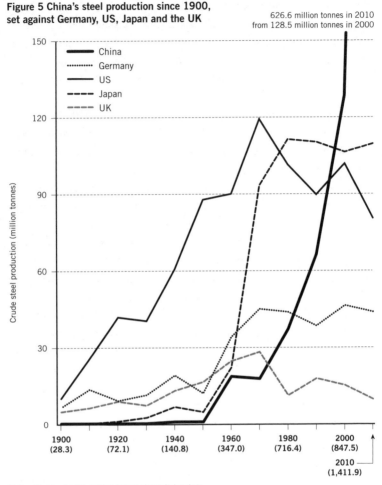

**Figure 5 China's steel production since 1900, set against Germany, US, Japan and the UK**

626.6 million tonnes in 2010
from 128.5 million tonnes in 2000

Crude steel production (million tonnes)

| 1900 | 1920 | 1940 | 1960 | 1980 | 2000 |
| (28.3) | (72.1) | (140.8) | (347.0) | (716.4) | (847.5) |

2010
(1,411.9)

**Notes:** World output in million tonnes shown in brackets.

**Source:** World Steel Association, International Steel Statistics Bureau.

biggest car producer. In the same year China also became the world's biggest market for cars. Wang Dazong, chief executive of Beijing Automotive Industry Corporation (BAIC), China's fifth largest car-maker, is among many senior industrialists in China who see little sign of a slowdown. China's automobile market will, according to Wang, nearly triple to 40 million cars between 2010 and 2020. By this time China will, he says, account for half the world's car output.[27]

## Pumping expectations

In 1990, China played a tiny role in sales of construction equipment. The country accounted for less than 5 per cent of the revenues for this industry. Twenty years on, the picture had changed remarkably. Underlying the extent of the country's building boom, sales in 2010 of construction equipment in China reached $25 billion, making the country by a long way the biggest market in the world for these machines, accounting for almost 40 per cent of global sales. China's impact is particularly marked in large crawler excavators, the workhorses of the construction sector. In 2010, 200,000 such machines were sold around the world – and of these, six out of every 10 went to customers in China. The importance of the country in this business has benefited many foreign suppliers, including Caterpillar and Komatsu, which have established their own Chinese plants. However, it has also sparked the emergence of a new set of Chinese manufacturers, which are starting to have an impact not just inside but outside China.

Among them are Sany and Zoomlion, both of which have grown enormously in the 'niche' field of concrete pumps. These are high-tech machines which pump concrete long distances using powerful hydraulic mechanisms mounted on trucks. For many years two German companies, Putzmeister and Schwing, dominated this industry globally. But more recently the two Chinese companies have used a twin-track strategy – pushing into overseas markets while also investing heavily in domestic sales – to challenge the German dominance. In 2006 Sany took over as the world's biggest concrete pump maker by sales, displacing Putzmeister. In 2011, it became one of the first Chinese machinery groups to build a plant in Europe, starting a factory for concrete pumps near Cologne, in Germany's industrial heartland.[28] In January 2012 it went one better, acquiring Putzmeister for $690 million in the biggest acquisition by a Chinese company of a German *Mittelstand* business. Sany's drive into Europe followed an earlier move by Zoomlion, which in 2008 acquired CIFA, a leading Italian concrete pump maker. The deal gave the company access to several CIFA factories in Italy as well as its global marketing network.

These ventures illustrate the increasingly outward-facing stance of many Chinese manufacturers. With the effort to build production bases overseas, often through acquiring companies with advanced technologies and well-known brands, has come an interest in changing the emphasis of Chinese business from low-tech to high-tech. At the centre of this strategy has been Europe. This might be because of the large number of European companies in fields such as machinery where the Chinese are eager to develop their expertise. There is a sense that Europe is more open to foreign participation in industry – with less of the protectionist sentiment that often features in the US. Clive Whiley, chief executive of Evolution Securities China, a London-based financial services group, says many European engineering companies are starved of investment funds.[29] As a result, there is an eagerness to engage with the Chinese and welcome the kind of cash injection that an expansion-minded new Chinese owner can bring. Franz Fehrenbach, chief executive of Bosch, the German engineering group, says he is well aware of the Chinese interest in Europe. 'I am expecting a massive attack from China in Europe in the next few years – particularly in the machinery sector. The Chinese will improve their quality and technology, but they will at the same time be extremely price-attractive.'[30]

Attempts by the Chinese government to bolster industries in China such as aircraft manufacturing, gas-fired power turbines and low-emission diesel engines are part of the strategy of moving into higher-value industrial sectors. In turn, the overseas companies that rely on China to manufacture goods that they then sell (often under their own brand names) often expect more in terms of technology and design. Gordon Wen, director of Fountain Set, a Hong Kong-based textiles business which operates factories in mainland China, says: 'In the past, customers would come to China with a specification of what they wanted to be made. Now they are coming and asking: "What have you got for us?" They are interested in buying the products that we've made using our own design resources.'[31]

An example of the new approach is in railway engineering. Big Chinese makers of rail locomotives and track signalling are increasingly trying to sell their products overseas, on the back of a decade of success in extending their operations in China, often with the help of technology partnerships with rail engineering companies from the West or Japan. Such Chinese companies include China North Locomotive and Rolling Stock (CNR) and China Southern Railways Sifang. 'They [the Chinese companies] have . . . taken the best of German, French and Japanese [railway] technologies and are now producing some very good equipment themselves,' says Michael Bostelmann, managing director of Fandstan Electric, a UK maker of railway equipment.[32] In the automotive industry, BYD, a fast-growing Chinese car-maker that also produces batteries for fuel-efficient electric cars, has linked up with Daimler, the big German car-maker, to work on new generations of low-carbon emission vehicles.

One company more than any other has set the tone for the two-sided Chinese strategy of overseas expansion, supported by efforts to develop higher-value, design-intensive goods. Lenovo is China's largest maker of computers, and the fourth biggest in the world. The company's most eye-catching move was its 2004 acquisition of the personal computer operations of IBM, the US computer giant. The $1.75 billion deal was the first large cross-border acquisition by a Chinese technology business. It was also the first big illustration of the 'reverse globalization' transactions that became a feature of the later part of the decade. The Lenovo takeover was the more remarkable since IBM had done more than any other company to invent the personal computer. It introduced a pioneering version in 1981, in a move that triggered the immense growth in sales of the machines in the 30 years afterwards.

Some features of Lenovo's style can be glimpsed inside three interlinked office buildings in Morrisville, North Carolina, where young computer engineers are playing table tennis. The table is at Lenovo's US 'centre of operational excellence.'[33] It was installed at the request of the employees' Chinese colleagues on the grounds that it would help them to relax.[34] The company's top executives divide their time between Morrisville and another set of offices in Beijing which serves as Lenovo's main office in China. The idea of the twin sites is to try to combine the best ingredients of US and Chinese business practices so as to form a strong global enterprise.

## A legend grows

The man who started Lenovo – and has been by far the biggest influence on the company – is Liu Chuanzhi, a determined and resourceful computer scientist.[35] Liu has coped with struggles of a kind that few Western executives have experienced. After graduating from a military-backed engineering college in 1966, he worked at the Chinese Academy of Sciences for two years. But then his stint as a research engineer was brutally interrupted by Mao's notorious 'cultural revolution'. Like millions of other educated young Chinese, Liu was forced to leave his job for two years of manual work in the countryside. In 1970, he was allowed back to his job at the academy, and eventually given permission to try to commercialize his research into a new family of computers that could process Chinese characters. In 1984, Liu and 10 other researchers at the academy's Computing Technology Institute started Legend – the company that would later become Lenovo – helped with $25,000 from state funds. Liu recalls that he and the other Lenovo employees threw themselves into the challenge with a gusto beyond that of even the normal hard-driven entrepreneur. 'Why would we work so hard . . .? Because the people of my generation, we were suppressed like crazy in the class struggle. Finally we could start doing some real work.' Liu also remembers the first time he had a business meeting with IBM. It was 1985. The US company was a much revered giant, and Lenovo a tiny start-up. 'I never imagined that one day we could buy the IBM PC business. It was unthinkable.'[36]

Lenovo gradually became the dominant player in China's fast-growing computer market. But it failed to make much headway in the US and Europe. These difficulties triggered the then-radical idea of buying the personal computer unit of IBM. Liu and the others running Lenovo thought the technology and marketing knowledge of the IBM workers who came in with the deal, plus the company's brand strength, would provide an immediate boost. However, the transaction failed to have the expected impact. Liu addressed the problem in 2005 – when he was chairman – by recruiting as chief executive William Amelio, an American manager who had previously been a vice-president of Dell, the Texas-based computer maker. Amelio established a 2,000-strong team of development engineers and designers, spread around the two headquarters buildings plus another office in Tokyo. Angela Qiu, the head of a Lenovo team in Beijing inquiring into new ideas in areas such as materials and software, says: 'If Lenovo is to move ahead as a company, it's vital for the company to make decisive advances in design and innovation.'[37] Even though Amelio left Lenovo in 2009, it appears some of the marketing and technology ideas that he introduced have taken root. Liu certainly appears to feel there have been benefits. As the company has evolved, he feels that one advantage of its exposure to US business practices is that the company is now more inventive and ready to learn. 'We grew up in China's era of reform and opening, we knew nothing and just had to learn by ourselves,' he says. Now he feels the company's product designers and managers have the ability to 'write recipes' – think of new ideas and apply them – rather than simply 'cook according to [existing] recipes'.[38]

A company that shares many of the same characteristics as Lenovo – and has followed a similar path – is Geely, one of China's biggest car-makers. Li Shufu – Geely's chief executive and founder – mixes homespun values with steely ambition. Fond of playing up his peasant roots, Li writes poems in his spare time. He decorates his office with some of his favourite lines of verse – including one entitled 'Who could choose a clearer way than Geely?'

Born into a farmer's family, Li started a manufacturing business in 1984 – the same year as Liu – with money from his father. His chosen industry was components for refrigerators, at that time starting to see the first signs of buoyant domestic demand. Later, he moved into motorcycles, another area of fast growth, through taking over a bankrupt state-owned producer. Geely graduated into four-wheeled vehicles, building its first car in 1998. Expansion was rapid: by 2009, its annual output reached 300,000. The following year, Geely made its big move into overseas markets. It paid Ford Motor $1.8 billion to acquire the Swedish-based automotive group Volvo, one of the world's most famous and upmarket vehicle brands. Li's plans are built around a strategy of maintaining Volvo's European manufacturing footprint, plus its close relationship with its continent-wide supply chain, while replicating the company's design and technology skills in his Chinese factories. While the China part of the operation can gain from this transfer of expertise, the European side should also benefit from the availability of cheap parts from China. Li says China should turn into a 'second home market' after Europe for Volvo. By 2015, he wants the combined Geely/Volvo sales volumes to reach 2 million vehicles.[39]

In discussing the Volvo link, Li stresses that the benefits of the deal stretch both ways – both into and out of China. Conveying a similar argument is Mark Day, the former managing director of Johnson Security,[40] a UK company purchased by Four Dimensions of China in 2007. Both Johnson and the Beijing-based company make armoured security vehicles for transporting cash for banks and retail chains. Four Dimensions – owned by its chairman Wang Yan, a Chinese entrepreneur – wanted to buy the UK company mainly for its advanced technology in areas such as special security screens and cash transfer systems. It felt also that the acquisition could provide a way of finding customers in the European market. But as Day points out, there were advantages for the UK company too. Between 2007 and 2010, Four Dimensions invested about $3 million in its UK offshoot. The money supported new product development and manufacturing improvements. The Chinese parent has also provided a sales outlet for Johnson's products in Asia, which it would have found difficult to engineer for itself. Day says that had Four Dimensions not arrived with its investment cash and a new route for potential sales, his company might have found survival difficult.[41] For Wang, meanwhile, the Johnson deal appeared to whet his appetite for European acquisitions. In 2010, his company added a further operation in the continent through the purchase of KFB Extramobile, a German maker of ambulances – another niche field of specialized vehicles.

Even more than was the case with Johnson, a Chinese deal involving Emag, a German machine tool producer, turned into a way to keep the European company in business. In the economic crisis of 2009, Emag experienced a precipitous drop in revenues that had Norbert Hessbrüggen, its long-time chairman and owner, searching for a partner that could inject new funds. He found one in Pan Xiping, an experienced Chinese businessman with interests in textiles and specialist components as well as machinery. The two men agreed that Pan's Jiangsu Jinsheng manufacturing business should take a 50 per cent stake in the German company. 'If you can't beat them, join them,' says Hessbrüggen. 'In the long run, we would have faced difficulties as a Europe-centred company.' Hessbrüggen says that with a Chinese partner – whose contacts in its home nation provide a better route to this fast-expanding market than Emag's previous sales operations – his company can face the future with more confidence.[42]

## Cultural fall-out

Moves by Chinese companies into other countries – just like efforts by European or US businesses to expand into China – often proceed in a way that is far from smooth. The problems arise as much from deep-seated cultural disparities as from the differences in the way managers approach the technical aspects of product development or marketing. Some of the difficulties became apparent with the 2008 purchase of UK-based Dynex, a maker of specialist electronic devices for controlling electric motors. The acquirer was China South Locomotive and Rolling Stock (CSR), a 'sister' company to CNR and another large railway engineering group. It has used the transaction to gain an in-house producer of devices that use digital control to cut greatly the energy consumed by railway drive systems. Paul Taylor, Dynex's chief executive, says he initially worried that the Chinese owner would 'strip out the technology, take it to China and close down the [UK] operations'. CSR chose instead to keep the UK business virtually intact, helping it to expand with a $20 million programme of capital investment and research and development. The cultural divide, however, has been considerable, Taylor admits:

> If you ask me what the differences are it's hard to pick out just one. It's not as if just one thing is different, as in the trees being blue rather than green. It's more that the business cultures [in the two countries] are completely alien. The landscape is altogether different, covering the way that meetings are conducted to how businesses deal with their staff or customers.

Taylor expands on what this means.

> The Chinese are very good at planning and setting long-term goals, which they do in a precise way. They look at their business in a holistic

way, with the emphasis on decisions being taken on a communal basis. What they lack is I think something of the entrepreneurial, individualistic approach which the British are better at.

The different approach means the UK side to the operation has to be more patient about the time taken for decisions, and use a lot of diplomacy when trying to win arguments. Taylor suggests the divide can be bridged with effort and hard work. 'What we've done is to expect both sides to change a bit and meet somewhere in the middle, while trying to adopt the best parts of each other's cultures.'[43]

Similar issues of cultural disparities are also evident at a huge chemicals site on the outskirts of the ancient Chinese city of Nanjing. The complex has about 1,400 employees and an output valued at about $2 billion a year. Of this, virtually all is sold to businesses or consumers based in China. The plant is a 50/50 joint venture between the German chemicals maker BASF and China Petroleum & Chemical Corporation (Sinopec), a state-owned energy and chemicals group. The joint venture was created in 1996, in one of the first big foreign manufacturing investments in the country. After a lengthy planning and construction phase, production started in 2005. Total investment in the site, shared between the two partners, is set to reach $4.3 billion by 2012.

The layout of the plant is modelled on BASF's flagship chemical complex in Ludwigshafen, southern Germany – the largest chemicals manufacturing unit in the world, employing nearly 36,000 people. The facility works according to what BASF calls the *Verbund* principle. This almost untranslatable word conveys the idea that everything is linked or integrated. Chemicals made in one part of the operation act as the starting materials for other reactions elsewhere. The Ludwigshafen site illustrates a special sort of manufacturing value chain, one in which all the processes are condensed into a small space, as opposed to being dispersed around the world. At Ludwigshafen, 200 individual factories make a similar number of key chemicals that form building blocks – or what BASF calls 'immortals'. The immortals form the basic building blocks for all the 100,000 chemicals that the company makes for a wide range of industries from water treatment to the car sector. Owing to its relative youth, the

Nanjing plant is now a tenth of the size of the Ludwigshafen operation, and makes only a small fraction of the 200 immortals. Over time, however, BASF wants to turn Nanjing into a 'new Ludwigshafen'. Bernd Blumenberg, a German chemist who headed the BASF/Sinopec venture between 1996 and 2011,[44] says the technological complexity of the Nanjing operations is gradually increasing. This is in line with the wider range of requirements for different types of chemicals from its customers.

BASF's experience illustrates the tensions that can sometimes occur in ventures such as this. Some of these issues can be expected to arise in virtually any joint undertaking between different companies. Others are more likely in the special circumstances of Chinese/European combinations. Blumenberg says that following the initial agreement, relations between the two companies were 'not particularly friendly'. There were suspicions on both sides about the other partner's ultimate goals for the operation. He says, for instance, that he had to veto a suggestion that the venture incorporate an office on the Nanjing complex for Communist Party managers. The office would have strengthened the party's links with workers, and acted as a 'listening post' to monitor what went on in the venture as a whole. One of the party managers' jobs would have been to feed workers with political messages – which could have extended into fields such as training or working conditions. Conflicts could then have built up between what workers were being asked to do by the Communist Party and BASF's own requirements. 'I said: No, we're not having this,' says Blumenberg. 'We thought it would not fit in with the normal way BASF seeks to operate.'

There have been other difficulties that have taken time to resolve. Getting Chinese managers to say what they really think can be a problem, says Blumenberg. 'If you ask for a view that might provoke discord then [Chinese workers] often evade the issue. Perhaps it's a question of being over-polite, or maybe it's an effort to stay away from potential trouble in a socialistic system.' But on the whole, Blumenberg is positive. He says the two companies have learned from each other and relationships are now fairly good.

They [Sinopec] send some of their best people to work at and manage the plant. Some of them look to me like future leaders. I'd say a lot of state-owned manufacturers in China are concerned mainly with maximising the output of their plants, but our partners are now learning about the marketing side of production too. Perhaps we [the BASF side of the venture] are teaching them something about the economic impact of what they are doing.[45]

From the point of view of BASF, it too stands to gain massively from the venture. Apart from the obvious benefits of gaining access to the fast-growing Chinese market for chemicals, the experience in running the plant is teaching the company about new requirements for chemicals arising from the demands of China-based customers. An example concerns materials used in producing insulation panels for the construction industry. The technical standards for such products in China are different to those elsewhere. Responding to these nuances in the case of the chemicals being manufactured at Nanjing has given BASF useful know-how that can be applied to other parts of its business. New ideas for chemicals being suggested by other Chinese customers are likely to push BASF into new directions that it might not otherwise have been aware of, says Martin Brudermüller, BASF's vice-chairman. 'A lot of our customers [in China] are switching from a copycat philosophy to [one that emphasizes] more innovative product areas. This puts pressure on us to devise more advanced materials to meet their requirements.'[46]

As Chinese and foreign businesses try to become more global, their interests will intersect increasingly often. The extended value chains that are often part of manufacturing will include China – or Chinese companies operating in other countries – more and more. Meanwhile the Chinese preoccupation with moving more products and processes towards the high-value end of the manufacturing spectrum will have implications for a range of businesses, both inside China and in other countries. For both the Chinese and non-Chinese sides in many of the new ventures, an interest in learning from each other and finding common points for cooperation will be necessary. The track record of European, Japanese and US businesses operating in China in a similar way to BASF is already fairly well established. However, the history of Chinese manufacturing ventures overseas is incredibly short. How such businesses as Lenovo and Geely will cope with the challenges of running their foreign operations – and developing the right blend of management methods to make them a success – is still very hard to assess.

China's return to a leading position in global manufacturing has come after an extremely short period of rapid growth. Comparisons are inevitably made with Japan's expansion surge in the 1970s and 1980s. This period led to a new set of management and production ideas pioneered by Toyota, built around just-in-time manufacturing and *kaizen*-style continuous improvement, that has been applied widely all around the world. It is not clear as yet that China's rapid growth in manufacturing will leave behind anything of such lasting value. Moreover, for all China's rapid rise, it seems unlikely that its manufacturing power will turn into a force that is completely dominant. The Chinese business model contains some inherent and potentially fatal contradictions. At its heart is an attempt to reconcile freewheeling capitalism with the close and undemocratic control of a country by unelected Communist leaders. It is quite possible that the model could unravel in a way that is difficult to foresee but could lead to China's industrial progress going into reverse. For this reason, companies in other parts of the world are unlikely to want to rely on the country too much for their production operations, and may well decide to switch more of their investments to other regions where the long-term political environment is easier to forecast.

Manufacturers in other countries have also learned how to compete with China better, and are doing so using ideas, such as designing new 'breakthrough' products and technologies, rather than purely trying to bring down costs to China's level.

Learning to live with China – sometimes in cooperation with Chinese interests and sometimes in competition – will become increasingly important for many businesses based around the world. For Chinese companies, trying to engineer the right approach to continuing the country's rapid period of growth will be an increasing preoccupation. Among the key influences shaping the new industrial revolution will be the connections that bind China to the rest of the world.

# CHAPTER 8

# Crowd collusion

## Pole position

Warsaw is a small town in Indiana that acquired its name in the 1830s, a result of the popularity of Poland in America at that time. The interest was almost totally due to Thaddeus Kosciuszko, a Polish-American engineer and political activist. Kosciuszko moved to the US from Poland in 1776, the year of the American declaration of independence. He felt inspired to offer his service to the US 'rebels' who were fighting Britain. Commissioned as a colonel of engineers by George Washington, Kosciuszko's talents lay in constructing military garrisons. He was responsible for improving the defences of the West Point garrison near New York, and also fortifying Philadelphia. The engineer lent his name, minus the 'z', to the area around Warsaw, which is called Kosciusko County. Kosciuszko extolled the virtues of working 'with reflection and intelligence', and in excelling in areas of science 'in which you should have true mastery'.[1]

While Warsaw contains today many of the characteristics that Kosciuszko found admirable, it has never had any sizeable Polish community. There is no evidence that the town – with a population of 12,000 – was ever visited by the man who might otherwise have been regarded as its 'favourite son'. Instead of seeking out signs of Polish connections, people come to Warsaw for another reason: to talk about hips, knees or shoulders. Warsaw is the global centre for a $40 billion-a-year business making replacements for these parts of the body.[2] Of the world's five biggest companies in surgical implants, three – DePuy, Zimmer and Biomet – have their headquarters in Warsaw. The three companies between them account for about a third of the orthopaedic device industry's annual sales. Another of the top five businesses is Stryker, based a two-hour drive to the north of Warsaw, in Kalamazoo, Michigan. (The fifth member of this business quintet is Smith & Nephew, whose head office is in London.) Warsaw contains about 100 orthopaedics-related enterprises, including device makers, suppliers and service businesses. Between them, they account for about 6,000 jobs within a radius of a few kilometres of the town centre.[3]

Warsaw's orthopaedic businesses constitute a manufacturing cluster. A cluster is a group of companies in the same industry, located in a small area.[4] Many of these groups of businesses have existed for decades, sometimes for centuries. The Institute of Strategy and Competitiveness at Harvard Business School has studied more than 800 clusters in some 50 countries.[5] Nearly all have evolved as a result of two basic mechanisms, which are sometimes intertwined: the development of new ideas, and the use of local materials. Warsaw is an example of the first type of cluster, as is a concentration of scientific instruments businesses in Göttingen, Germany, and a group of aircraft makers in Wichita, Kansas. Examples of the second type of cluster, which are in general by far the oldest, include businesses involved in brick-making in East Godavari in India; pulp and paper production in Sweden; and leather footwear around Oporto, Portugal.[6] Clusters are small ecosystems. Helped by face-to-face meetings, and the rapid transfer of both physical goods and ideas, clusters facilitate the interchange of know-how. The 'sharing' effects help the businesses within the clusters, whether they are new or well established, to develop new strengths and capabilities. It is perhaps the closest to a socialistic model of resource pooling that the capitalist-oriented business world knows.

It might appear that clusters fit poorly into a global manufacturing sector which is becoming more fragmented and dispersed. The two concepts are, however, compatible. Clusters and 'networked manufacturing' are mirror images of each other, one looking inwards to small communities of businesses squeezed into a small area, the other looking outwards to a dispersed value chain with nodal points in many countries. A specialized cluster can sometimes encompass all the main activities of a complete value chain, including research, product development, marketing and production. Equally, the businesses in such a group may work on just a small part of the span of activities needed for a complete manufacturing operation, such as making specialized components, with the rest of the processes done somewhere else. The growth of China is compatible with a global industrial model in which regional agglomerations of manufacturers are important. China has plenty of examples of industrial clusters[7] – the Pearl River Delta being probably the biggest.[8] There are also many examples of similar concentrations of industry elsewhere that radiate connections to China. One instance is the small group of companies in Poole in England that specialize in air bearings for specialized drilling machines for the printed circuit board industry. The development of these companies is driven partly by local connections, and partly by their links with electronics businesses globally, especially in China. In the new industrial revolution, many of the most potent changes will evolve from products and processes that are developed within regional concentrations of expertise, with the help of connections that span the world.

## Cluster dynamics

Orthopaedic implants add up to one of the fastest-growing sectors in manufacturing. As people live longer, the need to replace worn-out or defective body parts has risen. In 2010, about 2 million people worldwide had joints such as hips and knees replaced, with the figure having risen roughly threefold since the early 1980s. According to some projections, by 2030 the number of people having these operations each year could be about four times higher. Technological innovation and better manufacturing techniques have improved the effectiveness of joint implant surgery, as demand for the therapy has risen.[9] But why should so much of the world's orthopaedics expertise be concentrated in Warsaw?

The story begins with Revra DePuy, a pharmaceutical salesman, who was born in Grand Rapids, Michigan, the neighbouring state to Indiana. DePuy moved to Warsaw in 1895, for no other reason, it appears, than that he had visited the town in his sales job and had liked it. He started his own business, DePuy Manufacturing. The company's first products were wire-based splints for setting broken bones. DePuy later started producing slings, neck collars and braces. Early in the twentieth century, the company developed a specialized series of surgical instruments, and began making orthopaedic implants in the 1960s. Since 1998, DePuy has been part of Johnson & Johnson, the big US healthcare company. In 1927, one of DePuy's salesmen, Justin Zimmer, left to establish a rival orthopaedics supplier, which he called Zimmer. Since he had roots in Warsaw, he saw no reason to move away. Zimmer's first products were a new line of aluminium splints that the entrepreneur thought worked better than the rival items made by his old company. In the 1930s, Zimmer moved into bone fixation devices – special screws and fasteners that held together broken bones – before moving about 20 years later into joint replacements. In 2010, Zimmer had worldwide sales of $4.2 billion and more than 8,000 employees, just over a quarter of them in Warsaw. Biomet – the third of the Warsaw companies – was started in 1977 by Dane Miller and Jerry Ferguson, two Zimmer executives who felt the company had grown too bureaucratic, and two others from Orthopaedic Equipment, another Warsaw medical device business that Biomet later bought. Biomet – like the other two members of the Warsaw trio – decided that its future also lay in providing better and longer-lasting joint implants.

Stryker – located outside the cluster, but part of a related community of companies – was the creation of Homer Stryker. He was a surgeon-cum-inventor who was born in 1894 in a farming community in southern Michigan. In his childhood, Stryker was surrounded by people who liked tinkering with agricultural gadgets, such as ploughs and tractors. The engineering culture of the area was helped by the emerging automotive companies such as General Motors and Ford, based only a few hours' drive away in Detroit. After opting for a career in medicine, becoming Kalamazoo county physician in 1929, Stryker branched out into surgery. He was interested in both using existing devices and making new ones. He set up Stryker in 1941, initially to make walking frames and hospital beds, later moving into devices such as hip, knee and elbow joints.

The three big Warsaw implant makers – together with Stryker, located a short distance away – have spawned new companies that supply either products or services to these principal businesses. Some of these new companies have been offshoots of the first set of enterprises, while others have been drawn into the region by the attraction of potential orders, plus an established pool of technology and labour. Larry Gigerich, managing director of Ginovus, a US business advisory group, explains how this happens. 'The simple truth is that businesses tend to prefer to locate in areas where there are like businesses.'[10] The way in which Warsaw has evolved as a cluster has probably been helped by some of the non-business aspects to the town. It is regarded as a fairly quiet, safe place, with good transport links, decent education and pleasant countryside – all factors of interest to business people casting around for places either to set up new companies or to move to join existing ones.

The growth of the cluster has been driven by people such as Toby Buck, an engineer from Minnesota. After starting his career in the automotive and aerospace industries, Buck saw the relevance of medical implants to a world with more elderly people. As a result, he seized the chance to switch into a new discipline. He moved to the Warsaw area in 1991 to start Paragon Medical, a company making specialist components for the ortho-paedics industry. The company now employs more than 1,000 people, with 400 in Pierceton, just outside Warsaw, and the rest in other locations, including a plant in Changzhou, China, and a sales and engineering office in Switzerland. Referring to the 'collective intellect' of Warsaw, Buck says people are continually meeting to discuss new ideas, for either products or new ventures.[11] The ideas they spark off make the town and the surrounding region 'an incubator' for new entrepreneurial thinking. Rick Stetler, oper-ations director at Paragon, observes:

If an engineer [in a Warsaw implant maker] has an idea for a new product, he can pick up the phone [to a sub-contractor] and discuss it. Then five minutes later he can call round to show how the product should be made. It's a lot easier to do that kind of thing here than if the businesses were thousands of miles apart.[12]

Brian Emerick illustrates how businesses in a cluster can help to create new companies in related technologies. With a background in making dies and tools for a broad range of engineering industries, Emerick started Micropulse in Columbia City, a small town just outside Warsaw, in 1988. Micropulse specializes, like Paragon, in making precisely engineered parts for the main orthopaedic businesses in Warsaw and elsewhere. Added to this, Emerick has also become a small-scale venture capitalist. He has raised finance to back new companies in related areas of medicine, sometimes renting them space in Micropulse's headquarters. Emerick has a particular interest in the emerging science of orthobiologics: using a combination of biology, biochemistry and engineering to devise new therapeutic procedures. A company backed by Emerick that uses orthobiologics is Nanovis, located near Warsaw, which makes spinal implants. Rather than create the device from a conventional material that is 'passive' in the way it reacts with the body, the implant contains a thin layer of 'active' chemicals that influence some aspect of cell behaviour. For instance, some Nanovis bone substitutes incorporate an outer layer of special proteins that enable bone cartilage to repair itself.

In 2007, Nick Deeter, an orthopaedic specialist working at DePuy in Warsaw, chose the same approach as Justin Zimmer 80 years earlier: he decided to leave to start a new company called OrthoPediatrics, also based in the Indiana town. The company is developing new types of medical implant, for use specifically with children. According to Deeter, children with bone or joint problems have been poorly served up to now by medical devices created largely for adults. Now he aims to turn OrthoPediatrics into a 'commercializing engine' for products of this sort likely to have been invented by surgeons and other medical practitioners around the world but with the development rights ceded to his company.[13] Of all the possible locations where such strategies could turn out a success he believes Warsaw – due to its web of local and international connections – has probably the best credentials.

## Connections count

The easiest way for a cluster to lose its relevance is for the businesses in it to cut themselves off from researchers, rival companies and customers in the rest of the world. 'While proximity accounts for much of the informal learning that occurs within clusters, external connections are just as vital for bringing new information into the cluster,' according to Stuart Rosenfeld, principal of Regional Technology Strategies, a US innovation consultancy.[14] In Warsaw, the extent of the connections is illustrated by the stream of surgeons from around the world who fly in to the Indiana town every week for discussions with the medical device companies. Other links with outsiders have led to mergers and acquisitions that encourage growth both in Warsaw and outside.

Many of the early developments that helped the Warsaw cluster involved surgeons located some distance away. The hip joint was one of the first parts of the body that medical practitioners attempted to replace. Philip Wiles, a surgeon at the Middlesex Hospital in London, performed the first complete hip replacement in 1938.[15] Wiles used metal prosthetic devices to try to improve the lives of elderly people suffering from rheumatoid arthritis. Wiles's initial attempts had limited success. The stainless steel components used in the implants wore out quickly, leaving the patients in pain. However, others improved on Wiles's ideas. Paul Eichler, a Swiss-born surgeon, worked in hospitals in Massachusetts and Oklahoma, before moving to Indianapolis in 1948 to start his own medical practice. There he started consultancy work with Zimmer, which led to the company introducing its first hip prosthesis in 1950. Around the same time, Codman & Shurtleff, a Boston company that later became part of DePuy, started work on new implants for spines in conjunction with James Poppen and Ralph Cloward, two pioneering US neurosurgeons.

Sir John Charnley, a British surgeon, is regarded as the 'father' of the modern orthopaedics industry.[16] Charnley served in the British army medical corps during the Second World War, supervising production of splints for wounded soldiers suffering from bone fractures. Later, he joined the orthopaedic department of the Manchester Royal Infirmary, before moving in 1962 to the Wrightington Hospital in nearby Wigan. He replaced the steel used in Wiles's devices with other materials, including titanium and cobalt/chrome alloys that were more compatible with the human body and had better wear properties. Charnley introduced a poly-ethylene 'liner' to act as a shield between the different parts of the implant, so reducing erosion. He also devised new surgical techniques that made hip operations easier, such as the use of special cement to hold the implants in place, while cutting the risks of infection.

Charnley's ideas eventually fed through to Warsaw, via a link with DePuy. From the 1960s to his death in 1982, Charnley worked as a consultant to Chas. F. Thackray, a UK orthopaedic business based in Leeds, northern England. Some of Charnley's insights into making new kinds of hips benefited Thackray. It made a series of new implants, frequently in collaboration with other surgeons worldwide. In 1974, Corange, a private business in Switzerland with interests in the medical industry, bought DePuy. The change of ownership gave DePuy a set of new connections in Europe, and made the company more interested in partnerships in the continent. In 1988 DePuy bought Chevalier, a Swiss implant producer, and two years later it acquired Thackray, enabling the company to tap into the store of know-how the UK business had built up since Charnley's time. DePuy maintained a production base in Leeds until 2010, when the company shut it down, though it continued with a design and development centre. The Leeds-based activities of DePuy – and of Thackray before it – had a big role in helping to stimulate the current cluster of medically related companies in and around the city. The Leeds area now has about 100 medical businesses, most of them with fewer than 50 employees.[17] Many of these businesses have links to local hospitals and a network of small suppliers in the area. One prominent member of the Leeds cluster is Brandon, which is among Europe's biggest makers of specialized lighting for hospitals. Set up in 1946, Brandon had a series of early links with Thackray, as a result of which it developed high-intensity lighting for use by orthopaedic surgeons during operations.

After Warsaw, the world's second biggest concentration of specialist medical implant companies is in Memphis, Tennessee. Its evolution also has a connection to Justin Zimmer. The orthopaedics entrepreneur had a cousin, Don Richards, who worked as a salesman for DePuy in Memphis.

Possibly Zimmer's entrepreneurial ambition also prompted something similar in his cousin. In 1934, Richards left his employer to form a new business, which he decided would remain in Memphis. By the time his company, Richards Manufacturing, was sold in 1986, it was the world's third biggest maker of orthopaedic devices. The company that bought it was the UK's Smith & Nephew – in a move that catapulted it up the league table of the world's big orthopaedic suppliers. Smith & Nephew now bases its global implants operations in the Tennessee city, with its London global headquarters taking responsibility for the company's full product line, which also includes other areas such as wound care treatments.

Two other large medical device makers, both US owned, have their orthopaedics headquarters in Memphis. One is the bone implant division of Medtronic, a company based in Minneapolis which is best known for its heart pacemakers. The second is Wright Medical Group, which was formed in 1950 by Frank Wright, an engineer who used to work for Richards Manufacturing. Memphis is also the home of influential ortho- paedic institutes such as the Campbell Clinic, started in 1909 by Willis Campbell, and the Department of Orthopaedic Surgery at the University of Tennessee. The medical institutes and the three big implant companies have provided the 'seed' for the Memphis cluster. The Memphis cluster now has about 60 companies involved with implant manufacturing, providing combined annual sales of several billions of dollars.

Sometimes clusters connect. An example is the link between Memphis and Warsaw, transmitted by a series of events involving Zimmer and Medtronic. Danek was a specialized spinal implant business set up in Warsaw in 1983 by former executives at Zimmer, along with George Rapp, a local surgeon.[18] After purchasing a distribution business in Memphis in the late 1980s, Danek soon afterwards moved its headquarters to the Tennessee city, while maintaining most of its manufacturing in Warsaw. In 1993, Danek bought Sofamor, a rival French medical devices company. Six years later, yet another merger took place, with the newly combined Sofamor Danek business being purchased by Medtronic. This was the move that took the Minneapolis company into orthopaedics for the first time. Medtronic is now the world's biggest maker of implants for the spine – accounting for a share of about a quarter of a 'niche' of the orthopaedics business with sales in 2010 of more than $6 billion. Rather than turn its back on Warsaw, Medtronic has strengthened its operations in the Indiana town. This came through the decision in the late 1990s to build a new manufacturing and research centre there that employs 600 people.

## Material links

One of the world's oldest clusters is in Jingdezhen, in Jiangxsi province, in southern China. In this area, porcelain and pottery production – which has its roots in the good-quality clay found in the area – has been important for 1,400 years. A similar cluster is in Sassuolo, a town in central Italy. In 1533, Pierre Belon, a French traveller and naturalist, wrote after visiting the region: 'The soil hereabouts tends to stick tenaciously to the feet of passers-by as if it were damp. It is composed of coarse sand of a whitish colour.'[19] The material was fine clay with properties that made it especially useful for turning into ceramic tiles. Anyone driving into Sassuolo immediately notices what the town is famous for. A fine layer of white dust is visible on most exposed surfaces. The dust comes from the high-grade clay used as a raw material by the 100 or so tile manufacturers in and around the town. While local clay was used by the companies for a long time, most of the raw material now used locally comes from further afield, such as Ukraine or parts of Asia. The key feature helping to maintain Sassuolo's strength in this industry is nowadays not local supply of materials but expertise. While the local clay deposits are largely worked out or too difficult to gain access to, the engineering and technical skills in the local tile-making community have proved longer lasting. As a result, Sassuolo has remained one of the world's leading localities for tile companies. Large businesses in this sector which are based in the town include Panaria, Concorde and Marazzi. Stoke-on-Trent in England is another region where local clay deposits gave rise to a large concentration of companies specializing in ceramic items, mainly tableware. In the area around High Wycombe in southern England, wood from local beech forests stimulated the growth of a local furniture industry from the seventeenth century onwards. While both sets of clusters are much diminished compared to 50 years ago, important residues of these industries exist in both areas.

Besides clay and wood, other materials used by clusters have been metals, particularly iron and steel. From the 1850s to the 1950s, the world's biggest steelworks were mainly in inland areas of Western Europe and the US, often in fairly tightly constrained areas, close to sources of iron ore and coal. Particularly important was the area of northern Europe taking in parts of Belgium and Luxembourg, the French province of Lorraine and the Saarland area of Germany. Other key areas in continental Europe were the Ruhr/Rhine junction in Germany, and Silesia, Poland. In these regions, the presence of local materials stimulated not just steel production, but ancillary services and supply businesses that sold to the steel industry. The presence of metal ores and coal also had an indirect impact on promoting the emergence of enterprises in 'downstream' product sectors that used iron and steel as a raw material.[20]

In continental Europe, steel industry clusters are less important than they were. From the 1950s, the link between steel production and local supplies of iron ore and coal became weaker. The materials became depleted and harder to dig up. Also new supplies became available from further afield. As a result, the 1950s and 1960s saw a trend towards building new steelworks by the sea. The new sites included their own ports both to receive iron ore and coal shipped in from countries such as Brazil and Australia, and to export finished steel. The biggest steel mills in continental Europe now are relatively new coastal plants, such as those in Ghent in Belgium, and Dunkirk and Marseilles in France, all of them run by ArcelorMittal, and the Taranto site in southern Italy owned by Riva, Italy's biggest steel company. The US is to some degree an exception. Large steel plants continue to be clustered near the Great Lakes. The region's water links provide useful connections to the outside world both for raw materials and finished products. The region is also helped by its closeness to sizeable deposits of iron ore.

In Britain, the move towards building large steelworks on the coast started earlier than in most of the rest of Europe. Much of this was due to the UK's island characteristics and good shipping links. Examples include the giant Teesside steelworks, built in 1917, which in 2011 was sold to Sahaviriya Steel Industries of Thailand, and the Port Talbot plant in South Wales, which dates back to 1901 and is owned by Tata of India. But in the

UK, the idea of the steel cluster – not so much involving steel-making but companies that use the metal – has never died out completely. It lives on in Sheffield, the place where much of modern steel-making started. Well before Henry Bessemer's breakthrough in mass-production steel-making technology in the 1850s, Sheffield had a sizeable industrial community making iron and steel products.

One of city's specialities was cutlery, a field where Sheffield has had a presence since the fourteenth century. Reflecting this expertise, the Company of Cutlers in Hallamshire, a trade group which still exists, was incorporated by an Act of Parliament in 1624 to regulate the local industry.[21] After it became feasible to make steel in larger amounts towards the end of the nineteenth century, high-volume steel-makers based in Sheffield started to thrive. In 1856, John Brown, a local entrepreneur who ran a company of the same name, opened the Atlas Works in the city, and quickly converted it to the new Bessemer technology. Nine years later, the Vickers company built the huge River Don steelworks, later taken over by British Steel (now Tata). Other big steel-makers that developed in the city in the late nineteenth century included Thomas Firth & Sons, Davy Brothers, and Daniel Doncaster.[22] Many of them had subsidiary operations making steel products, particularly for the heavy armaments industry.

Today, little basic steel-making remains in Sheffield. The city produces less than 1 million tonnes a year of the material, with most of this coming from two sites, one run by Tata and the other by Outokumpu, a Finnish company.[23] But the city retains strengths in several downstream steel-related businesses. In Sheffield and nearby Rotherham there are about 500 companies in sectors linked to steel forgings and castings, specialized machining, materials supply and testing. Several of these can trace their roots to the old-established steel-makers. The companies include Sheffield Forgemasters, which makes large steel parts for industries such as power generation, and occupies the same site by the Don River as Vickers did in the late nineteenth century. Others are Firth Rixson, a specialist in metal forgings for aircraft, which was formed from parts of Thomas Firth; DavyMarkham, a company that makes huge steel parts for bridges and similar structures, and which emerged from Davy; and Doncasters, another forgings business that is based on divisions of Daniel Doncaster. Additional companies in the Sheffield metals cluster, with only indirect links to these old-established businesses, include Independent Forgings & Alloys, an exponent of a specialized form of steel-rolling technology with a history going back 200 years; HD Sports, one of the world's biggest makers of ice-skate blades; Arnold Wragg, a maker of high-strength nuts and bolts used in products such as unmanned flying 'drones' used for surveillance missions; and Bromley, which produces bobsleighs for Olympic athletes.[24]

Sheffield's cutlery traditions remain in evidence, not only in the form of companies that continue to make specialist knives but in the shape of businesses in the related field of surgical instruments, including scalpels, tweezers and scissors. Swann Morton, the world's biggest maker of scalpels, which was formed in 1932, is based in the city. Other companies in surgical hardware in Sheffield include Sheffield Precision Medical, Barber, Platts & Nisbett and Heeley Surgical. Sheffield also has its own link with Warsaw. In 1895, George Thornton, a Sheffield entrepreneur, established G. W. Thornton to make steel cutlery. Thornton had a spell in the 1970s and 1980s as part of Bramah Engineering, a company that was owned by descendants of Joseph Bramah, the eighteenth-century locksmith and inventor.[25] Since 2003, however, Thornton has been part of Warsaw-based Symmetry Medical, a specialized maker of orthopaedic components. The company's Sheffield plant makes a range of high-precision parts, some of which fit into aerospace engines, with others ending up in hip implants.

## Ring cycle

Squeezed into a circular area centred on Lucerne in Switzerland and extending for about 250 kilometres is the 'Alpine Ring'.[26] It takes in most of Switzerland, and parts of Germany, Italy, France and Austria. The largely mountainous area is a cluster of clusters: an agglomeration of 20 or so individual industry concentrations in sectors from watches and surgical instruments to bath taps and car parts. Inside the Ring are some 3,000 predominantly small to mid-sized companies involved in specialist areas of engineering or manufacturing. Nearly all are privately owned. Several areas inside the Ring or on its fringes have been shaping parts from metals for hundreds of years. This activity has almost always been linked to local supplies of raw materials, mainly iron ore. The small town of Le Brassus in Switzerland was one such focal point. Le Brassus – in the Jura mountains – is 20 kilometres from the iron ore deposits of Vallorbe, where iron was first mined in the late thirteenth century. A second notable area is around Aalen, in southern Germany, close to the north-western fringe of the Ring. Aalen was where Schwäbischen Hüttenwerke, one of Germany's oldest industrial enterprises, was set up in 1365 to smelt local iron ore.

A third centre for metalwork in the Ring developed in northern Italy, around Brescia. Gun-making – based on local iron ore – has been important in the region for 500 years. Beretta is a company started near Brescia in 1526 by the gunsmith Maestro Bartolomeo Beretta. Its first big contract was to make arquebus barrels, specialized weapons bought by the Venice Arsenal for fitting to ships. Slightly to the west of Brescia, around Lake Orta, is another region of northern Italy noted for metals production. Here, the key material is locally mined copper. The companies that evolved in this region from medieval times developed a specialist interest in making bronze bells for local churches.

A fifth important district for metals in the Ring developed during the 1850s. This is the area around Tuttlingen, a small German town just south of Stuttgart. Skills in using local iron deposits for a range of metal goods (including farm implements and industrial tools) led local entrepreneurs to set up plants for making cutlery, replicating what happened in Sheffield. In 1867, Gottfried Jetter, a Tuttlingen cutler, set up Aesculap, a maker of surgical instruments such as forceps, tweezers and scalpels. In this development, the Tuttlingen companies again followed a similar pattern to their counterparts in Sheffield, moving into new fields marked by more advanced technical processes and where they could see the chance of gaining a competitive advantage on an international scale.[27]

One factor that – over several centuries – has helped lay the foundation for businesses in the Ring has been its geography. For centuries, the Alps have been a key staging post on migratory routes. As people travelled, they took with them new ideas, often involving novel products and technologies. An important set of ideas concerned watch and clock making. The transfer of this know-how into Switzerland led to the start of the Swiss watch industry – which accounts for the Ring's most important group of companies. This agglomeration of activity involves about 600 companies, counting both assembly businesses and suppliers. Invented in China, the technology of mechanical clocks reached Europe in the thirteenth century. The main clock production centres were initially Britain and Italy. By the mid-1500s, France, and especially the area around Paris, also became a watchmaking stronghold. Making clocks involved disciplines that included metals refining, precision cutting and miniaturization. Much of the skill base was applicable to other industries. For this reason, Lewis Mumford, the historian and critic, called the clock 'the key machine of the modern industrial age'.[28] Watches – small and mobile clocks – appeared in the early 1500s. Making them required even more refined production techniques. People who were good at watchmaking would often at some stage move to other early industries. Watchmaking in the medieval era was a 'school for skill', according to David Landes.[29]

But how did a sizeable watchmaking industry – in fact the world's biggest by value of production – end up in Switzerland? The explanation lies in religious strife. In the sixteenth century, Geneva was an independent republic that had yet to be subsumed into Switzerland – which happened only in 1815. The city had acquired a reputation as a centre for craftsmanship in fields such as jewellery and enamelling. In 1685, the French king Louis XIV revoked the Edict of Nantes that nearly 100 years earlier had permitted Protestants freedom of worship. French people who practised this faith were suddenly exposed to potential attack, and some feared for their lives. Many of these people worked in craft disciplines, including watchmaking. Geneva – because of its existing industrial focus – was regarded by large numbers as an attractive destination where they had a good chance of finding work and putting down new roots.

Aided by the influx of people and ideas, Geneva's craft workshops emerged after the late seventeenth century as a key centre for the European watch industry. Businesses in the city specialized particularly in the production of the ébauches, or movements, that are the vital 'engines' for mechanical watches. To help cut costs, work in watch and ébauche assembly was contracted out to the inhabitants of the towns and villages of the nearby Jura mountains – where wages were lower. Many of the people who entered the industry on the assembly side were farmers who split their time between their conventional jobs and the new activity of watch production. Luckily for the owners of the Geneva-based watch businesses, the agricultural workers turned out to be sufficiently dexterous and diligent to do the work to a high standard.

Other key factors concerned local supplies of iron ore, and expertise in using this as a basis for watch components made from iron or steel. The availability of these resources helped the industry to expand. As this happened, and with assembly operations already moving into the Jura, the centres of watchmaking in Switzerland spread from Geneva into several other nearby localities which had sources of finance and skilled labour. The areas where watchmaking expertise was replicated in the 1700s and 1800s fit closely into the shape of the current-day Swiss watch cluster. The watch business in Switzerland is now centred on four areas, located around Neuchâtel and Berne as well as Le Brassus and Geneva. About 80 per cent of the Swiss watch businesses are based in these places.[30] Strictly speaking, it is therefore correct to think of not one but four Swiss 'mini-clusters' for watchmaking, all of them fitting into the much broader Alpine Ring.

Other ideas were transferred into the Swiss watch industry. Particularly important was knowledge linked to Benjamin Huntsman's crucible process for making high-quality steel. The Sheffield steel-maker had developed the technology in the mid-eighteenth century. He tried to keep his ideas secret. However, the know-how leaked out after he started exporting goods such as hand tools for industrial use. Customers in countries such as France and Germany were intrigued by the high quality of the material in these goods. They started to wonder how the steel had been made. They found at least some of the answers by in-depth examination of the metal, and also through launching the equivalent of 'industrial espionage' operations to arrive at important clues. For instance, Sheffield workers knowledgeable about Huntsman's methods were sometimes bribed to hand over to the Swiss competitors key details of the technology. By the end of the eighteenth century, Swiss watchmakers had learned enough about Huntsman's ideas to be capable of replicating some aspects of his production technology. This was crucial to enabling them to improve their own products. During the 1880s, Switzerland took over from the UK as the world's biggest watchmaker, a position the country has maintained.

## Ideas in time

In a similar way to watchmaking, the other main Ring clusters have evolved to become pockets of expertise in specialist areas of manufacturing. In the Aalen area, Schwäbischen Hüttenwerke is now a maker of high-tech car parts. The company is part of a cluster of automotive parts businesses, many of them supplying the Stuttgart-based vehicle makers Daimler and Porsche. Among the leading members of the cluster are Robert Bosch, Behr, Eberspächer, Mahle and ZF.[31] Close to Brescia, Beretta is still based in the small Alpine town of Gardone Val Trompia. Now in its fifteenth generation of family ownership, the company remains one of the world's biggest gun-makers. It is part of a cluster of companies that specialize in weapons and other goods made from iron and steel. Underlying the linkages, in close-by Cominica to the north of Lake Iseo are three steelworks, at Selleo, Cerveno and Malegno, run by Riva, Italy's biggest steel producer.

In the Lake Orta district, the metalworking skills of the past have stimulated the growth of an industry making valves and taps, mainly from brass. An area close to the lake is known as the Valley of the Valves. It contains about 150 companies in valve manufacturing, including the supply of special parts and materials. Marco Paini, chief executive of Paini, a tap maker in Pogo, close to Lake Orta, points out that the local valve and tap producers would be much less capable of competing on a global scale without the many suppliers in the neighbourhood in fields such as specialized cutting or metal polishing.[32] Maurizio Meloda, general manager of Ottone Meloda, a family-owned tap business in the area, says: 'Having these skills together is a definite advantage for us.'[33]

Of the other Ring clusters, the one close to Tuttlingen in south Germany has developed into the world's leading centre for surgical instruments. 'If you are a surgeon anywhere, then you will have heard of Tuttlingen,' says Karl Leibinger,[34] president of KLS Martin, one of the biggest businesses in the district. Leibinger's company is among about 300 companies in Tuttlingen and nearby towns that make either complete surgical devices or components for them. The biggest of these groups is Aesculap – which is now also the largest producer of surgical instruments in the world. Aesculap retains its main manufacturing centre in Tuttlingen, where it employs roughly 1,000 people out of the 10,000 in the cluster. The other clusters in the Ring have developed largely as a result of skills transfer from other specialist centres locally, buttressed by expertise developed inside each area. In the Arve valley in France, to the south-east of Geneva, about 300 small businesses make components for products such as cars, aircraft or medical equipment. Companies in the Arve region started to build up expertise in engineering in the eighteenth and nineteenth centuries, when they made components for Geneva-based watch producers based some 40 kilometres away. A refocus on newer industries took shape during the twentieth century. Leading businesses in the cluster now include Somfy, which at one time made precision parts for clocks, and now uses related skills in forming metals to produce specialized motors for controlling blinds and shutters. Other businesses in the cluster include Anthogyr, which makes dental implants; MicroWeld, a producer of components mainly for medical equipment; and Antho Deco, which specializes in parts for hydraulic pumps and related products.[35]

In the Franche-Comté area of eastern France, on the other side of the Jura mountains, companies have again used a mix of old and new ideas to create another cluster. Here, several hundred small companies have evolved to make tiny parts for watches and related industries that require high-precision components. Rubis Précis in Charquemont, near Besançon, was established in the 1940s to provide ruby-based components for the Swiss watch industry. It has graduated into making a range of components for other sectors, including telecommunications systems and medical devices.[36] Within Switzerland, many of the precision engineering skills in watchmaking have been important in the formation of yet another cluster. This is based on medical equipment – much of which relies on the detailed creation of small parts and advanced engineering skills. The medical cluster in Switzerland involves about 500 companies in sectors such as special pumps and orthopaedic implants.[37] Zimmer, DePuy, Stryker and

Medtronic – all of the leading US implant makers with the exception of Biomet – have acquired or started development or manufacturing operations in Switzerland to tap into the local expertise.[38]

No company in any cluster should think it is in such a strong position that it does not sometimes have to adapt. A critical period for the Swiss watch industry was the early 1980s, when many local companies were in a state of crisis. Swiss exports of watches and movements plummeted from 91 million units in 1974 to 43 million in 1983. The poor results led to several leading companies disappearing. The problems were due to new competition and new technology. The competition came in the form of Japanese companies led by Citizen, Sharp, Casio and Seiko. They based their products on digital, rather than analogue, displays, and the use of electronically controlled quartz crystals for watch movements, rather than the conventional mechanical ébauches favoured by the Swiss businesses. Not only were the Japanese-made watches cheaper, but many consumers liked their novelty. The market share of the Japanese began to rise appreciably, with a corresponding decline for the Swiss businesses. For some time it appeared that Japanese manufacturers were about to destroy one of Europe's best-established specialist industries. But the Swiss watch business recovered, with the rescue efforts led by an outsider.

Nicolas Hayek was the Lebanese-born owner of a Zurich consulting firm, Hayek Engineering. He admitted he knew little about watchmaking – but he knew a lot about restructuring businesses in chemicals, consumer goods and cars. Hayek was asked by bankers to take over running the combined forces of Switzerland's two biggest watchmakers, which he formed into a new company that he later called Swatch.[39] The company was revitalized with the help of a team of new managers, many of whom came from outside the watch business, including Ernst Thomke, a former pharmaceutical salesman with a gift for marketing. With the help of two engineers, Elmar Mock and Jacques Müller, Hayek introduced a new quartz watch based on just 51 components (compared to twice as many for comparable Japanese models) and called it the Swatch.[40]

Using automated manufacturing techniques, the watch could be produced in Switzerland (despite the country's high wages) and sold for around $40. The design featured coloured parts made out of plastic, and as stylish as possible: one design, called the Jellyfish, had a transparent case to make a feature of the parts inside. The products went on sale in department stores, boutiques and fashion houses. Swatch sales rose from just over 1 million units in 1983 to 12 million in 1986. Hayek's approach prompted the rest of the Swiss watch industry to introduce new thinking. Other companies improved their sales and promotion campaigns, and put more effort into design and production. By 1990, Swiss watch exports had recovered to reach more than 90 million units. In 2010, the Swiss industry pushed up its sales by a fifth compared to the previous year. It ended the decade comfortably ahead in watch sales compared with other countries such as France, Germany and China. In 2010, Swiss-based watch companies employed some 35,000 people and accounted for sales estimated at just over $17 billion, equivalent to roughly a third of the revenues of the world watch industry.[41] The industry leaders include Jacquet Droz, Vacheron Constantin, Breguet and Dubois & Fils, all of which started in the eighteenth century. Driven by strong demand for high-price time-keeping devices from around the word, and by 300 years of experience in complicated metals and engineering technologies, the Swiss watch industry shows few signs of giving up its lofty position.[42]

## Clever people, new ideas

One of the best places to observe how industrial clusters are likely to develop is Cambridge in the UK. The area in and around the city is home to about 1,500 technology businesses. Most of them have fewer than 50 employees. Many have close links to science and technology departments at the University of Cambridge, one of the world's top academic institutions.[43] Another key ingredient of the 'ecosystem' of the Cambridge cluster is the network of research and development centres set up in the city by global businesses, including Unilever, Hitachi, Rolls-Royce, Philips, Schlumberger and Microsoft. In the past 20 years, a strong support structure for the smaller companies has emerged in the form of service businesses such as legal and accountancy firms, and financial groups offering sources of venture capital. Walter Herriot is a bank manager-turned-business adviser who has been involved with the Cambridge cluster for 40 years. Herriot likens the chain of linkages within the cluster to a sequence of chemical or biological reactions. 'When you put a lot of bright people together, give them access to business know-how and sources of funding, it's amazing the new ideas that will emerge.'[44]

Many of the Cambridge companies are involved in the development or design-related parts of the manufacturing value chain, rather than in physical production – which in these cases is left to other localities, sometimes outside the UK. A key characteristic is an interdisciplinary style of working. Such businesses take ideas from separate business sectors or branches of science and technology. They then blend the features to create new products or business types that would be difficult to devise in any other way. The interdisciplinary style has emerged as a result of the mix of scientific and technical disciplines that has taken root in Cambridge over several hundred years. A key event was the university's establishment in 1874 of its Cavendish Laboratory in experimental physics. Under the initial direction of James Clerk Maxwell, the laboratory ushered in a new way of approaching physics in which the discipline was aligned with practical engineering techniques such as machining, materials processing and metallurgy. A range of new ideas in semiconductors, molecular biology, radio communications, medical physics and materials processing have emerged from the laboratory, many of them benefiting local companies. Added to this has been the more recent interest among researchers in the city in the cross-sectoral collaboration that often eludes scientists and engineers elsewhere.

A strong influence involved Tim Eiloart, a Cambridge University chemical engineering graduate during the late 1950s. An unconventional and adventurous character, Eiloart had taken part while a student in a failed attempt to cross the Atlantic in a balloon.[45] Then in 1960, after finishing his degree, he established Cambridge Consultants. The business's aim was to bring together ideas from many parts of science and technology to help companies in sectors from dishwashers to windscreen wipers. It gained a following from both British and overseas customers prepared to put money into funding technology projects that involved lateral thinking and an agglomeration of technical ideas. An early project, for instance, involved producing a design for one of the first self-service petrol stations, using a mix of novel control systems and telecommunications devices.[46] Cambridge Consultants was one of the first UK companies to use semiconductors rather than valves for electric circuits. Under Eiloart's stewardship, the company eventually ran out of money, and was bought in 1971 by Arthur D. Little, a big US consultancy, after which its founder resigned. Later on, three other similar technology consultancies evolved in the Cambridge area, all of them tracing their links to Cambridge Consultants. The four groups are now the among the world's leading technology consultancies, employing about 900 people in their Cambridge offices and laboratories, plus another 250 elsewhere in the world. While the companies' combined sales in 2009 were $200 million, the products and services they have made possible in sectors from electric motors to pregnancy test kits have estimated annual sales running to several billions of dollars. Among the big companies that have benefited from this work are Fiat, Bosch, 3M, Vodafone, Motorola and Bayer. The work of the four consultancies underlines how the best clusters bring together people with skills and imagination. These people use their combined talents to devise products and processes that can be applied worldwide.

Examples of successful companies based in Cambridge that have evolved in this manner include ARM Holdings. The company invented a way to create new types of semiconductor for 'internet-enabled' mobile phones. Its business is based on licensing the designs to phone makers so they can incorporate the chips in their devices, with ARM taking a fee for each one that is used. Crucially, ARM does no manufacturing, saving itself the expense of having to set up and operate one or more integrated-circuit plants, but arranges for the chips to be made by contractors. ARM's business model requires it to behave as a hybrid of research group, wholesaler and consultancy – with knowledge of manufacturing added to the mix. It also requires a broad knowledge of different aspects of electronics, from circuit design to new materials.

Other Cambridge businesses that have evolved in an analogous manner include Domino Printing Sciences, which introduced 'ink-jet' printing techniques to the packaging industry by combining ways to create ink particles with novel methods of electronic control, and Abcam, which has merged internet sales techniques and advanced chemicals production to sell more than 70,000 types of specialist proteins to 10,000 customers in the pharmaceutical industry and university research community. Other businesses that are less well established but appear in a good position to expand include Ubisense, which uses computer-aided design software and satellite communications techniques to monitor the location of components in car factories; Blue Gnome, a business combining computerized image processing with biotechnology to make test kits for the chemicals industry; Ultravision, which has devised a new type of contact lens by bringing together advanced optics and materials processing; and Owlstone, which uses sensor, materials and electronic technologies to develop tiny chemical detectors for applications in military equipment and healthcare.

The Cambridge connections have happened virtually by accident, with very little planning. The most influential moves to help the Cambridge cluster in recent years have included continuing strong investments in the city – from both government funds and private-sector initiatives – in improving its role as a leading centre for new thinking in science and technology. Keeping in the forefront of science and engineering is often vital for the key organizations in clusters if these areas are to continue to be relevant in a world that is changing fast. A second key activity which has bolstered the city's standing as a cluster is the development of a number of networks in Cambridge that encourage people to meet to discuss new ideas. The most highly developed of these is the Cambridge Network, a business organization with 1,000 corporate members from across many areas of business and academic research. Other groups of people can be brought together around a nexus of individual companies or university departments. The local connections – important even in a globalized world – count more than sometimes is recognized. While few places in the world have the advantages conferred on Cambridge from its long history of scientific and technical strength, many others have the chance to bolster their credentials as industrial clusters by stepping up efforts to collaborate on a local basis.

An example of how this can happen on a small scale is a 10-company group called Midlands Assembly Network, based in the industrial centre of Birmingham in the UK. Each of the 10 companies is in a different field of engineering and manufacturing, ranging from making electronic control panels to precision cutting. The companies collaborate on projects for much bigger companies around the world and share ideas in areas such as new processes, as well as letting the others in the network have access to their top suppliers. 'As a result of the network, all of us who have access to it have been able to perform better than we would have done as individual businesses,' says David Spears, managing director of Brandauer, one of the 10 companies.[47]

Most of the world's leading industrial clusters have histories measured in decades, with some of them stretching to centuries. Understanding what has happened to the companies in these industrial concentrations in the past is important to working out how they operate now, and also what is likely in the future. In each case, an ability to focus on several things at once will be necessary for the businesses in the various clusters. They need to be alive to new developments in technologies in areas relevant to their businesses, often spanning a wide spectrum of disciplines. The companies need to look inwards to activities taking place close by, to see to what degree the businesses themselves can adapt to local trends. They also have to divert attention to linkages that can be important with businesses in many parts of the world. Such a range of preoccupations may be extremely hard to manage at the same time as operating the business on a day-to-day basis. Businesses in clusters can be regarded as regional 'anchor points' in a world where making connections has become physically easier, while at the same time harder to make a success of because of the many complexities involved. In the next 30 years, the degree to which clusters develop – in both the established developed countries and the emerging economies – looks likely to have an influence on how well all these regions progress in industry generally. During the new industrial revolution the performance of clusters will be increasingly important to economic success or failure.

# CHAPTER 9

# Future factories

## Liquid assets

Anil Jain is managing director and part-owner of Jain Irrigation Systems (JIS), a company based in India that is the world's second biggest maker of micro irrigation equipment. Micro irrigation – also called drip irrigation – is an embellishment of the techniques for using water to improve crop yields that have existed for thousands of years. It requires technologies in fields such as pumps, control systems and filters, supported by know-how related to specific types of crop. 'We are putting product engineering together with agricultural science,' says Jain.[1] Nearly three-quarters of global water consumption is used in agriculture. The big expected rise in the world's population in the next 50 years – from 7 billion in 2011 to 9 billion in 2050 – will put even more pressure on supply. Changes in weather patterns linked to global warming may limit rainfall in many of the regions that most need it.

Micro irrigation supplies water through plastic pipes, often in tiny amounts, in such a way that it goes directly to plant roots. The water flow can be varied to fit in with local conditions, concerning the quality of the soil and the closeness to the surface of the water table. The technology is useful in helping farmers gain the maximum benefits from limited water supplies. Micro irrigation has existed in a fledgling form since the 1960s.

However, the business appears to be on the brink of a big expansion, driven by changes in the design of equipment, lower costs and advances in agricultural science. The easier access to water that micro irrigation makes possible should help to alleviate food shortages and poverty. At the same time, producing micro irrigation systems, and providing the service support needed to make the hardware useful, has the potential to turn into a large industry, adding to wealth creation and jobs.

The business of micro irrigation was invented in the 1960s by Simcha Blass, an Israeli engineer. Blass observed that a slow and balanced drip effect led to sustained growth of crops such as cotton, fruit and cereals. The key to this was a device that Blass developed that sounded simple: a small, precisely engineered tube that slowly releases water through perforations. The modern forms of these devices are 'micro emitters': small plastic devices linked to miniature pumps that distribute water at the rate of as little as a few cubic centimetres an hour. Based on Blass's ideas, Netafim – now the world's biggest maker of micro irrigation systems – was started in Israel in 1965. About the same time, Jain's father set up a small agricultural distributor in northern India. Later this moved into irrigation technology to form the basis for JIS. The company has modelled itself on Netafim's approach. It has a target of reaching annual sales of $5 billion before 2020, and as a result overtaking Netafim to become number one in the industry.

Jain explains that micro irrigation is far from the stereotypical mass production industry. Individual systems have to be fine-tuned to meet the needs of the farmers the company works with. 'We have a customized approach, where what we do has as much of a connection with the services industry as with manufacturing. To assemble a complete system, we use thousands of different components to engineer a product that fits in to what our customer needs.' The company has been helped through 20 acquisitions since 2005, with most of the deals involving companies based outside India. The transactions have brought in specialized production and process know-how, together with factories in the US, Brazil, Turkey, Australia and Spain. Particularly useful was the purchase in 2008 of Thomas Machines of Switzerland, a leader in the niche technology of making high-speed production machines for plastic 'drip feed' pipes.

Micro irrigation will be among a number of growth industries of the twenty-first century. All these industries will be in areas of activity where the potential market is large, and where the needs they are attempting to satisfy are a long way from being met. The areas of industry that will emerge will largely address the 'four big needs' of humankind: comfort, energy, security and information. Comfort centres on food, shelter and clothing. Energy is needed to provide mobility, light and heat. Security covers healthcare, weaponry and reduction in environmental threats such as global warming. Information – or more specifically its acquisition and transfer – is vital to human development. More technologies will be available to drive on these industries; the technologies will overlap more, and work more quickly. In some cases, several technologies will combine to alter the characteristics of existing industries, or create new ones. The new and emerging industries will provide a broad platform for wealth creation, with opportunities not limited to a few countries, but spread globally. These expanding business sectors will be among the most visible features of the new industrial revolution.

## Small is bountiful

Nanotechnology applies to techniques to manipulate materials at an atomic level. The range of sectors it could affect is considerable. Among these are textiles and clothing – an area for exploitation for Nano-Tex, a company started in California in 1998. Underscoring the links between old and new industries, Nano-Tex's chairman is Wilbur Ross,[2] a US financier who is a leading steel investor and an ArcelorMittal board member. The company has devised methods to impregnate tiny polymers into the fibres of materials such as cotton or polyester. The size of these particles is measured in nanometres, or billionths of a metre. The polymers are chosen for their special properties. For instance, they might resist stains by having a surface that repels liquids. Because of an especially porous structure, they could be good at absorbing sweat, so making them useful in sports clothing.

In alternative applications for nanotechnology being pursued by others, tiny chemical molecules called nanoparticles are used in some sunscreens to block ultraviolet light. Computer disk drives have 'read heads' (the styluses that decipher digital code) made with films that are about one atom thick. Premium tennis balls are sealed with nano-sized grains of material to make them last longer. Other products include paints, medicines, luggage and toys. World sales of 'nanotechnology enabled' products in 2008 have been estimated at $254 billion. However, this figure is expected by the US's National Science Foundation to climb to $3,000 billion by 2020. By this time, making and selling nanotechnology-derived products could employ 6 million people, up from 400,000 in 2008.[3]

In some senses, nanotechnology has been around a long time. Many manufacturing activities, especially concerning chemicals, involve the production of materials on an atomic basis. However, until recently scientists and engineers have had a limited ability to control with any accuracy how such structures are made. The US physicist Richard Feynman, in a lecture in 1959, looked at the possibilities. Science and industry had up to then centred on extracting minerals from the earth, then processing them using orthodox physics and chemistry. The opportunities were always circumscribed by the construction of the atomic layers in these materials. Feynman posed a bold question: 'What would the properties of materials be if we could really arrange the atoms the way we want them?'[4]

Soon, answers became apparent. In 1974 the Japanese materials scientist Norio Taniguchi defined nanotechnology as 'the processing of, separation, consolidation, and deformation of materials by one atom or by one molecule'.[5] In 1982, the invention of the scanning tunnelling microscope meant scientists could visualize atomic structures, a job beyond previous instruments. The discovery in 1985 of fullerenes triggered more interest in nanotechnology. Fullerenes are molecules composed entirely of carbon, in the form of a hollow sphere, ellipsoid, or tube. Cluster science emerged as a relevant discipline. It described efforts to understand interactions between atoms, and to influence them. Some of the ideas became practicable. In a book in 1986 the engineer Eric Drexler said old ideas of 'bulk engineering' were being superseded by new nanotechnology methods that were far more precise and would 'change our world in more ways than we can imagine'.[6]

Yury Gogotsi is a Ukraine-born materials expert who is chairman and founder of Y-Carbon, a company based in Philadelphia. Its speciality is 'carbon nanotubes', naturally occurring types of carbon discovered a few years after fullerenes. Like these structures, nanotubes can be made in many variants with multiple applications. Nanotubes consist of pure carbon, filled with tiny cavities. Gogotsi's company has devised a suite of procedures to make its materials with a pore size matched to whatever application is needed, and accurate to within 0.1 nanometres. Gogotsi describes Y-Carbon's procedures as 'customized manufacturing on an atomic scale'.[7]

Ten million of Y-Carbon's nanotubes can be lined up next to each other within 1 centimetre. Each has a cross-section of roughly one ten-thousandth of a human hair. Because it is made up of small cavities, densely packed together, a block of nanotubes is mainly empty space. The internal 'walls' to the voids add up to an immense area. One gram of the nanotubes made by Y-Carbon contains an internal 'real estate' of 3,500 square metres. One way to make use of this is in electricity storage, Gogotsi says. In these instances, each nanotube becomes a tiny capacitor – a device for entrapping electrons. Such capacitors could be used in place of orthodox batteries, powering consumer equipment or new generations of electric cars. Nanotube-based capacitors could become small and cheap enough to be incorporated into many kinds of machines to store energy that would otherwise be wasted. Such 'energy recycling' mechanisms could, for example, transform the operation of conventional petrol-driven cars. Gogotsi sets out the possibilities. 'The energy generated in the brakes as a car slows down, and which is normally wasted as friction, could be channelled into a high-energy capacitor, and diverted into helping to drive the vehicle's engine. This could cut 40 per cent off the vehicle's fuel bill.' The technology is being investigated by makers of high-power capacitors such as Maxwell Technologies of the US and Japan's Panasonic. Other companies interested in nanotubes in energy applications include Saft, the French battery producer, and Kuraray, a Japanese company which makes high-purity carbon for a range of applications.

Outside energy storage, other uses for carbon nanotubes could include catalysis. The large internal area inside these structures would be coated with special materials to speed up the reactions that take place inside chemicals plants. Nanotubes can also act as filters, to remove unwanted materials in healthcare or chemicals manufacturing, or even as semiconductor memories or sensors. Carbon-based nanotubes could turn into a big industry in the twenty-first century, says Gogotsi, creating employment in both their production and their use. Nanotechnology, he says, provides a new vehicle for making use of carbon – one of the most abundant materials on the planet and vital for mankind's energy use as well as for life itself, but one where many potential applications are only now becoming apparent. It is not being too fanciful to suggest, he says, that the twenty-first century could herald the start of a new 'carbon age'.

## Chemical toolkits

A typical product made by Ralf Wagner's company weighs 10 micrograms and costs $800. Discussing what his products are used for, Wagner says his company 'sells information'.[8] He is chief executive and co-founder of Geneart, a German company that is the world's biggest manufacturer of synthetic genes. They are man-made versions of the long sequences of deoxyribonucleic acid (DNA) present in the cellular tissue of plants and animals. Genes – invisible unless analysed with powerful instrumentation – carry a code that depends on the positions of different chemical 'building blocks' inside the DNA. The code provides information identifying the species the plant or animal belongs to. Variations in the sequence of chemicals in the code give instructions for a range of biochemical processes inside cells, for instance the manufacture of the proteins vital to life. Engineers are now using genes, or more pointedly the genetic codes they carry, to make a range of new materials. In these processes, the genes are equivalent to the software in a computer, providing the essential information needed for its useful operation. The broad description for the processes at the heart of these new ideas is synthetic biology.

Synthetic biology is a term that first came into use in the 1970s.[9] It is defined as the application of engineering principles to biology. Since synthetic biology is based around manipulating molecular structures on a microscopic level, it can be regarded as a subset of the wider discipline of nanotechnology. A leader in this field is Synthetic Genomics, a US company started in 2005 by Craig Venter, a biochemist who is among the world's top 'bio-entrepreneurs'.[10] Venter has set a goal to 'create products with trillion-dollar [$1,000 billion] markets that use a series of novel biochemical processes to replace the products of the petrochemical industry'.[11] Among the families of carbon-based substances that could be made in this way are pharmaceuticals, catalysts, fuels and various novel materials to replace plastics used in a range of applications from construction to packaging. As with nanotechnology, synthetic biology has not appeared suddenly. For thousands of years, mankind has used biochemical processes – often labelled biotechnology – to make foods such as bread, cheese and beer. Plants have been used as the raw materials for industrial products such as fuels or plastics since the late nineteenth century. In these instances, the starting materials have included naturally occurring sugar cane, rapeseed and cellulose derived from wood. They normally work in conjunction with microbes such as yeast, the microbes' function being to trigger the key biochemical reactions needed to make the product. The products made in this way – where no genetic modification is involved – are called first-generation bioproducts. Of these, the best known are fuels. Petrol and diesel made from biological sources such as ethanol derived from plants have become a large industry in many countries.

The true products of synthetic biology – where adjustment of cell structures is done using genetic techniques – are called second-generation bioproducts. The first steps in this direction came with the identification of the structure of DNA in 1953 by James Watson and Francis Crick at Cambridge University. A further move was the invention in the 1970s of 'recombinant DNA', procedures for manipulating genes, which became known as genetic engineering. Through such ideas, genes could be inserted into the chemical structures of existing organic materials to create new products, which initially were mainly medicines. Synthetic biology takes these techniques beyond the use of individual genes, and towards engineering large numbers of genes simultaneously. It is particularly applicable for working with genomes, the complete set of genes required for identifying a plant or animal species. Methods have now been devised for assembling complete genomes of new forms of plant and other organisms, and then finding ways to produce these molecules either in the laboratory or in commercial operations.[12]

Synthetic Genomics is, for instance, trying to create genomes for new plant types that would be variants on seaweed, corn or switchgrass. Assuming the new plants could first be identified and then grown and harvested, they could form the raw biomass from which new forms of plastics or fuels could be made with tailored properties. For instance, a plastic could be designed so as to provide a particular kind of structural characteristic, such as for use in construction or packaging. Similarly, a new fuel could produce a specific energy output per unit of mass. Another of the company's projects is to develop new forms of microbes (such as yeast) that would react with biomass to make defined organic materials. 'Rather than use the microbes that happen to exist in nature, it would be much better to design and make them ourselves, so they work in the way we want them to,' explains Aristides Patrinos, Synthetic Genomics' vice president.[13] Using such ideas, says Patrinos, biochemicals could be manipulated in a customized manner to 'act as factories turning out specific types of bio-based products'. Synthetic Genomics is working with several businesses, including BP, ExxonMobil and the Asiatic Centre for Genome Technology, a company in Malaysia, to discover how to create new substances using these ideas.

Some critics have voiced fears that synthetic biology could create genetic modifications in plant types or animals which could – through reproduction and subsequent proliferation – cause long-term health hazards. The possibilities of creating new forms of living material – perhaps even human life – through artificial means carry serious ethical considerations.[14] But more positively, synthetic biology can be viewed as a further step to making at least some forms of manufacturing more environmentally benign. It could lead to widespread alternatives to existing processes for making industrial goods that are based on fossil fuels. Such processes frequently involve the release into the atmosphere of carbon dioxide, as well as depleting the earth's natural carbon reserves. Added to this, growth of the specially tailored biomass needed for synthetic biology involves, as a part of the natural process of photosynthesis, the *extraction* of carbon dioxide from the atmosphere. So synthetic biology, if introduced on a large scale, could help in the goal of lowering the concentration of greenhouse gases in the atmosphere, while also ushering in a range of opportunities for making goods in a radically different manner.

## Material solutions

Up to now biotechnology has been applicable only to creating organic materials – those formed from biological processes and containing carbon bonds. But now some scientists are trying to devise related processes that work with materials not derived from biology and so regarded as inorganic. Such substances could include many metal-based chemicals, and even the metals themselves. Lee Cronin, a professor of chemistry at Glasgow University, says reactions of this sort follow the principles of 'inorganic biology'. Cronin is referring to processes that occur in nature, involving reactions between atoms such as carbon, oxygen and hydrogen, but which scientists have adapted to work instead with compounds of metals, including iron or aluminium.[15] Through such mechanisms, new metal-based chemicals could be produced through biology-based processes of cell division and multiplication. They could be made to adapt or 'evolve' – using pathways similar to those in life processes – so they are capable of working in different conditions. In such a way, a metal-based material with the potential to act as a catalyst or anti-corrosion coating could be made to function at high temperatures, or in an atmosphere contaminated by salt or noxious chemicals. New routes based on inorganic biology could be found for making many metal-based industrial chemicals with novel applications.

Such ideas may take decades – or even longer – to come anywhere close to creating commercial products. However, some other new manufacturing methods for related materials are somewhat closer to realization. Here, the goal for engineers is to devise new ways to make metals used as the basis for a huge range of industrial products. Among the pioneers in this work is Giovanni Arvedi, chairman of Arvedi Group, a steel company he started in 1963 in the ancient Italian town of Cremona. The company's main steel mill is a short distance from the ornate sixteenth-century palace that serves as both Arvedi's family home and the headquarters of his company. Arvedi is an accountant-turned-engineer who speaks in an animated fashion and whose angular frame bristles with determination. Since the early 1980s, he has spent $600 million devising a new process for making steel that could greatly lower the cost of production, as well as reduce the environmental impact of existing processes.[16] It has been a tough struggle, Arvedi admits. 'I travelled the world talking to people about new approaches [to steelmaking]. I observed what others had tried, put together the processes that worked and eventually made progress.'[17]

Arvedi has built a production line at Cremona that uses his new principles and which he thinks could be the prototype for other plants. It could, he says, lead to new plants that make sophisticated steel rolled into thin sheets, and which operate on a reduced scale compared with conventional mills. 'The new types of steel factories would be less obtrusive than the plants we are used to, use less energy and cause less pollution.' The Italian industrialist has linked up on this project with Siemens, which since 2009 has had an agreement to try to sell the intellectual property behind the process to global steel-makers. The new plant at Cremona is based on a process Arvedi calls 'endless strip production' (ESP), which can make up to 3 million tonnes of steel a year. The technology is centred on effecting changes to the final processing stages of steel production when hot and semi-molten metal is cast and rolled. The system eliminates the breaks that normally feature in these processes. It uses novel automation techniques to ensure the steel flows continuously, allowing for changes as this happens in the temperature, shape and structure of the liquid metal. In conventional steelworks, steel enters these different stages after passing along different processing lines. The breaks are necessary to reconcile the various changes in the structure of the material as it flows between stages. They allow time to slow down the passage of the metal, or change conditions of thickness and temperature to put the material in the right physical state for a specific process. The gaps in production can take hours or sometimes days. But the stops and starts in conventional processes not only slow production, but increase the space needed for the necessary equipment. Also, energy is wasted, due to the continual need for cooling and reheating between adjacent processes.[18]

Arvedi has tackled the problems by ensuring that steel in the finishing stage of manufacture is modified much more quickly than in orthodox steel-making. This is done through new systems of sensors and computer controls, plus modified heating and cooling procedures. With the improved design, Arvedi believes the cost of constructing steelworks could be cut by up to half, with operating costs falling by a similar amount, helped by a reduction in the need for energy and plant labour. Arvedi's vision is that, with the new ideas, steel mills could be constructed on small edge-of-town sites close to where the metal is needed, as opposed to being built as large facilities long distances away from the places where customers are based. He thinks the ESP process could lead to a new economic basis for steel production that would also offer the prospect of lower energy use and lower emissions of carbon dioxide. The Italian industrialist has high hopes that plants based on his ideas could be built around the world, especially in 'emerging economies' where steel demand is rising fast. 'Many nations that are newly industrializing have a particular need to make steel in a more environmentally responsible manner, based around lower pollution and creating production close to where the metal is needed.'[19]

While Arvedi is working on a new way to make a metal with an extremely long history, Guppy Dhariwal is trying to perfect a new process for a material that has been in use for a much shorter period. Dhariwal is chief executive of Metalysis, a company based near Sheffield. Metalysis is attempting to commercialize a method to make titanium that could substantially reduce its costs and lead to a big increase in applications. Titanium is named after the Titans: mythical, ultra-powerful deities from Greek legend. The name is apt since the metal is often regarded as a 'wonder material'.[20] Mineral forms of titanium are widespread; titanium is the ninth most abundant element found in the earth's crust. But its use has been held back by the difficulty of producing it in a pure form, which was first done only in 1910.

Titanium is strong, durable and light. It is also highly resistant to corro-sion. These characteristics make the metal suitable for many structural applications, for instance in aerospace. Here, titanium can form part of the 'stiffening' struts and other elements that hold aircraft together and where the need to save weight is crucial. Titanium is also 'biologically compatible'. It can be put into the body without interacting with blood corpuscles or cell structures and thereby damaging the immune system or causing other damage to normal biological processes. As a result, one big application for titanium is in orthopaedic implants, such as artificial hip joints. But even with the metal's extensive list of good properties, world consumption of titanium is low by the standard of many other materials. In 2009, supply and demand came to only about 100,000 tonnes, as against 40 million tonnes for aluminium and 1.2 billion tonnes for steel.

The reason for the small amounts of titanium that see use is simple: as a result of the complexity and cost of current production methods, titanium is very expensive. In 2010, the metal sold for $35,000 a tonne, 15 times more than aluminium and 60 times more than steel. Dhariwal thinks he can change matters. His company – formed in 2001 and with a staff of 60 – is trying to turn into an industrial process an electrolysis-based method to make titanium that was invented in the 1990s by three chemists at Cambridge University led by Derek Fray. The current method for manufacturing titanium uses the Kroll process, devised in 1932 by William Kroll, a Luxembourg-born scientist. It uses a lot of energy, and produces only small quantities of the metal. It involves reacting chlorine at about 1,000 degrees centigrade with titanium dioxide, the main source of titanium. Many of the reactions are hazardous, so have to be carefully monitored and enclosed in expensive structures to cut the risk of explosions. The Fray technology – at least in theory – is a lot simpler. An electric current is passed through a bath of calcium chloride. A solid plug of titanium dioxide acts as the cathode – the negative terminal in the cell. As part of an electrolytic reaction, oxygen is removed, leaving a solid lump of pure titanium at the cathode.

Dhariwal thinks the process – assuming it can be made to work on a large scale – could greatly change the economics of titanium production and lead to a big boost in its use. His plan is that titanium plants based on the company's ideas could be set up on a global basis. Under one possibility, users of the technology could pay a licence fee to the UK company to permit them to operate their own versions of Fray-based electrolytic plants. Enthusiasts for the Fray process think that if Metalysis succeeds in turning it into a commercial reality, the price of titanium could halve by

2020, followed by sharper reductions after this. As a result, applications could rise considerably – not just in fields such as aircraft components and aero-engines but in other more mundane products, including car parts, toys and sporting goods. 'We have a huge opportunity to push on with a technique that could lead to a big expansion in applications for titanium, and make the metal much more like steel in terms of its usefulness,' Dhariwal says.[21]

## High fibre

In a giant aerospace plant near Preston in northern England, a $9 million machine tool is going through its paces. It is cutting large pieces of titanium that will be used in some of the world's most advanced and expensive aircraft. The tool is the result of a 10-year collaboration between BAE Systems – the British military equipment manufacturer that operates the plant – and StarragHeckert, a Swiss machining specialist which built the equipment. The tool has been developed to cope with the difficulties of cutting titanium accurately and quickly. As well as being tough, titanium has unusual thermal properties, as a result of which heat is transmitted through it extremely fast. Because of this, the high temperatures generated when the metal is being cut are hard to dissipate without the use of special cooling mechanisms. The new machine uses a range of technologies – including a novel heat transfer system – to cope with these challenges. It is being used to make parts for one of the world's most advanced defence technology projects: a US-led $380 billion programme to build F-35 Joint Strike Fighter aircraft. Each aeroplane – in a project organized by the US Department of Defense with a team of contractors including BAE – will cost $200 million.

Since the 1990s, StarragHeckert has acquired a reputation as one of the leading makers of sophisticated machine tools, especially for the aerospace industry. The experience it has gained through the project with BAE could help it to develop a range of other novel machining systems, for cutting both titanium and other materials. It illustrates how applications in one area of industry – in this case the use of titanium in a high-tech aerospace programme – can stimulate the creation of new opportunities in a related business sector. There are other materials apart from titanium where transfer of ideas between different industrial sectors seems likely to stimulate economic growth. Some of the best examples feature carbon fibre, wafer-thin strands of carbon that look likely to turn into a big business in the early part of the twenty-first century.

Carbon fibre provides another example of carbon's versatility. First discovered in 1879, carbon fibre consists of chains of carbon atoms, locked in almost perfect alignment. The material provides extreme strength, stiffness and lightness. However, for many years it was impossible to make it in high volumes. As production processes improved, from the 1960s onwards applications for the material started to multiply.[22] From around this time, carbon fibre has been made mainly from a starting material of polyacrylonitrile, a polymer synthesized from oil or natural gas. In 2009 three Japanese companies – Toray, Mitsubishi Rayon and Teijin – accounted for approximately 70 per cent of world carbon fibre output. Like many new materials, carbon fibre has seen its production costs fall as more of it has been made. In the mid-1970s, 1 kilogram of carbon fibre sold for $2,000. By the late 1980s, when world production was about 5,000 tonnes a year, the price had fallen to $100 a kilogram. In 2009, when output came to 40,000 tonnes, the price had fallen to $25 a kilogram. Growth in uses of the material looks set to continue. Industry forecasts indicate that global demand for carbon fibre will expand from 46,000 tonnes in 2011 to 140,000 tonnes by 2020.[23]

By itself, carbon fibre has limited uses. In most applications it has to be formed into a mesh which is then encased inside plastic resin. The carbon strands in this arrangement act as reinforcing layers, in much the same way as steel rods act as supports inside reinforced concrete. Compared to a component made from steel, the same product based on a carbon fibre resin weighs 75 per cent less, but is three times stiffer and 10 times stronger. Relative to aluminium, which since the 1950s has been the main material used in aerospace due to its lightness, an equivalent carbon fibre item is 20 per cent lighter and six times stronger. The usefulness of carbon fibre resin is linked to the way it can be formed into a variety of components of different shapes and strengths, dependent on the design of the mesh and how the final piece of resin is fashioned. In aerospace applications, a crucial point is that it can be bonded to titanium without difficulty – avoiding the problems of corrosion that sometimes occur when carbon fibre is joined to structures made from aluminium.

Carbon fibre components will form a large part of the Boeing 787 and Airbus A350 passenger jets that look like turning into two of the biggest workhorses of the commercial airline industry in the first half of the twenty-first century. Thanks partly to the use of carbon fibre, which will account for up to half the weight of both aircraft, the jets will use significantly less fuel, adjusted for the number of passenger kilometres flown, compared to previous generations of airliners. Away from the aerospace industry, use of carbon fibre looks set to expand in many areas of manufacturing where lightness and strength are important, along with the ability to tailor designs to meet the requirements of individual customers. Examples of industries where the material is seeing increased use include sporting goods, boats, specialist vehicles (for instance high-performance racing cars), wind turbines and machine parts.

One leader in using carbon fibre is Armor Designs, based in Phoenix, Arizona. The company makes lightweight body armour based on resins impregnated with a lattice-like carbon fibre structure. The way the fibres are interwoven in a series of complex patterns is controlled by specialist software, invented by James St Ville, Armor Designs' chairman and founder. St Ville is an unusual polymath who started out as an orthopaedic surgeon, and then became a computing expert, before branching out into carbon fibre. He says his company's capabilities centre on its software. The way the code is built up can be changed depending on the envisaged use of the final product. 'If our customers tell us the kind of bullet they want to stop [through the use of protective armour], we'll design a product to do it,' St Ville remarks.[24]

Growth in use of carbon fibre has stimulated many companies such as Armor Designs that specialize in using it in specialist products. Another is Lola, a UK business which uses carbon fibre in racing car designs, and also in components for the unmanned drone aircraft that could be used to prosecute future wars. Another group of companies has concentrated on the branch of the industry that involves production of so-called 'prepreg': resin already impregnated with carbon fibre and which is shipped to customers in fields such as aerospace to be made into final products. A third set of companies develops different types of machines used in the industry. Some genres of equipment are needed to work with the fibre itself, in which case it threads the material into set patterns using such processes as weaving, knitting or 'layering' the fibre in multiple bands. Other machinery can be used – in a manner analogous to how StarragHeckert's tools are used to cut titanium – to fashion the end product. The existence of this large number of discrete business sectors, all forming a broad 'ecosystem' built up around the carbon fibre industry, illustrates how a single area of materials development can trigger wider economic activity.

## Energy source

In 2010 several of the world's biggest makers of gas-fired central heating boilers announced plans to sell novel combined heat-and-power (CHP) appliances for homes. The machines operate in a particularly efficient manner to supply central heating and also electricity – the latter being created through the use of waste heat driving a turbine. Due to this novel method of operating, the equipment promises cuts of up to a quarter in household energy bills. The new models were put on sale by three competing engineering consortiums with members drawn from around the world. In each case they were based on designs for 'heat engines' that derive from a patent published in 1816 by Robert Stirling, a Scottish clergyman.

Stirling's engines are an example of a long-established idea that has taken a long time to look suitable for real-life use. The pastor believed his design could rival the steam engine of James Watt, a fellow Scot who died just three years after his patent appeared. Like Watt's machine, the Stirling design applied energy to a fluid trapped inside a cylinder. Since it was based on reusing heat that would normally be wasted, the efficiency of the system was substantially higher than that of the Watt engine. While Watt's system featured water as the working fluid, his rival chose air. The Stirling design avoided the use of boiling water and high-pressure steam, a combination that sometimes caused accidents. For all these reasons, the clergyman's ideas stirred a lot of interest. But for all their promise, until the early years of the twenty-first century, outside the realm of prototypes and demonstration systems, only a handful of fully operational Stirling machines had been built.

The problems went back to the design. It required highly engineered components including special springs, gas seals and bearings. They were beyond the capabilities of anyone in the nineteenth century to make, at least at an acceptable quality and cost. By contrast, Watt's steam engine was fairly easy to manufacture. It was replicated in large numbers around the world, helping to drive on economic growth. Even later, the difficulties in making working Stirling machines persisted, as technology failed to move fast enough to make them practicable. But by 2000 the outlook had changed. Advances in several areas of engineering meant Stirling's ideas had a chance of being put to use. The high-strength steels needed for the springs had become available. Coatings made from polymer, metal or ceramics could be used to create the airtight barriers needed for the machine's gas seals. Virtually friction-free bearings, working without the need for lubricating oil, were also on the market. Such oil-free bearings were needed in Stirling machines, since oil coming into contact with the complex working parts had to be avoided. As a result of the advances, in around 2010 three sets of company alliances were established to make Stirling-based CHP systems for domestic use. Among the partners in the consortia, the best-known companies were makers of central heating boilers such as Britain's Baxi and Vaillant, and Bosch of Germany.

Each group of companies adopted a different manufacturing strategy. One of the consortia uses a form of Stirling system devised by Whisper Tech, a company in New Zealand. This particular group of companies opted to make its products in a factory in Spain. The location was prompted by the relative closeness of the factory to the European countries considered the most obvious markets for the products. The second consortium used a Stirling design from Sunpower, a technology business in the US. It based its plant in China, since this promised lower costs. The third group, using technology from Infinia, another US company, selected Japan for its main production location. Behind this was the logic that Japan – with its exceptional record in precision engineering – was the best place to site the manufacture of such a complicated machine. The CHP systems from the three consortia all cost up to $15,000, making the products' 'up-front' price at least twice as high as that of a conventional gas boiler. However, the potential of the Stirling designs to save on running costs for heating, as well as provide a 'free' source of electricity, could make them popular, especially if prices fall with rising production.[25]

In another branch of the energy business, Richard Yemm is also upbeat about prospects. The sandy-haired, unassuming physicist is founder and commercial director of Pelamis, a company based in a dockside factory in Edinburgh. Its products are 180 metre-long articulated steel tubes designed to float out to sea. They are one answer to the urgent issue of finding ways to produce energy without ruining the environment. Formed in 1998 and named after a species of tuna fish, Pelamis is backed by $67 million in investment capital. It is one of the leaders among a disparate group of companies making machinery for producing energy from the oceans' waves. When in operation, Pelamis's red and yellow machines look like giant sea snakes. Each costing up to $10 million, they use wave movement to power hydraulic rams encased in the joints of the articulated tubes. The rams transfer the energy into hydraulic fluid which is used to power turbines and so create electricity.

Wave power adherents such as Yemm believe the technology is on the brink of becoming a realistic commercial proposition. One of wave power's advantages, he believes, is its relative accessibility.

Waves deliver their energy close to the shoreline, in many cases near to where people need it. If you study a map of the world, you will find that the places where wave power looks most suitable [in terms of the height and strength of waves] are close to some of the biggest centres of population, such as the east and west coasts of North America, the southern part of South America, and large parts of Western Europe.[26]

Wave power was first studied seriously in the 1970s. Its supporters postulated that the sea was one of the most obvious sources of 'free' energy, if only a way could be found to harness it effectively. Wave power ultimately derives its energy from the sun. This is done through the sun giving up roughly one-hundredth of its energy to heat air molecules, with the temperature gradients present in the atmosphere giving rise to air currents. These currents – wind – transfer approximately one-hundredth of their own energy to the surface of the sea. As a result of this sequence of linkages, wave energy is sometimes thought of as 'concentrated solar power'. But the first wave power devices were largely unsuccessful. Wave machines are required to operate continuously while being battered by the sea. At the same time they have to produce electricity reliably, at an acceptable cost. The technologies behind the machines were initially not sufficiently developed to achieve these goals.

In the years that followed, however, improvements have been made. Costs of providing power from the waves have fallen. This has encouraged hopes that by around 2020 the price of electricity from wave machines could be no higher than that from mainstream sources, chiefly from fossil fuel plants. In 2011, Pelamis was near the end of trials with a machine bought by the German energy group Eon. It was also preparing to hand over a further wave system to the UK group Scottish & Southern, with more machines in the pipeline due to be sold to Vattenfall, a Swedish energy group. Similar progress is being made at several other companies that are pushing on with wave power developments. According to Yemm's projections, the value of wave equipment that could be in place in the sea around the UK could reach $1 billion by 2020 and – a decade later – 10 times this figures. 'In a country like Britain that is surrounded by sea, wave power could turn into a huge industry, producing goods worth hundreds of million of dollars a year while employing tens of thousands of people.'

Another energy-related sector that could benefit from rapid changes in technology is solar-powered lighting. The products are targeted at the 2 billion people who live in homes where electricity is either unavailable or intermittent. One of the leaders in this new industry is D.Light, a company based in Hong Kong. Its electric lamps sell for $10–20, mainly in India and Africa. 'We've made a connection between new technologies, design and manufacturing. As a result we're making a difference to the way people live,' proclaims Sam Goldman, one of five graduates from Stanford University who founded the company in 2007.[27] D.Light has a design centre in Hong Kong, a factory in southern China, and sales offices in India and East Africa, and is opening a research laboratory in California. Goldman calculates that each lamp his company sells is used by an average of five people, mainly a family. On this basis, he reckons that in early 2011 D.Light's products – based on cumulative sales to this date – were being used by 3 million people who would have otherwise been denied access to illumination. He has ambitious goals for the next few years. 'By 2015 we want to bring [the number of users] to 50 million people, and to 100 million five years after this.'

D.Light's products have three main components: solar power collectors, small electronic control units, and a new form of light source, the light-emitting diode (LED). Based on semiconductors, LEDs provide light at a specific wavelength when subjected to an electric charge. Their chief advantage is that virtually all the electrical energy emerges as light. Little is wasted as heat, as happens with traditional filament-based bulbs. As a result, the efficiency of LEDs is much higher than conventional light sources, while carbon dioxide emissions – even when LEDs are connected to orthodox power grids as opposed to receiving energy from the sun – are much lower than with conventional light sources. The solar power lights illustrate what is possible when a number of technologies are put together. They indicate how equipment to produce or disseminate energy more efficiently – and on a more sustainable basis – will become a big industrial opportunity.

## Revolutionizing medicine

One of the most promising areas for manufacturing involves healthcare. As the world population grows richer and older, tackling disease, and preventing people from succumbing to it, will be a priority. Now, techno-logical changes are helping industry to respond to the challenges. Some of the most far-reaching applications for the genetic engineering techniques at the heart of synthetic biology could come from combining these ideas with computer science, medical imaging and electrical engineering. As a result, processes for recognizing and combating disease – diagnostics and therapy – are starting to overlap. In the process, opportunities in the healthcare industry are becoming transformed. The convergence between diagnostics and therapy is affecting a range of companies, involved in both the manufacturing and services arms of healthcare. One group concerns businesses in chemical-based diagnostic testing. Their basic area of activity consists of examining biological samples – normally in a laboratory – to look for indications of disease or other medical conditions. A second set of companies consists of the world's biggest makers of medical diagnostics equipment, including General Electric, Philips, and Siemens. Their main products are imaging systems such as X-ray and magnetic resonance imaging (MRI) machines. A further group comprises suppliers of medical implants such as heart valves, and includes Medtronic and St Jude Medical. Such businesses make 'active' implants designed to influence medical conditions, for example electronic systems influencing the operation of organs such as the heart or brain, or pumps supplying drugs internally. It is also possible to visualize some of the businesses that produce non-therapeutic or 'passive' implants – such as hip joints – entering this branch of the diagnostic/therapy industry at some stage. A fourth group of companies encompasses big pharmaceutical manufacturers such as GlaxoSmithKline and Pfizer.

Some of the early moves in diagnostic/therapy integration took place in the late 1980s. The focal points were two academic institutes in California: the University of California, Berkeley, and Stanford University. Several groups of scientists – with the biochemist Stephen Fodor prominent – were responsible for the ideas behind devices known as genechips.[28] The products incorporated a set of procedures for uncovering information about a person's genes.[29] This led to ways to find out about defects in the gene structure that could lead to medical disorders, and to treat either the cause of the problems or the symptoms once they appeared. Genechip manufacturers use techniques from microelectronics production to create tiny cavities etched into the surface of a semiconductor-type surface. These microscopic 'wells' hold in place thousands of different biochemicals with known DNA structures. Scientists investigating the identity of materials bring samples into contact with the chemicals in the wells. Sensing devices backed up by the computing functions on the chip monitor the subsequent reactions. In this way, it is possible to acquire knowledge about the genetic structure of the samples. Genechips – made by companies such as US-based Affymetrix, of which Fodor is now chairman – now constitute a large industry. But the devices seem capable of a lot more development.

New versions of genechips offer the possibilities of becoming miniature 'test rigs' for the mass screening of biochemicals. The materials could be molecules that are candidates for drug treatments. Or they could be samples of biological tissue taken from people, where analysis of genetic fragments might indicate health disorders. Similar systems can be used to 'read' the genetic information in body cells to monitor how well patients are responding to drug treatments for specific conditions. For instance, if someone has cancer, he or she might be treated with a drug designed to bring about a specific change in the DNA code in specific parts of the body. Suitably designed genechips give doctors the opportunity to work out how well the treatment has been working, and change it if necessary.

Increasingly, genechip technology is being used in 'real-time' monitoring systems, for instance of hospital patients. One idea is to incorporate the genechips in small machines (about the size of a portable credit card reader) so the examination can happen by the patient's bedside. Another possibility is to put the devices in instruments implanted in the body to allow for a continuous check to be made of a person's medical conditions using telecommunications signals. The alignment of diagnostics and treatment has also stimulated 'fast feedback' ways to deal with people suffering from chronic health problems. This happens by linking remote methods of health monitoring to therapeutic treatment. In the case of diabetes, sufferers are conventionally treated by insulin, given in accordance with sugar levels in the bloodstream. Insulin pumps worn on the body are now capable of pumping into the bloodstream carefully administered doses which can change from day to day. The amounts of insulin can be altered automatically to fit in with data about the individual's blood sugar concentration – with these data coming from monitoring instruments now capable of being implanted in the body. A further layer of control of the monitoring can now be added, since it is possible to link the instrumentation on each person to a remote medical centre via radio networks. In this way, computerized monitors would check that the 'closed loop' feedback systems involving the sensor/pump combination were working effectively.

Assuming these ideas reach fruition, people suffering from specific ailments could find themselves being monitored round the clock by a combination of implanted sensing devices and computers, supported by doctors sitting at their desks possibly hundreds or even thousands of kilometres away.

A further step in the progression of medical technology – and the manufacturing needed to make it useful – concerns the design of pharmaceutical treatments. Usually, drugs for medical conditions are 'one size fits all'. No effort is made to ensure the medicine fits in with the specific DNA characteristics of an individual. However, with knowledge about personal genetic identity, a particular patient could have a medicine designed for him or her specially. Such products would be made by starting with a base pharmaceutical, which would be modified on the basis of different people's genetic identity. Assuming the economics could be made to work, such tailored medical procedures would fit in with the idea of more detailed monitoring of people's physiology using methods based on genetics. It would be through these investigations that detailed know-how would arise of the medical problems from which a person is suffering. Then a specific pharmaceutical would be made to suit that patient – and that patient alone. The emergence of these ideas is part of the trend seen in the whole of manufacturing leading to greater customization or even 'personalization' of products.

## Paper profit

One of the oldest and most useful manufactured products is paper. Made from carbohydrate material from plants, paper was the first information transfer device. It is also the most widely used. Could it ever be superseded? Hopes rest on creating a form of 'electronic paper' that is 'readable' and 'writeable'. A way to make an electronic device resembling paper with information capable of being easily assimilated – and altered – has been a key ambition for decades. Such electronic paper would be easy to handle, ultra-flexible and almost impossible to break. Small and thin computer tablets – such the Apple iPad or the Amazon Kindle book reader – have brought the vision a step closer. However, tablets have yet to provide the convenience and transportability of paper. One reason is that the displays in tablets continue to be based on liquid-crystal devices, based on glass sheets. Glass is inherently fragile and relatively heavy, making it not an obvious material for electronic forms of paper. As a result, engineers have been inquiring into the possibilities of using other materials as the basis for such products. In the lead in terms of the potential is plastic.

Ahead of others in the effort to introduce a new kind of display device – using extremely thin plastic – is Plastic Logic. The company has a headquarters split between the UK and US and its main factory is in Germany. It has its origins in electronics and materials research at Cambridge University. Backed by $200 million in investment, mainly from US-based venture capital companies and large businesses such as Intel and BASF, the company was started in 2000 to capitalize on ideas to 'print' electronic circuits on sheets of plastic. The first area of application for the products is light and flexible display screens. The materials Plastic Logic uses in its devices are polythiophenes, part of a class of materials known as conjugated polymers. The chemistry of the polymer layers is changed by firing at them tiny particles of other types of plastic, using a technique similar to ink-jet printing. The final shapes of the plastic-based electronic circuits are made with lasers. One of Plastic Logic's strategies is to use the plastic circuitry to control the position of tiny particles – suspended inside another layer of plastic film – that act as 'electronic ink'. In this way, words, pictures and diagrams can be built up on the display as though they were on paper. Plastic Logic is collaborating on this technology with E-Ink, a Taiwanese company that is the biggest maker in the world of electronic ink products.

The Cambridge company hopes to make headway in a number of different technological directions. Its ideas related to displays could interest many companies in the consumer electronics industry. However, a still more exciting vision focuses on the idea of using plastic-based electronics as a substitute for conventional semiconductors based on silicon. Hermann Hauser is an Austrian-born physicist-turned-electronics entrepreneur who is a Plastic Logic director. Hauser is one of the world's top experts in how industry is being affected by technology developments. He is a big enthusiast for the concepts behind plastic electronics, which he says could ultimately end the dominance of silicon as the main material for the microchip industry. 'Because plastics are much cheaper materials than the high-purity silicon used in conventional semiconductors, and also because the processing steps required for a plastic semiconductor are so much less expensive than for silicon, new plastic-based chips could turn out 90 per cent less costly than silicon-based integrated circuits.'[30] One application for plastic chips selling for just a few cents each could involve their incorporation into clothing or personal goods. As a result, each item – perhaps a shirt or a children's toy – would then contain some rudimentary 'intelligence'. Directing a radio scanner at the articles could trigger a response (via a voice synthesizer) with instructions about how it should be used or maintained, while also saying who it belonged to. Such tags could be used to keep a check on virtually every manufactured product once it had left the production line and finished up in a home, factory or office.

In 2011 the Plastic Logic story took a new twist. Rusnano – Russia's state-backed nanotechnology corporation – announced it was taking a 25 per cent stake in the company in exchange for a promised $650 million investment.[31] As part of the deal, Plastic Logic is to build a factory in Moscow, which should be ready by 2013. Rusnano was keen to become involved on account of Russia's interest in expanding in new technologies that could lead to new industries. The Russian group announced it was taking its stake after a protracted negotiation in which Plastic Logic also sounded out other potential big shareholders. Others in the discussions included Chinese state-owned entities attracted by the potential of plastic electronics.

The emergence of the new Russian investor in Plastic Logic underlines the global nature of modern industry. Plastics-based microelectronics is among many areas of manufacturing which will have big opportunities to expand in the twenty-first century. In 2010, while the discussions over expanding Plastic Logic's shareholder base were taking place, China's government disclosed some of its broad thinking on the kinds of industries worth backing for the future. State planners published a list of seven 'new strategic industries' that Beijing thinks will propel the country's transition from a low-cost workshop into a producer of high-value, high-technology goods.[32] The list covers biotechnology, advanced mate-rials, alternative energy, new generations of cars, 'high-end' industrial equipment, environmental industries and new forms of information tech-nology, the latter including plastic-based chips. All are businesses aimed at satisfying central human goals. They use an array of new technologies, involve a mix of products and service disciplines and have potential markets spread around the world. By using new thinking to improve in each area, China's rulers think the country can expand its economy, become more competitive and boost employment – goals that appeal to every government.

While China has a more prescriptive approach than many countries, it is not alone in trying to draw up plans for the businesses that will be important in the next 50–100 years. Such exercises are considered all the more necessary given the traumas of the 2008–9 financial crisis and the deep recession that followed. The twin calamity was triggered by a build-up of indebtedness and an over-reliance on the finance sector to provide for economic expansion. The worst failings were in the UK and US, although other countries too suffered as a result of these policy errors. Politicians and government officials have tried to absorb lessons from what went wrong. Faith in the capability of service industries to lay the basis for growth has been shaken. As governments attempt to set a course for the future that involves a bigger place for manufacturing, the pattern of the new industrial revolution will provide a useful road map.

# CHAPTER 10

# The new industrial revolution

## Product placement

Since manufacturing started in its modern form in the late eighteenth century, four big periods of change have had an impact. The new industrial revolution will be the fifth. It started around 2005, and will last until about 2040, though it may be the end of the century before the changes have their full effect. Most of its important elements are related to previous eras of change. It would be hard to describe many of these individual features as completely new. The impact will come from these factors taking effect at the same time, and the way they interact. There will be more opportunities for customization – with many companies offering a mix of 'mass customization' and 'mass personalization' to widen choice. The way goods are designed and made will become more complex. Processes such as development, production and service will be spread across a global 'value chain' of operations. Across this value chain, there will be opportunities for businesses based in many countries, both high-cost and low-cost, to play a part. The possibilities for making and selling products in narrow 'niches', aimed at specific groups of customers, often widely spread globally, will be greater. This will give companies – many of them based in the high-cost regions – more opportunities to specialize.

Manufacturers will demonstrate a greater awareness of the environment, attempting to make things on a sustainable rather than a destructive basis. The idea of materials being recycled between industrial residues and new products will become more commonplace. The proportion of world manufacturing that takes place in China and other 'emerging economies' will continue to increase. This is natural as these regions account for a larger share of the world economy. There will be more of an emphasis on locating productive capacity in regions where the goods being made will be used, rather than on transporting the products long distances from such plants.

Therefore, while China is likely to continue to be the world's biggest manufacturer for a long time, the rate at which the country increases its global share of factory output will slow. The advantages of locating production in China for export – especially to Europe or the US – will, as part of this change, become less obvious. As for the high-cost regions, the benefits from basing production and design jobs in these places – at least in certain types of industries – will start to become more clear-cut. Many of the successful manufacturers that feature in high-cost regions will be part of 'clusters' of manufacturing businesses concentrated in small areas.

Compared to the previous four periods, the new industrial revolution will be the first where the impact is felt in a homogeneous way: its effects will be spread globally, as opposed to being concentrated among a limited group of developed or rich economies. As a key part of this trend, the places where many types of products are capable of being made will become much more diverse. Reflecting this move to homogeneity, companies will increasingly spread their manufacturing between emerging economies and 'developed' nations in a 'hybridized' style. The new period will be an age of 'industrial democracy' in its truest sense.

Behind hybridization strategies will frequently be companies' need to gain maximum access to the growing markets in the developing part of the world. There will be an interest in deriving benefits from the lower costs that production in these places entails. But frequently companies will not want to lose the advantages that come from plants and development operations in traditional industrial regions. The negative effects of high costs in these regions will often be offset by advantages derived from the availability of advanced technical skills, as well as closeness to important markets.

In the twenty-first century, as costs, production disciplines and technologies show more signs of convergence, new ways of describing countries' manufacturing prowess will be required. The differences between 'developed' and developing nations will start to erode. What will count are the details of which products are best made in specific places, how manufacturing functions are split up globally and the types of skills and suppliers that are needed to support specific operations in set locations.

Due to greater efficiencies and use of improved automation technologies, the number of people involved in manufacturing will stay relatively low as a percentage of the world population. However, a growing proportion of the industry workforce will have technical qualifications and be in jobs where the emphasis is on learning new skills.

The need for craft-based disciplines – centred on traditional concepts of 'touch labour' – will continue to be strong. There will be plenty of opportunities for companies to progress in product areas that require these skills. This will happen, even in parts of the world where labour costs are high, so long as companies choose industrial sectors to compete in where customers are happy to pay relatively high prices.

Manufacturing will continue to exert a strong influence in the global economy. It will stimulate the use of new technologies, some of which will be taken up by other sectors – in services, agriculture, construction and energy exploration. The new products that emerge from industry will help to increase productivity in these other parts of the economy, thereby adding to overall economic growth. Theoretically, a single country could allow its own manufacturing industry to disappear. It could leave this area of activity largely to others. But then it would miss out on the local transmission effects that are important when groups of companies interrelate. It would also have to import a lot of the goods it needs for its economic well-being and miss out on a chance to boost the size of its own economy. In the coming decades, manufacturing will have plenty of opportunity to grow in size and influence. A vigorous and resourceful manufacturing sector will be vital to any country that wants to be regarded as a twenty-first-century success.

## Ages of improvement

Prior to the first industrial revolution – or the Industrial Revolution – countries' levels of skill, and the technology they had to offer in production-related disciplines, varied only by small amounts. As a result, the amount of output of man-made goods in specific countries or regions was more than anything a function of population. The Industrial Revolution changed matters. It was, initially, a British phenomenon. From the revolution's start in about 1780, its effects spread within 50–100 years to a limited number of other countries. The impact was felt almost exclusively in the 'developed' nations, chiefly other parts of Europe, and North America. By the end of the nineteenth century, the so-called developed world had become responsible for by far the biggest share of world manufacturing. Other regions retained only a small share of the global output of factory goods, in spite of their large populations. The pattern was to stay much the same for the next 100 years.

Helped by advances in energy transfer linked to steam engines, the first revolution led to large factories making goods according to standardized designs and production methods. It made possible fairly simple products, using relatively large numbers of people. It was the major force turning agrarian-based communities into industrial ones. A key indicator was large-scale migration from the countryside to towns. There was little regard for environmental impact, in terms of either how products were made or what they did when in use. Most production coexisted with design and development. The idea of trying to separate these functions by more than short distances would have been regarded as foolish or close to impossible. The second big historical change was the transport revolution of the mid-nineteenth century. Again, this started in Britain. It was triggered by the invention of the railway locomotive, and the establishment of the necessary infrastructure of a rail and signalling network. Canals and steel-hulled ships appeared at roughly the same time.

The new modes of transport opened up fast communications links for people and goods. Transport became a lever for the expansion for businesses of many kinds, including those in manufacturing but also services, agriculture and mining. The scientific revolution started in about 1860; to some degree it overlapped with the transport revolution. Its biggest feature was electricity. Such a convenient and clean form of energy, capable of being produced on demand and relatively cheaply, had not previously existed. The scientific revolution stimulated the advent of cheap steel, aluminium, new building materials and modern chemicals, including pharmaceuticals. It made possible many new products and processes that led to growth in a range of industries outside manufacturing, from retailing to construction.

The computer revolution started in about 1950, almost a century after the transport revolution. It led to small, cheap data-processing machines, including personal computers, the Apple iPad and the internet routing equipment that facilitates the worldwide web. By making possible new and cheaper control processes for activities from telecommunications to industrial production, the computer revolution changed the nature of many business sectors. It enabled businesses or people to do things that previously would have been impossible, from using electronic exchanges to place phone calls easily and cheaply with individuals around the world, to harnessing the power of computerized machine tools to cut metal parts extremely fast and to high precision. Through all these mechanisms, the computer revolution had an immense catalytic effect on the global economy.

One conclusion from the first four industrial revolutions is that such concerted periods of change invariably take a long time to have their full effect. The impact of the first industrial revolution was initially focused on a few sectors, such as metals, textiles and heavy machinery. It became relevant to other fields of industry, sometimes many years later. To start with, its geographical spread was limited. The revolution began in Lancashire, the centre of Britain's late eighteenth-century textiles industry. It was several decades before its impact was recognized – not just in other parts of the world but in some UK regions also. In the case of the revolutions that followed, there were similar time lags. A key product that grew out of the transport and scientific revolutions was the aircraft, helped by advances in materials such as aluminium plus new engines. But the concept of air travel for most people, even in the rich Western world, remained a novelty until the 1970s, more than a century after the transport revolution began. The first electronic computer was developed in 1946. But the power of the computer became evident to most people only after the invention of the microprocessor 25 years later. It took another quarter of a century after this – to the late 1990s – for the first signs of the internet to become evident. Other applications for the internet – including Twitter or Facebook – began to appear some years after this.

For long periods, all the first four industrial revolutions were unfinished. It is wrong to think of these as sudden bursts of change, with few links between them. They were also driven by many factors. It is too simplistic, according to Joel Mokyr, to characterize the first industrial revolution as the 'age of cotton, or the age of steam'. Rather, it was the 'age of improvement' covering many activities, many of which had their roots in events which had taken place years earlier.[1] In 2003, discussing the computer revolution, the US economic historian Nathan Rosenberg observed that he was convinced that 'the full impact of the computer, even now, lies well into the future'.[2] In a similar way, the new industrial revolution will draw heavily on some of the technologies that became established in previous periods of change. The fact that the new revolution has so many roots will add to its potency.

## Technology push

Of the essential ingredients of the new period of change, technology is the most crucial. The application of new scientific thinking will play an increasing role in the way products are designed and made. As each stage of industrial development is reached, technological sophistication rises by a notch or two. This both provides a platform for the developers of future products, and sets the bar higher in terms of standards of achievement. In the realm of technology development, several key factors are important. More ideas than ever before are making their way from the research stage to development. Tied to this is the increase in resources being directed towards science and technology research.

In 2010, the world spent about $1,200 billion on research and development, over 25 per cent more than the annual figure in the mid-1990s.[3]

The total includes money spent directly by industry, aimed at explicit commercial goals, as well as 'pure' research in government laboratories and academia. In 2010 there were at least 7 million people working in science and technology globally, up more than 40 per cent compared to 1995. In 2008 these people produced 1.5 million papers for scientific journals, a more than threefold rise on the figure 20 years earlier. Of the most recent stock of papers, a third of them involved collaboration between scientists and technologists from different countries.[4] The annual number of patents granted by the US Patent Office rose by 143 per cent between 1990 and 2010, indicating a big rise in development activity.[5] Not all of this scientific and engineering activity works its way into manufacturing, but a lot does.

Scientists and technologists rarely discover anything completely new. They generally build on what is already known. A small number of technologies have been central to human progress. These are the so-called 'general purpose technologies' (see Figure 6).[6] The steam engine, Bessemer-produced steel and the computer are all examples of general purpose technologies that have had an impact, out of 30 so far identified. Of these, 11 emerged during the twentieth century – and of this number, seven made their presence felt only in the final half of the century. The relatively recent general purpose technologies include the computer, as well as the laser, biotechnology and nanotechnology. It often takes several decades for general purpose technologies to exert their full effect. For instance, improvements in many industries powered by electricity – a general purpose technology of the late nineteenth century – became evident only 50 years or so later. In all these cases, the 'learning disciplines' influencing how technology permeates through the economy took time to become properly assimilated. The way the delayed impact of newly devised technologies will unwind in the early years of the twenty-first century will give the new industrial revolution a key stimulus.

Another change concerns how technology programmes are being managed. In past eras, research and development was a process organized largely separately from the commercial work of companies. This was the case whether the businesses did the research by themselves or in collaboration with partners such as academic institutes. In either case, the

**Figure 6 Types of general purpose technologies**

| General purpose technology | | Date | Type of GPT |
|---|---|---|---|
| 1 | The domestication of plants | 9,000–8,000 BCE | Pr |
| 2 | The domestication of animals | 8,500–7,500 BCE | Pr |
| 3 | Smelting of ore | 8,000–7,000 BCE | Pr |
| 4 | The wheel | 4,000–3,000 BCE | P |
| 5 | Writing | 3400–3200 BCE | Pr |
| 6 | Bronze | 2800 BCE | P |
| 7 | Iron | 1200 BCE | P |
| 8 | Mechanical pulleys/gears | 500 BCE | P |
| 9 | Heavy plough | 8th century | P |
| 10 | The water wheel | early medieval period | P |
| 11 | The three-masted sailing ship | 15th century | P |
| 12 | Printing | 16th century | Pr |
| 13 | The steam engine | late 18th–early 19th century | P |
| 14 | The factory system | late 18th–early 19th century | O |
| 15 | The railway | mid 19th century | P |
| 16 | The iron steam ship | mid 19th century | P |
| 17 | The internal combustion engine | late 19th century | P |
| 18 | Mass production steelmaking | late 19th century | Pr |
| 19 | Electricity | late 19th century | P |
| 20 | The motor vehicle | 20th century | P |
| 21 | Chemical synthesis | 20th century | Pr |
| 22 | Aircraft | 20th century | P |
| 23 | The mass production, continuous process, factory | 20th century | O |
| 24 | The computer | 20th century | P |
| 25 | Semiconductors | 20th century | P |
| 26 | Laser | 20th century | P |
| 27 | Lean production | 20th century | O |
| 28 | The internet | 20th century | P |
| 29 | Biotechnology | 20th century | Pr |
| 30 | Nanotechnology | 20th century | Pr |

**Note:** The 30 general purpose technologies since 10,000 BCE. The GPTs can be divided into different types, where P equals product; Pr equals process; O equals organization.

**Sources:** The list is based on Lipsey, Carlaw and Bekar, Economic Transformations, with modifications by the author.

research scientists and engineers were generally kept away from marketing people and 'applications engineers', the latter having the job of adapting new ideas to meet the needs of customers. Now, however, the emphasis is on linking development operations much more closely to what customers expect and require. The same trend can be seen in the number of academic researchers who have partnerships with companies so the two groups work together. Such arrangements – part of the trend towards so-called 'open innovation'– help to speed the flow of new ideas to the commercial sphere.[7]

Linking in with this overlap between the kinds of people who work on product development is the way in which more technologies are being investigated in combination with others.[8] The new areas of nano-technology and synthetic biology illustrate the trend. Key aspects of how these technologies work involve the mixing of ideas from several disciplines. For instance, a research engineer working on a new product in synthetic biology might draw on materials science, information processing, biochemistry, computer-aided design and mechanical engi-neering. There are now many product fields where 'parallel processing' of technologies are highly relevant to how engineers are trying to improve them. Examples include miniature pumps, used in the healthcare industry, where key technologies include computer-aided design and micro-machining. In military hardware, the development of self-guided 'smart bombs' is driven by miniature jet engines, high-speed data transfer and new materials.

A further feature is the number of new countries that are becoming more active in technology development. Up to about 1990, the nations that played a part in technology development were broadly the same as the 'industrialized' nations. Now, the talent pool has become broader. In 2010, about 1.5 million of the 7 million science and technology workers were in China, about the same figure as in the US. In 2008, Chinese scientists and engineers were responsible for 10 per cent of the world output of scientific papers, up from 1 per cent in 1988. The US was still a long way ahead, accounting for 21 per cent of the 2008 total, but its dominance had slipped massively since the end of the 1990s, when the country's share was roughly twice as high.[9]

China is not the only country moving ahead. In 2008, researchers from Brazil, Taiwan and South Korea each accounted for 2 per cent of the world's scientific papers by authorship, in each case more than 10 times the comparable figure 20 years earlier. In 2008 India accounted for 3 per cent of scientific papers by authorship, giving the country a stronger position than most of the lower-rank nations. However, India started from a higher base, given that in 1988 the comparable figure was

2 per cent.[10] Big companies such as General Electric, Electrolux and ABB are channelling more of their spending on research and development into countries such as China, India and Brazil by setting up research and technology centres. The fresh thinking is having an impact in such product areas as medical scanners, low-energy motors for refrigerators and high-conductivity cables. The greater involvement of a wider range of countries in science and technology looks likely to provide more ideas – of an increasingly disparate nature – for the world's manufacturers to work on. In time, they will evolve into new products and services for companies to sell, which will have an impact on the world.

## China's rise

In 2010, China reacquired the title of the world's largest manufacturing country by output.[11] It took this position (by a fractional amount) from the US, which had been the manufacturing leader since just before 1900. The last time China had been number one was in the early nineteenth century, after which it ceded the title to Britain. The scale and speed of China's rise have been unparalleled, even by the standards of Britain's surge as a manufacturer in the late eighteenth and early nineteenth centuries. In 2010, China had about 130 million people working in manufacturing, or roughly 40 per cent of the total world manufacturing workforce of about 328 million.[12] In the same year, China's exports of merchandise goods (mainly consisting of manufactured items but also comprising oil and related products) accounted for 10 per cent of the global figure. They were greater than those of any other country, adding up to $1,581 billion – ahead of the US with $1,280 billion and Germany with $1,270 billion. In 2010, China had a trade surplus with the rest of the world on goods of $183 billion. The surplus was the second biggest in the world after Germany with $202 billion, and ahead of Russia with $152 billion (where the goods were mainly oil) and Japan with $77 billion. In 2010, the US in contrast had a goods deficit of $690 billion; for the UK, the deficit was $153 billion and for France, $87 billion.[13]

The size of the turnaround in the China/US trade position over 30 years underlines the magnitude of what has happened. In 1980, China's manufacturing role was so weak that the US imported from this country just $1.1 billion of goods, representing a minuscule 0.4 per cent of the US's $257 billion imports bill. By 2010, so great had China's manufacturing power become that the US's goods purchases from China came to $364 billion, or 18 per cent of the US's total imports. In 1980, demand for US goods in China easily exceeded the flow of products going out the other way. Since US goods exports to China were $3.8 billion, the US had a sizeable surplus in that year on its China trade of $2.7 billion. By 1985, China's flow of goods being sold to the US had increased so far that the US had, for the first time, a small deficit with China of $6 million. From this point, the deficit has kept on rising, to reach $10.4 billion in 1990, $83 billion in 1990 and $273 billion in 2010.[14]

Between 1990 and 2010, China increased its share of world manufacturing by a factor of more than six, from 3 per cent to 19.4 per cent. The move pushed it up from seventh place in the 'league table' of countries ranked by manufacturing output in 1990, to its newly held number one position. In contrast, the changes in other countries have generally been far less impressive. While some developing countries have moved in the same direction, albeit by smaller amounts, most established industrialized nations have seen their shares fall. Over the 1990–2010 period, South Korea's share of global manufacturing output rose from 1.5 per cent to 2.6 per cent, India went from 1.1 per cent to 2.5 per cent and Indonesia from 0.7 per cent to 1.8 per cent. During these 20 years, only Russia showed a particularly marked rise in its share to rival the change in China. The change in Russia's case was from 0.2 per cent to 2.1 per cent. However, much of this can be explained by Russia's extremely low figure for 1990, which was related to the economic shocks triggered by the collapse of Communism. Even though the share for Brazil moved around over the 20-year period, its share of world manufacturing output in 2010 was 2.7 per cent, the same as it had been in 1990. As a result of the various shifts, Brazil and South Korea have moved from being the eighth and eleventh biggest countries in manufacturing output respectively in 1990 to numbers six and seven in 2010 (see Figure 7). India and Russia climbed over the same period from being sixteenth and unranked (outside the top 25) in the league table to the eighth and eleventh slots.

**Figure 7 Leading countries by manufacturing output, 2010**
(by percentage share)

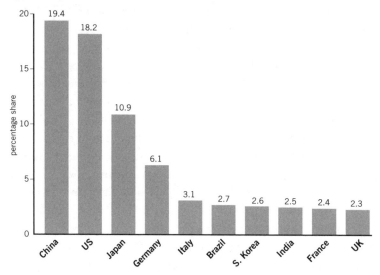

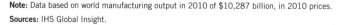

**Note:** Data based on world manufacturing output in 2010 of $10,287 billion, in 2010 prices.
**Sources:** IHS Global Insight.

The changes have moved Britain – the number one in manufacturing in the late nineteenth century – from joint fifth position both in 1990 and as recently as 2006 – to an unimpressive looking tenth in 2010. Its share of the world total has fallen from 4.8 per cent in 1990 to 2.3 per cent in 2010. Japan and Germany came in as numbers three and four respectively in the 2010 world manufacturing league table, having been in second and third slots 20 years earlier. Italy and France were the fifth and ninth largest in 2010, having previously been in fourth and joint fifth positions. The shifts mask pronounced changes by these countries in their overall shares of world manufacturing output. In the case of Japan, this proportion fell between 1990 and 2010 from 18.8 per cent to 10.9 per cent, with comparable figures for Germany, Italy and France being falls from 10.4 per cent to 6.1 per cent, from 5.6 per cent to 3.1 per cent, and from 4.8 per cent to 2.4 per cent. But perhaps the biggest loser – if not in purely statistical terms so much as in national self-regard – has been the US. In 1950 the US accounted for not far off half – 44.7 per cent – of the world's total goods output. In 1990, the US remained the world's biggest manufacturer, with a share of 23.1 per cent as compared to Japan in second position with less than 19 per cent. However, by 2010, due to China's strong progress over the previous 20 years, the share of the US had contracted to a relatively meagre 18.2 per cent. This pushed the country into the number two slot in the global manufacturing league table – it was the first time since the end of the nineteenth century that a country other than the US had taken the title of the world's largest maker of factory products.[15]

During the twenty-first century, many of the countries previously outside the leading positions in world manufacturing will probably continue to increase their share of total production. But of these only India – as a result of its large population – looks likely to come even close to challenging China in terms of leadership. In the developed world, the US will continue to be not too far away from China in terms of its share of the total world output. But it is highly unlikely that – at least for the foreseeable future – the US will regain its crown as the world number one.

## People power

One key factor behind the idea that China's position is close to unassailable is the straightforward matter of population. China's large number of people has contributed a lot to its rise as a production behemoth. China accounts for a fifth of the world's people. Given this state of affairs, its record of punching so far below its weight for most of the twentieth century has been an anomaly. On the assumption that standards of technology and organizational competence are reasonably spread out, then the capabilities of a person in one country to do productive work should bear at least some resemblance to the equivalent potential in other countries. The fact that China's share of factory production is now roughly equal to its share of population suggests that some levelling in capability has indeed been occurring. In the next 100 years, although India will come close to it, China's population is almost certain to remain well ahead of that of the US. For this reason, on the assumption that no big political or technology shock takes place, China's manufacturing production is likely to remain some way in front of that of the US.

In explaining China's advance, lower costs have been an important element. Since living costs in China are substantially lower than in most developed nations, wages are also much less. In 2009, the average cost of employing someone to work in a factory in China (including social security and related costs) was $1.36 an hour, compared to $53.80 in Norway, $40.10 in France, $33.50 in the US and $30.80 in Britain.[16] Wages are by no means the only determinant of overall product costs, other key factors being the costs of materials, energy and plant. But in many industries, wages may account for 25–30 per cent of total costs. As a result of China's low wages, the costs of making a product in China are sometimes (depending on the product) as little as half the comparable figure for making the item in a high-cost nation such as the US. This has provided an obvious incentive for many companies to put more of their global manufacturing in China, both for sale within the country and for export.

As China's share of output has risen, its impact has been more widely felt. The idea of the 'China price' – the cost of having a specific item made in China – being a lot lower than elsewhere has helped to drive down manufacturing costs all over the world. It has encouraged more production to migrate to China and, to a lesser degree, other low-wage countries. The pressure on other businesses has sometimes been brutal, leading to factory closures in many Western nations and in some cases losses of tens of thousands of jobs. But the underlying pressure has not been too different from what took place in other periods of intense price competition during the twentieth century. The mantra of the experience curve is that prices for manufactured goods generally fall, at least in relation to other parts of the economy, and sometimes by large amounts. Companies that cannot shift their cost structures to cope with these price changes – unless they can find a niche in the market which offers an escape route – have always found it tough to survive.

A third aspect helping China has been government assistance for China-owned and China-based manufacturers. Beijing has directed overt help to these groups as a way to aid national competitiveness and employment. Making China the world's mightiest manufacturer has fitted in with government aspirations to improve the country's overall international position, and rival, or surpass, the US as a superpower. Government aid has manifested itself in many ways, from low-interest loans to a range of tax incentives. Some critics, particularly in the US, also maintain that the value of the renminbi has been kept artificially low by government intervention on currency markets, thereby boosting the competitiveness of China-based manufacturers in relation to foreign rivals. In the 1960s and 1970s, Japan aided its economic advance through programmes of support to domestic manufacturers, chiefly administered by the all-powerful Ministry of Economy, Trade and Industry (MITI). Similar programmes were later put into operation by other 'developing' countries seeking to move ahead in manufacturing – and in other areas of technology or knowledge-based business – such as South Korea and Singapore. It has been generally acknowledged that such state initiatives are acceptable as 'emerging' economies attempt to increase their living standards and technological prowess.[17] But in the case of China, its more vociferous critics contend that the nation has moved past the status of a 'developing' region. According to this argument, Beijing should by now have reined back on some of the policy instruments, so as to comply with international guidelines about removing preferential treatment for local companies and helping fair trade. Few topics related to economic policy have sparked greater debate, especially in the US, in recent years.[18]

A final factor assisting the country's rise has been the government's interest in opening the country to the influence of foreign companies. They have brought new ideas in technology, organization and management. Together with heavy state spending on roads, ports and other infrastructure to support industry, the foreign involvement from the early 1990s acted as a catalyst for a rapid rise in industrial output. The result of this foreign involvement in China was that in 2008 about a quarter of the country's overall manufacturing was controlled by non-Chinese-owned businesses. According to statistical convention, production from factories based in China is counted as being 'Chinese'. This is irrespective of the ownership of the company which holds title to the goods. The same happens in other countries; output of products made in a factory in the

UK owned and operated by a French company helps to increase Britain's gross domestic product, not that of its European neighbour.

It follows that the impact of heavy foreign participation in China's manufacturing economy has been felt in two main ways. It has helped to increase China's emergence as the global manufacturing leader. At the same time, the foreign companies that have put down roots in China have gained significant benefits themselves. This has happened through the use of China-based factories (either their own, or belonging to suppliers) to make many types of goods for less than is the case in other countries, and also to use the plants as a base for helping increase sales in the expanding China economy. For instance, in 2010 General Motors for the first time sold more cars in China than it did anywhere else, including the US.[19] For those companies that have made the effort to involve themselves in China in this way, the country's rapid growth has provided opportunities as well as threats.

## Chain reaction

A description of China's role underlines how it has become a vital part of the value chains that have featured as manufacturing has become a 'networked' activity. Value chains involve multiple players in many countries, with the key tasks spread globally rather than squeezed into one place.[20] The functions include research and development, production, marketing and sales and 'after-service', the latter possibly taking the form of maintenance contracts in the case of complex pieces of equipment such as gas turbines or aircraft. These tasks may be done by the company that 'owns' the product – by having legal rights to intellectual property, or controlling the item's manufacture; alternatively, the functions can be left to external contractors. It is evident that China has in recent years become a highly important member of the club of 'manufacturing-capable countries', or MCC. Others have followed a similar path. The more nations that can be regarded as part of the MCC club, the more options are open for them to participate in broadly spread value chains, and the healthier will be the overall state of global manufacturing.

When it comes to analysing the huge value of exports emanating from China that have helped the country status as a top manufacturer, it is worth examining the ole of value chains. Many of the goods sold by China as exports are assemblies of items where the main value has came from outside the country. In some cases, the biggest part of the component's value derives not from the act of manufacturing, but the development activity that makes it possible. The 'value added' of the productive work done in China frequently accounts for only a small proportion of the total traded price of the product.[21]

The overall impact of these effects is hard to unravel quantitatively. To do this properly would involve examining the detailed value chains for a huge number of products. However, several studies have been made of items made by Apple – with the help of value chains – that illustrate some of the forces at work. Most of the Apple product's value is due to the innovation and skills locked inside the minds of its employees – virtually none of whom work in physical production as normally defined. Apple operates no factories of its own, apart from small plants for prototypes. In economic jargon, it is a 'factoryless goods producer' or a 'virtual' manufacturer.[22] Apple's products are made under contract by other companies, mainly in China, using value chains that involve many manufacturers of components in other countries. The products can be used to illustrate where much of the true 'value added' in manufacturing often lies, with the picture frequently different from that told by raw trade data.[23]

Among Apple's best-selling products are its iPhone 'smartphones'. In 2009, 11.2 million iPhones were assembled in China and shipped to the US at a factory transfer price – roughly corresponding to the cost of manufacturing – of $179 each. In the US, the devices went on sale for approximately $500 each, giving Apple a gross profit margin per unit of $321. The value of the exports from China to the US attributable to the iPhone shipments came to $2 billion. However, the exports were offset by $121.5 million of components made by the US companies Broadcom and Numonyx and shipped to China to be assembled into the finished phone. The net effect of the transactions was that in 2009 – under the conventional way of counting trade data – the iPhone contributed $1.9 billion to the US's net trade deficit with China, or 0.8 per cent of the country's total $226 billion China deficit for the year. But picking apart the supply chain for the iPhone leads to a more nuanced view of what is happening in the production processes. Of the $179 factory transfer price for each phone, only $6.50, or 3.6 per cent, came from the physical aspects of the final assembly process. These costs consisted of employees' wages at the contractors doing the assembly work, together with these companies' overheads and profits. Of the remaining $172.50, most came from the value of components made not in China but in other countries, including Japan, South Korea and Germany. Taking into account these factors, the 'added value' of China's exports to the US linked to the iPhone came to just $73.5 million in 2009. This low figure sums up the small amount of engineering and manufacturing effort that China put into fulfilling its part in the production operation. If these additional factors are taken into account, the US's trade with China on the iPhone on a value-added basis consists of exports to China of $121.5 million of components, offset by $73.5 million of engineering effort as manifested by the assembly operations taking place in China. The result is that what appears – on the normal basis of calculating trade data – to be a deficit with China of $1.9 billion on the iPhone turns into a net surplus with this country of $48 million.[24]

The recalculation does not alter the fact that, due to the use in iPhones of substantial amounts of parts made in Japan, South Korea and Germany, the US's 'value-added' trade deficit with the rest of the world remains substantial. However, much of the deficit should, under this new method of calculation, be linked to nations other than China, in a change that would illustrate more realistically the contribution of different countries to how the iPhone is produced. If such calculations were applied to the many other types of goods made in China and shipped to the US for final sale, but which contain substantial amounts of 'bought in' parts and software produced in other countries, the extent of the US's trade deficit with China would be depicted as being a lot lower than is commonly thought.[25]

From other financial details about the iPhone, other inferences can be made about where the value behind the device really lies. Of the $321 gross margin, probably about half – about $160 per phone – went to the distributors and retailers involved in the sales supply chain. The other $160 was kept by Apple. It paid for sales and marketing expenses, along with the technical and design work done by the several thousand engineers working on the iPhone.[26] The money left over from these expenses was retained profit. Apple chooses not to break down exactly how the $160 is divided up. But an educated guess is that about $100 of the $160 came from paying for the technological development that made the device possible. If the 'technology cost' per phone is indeed about $100, that equates to about a fifth of the retail price of each gadget – and is roughly 15 times higher than the sum paid for the iPhone's physical production.[27]

Details related to Apple's iPod music player provide other insights into what is meant by the 'value' of products and who gains the most from creating this value. Like the iPhone, the iPod is assembled largely in China and built from components that are mainly made in places other than the US. Nonetheless, the value that flows into the US – due to intangible aspects to manufacturing – remains considerable. In 2006, 41,000 jobs worldwide were supported by work divided up along the value chain of the iPod. Of these 13,900 were in the US, half of them highly paid engineering and other professional jobs, mostly within Apple itself. The other 27,200 jobs were split between countries such as China, which was responsible for almost half, with the rest being mainly in the Philippines, Japan and Singapore.

In 2006 the total wages paid to the 41,100 people employed in iPod-related work came to about $1 billion, or roughly $25 per device sold. Even though the US had half as many jobs from the iPod as the rest of the world, the total wages paid in that country related to the device came to $750 million, more than double the $320 million paid to people in other countries. More than two-thirds ($525 million) of the earnings in the US went to comparatively well-paid professional employees, either at Apple or in companies working for it.[28] If China had not surged ahead as a manufacturing power, Apple would still have invented new products. It would have found a way to manufacture them, even if this did not involve China. The country's great leap in manufacturing has made a big difference to Apple's ability to make, and sell, its products. But a lot of the value locked into the full extent of Apple's manufacturing operations has remained in the US. While Apple's success has given China some economic benefits, the positive impact on the US economy has been much greater.

## Shock treatment

The story of manufacturing has been one of a hugely productive sector driving on the global economy by delivering cheaper and more versatile goods, while also employing relatively few people. The relative paucity of people in manufacturing – not just now but in the past – underlines how a small segment of the world population has acted over the past 200 years as a form of economic 'shock troops'. In creating new forms of goods more cheaply, the manufacturing workforce has delivered an economic boost that has gone far further than the small numbers employed would indicate. Put simply, one person in a manufacturing job has delivered more economic benefits than people working in other sectors. All the indications are that the impact of manufacturing will continue, even though important shifts have been occurring in terms of the regions of the world where the most important elements of the work have been taking place.

The impact of manufacturing is manifested most graphically by economic data that compare what has happened in the world of making things with overall economic activity over the past two centuries. Between 1800 and 2010, global manufacturing output rose by an annual average of 2.6 per cent.[29] This is well above the comparable 2 per cent annual increase in gross domestic product – measuring the productive effort of the entire global economy – over the same period. It is also three times higher than the comparable 0.9 per cent average yearly rise in global population. Between 1800 and 2010, output per worker in manufacturing increased by an average of 1.7 per cent per year. Over the same period, the rate of increase of global gross domestic product per person – a measure of the world's overall capability to create wealth – rose by just 1.1 per cent annually. The figures indicate that output per person in manufacturing – representing productivity – has risen substantially more than living standards. In other words, manufacturing has made itself more efficient at a rate above what has happened elsewhere in the economy. As a result, prices of manufactured goods have tended to decline, at least in relation to costs in other parts of economic output. At the same time, their sophistication has gone up. This is another manifestation of the manufacturing experience curve, explaining how costs fall as experience, or learning, rises.

The US consumer price index[30] is one of the best measures of price changes for consumer goods and services not just in the US but globally. Studies of the index over the past 50 years have shown a more marked rise for prices of services than for most kinds of factory-made products. However, the trends have become even more marked in the early years of the twenty-first century. Between 2000 and 2010 the consumer price index for all goods and services rose by 22.5 per cent. Over the same period, the index as measured separately for durable goods – covering items from furniture to home computers – fell by 18.2 per cent. The price-depressing impact of China – both due to the lower costs of goods made there and the country's competitive impact in forcing down costs elsewhere – has clearly had an effect. However, China's influence has merely made more marked a trend that has been in evidence for a long time.

In 2010, there were more manufacturing workers than ever before. But at 328 million out of 6.9 billion, the number equated to just 4.8 per cent of the world population. On the assumption that roughly half the world population is available for employment, in 2010 the proportion of the global workforce in manufacturing was about 10 per cent. If this figure seems low, this is nothing new. Over the past 200 years manufacturing employment – expressed as a percentage either of the world's population or of the workforce – has stayed fairly stable. Historical evidence suggests the figure as a proportion of population has generally been between about 2.5 per cent and 8 per cent, while as a proportion of the total workforce it has been between about 5 per cent and 15 per cent.

In 1800 the number employed in manufacturing came to 47 million, just 4.7 per cent of the world population of 1 billion. By 1900, due to big increases in productivity in the 'developed' countries that were the main beneficiaries of the Industrial Revolution, the numbers working in manufacturing had fallen slightly to 45 million. Meanwhile, however, the global population had risen to 1.6 billion. Therefore, in 1900, the proportion of the world stock of people employed in manufacturing fell to as low as 2.8 per cent. During the twentieth century, factory output rose immensely, at well above the rate of growth in the manufacturing workforce. Between 1900 and 2000, manufacturing production increased almost fifty-fold, while the numbers working in the sector rose only by about six times.[31]

For most of the past 200 years, the rich, developed nations have been the unrivalled leaders in manufacturing. They have been most influential in promulgating new ideas in this discipline, and the biggest beneficiaries of the changes that have resulted. Over the 210-year period to 2010, factory production in the developed countries rose by an average of 2.9 per cent a year, compared to 2.3 per cent a year in the rest of the world. The two figures indicate how, as a broad trend, the developed regions have increased their share of manufacturing over a long period. However, in recent years there has been a shift in power in manufacturing. The 'have nots' in factory output have been catching up on the 'haves'.

## The stage shifts

The 210-year period started with what are now known as the 'industrialized' regions in a weak position. In 1800 – after the Industrial Revolution had begun but before it had much effect – the developed countries were responsible for just 29 per cent of world manufacturing output. The 'emerging' nations as they are now called – with China and India in the lead – accounted for the remaining 71 per cent.[32] In the century after this, the changes triggered by the Industrial Revolution worked their impact. But almost all the effects were focused in the developed high-cost nations. During the nineteenth century, manufacturing in the poor, emerging nations fell back. The result was that by 1900, the developed regions were responsible for 87 per cent of world factory output, with just 13 per cent coming from everywhere else.

During the twentieth century, the extent of the rich countries' dominance fell slightly. This reflected some sharing out, from the developed nations to elsewhere, of the advances from the first four industrial revolutions. However, the move in this direction was fairly weak. By 1980 the proportion of manufacturing emanating from the rich world was still as high as 66 per cent. In the following 20 years, the figure went up a little more, to reach 73 per cent in 2000. But then the balance of power started to shift. Between 2000 and 2010, manufacturing output in poor countries moved ahead extremely quickly, by 6.3 per cent a year.

During the same 2000–10 period, as a result of generally weak growth exacerbated by the 2008–9 recession, production in rich nations fell by 0.2 per cent a year. By 2010, as a result, the share of the developed world in total manufacturing output went down to 59 per cent. The proportion of manufacturing coming from the poor, emerging economies was consequently 41 per cent – the highest it had been for some 150 years. The surge in factory output from China was the main reason for the turnaround, but not the only one. Other countries – including India, Brazil and Russia, previously considered to be in the second lane in manufacturing – began to show their own increases in production.

The changed conditions have also shown up in productivity data giving the detail of what has been happening in different parts of the world. The big increase in output per worker in the history of manufacturing has been largely a 'developed region' phenomenon. Between 1800 and 2010, manufacturing output per worker in the developed nations increased by 2 per cent a year on average. Over the same period, the comparable average productivity improvement in the emerging economies was much weaker, at 1.4 per cent. For much of the twentieth century, the productivity advantage of the developed nations compared to the emerging economies kept increasing. This happened as the rich nations gained most of the rewards from the increasing technological content of manufacturing. In 1900 the relative advantage of the developed world in productivity – expressed numerically by output per worker in one region, as a ratio of the equivalent figure in the second set of countries – was 6.9 times. By 2000, the comparable number had grown to nine times.

Around the end of the twentieth century, however, productivity changes in the emerging nations started to pick up to match – if not surpass – the year-on-year increases in the rich world. Between 1990 and 2000, manufacturing output per person in the developed regions rose 3 per cent a year. However, between 2000 and 2010, the figure fell back to 2 per cent a year. In the emerging nations, productivity rose by 2 per cent a year in the first of these 10-year periods, and then moved ahead 3.5 per cent a year between 2000 and 2010. This was a sign of the developing regions starting a significant 'catch-up' with the rest of the world. It was driven by the spreading out of technologies and organizational capabilities.

The shifts were accentuated by the increasing importance of value chains and manufacturing networking, involving both large multinationals and smaller players. By 2010, as a result of the changes, the productivity advantage of the rich countries as compared to the poor ones had slipped back to a ratio of 7.8. As a result the rich world's relative advantage regarding output per person in 2010 was significantly less than it had been just 10 years earlier, and not that far ahead of the advantage it had had in 1900.[33] The fall in the productivity advantage enjoyed by the rich nations was partly a factor of declining output in the industrialized world. The fact that it was not any worse was due to a substantial reduction in employment in rich countries, part of a longer-term trend. In 2010, it would be difficult to pretend that the rich world was anything other than substantially ahead of the rest of the world on manufacturing output per worker – a vital part of wealth creation. However, the beginning of a greater degree of uniformity between productivity trends in the two sets of nations – even allowing for the continued lead by the most developed regions – is part of the broad platform of technological and economic factors that will allow the new industrial revolution to flourish.

## Employment fall-out

Between 1900 and 1980, manufacturing employment in rich countries rose more than threefold to reach 71.5 million. But from 1980, employment dropped by almost 7.5 million to 63.9 million in 2000. After this came a still deeper decline, with the number of jobs plummeting 12.8 million by 2010 to 51.1 million, a 20 per cent fall. The job reductions happened as Western manufacturers went to still greater lengths to make themselves more efficient and competitive. Particularly large drops in numbers were recorded in the US – where employment fell from 17.2 million in 2000 to 11.5 million in 2010, a decline of 5.7 million, and in the UK, where the numbers went down from 4 million to 2.5 million, a 1.5 million fall-off. Japan saw a decline of 2 million, from 12.3 million to 10.3 million, while in Germany the decline was a more muted 800,000, from 8.1 million to 7.3 million.[34]

The gloomy data related to employment in manufacturing in the rich countries do not tell the complete story of what has been happening to the manufacturing workforces in these nations. While total jobs have been falling, the numbers of relatively well-paid, highly skilled posts in fields such as engineering have been rising. The US is symptomatic. Here, manufacturing employment among workers with a college education has held up a lot better than manufacturing employment generally. Between 1992 and 2009, the number of employees with an advanced college degree increased from 841,000 to 1.2 million, an increase of 43 per cent. Over the same period, the number of workers with relatively low skills as measured by their school qualifications fell by a similar proportion, from 11.3 million to 6.7 million. Instead of employing large numbers of relatively poorly paid, and often low-skilled production employees, companies are more likely to have a higher proportion of their workers in fields such as development, sales and marketing. Here, typically, people are paid more, but also contribute more in terms of ideas and adaptability.

In terms of the jobs balance in manufacturing between developing and developed countries, a clear shift has been taking place. Between 2000 and 2010, manufacturing productivity in the countries outside the main industrialized world moved ahead fairly briskly, but with output going up even more. The result was a substantial increase in manufacturing employment in the so-called developing – or poor – regions. Between 2000 and 2010, employment in these areas went up 29.4 per cent, with 63 million jobs being added in this period, taking the total from 214 million to 277 million. Of the 63 million new jobs over this period in the poor countries, 35 million – more than half – were in China, which saw its own workforce in manufacturing expand during this time from 95 million to 130 million. Of the 2010 total number of manufacturing workers in poor countries of 277 million, about 47 per cent were in China, with almost 20 per cent, or 51 million, in India. Coupled with the 12.8 million decline in manufacturing jobs in the 2000–10 period in the established industrialized nations, the overall increase in employment over this time for the whole world has been slightly more than 50 million. This has taken the global total from 278 million to 328 million, a rise of 17 per cent over the period. While in 2000, the rich countries accounted for 23 per cent of the world manufacturing workforce, with the poor, developing nations accounting for the rest, the split just 10 years later had changed dramatically: in 2010, only about 15.5 per cent of global employment in manufacturing was in the main developed nations, a share that was about the same as the prevailing figure in 1800. Even so, care needs to be taken in the way this number is interpreted. The population of the rich countries as a proportion of the world total was about 12 per cent in 2010. Therefore, even with the decline since 2000 in the share of total manufacturing employment in the main developed nations, the figure for 2010 is still slightly above what might be expected if employment trends in manufacturing were to mirror precisely the overall distribution of global population. It is a sign, along with others, of how the pattern of activity in manufacturing generally has started to become somewhat more evenly spread between the rich and poor parts of the world.

While the change in the jobs balance has been taking place, the proportion of most nations' gross domestic product – total economic output – accounted for by manufacturing has been falling steadily. This is fairly easy to explain. In most areas of manufacturing, wages account for the largest proportion of economic output. The numbers employed in manufacturing, at least in most rich countries, have been falling for some time. As employment has come down, so too have total wage costs in relation to the rest of the economy – especially when compared to areas such as services which are much more labour intensive. The fact that the percentage of most developed nations' economies represented by manufacturing is less than it was turns out to be a factor mainly of falling employment. That manufacturing has become more efficient – as a result of which it has needed fewer people – is the main reason for the overall change. The higher efficiency and smaller workforces have pushed down the prices of manufactured goods – an important phenomenon linked to the experience curve.

Another way of analysing what has been happening is to start with a discussion of price changes. Lower prices mean the total amount of economic output from manufacturing is depressed in statistical terms, regardless of the actual technological or social 'worth' of the goods being made. A corollary of this is that the percentage of manufacturing showing up in total output figures inevitably goes down. Another factor has been social change.

As people around the world have grown richer, they have preferred to spend a greater part of their incomes on services of different kinds – such as travel, leisure and retail. Even though virtually all services are dependent on manufactured goods, higher expenditure in these fields has naturally tended to 'crowd out' the component of manufacturing in total output.

While such changes are fairly general, the degree of the downward shift in the proportion of gross domestic product covered by factory production has been much more marked in developed economies than elsewhere. Between 1980 and 2010, the proportion of total world output accounted for by manufacturing dropped by nearly 30 per cent, from 24.1 per cent to 17.6 per cent. In 1980 in Europe, 25.5 per cent of the economy was represented by manufacturing, a figure that dropped to 15.1 per cent by 2010, a fall of more than 10 percentage points. But the comparable decline in the Asia-Pacific region – which, while including Japan, also covers large parts of the emerging economies, including China – was a lot less severe. In 1980 Asia-Pacific factories accounted for 26.8 per cent of the region's total economic output. By 2010 the comparable share was 24.3 per cent – a decline of only about 2.5 percentage points.

The nation that experienced one of the biggest falls in terms of shares of its economy represented by factory output was the UK – the world's industrial cradle. Here, the decline was by more than half, from 24.9 per cent in 1980 to 11.7 per cent in 2010. In the US and Germany, the fall was almost as severe, with the proportions in these two countries dropping over the period from 20.7 per cent to 11.8 per cent, and from 37.3 per cent to 20.8 per cent. In Japan, the shift was less marked, from 28.3 per cent to 20.2 per cent. In China, the comparable move over the 30 years was from 40.5 per cent to 32.5 per cent. Among the few countries to buck the trend were India and South Korea, both of which saw the proportion of their economies accounted for by manufacturing rise over the 30 years. In India the figure went up from an extremely low 14.5 per cent in 1980 to 26 per cent in 2010 – a number that reflected the country's relatively recent interest in expanding manufacturing as a growth engine and as a result move away from its historical dependence on agriculture. In South Korea, the proportion of the economy comprising manufacturing increased over the period from 21.7 per cent to 29.8 per cent – the result of many companies based in the country increasing considerably their competitive efforts in a range of sectors, including cars, steel and electronics, and performing better in these activities than overseas rivals.[35]

Comparisons are sometimes made between manufacturing and agriculture. In the nineteenth century and for most of the twentieth century, agriculture accounted for extremely large proportions of employment totals in most countries, including the rich developed ones. As productivity improved, job numbers shrank, as did agriculture's share of gross domestic product. But the apparent parallels between the two sectors should not be taken too seriously. Agriculture provides hugely valuable resources – food – for the world. Big technical advances mean the numbers of people needed for the world agriculture industry are a lot lower than before. But the possibilities of creating new manufacturing products are virtually endless, while the number of potential crops to grow or animals to rear is much more limited. Manufacturing will continue to provide a base for new and improved products, with economic benefits spiralling out far and wide into people's lives, in a way impossible to imagine in the case of crops and the rearing of animals.

Manufacturing as an important activity started in earnest little more than 200 years ago. It has been one of the most compelling narratives in economic history. It has centred on new technology plus new methods of organization originating in a small group of countries. The growth of manufacturing has provided huge economic benefits, with the capability to deliver these advances having spread out in recent years to include a much wider range of countries than before. Manufacturing standards – in terms of technical, managerial and organizational competence – have started to converge. The similarities between groups of nations are becoming more noticeable than the differences. The changes have provided a platform for the future.

## Towards 2050

In the 30 years to 2010, the global manufacturing landscape saw a seismic shift. There is now much more of a 'level playing field' between manufacturing capabilities in many countries. This provides a more even base for the development of the world's manufacturing capabilities. China's surge in production during the final years of the twentieth century and the early part of the twenty-first has been a big part of this trend. The change has been highly positive for China. But it has alarmed some onlookers in the rich, developed countries. The worries have been exacerbated by the period of subdued economic growth that began in many rich nations around 2009, a reaction to the bank failures and severe credit constraints that triggered the 2008–9 financial shocks. Other associated elements have been a lingering crisis in Europe about the future of the euro, plus fears in the US about excessive government debt. With much of the world struggling to return to sustained economic expansion, anxiety has set in that the well-off nations' long period of strength in manufacturing has finished.[36] A particular flurry of concern on this score has been evident in the US.[37]

Such fears are unfounded. The opportunities for the established industrialized world are as great – perhaps still greater – than ever before. The advanced countries retain many advantages, technical, social and economic. They have the ability to participate in dispersed manufacturing operations with many other nations in other parts of the world. The rapid strides China has made have been admirable. But China will not continue to expand in manufacturing in the way it has done in the recent past. The signs are that the rate of increase in factory output will slow down, under the pressure of higher wage and energy costs and deepening environmental challenges.

Some indications of this became evident in 2011 in the US where Boston Consulting Group published a study predicting 3 million new jobs in the US by 2020 as a result of a 're-shoring' of production transferred to China over the previous decade.[38] It is likely that the large increase in productivity that took place in 2000–10 in the low-cost nations will not be repeated in the 2010–50 period. Productivity will continue to rise, in all countries, but at a rate that is more evenly spread. Employment trends in manufacturing in the decades ahead are likely to show a marked difference compared to 2000–10 – a decade which saw a big shift in the proportion of total factory employment, with the poor countries gaining at the expense of the rich ones. As productivity trends continue to become more even, and as wages and standards of living in the developing areas of the world start to edge up, the proportion of global manufacturing employment in the established industrialized countries is unlikely to continue to show a fall, and may very well start to inch up from the 15.5 per cent figure in 2010. During the nineteenth century, the proportion of the total manufacturing workforce that was in the rich part of the world rose from 15.9 per cent in 1800 to 49.3 per cent in 1900. While over the 100 years from 2010 it would be extremely fanciful to expect anything like such a marked shift, it could well be the case that by the end of the 2000s the proportion of overall manufacturing employment in the countries currently categorized as rich will be a lot higher than was the case at the beginning of the century.

The way companies switch their approach to suit the broader platform for global manufacturing will be central to their, and the world's, future. 'Design-only' manufacturers will become a more substantial and dynamic group. Such businesses, predominantly located in the high-cost regions, will employ large numbers in product development. They will leave physical production to others, mainly in parts of the world with lower wages. Increasingly, companies of this sort will be part of complex value chains in which the different manufacturing elements are split up and spread globally, with individual operations taking place where factors such as skills and costs are most appropriate to the task in hand. Most manufacturers, whether based in the rich or the poor countries, will need to develop an international strategy. The companies will have to become increasingly adept at thinking on a global basis, in terms of finding suppliers, customers and collaborators.

The development and assimilation of technology will be critical to the way manufacturing develops. Transfer of technological ideas – perhaps as designs or know-how that are communicated as ideas rather than being part of physical products – will become an increasingly important part of the global value chains that will drive on much of manufacturing. The technological component to products will increasingly have a bearing on the ease with which they can be used after they are made, together with how they affect the global ecosystem. But technology will also affect decisions over where to put physical production. Other related factors will include the amount of factory labour required in production, the availability of relevant skills and suppliers, and the degree to which products require frequent design changes to suit them for their final use. Items that have a high technology component, use little direct labour and require a lot of variation will often continue to be made in high-cost countries – at least for sale in these locations – rather than be shipped in from relatively faraway low-cost nations. The likelihood that operating plants in a high-cost country will make economic sense becomes all the greater if the products in question sell for high prices – perhaps because they are part of a narrow niche where competitors are few.

Increasingly, a mix of manufacturing processes will feature production in both high-cost and low-cost nations – 'hybridized' manufacturing. Such an approach will be part of the way of operating not just of large businesses but also of small companies. The notion of 'micro-multinationals' – small companies which mimic much larger ones in the way they operate factories, technology partnerships and selling operations on a global basis – will become more familiar. Combining high- and low-cost operations through hybridization strategies illustrates that in the new industrial revolution there will be no single blueprint for success. Many different approaches, assuming they are backed up by intelligence, resourcefulness and imagination, will be possible.

The advantages of maintaining production and design jobs in the high-cost regions, where modern manufacturing started in the late eighteenth and early nineteenth centuries, will become more evident. The benefits will be that much more apparent when goods being made are for use in the same country or close by. It follows that 'localism' – making goods for local consumption – will become more of a feature. Many of the successful high-cost manufacturers that exhibit this characteristic will be part of small and concentrated 'clusters' of production businesses.

Clusters will be concentrated in specific localities that are often centred on small towns, surrounded not by traditional heavy industry but by countryside. Such concentrations of industrial skills will frequently – though not always – have their roots in past periods of industrial growth. The companies in these areas will make similar sorts of products and gain benefits from sharing technologies, suppliers and customers. By a combination of ingenuity and forward thinking, some clusters, and the businesses in them, will thrive, while others may well fall away.

While localism is making an impact, there will continue to be a big role – especially in the high-cost nations – for exporters. This is on the grounds that many of them are making items in relatively narrow fields, where competition is limited. Since demand exists for their products the world over, it makes sense to send them there. Also, for many companies of this type, product quality is high, giving them a big advantage. In the likely absence of large numbers of competitors that can match this level of quality and also have lower costs, the pressure on such companies to cut prices is low, sometimes to the point of being virtually non-existent. There is no disconnect between 'cluster thinking' and dispersed value chains. In the new industrial revolution, both will operate, with companies capable of switching between either system of production depending on circumstances.

As the basic act of producing items in factories becomes a less important part of the overall activity of manufacturing, other parts of the value chain will come to the fore. More companies will combine manufacturing with services, as a way to find more innovative ways to make themselves valuable to their customers. Increasingly, manufacturing businesses will act like consultants. The businesses will spend a great deal of time and effort in discussing with the customer its requirements – before creating the goods it needs. A good analogy is with the medical profession. The best doctors use empathy and knowledge to find out how a patient needs to be treated. They then supply a range of goods – medicines – and services – clinical treatment – to improve the condition. Manufacturing managers will increasingly resemble physicians.

As the new industrial revolution gathers force, governments will need to be adroit in following the changes – and guiding them to suit the best interests of their countries. The severe 2008/9 global recession was sparked more than anything else by an implosion in finance-based industries. Many countries – led by the US and UK – had looked to these sectors to provide the bulk of economic growth. Now, a new interest has emerged in stimulating production-based industries in fields that combine novel technologies and big global challenges.[39] How to lay the basis for this involves a series of different strands of policy. It is difficult to be too prescriptive about what is needed. Specific countries will require different sets of ideas. In the US, President Barack Obama in early 2012 set the tone for his re-election campaign later that year with a call to use a series of policy initiatives to increase the amount of manufacturing in the US through 're-shoring' or 'insourcing' strategies.[40]

'The overall numbers of people employed directly in manufacturing will remain fairly small as a proportion of the world population. But within the total, fast-growing parts of manufacturing that meet new needs or which are based on novel technologies will create large numbers of jobs that could, for specific sectors, run to hundreds of thousands, if not millions. A feature of these jobs will be their technological component. Workers will be predominantly able, academically qualified people, with skills in engineering and technology, along with the personal capabilities to apply them to a wide set of challenges. So making sure sufficient people of the right capabilities emerge from the education system to staff the manufacturing businesses of the future will be essential. A lot of this involves training the right kind of engineers – people who can combine skills in the 'hard' aspects of physics, chemistry and metallurgy with the capabilities in communication and working in teams that are increasingly necessary in a globalized world.

Greater emphasis should be given to deepening the role of technology, design and manufacturing in countries' national cultures. Nations such as Germany and Japan are further ahead in this effort than others such as the US and Britain. In a general way the notion of *monozukuri* – the Japanese word for the art and science of making things – needs to become more deeply entrenched.

State-backed financial support for new private sector manufacturing operations where conventional funding is hard to come by will often be a useful and justified part of government policy. Manufacturers themselves also have a role. They should try harder to make themselves more visible and attractive to young people who might at some point become important recruits. The overall emphasis should be on self-help, aided where necessary by modest government initiatives. A case in point involves clusters. Such local networks work best not only where concentrations of talented people and well-resourced institutions exist, but where the contacts between them are as rich and fluid as possible. Governments have a part to play in encouraging such networks to work well – for example, by handing out grants to encourage programmes of visits by different companies to others' facilities, as well as through providing the necessary funds for educational institutes that often play a part in clusters.

In the new industrial revolution, there will be immense opportunities for manufacturing to play a big part in boosting the global economy. The fruits of this activity will be products that help people to live happier and healthier lives, without causing undue environmental harm. The potential to participate in the new era for manufacturing will be shared out much more evenly among the earth's inhabitants than has ever been the case in previous big periods of change.

Manufacturing is the art and science of transforming materials to make new products and meet new needs. For 3,000 years it has experienced periodic shifts that have had an immense impact on the way civilization has developed. Now manufacturing is going through another all-encompassing process of change. In the new era, what is required more than anything is recognition of how some of the accepted patterns to production industries are altering, and an understanding of how best to gain the maximum benefits from these shifts. For the most talented, imaginative and technically qualified people, the new industrial revolution will create huge opportunities that will turn out no less exciting than those that changed the world during the original industrial revolution of the late eighteenth century.

# Notes

Fuller web information for many of the references in the notes can be found in the bibliography. All urls were current as of December 2011.

### 1 The growth machine

1. Rudyard Kipling, 'Cold iron'. The story was first published in *The Delineator*, Sept. 1909, before being collected in *Rewards and Fairies* the following year.
2. The 43 billion tonnes is the cumulative total weight of all the iron and steel yet produced, including recycled goods. Of the 43 billion tonnes, about 33 billion tonnes has come from iron dug from the ground, with the rest coming from recycled products made from scrap steel. Steel production data from 1900 are from the International Steel Statistics Bureau (ISSB), London. Earlier details from History Database of the Global Environment, Netherlands Environmental Assessment Agency (http://thema-sites.pbl.nl/en/themasites/hyde/productiondata/metals/index.html). Of the 33 billion tonnes of iron so far used to make goods containing iron and steel, virtually all is trace-able, somewhere on the planet. NB: iron and steel production data can be found in this database by searching under details for aluminium, copper, etc. The assumption is that a cumulative 130 million tonnes of iron goods were made prior to 1890. Estimates are from the author's calculations, aided by conversations with Robert Hunter.
3. The mass of the earth is normally regarded as $5.98 \times 10^{21}$ tonnes or about 6,000 billion billion tonnes (throughout this book, 1 billion = 1,000 million). More details from the US Department of Energy's Thomas Jefferson National Accelerator Facility (http://education.jlab.org/qa/mathatom_05.html); for more information about the mass of the earth, http://nineplanets.org/earth.html. These websites put the proportion of the earth that consists of iron as 35 per cent and 34.6 per cent respectively. Jules Verne, *Journey to the Centre of the Earth* (1864), provides a fanciful account of a journey under the planet's surface.
4. The earth's crust extends to about 30 kilometres beneath the surface. It has a total mass of some 26 billion billion tonnes. Of this, iron is about 5 per cent (Jürgen Schieber, 'Earth: our habitable planet', Indiana University, 2007, ch. 5 (http://www.indiana.edu/~geol105/1425chap5.htm). At an exploitation rate of about 1 billion tonnes a year, roughly the annual extraction in 2010–11, the iron should last 1 billion years. However,

the amount of iron regarded as being easily extractable by orthodox mining is a lot less than this, and is put at 230 billion tonnes – at which rate the iron would run out in around 2200 (World Steel Association, 'Fact sheet: raw materials', Brussels, 2011).

5. Possibly the insulation comprised animal skins, added to a layer of ceramic. Also helpful may have been rudimentary bellows, used to blow air into the furnace to keep the inside hot.

6. Calculations based on Robert Hunter, 'The value of iron', Metal Bulletin conference, Rotterdam, 2004. See also Robert Hunter, 'Riding the super cycle on a roller coaster, or reflections on the commodities boom', Metal Bulletin conference, Monaco, 2008. Hunter also assisted the author via email.

7. Reginald Bashforth, *The Manufacture of Iron and Steel*, vol. 2: *Steel Production* (London: Chapman & Hall, 1959); William Alexander and Arthur Street, *Metals in the Service of Man* (London: Penguin, 1979).

8. Joel Mokyr, *The Lever of Riches* (Oxford: Oxford University Press, 1990), p. 210. Also Donald Wagner, 'Early iron in China, Korea, and Japan', paper to annual meeting, Association for Asian Studies, Los Angeles, 1993, and Donald Wagner, *The Traditional Chinese Iron Industry and Its Modern Fate* (Copenhagen: Nordic Institute of Asian Studies, 1997).

9. David Hey, 'The South Yorkshire steel industry and the Industrial Revolution', *Northern History* 42:1 (Mar. 2005).

10. 'Output' in an economic sense is defined in this book as 'value-added' output – which for a company equates to revenue minus costs of purchasing goods and services. Gross domestic product for a country or group of countries is always put in value-added terms. 'Manufacturing output' is a component of GDP. Care must be taken not to try to compare measures described in value-added terms – such as GDP and manufacturing value-added output – with descriptions of gross revenues. Thus attempting to put nations' GDP alongside details of companies' sales is nearly always nonsensical.

11. P. Bairoch, 'International industrialisation levels from 1750 to 1980', *Journal of European Economic History* 11 (1982), figures quoted in Paul Kennedy, *The Rise and Fall of the Great Powers: Economic Change and Military Conflict from 1500 to 2000* (London: Fontana, 1989); see in particular tables 14, 15, 17, 18, 26, 28, 30. See also Nicholas Crafts, *Globalisation and Economic Growth: A Historical Perspective* (Oxford: Blackwell, 2004). Output data used in this book up to roughly 1900 are based on Bairoch's statistics. These are generally regarded by economic historians as imperfect but the best data available.

12. For the flow of history prior to the Industrial Revolution, Carlo Cipolla, *Before the Industrial Revolution* (London: Methuen, 1976); Jean Gimpel, *The Medieval Machine* (Aldershot: Wildwood House, 1988); Abbott Payson Usher, *A History of Medieval Inventions* (New York: Dover, 1988).

13. Ben Marsden, *Watt's Perfect Engine* (Cambridge: Icon, 2002).

14. Richard Lipsey, Kenneth Carlaw and Clifford Bekar, *Economic Transformations: General Purpose Technologies and Long Term Economic Growth* (Oxford: Oxford University Press, 2005).

15. T. S. Ashton, *The Industrial Revolution, 1760–1830* (Oxford: Oxford University Press, 1948).

16. The machines mainly centred on new equipment to automate spinning of cotton, including James Hargreaves's spinning jenny and Richard Arkwright's water frame. The historian Robert Allen has summed up important points linking these inventions and the wider context: 'The crux in explaining why the industrial revolution was invented in Britain is, therefore, explaining why British inventors spent so much time and money doing research and development ... to operationalize what were often banal ideas. The key is that the machines they invented increased the use of capital to

save labour. Consequently they were profitable to use where labour was expensive and capital was cheap, that is, in England. Nowhere else were the machines profitable. That is why the Industrial Revolution was British' (Robert Allen, *Global Economic History: A Very Short Introduction* (Oxford: Oxford University Press, 2011), p. 33).

17. Angus Maddison, private communication, 9 June 2006.

18. Bairoch, 'International industrialisation levels'.

19. Computerized scan of Shakespeare's work carried out by the author in March 2011.

20. For details of etymology, see http://www.etymonline.com/index.php?term=manufacture. This defines 'manufacture' as first seeing use in the 1560s, meaning 'something made by hand'. The word was derived from the Latin *manus* ('hand') and *factura* 'a working'. See also for definitions and derivations of 'industry', http://www.thefreedictionary.com/industry. According to this, 'industry' derives from the French *industrie*, meaning skill, which in turn comes from the Latin *industria*.

21. An immense literature has been created about the UK's Industrial Revolution. According to E. J. Hobsbawm, the Industrial Revolution 'marks the most fundamental transformation in the history of the world recorded in written documents' (Hobsbawm, *Industry and Empire* (London: Penguin, 1969), p. 13). See also Peter Matthias, The *First Industrial Nation: The Economic History of Britain 1700–1914* (London: Routledge, 1983); A. E. Musson, *The Growth of British Industry* (London: Batsford, 1978); W. H. B. Court, *A Concise Economic History of Britain: From 1750 to Recent Times* (Cambridge: Cambridge University Press, 1967); Keith Dawson, *The Industrial Revolution* (London: Pan, 1972); Maxine Berg, *The Age of Manufactures, 1700–1820: Industry, Innovation and Work in Britain* (London: Routledge, 1994).

22. Robert Bruen, 'Overcoming greatness: the decline and recovery of British mathematics in the post-Newton era', 1995 (http://www.lucasianchair.org/papers/newton-effect.html). See also for Babbage's time at Cambridge, http://www.bbc.co.uk/history/historic_figures/babbage_charles.shtml.

23. Charles Babbage, *On the Economy of Machinery and Manufactures* (London, 1832), p. 7.

24. Henry Bessemer, *Sir Henry Bessemer, F.R.S.: An Autobiography*, 1905.

25. James Mitchell, The Bessemer Centenary Lecture, Royal Institution, London, 1956.

26. Hobsbawm, *Industry and Empire*, p. 116, also diagram 24.

27. Bessemer, *Sir Henry Bessemer*.

28. Henry Bessemer, 'The manufacture of malleable iron and steel without fuel', paper delivered to the British Association, London, Aug. 1856.

29. In 1867, William Siemens, a German engineer working in the UK, made steel from pig iron in a reverberatory furnace – the precursor of what became known as the open hearth furnace. (William, who was later knighted, was a younger brother of Werner von Siemens, the electrical engineer who founded the Siemens engineering company in Berlin in 1847.) Also in 1867, the French manufacturer Pierre-Émile Martin used the idea to produce steel by melting wrought iron with steel scrap. A combination of the ideas from the two men is at the heart of open-hearth steel-making, a way of making steel which minimizes heat losses and also provides a way to make use of scrap steel as a raw material. The open-hearth process became the main steel-making method by the 1890s. Later the basic oxygen process – a new variant on the steel-making procedure – superseded both these methods. The basic oxygen process is the main steel-making procedure today, using pig iron from blast furnaces.

30. Obituary of Carnegie, *New York Times*, 12 Aug. 1919, http://www.nytimes.com/learning/general/onthisday/bday/1125.html.

31. Data for world steel output from 1900 onwards from ISSB.

32. For details of the US's overtaking the UK, George Wallis and Joseph Whitworth, *The American System of Manufactures* (Edinburgh: Edinburgh University Press, 1969). See also Martin Wiener, *English Culture and the Decline of Industrial Spirit, 1850–1980* (Cambridge: Cambridge University Press, 1981).

33. Bairoch, 'International industrialisation levels'; also see ISSB data.

34. In 1890, Abram Hewitt, a US steel-maker and engineer who went on to become a mayor of New York, paid Bessemer this tribute: 'A very few considerations will serve to show that the Bessemer invention takes its rank with the great events which have changed the face of society since the time of the Middle Ages' (http://www.history. rochester.edu/ehp-book/shb/hb11.htm).

35. The notion of the world having been subjected to periodic episodes of major technology-driven change – which could be labelled new 'industrial revolutions' – goes back to the early twentieth century. In the 1920s the Russian economist Nikolai Dmitrijewitsch Kondratieff noted the emergence of concerted periods of growth sparked by new thinking aided by technology. Later these periods were christened 'Kondratieff waves' (http://faculty.washington.edu/krumme/207/development/long-waves.html). Following on from these ideas, it became possible to conjure up the notion of new industrial revolutions following the first one in the eighteenth century. Also Peter Marsh, *The Robot Age* (London: Abacus, 1982); Alvin Toffler, *The Third Wave* (London: Pan, 1981); Peter Schwartz, Peter Leyden and Joel Hyatt, *The Long Boom* (London: Orion, 2000).

36. For insights into the chemicals industry and its contribution to the global economy, Ashish Arora, Ralph Landau and Nathan Rosenberg (eds), *Chemicals and Long-Term Economic Growth: Insights from the Chemical Industry* (London: John Wiley, 1998); Peter Spitz, *Petrochemicals: The Rise of an Industry* (London: John Wiley, 1988); British Plastics Federation, *The World of Plastics* (London: British Plastics Federation, 1986).

37. The broad notion that as experience in manufacturing went up, costs went down, had been known about for many years. In *An Inquiry into the Nature and Causes of the Wealth of Nations* (1776), Adam Smith pointed out: 'It is the natural effect of improvement, however, to diminish gradually the real price of almost all manufactures. That of the manufacturing workmanship diminishes, perhaps, in all of them without exception. In consequence of better machinery, of greater dexterity, and of a more proper division and distribution of work, all of which are the natural effects of improvement, a much smaller quantity of labour becomes requisite for executing any particular piece of work, and though, in consequence of the flourishing circumstances of the society, the real price of labour should rise very considerably, yet the great diminution of the quantity will generally much more than compensate the greatest rise which can happen in the price. There are, indeed, a few manufactures in which the necessary rise in the real price of the rude materials will more than compensate all the advantages which improvement can introduce into the execution of the work. In carpenters' and joiners' work, and in the coarser sort of cabinet work, the necessary rise in the real price of barren timber, in consequence of the improvement of land, will more than compensate all the advantages which can be derived from the best machinery, the greatest dexterity, and the most proper division and distribution of work. But in all cases in which the real price of the rude materials either does not rise at all, or does not rise very much, that of the manufactured commodity sinks very considerably.'

38. Wright published his ideas related to the experience curve in the February 1936 *Journal of the Aeronautical Science*. Louis Yelle, 'Adding life cycles to learning curves', *Long Range Planning* 16:6 (Dec. 1983): 82.

39. Boston Consulting Group, with foreword by Bruce Henderson, *Perspectives on Experience* (Boston: Boston Consulting Group, 1972).

40. Vannevar Bush, 'As we may think', *The Atlantic*, July 1945.

41. For details of Eniac, Peter Marsh, *The Silicon Chip Book* (London: Abacus, 1981), p. 4. For more insights into microelectronics technology, T. R. Reid, *Microchip: The Story of a Revolution and the Men Who Made It* (London: Pan, 1985); Tom Forester (ed.), *The Microelectronics Revolution* (Oxford: Blackwell, 1980).

42. Throughout the book, monetary figures are given in dollars, with conversions from other currencies done at prevailing exchange rates.

43. Details of numbers of computers, Ernest Braun and Stuart MacDonald, *Revolution in Miniature: The History and Impact of Semiconductor Electronics* (Cambridge: Cambridge University Press, 1978), p. 114.

44. *Scientific American* 237:3 (1977), *Microelectronics* issue, p. 5.

45. The author was responsible for extensive coverage in the *Financial Times* of the Mittal Steel/Arcelor bid battle in 2006. See for instance *Financial Times*, 28 Jan. 2006, 24 Feb. 2006, 26 May 2006.

46. Dollé had worked for most of his career at Usinor, a big French steel-maker that in 2002 merged with two other big European steel producers to form Arcelor.

47. Peter Marsh, 'Man of steel with a showman's flair for flying in the face of the improbable – FT Man of the Year Lakshmi Mittal', *Financial Times*, 23 Dec. 2006.

48. *Financial Times*, 27 Oct. 2004.

49. *Financial Times*, 4 Feb. 2006.

50. *Financial Times*, 5 Apr. 2006. For a slightly breathless account of the takeover battle, see Tim Bouquet and Byron Ousey, *Cold Steel: Britain's Richest Man and the Multi-Billion-Dollar Battle for a Global Empire* (London: Little, Brown, 2008).

51. *Financial Times*, 26 June 2006.

52. In 2000 BCE, with its price put into 2010 monetary values, to adjust for inflation over the past 4,000 years, iron sold for $10,000 a kilogram. With changes in technology, the price of 1 kilogram of iron in 1000 BCE was $500 (at 2010 prices). At the time of the Norman Conquest, 2,000 years later, it was $70. By 2010, the price was 50 cents a kilogram. Over the 3,000 years to 2010, the price of iron fell by an inflation-adjusted 99.9 per cent. Over 4,000 years to 2010, the price adjustment was 99.995 per cent.

53. Historical details of world manufacturing output are from IHS Global Insight, 'Global manufacturing output data 1980–2010, with split between different countries/regions', dataset made available to the author, Aug. 2008, with additional figures provided 20 Oct. 2011. In the opinion of the author, the IHS data give a more complete view of world manufacturing output than comparable figures available from the United Nations Statistical Division and World Bank.

54. The way of dividing the world into 'developed' and 'developing' economies – with variants such as 'rich' and 'poor' also capable of being used – dates to the 1960s. Asa Briggs, in chapter 1 of Briggs et al., *Technology and Economic Development* (London: Penguin, 1963): 'A circumstance new to history stretches the tensions of contemporary world politics. This is the widespread awareness of the divisions of nations into two classes, "developed" and "developing" in the parlance of the day or, in plainer words, rich and poor' (p. 15). Briggs put into the developed category 'the nations of north-western Europe and those elsewhere in the temperate zones that were settled and organized by people of the same stock: the US, Canada, Australia, and New Zealand', together with Japan and the USSR. All others were in the 'developing' regions. Briggs estimated that in the early 1960s the developed nations produced and consumed more than two-thirds of the world's goods.

55. IHS Global Insight dataset. In 2010, according to data from IHS, China was responsible for 19.4 per cent of world manufacturing output, ahead of the US with 18.2 per cent. Comparable UN data, available 31 December 2011, agree that China took over from the US in 2010 as the world's largest manufacturing nation by output. The UN data put China's share of factory output in 2010 at 18.6 per cent, compared to the US's share at 18.1 per cent.

## 2 The power of technology

1. Hans Bünte, *300 Years of Dillinger Steel Works* (Dillingen: Dillinger Hüttenwerke, 1985).

2. The postwar restructuring of Europe's iron and steel industry led, in 1948, to Dillinger Hütte coming under the control of the Société Lorraine de Laminage Continu (Sollac), a company headquartered in Paris but with operations scattered through France. (After the Second World War, the Saar area was transferred from German control to that of France, although Germany resumed ownership in 1957.) In 2001 Dillinger became partly owned by Arcelor, the pan-European steel-maker created by a merger of the three biggest steel companies of France, Luxembourg and Spain.

3. *Financial Times*, 11 June 2008; also *FT*, 15 Dec. 2008.

4. *Financial Times*, 27 Apr. 2005; also *FT*, 12 Oct. 2004.

5. Calculations based on estimates by Davies.

6. John Weston and N. E. Otter (pseud.), *Otter: The First Forty Years* (Buxton: Otter Controls, 1986).

7. Strix, *Strix Group: The First Fifty Years* (Isle of Man: Strix, 2001). The publication marked the fiftieth anniversary of the start of what had originally been an Otter factory, established in Castletown, Isle of Man, in 1951. John Taylor moved from the UK to run this factory in 1979. In 1982, he started Strix as a breakaway business from Otter. In the process he took control of the Castletown factory to make it part of the new company.

8. *Financial Times*, 27 Apr. 2005.

9. Hussey interview with author, Isle of Man, 2 July 2009.

10. Capela interview with author, São Paulo, 28 Sept. 2006.

11. Computer-aided analysis is an all-embracing description for the full range of software-based techniques useful in manufacturing. Computer-aided design (CAD) – a way of designing products in three dimensions – is a better-known term for a big part of what computer-aided analysis encompasses.

12. Spending on product development and computer-aided analysis software are estimates by the author, aided by telephone interview on 27 Jan. 2012 with Carl Bass, chief executive of Autodesk, a large US producer of software for computer-aided design.

13. Lang telephone interview with author, 19 Nov. 2011. Lang gained his first experience in three-dimensional CAD from 1963 to 1965 at Massachusetts Institute of Technology and then from 1965 to 1975 at the Cambridge University computer laboratory. In 1974 he was a co-founder of Shape Data, a Cambridge CAD company which was an early leader in this field, later helping to start Three-Space, another company in the same discipline.

14. John Gantz and David Reinsel, *Extracting Value from Chaos* (Framingham, MA: IDC, 2011).

15. According to Google, the number of books written up to 2010 came to 130 million. An average size modern book contains about 800 kilobytes. One byte equals 8 bits, the smallest amount of information recognizable by a computer. A rough rule is that one average English word requires 8–10 bytes to be described in digital form, including necessary punctuation and formatting information. See http://booksearch.blogspot.com/2010/08/books-of-world-stand-up-and-be-counted.html.

16. The first 787 jet was delivered to the Japanese airline ANA in September 2011, three years late. Boeing then had an order book for 800 of these new wide-body aircraft, worth about $100 billion, *Financial Times*, 11 Nov. 2011.

17. Siegfried Giedion, *Mechanisation Takes Command* (London: Norton, 1969).

18. Historical details for the CAD industry in Viktor von Buchstab, 'Fifty years of CAD history', *Design Engineering* (Oct. 2005). See Peter Marsh, 'A dream they never sold', *Financial Times*, 9 June 1986.

19. On the assumption that the average person in 2010 eats food containing 1,500 kcals (6.3 megajoules) a day, roughly equivalent to the energy stored in a third of a tonne of a typical food crop, the energy consumed and used by the average person during 2010 was 2.3 gigajoules. For all 6.9 billion people this works out at 15.8 billion GJ, or about 3 per cent of the world's total modern energy requirements.

20. A joule is a basic unit of energy. It is roughly equivalent to the work done by a person lifting a tennis ball 2 metres off the ground. The joule is named after James Prescott Joule, a nineteenth-century English physicist and brewer. See M. T. Westra, *Energy, Powering Your World* (Rijnhuizen: Institute for Plasma Physics, 2005). Another useful guide is the HyperPhysics website organized by the Department of Physics and Astronomy, Georgia State University (http://hyperphysics.phy-astr.gsu.edu/hbase/work.html).

21. Usher, *A History of Medieval Inventions*.

22. In the late eleventh century, according to John Ziman, 70 per cent of Europe's energy needs (excluding energy developed by people's muscles) came from animals, with the remaining 30 per cent attributable to watermills: John Ziman (ed.), *Technological Innovation as an Evolutionary Process* (Cambridge: Cambridge University Press, 2000), p. 77.

23. Mokyr, *The Lever of Riches*, p. 60.

24. Boyan Jovanovic and Peter Rousseau, 'General purpose technologies', in Philippe Aghion and Steven Durlauf (eds), *Handbook of Economic Growth*, vol. 1B (London: Elsevier, 2005).

25. Lynn White, *Medieval Religion and Technology* (Berkeley: University of California Press, 1978).

26. Lewis Mumford, *Technics and Civilisation* (London: Routledge & Kegan Paul, 1934).

27. In 1725, Leupold wrote that the 'best machines are those which consist of the fewest parts, or which are the simplest, which produce less friction, which are not too heavily loaded, and where power can be applied without any waste.' Leupold's comments are cited in Friedrich Klemm, *A History of Western Technology* (London: George Allen, 1959).

28. Von Siemens's comment in James Carey, *Communication as Culture: Essays on Media and Society* (New York: Routledge, 2009), p. 96.

29. David Landes, *The Unbound Prometheus: Technical Change and Industrial Development in Western Europe from 1750 to the Present* (Cambridge: Cambridge University Press, 1969).

30. Charles Parsons, *The Steam Turbine* (Cambridge: Cambridge University Press, 1911).

31. John Zink, 'Steam turbines power an industry: a condensed history of steam turbines', *Power Engineering* (1 Aug. 1996).

32. American Society of Mechanical Engineers, 'The world's first industrial gas turbine set, GT Neuchâtel: a historic mechanical engineering landmark' (http://files.asme.org/asmeorg/Communities/History/Landmarks/12281.pdf).

33. Siemens, 'Materials for the environment – world's largest gas turbine', Siemens, 2007.

34. Drew Robb, 'Combined cycle gas turbines: breaking the 60 per cent efficiency barrier', *Power Engineering International* (1 Mar. 2010).

35. R. U. Ayres and B. Warr, 'Accounting for growth: the role of physical work', *Structural Change and Economic Dynamics* 16:2 (2005): 181–209. See also 'The price of age', *The Economist*, 21 Dec. 2000 (http://www.economist.com/node/457272?story_id=457272); and http://www.santafe.edu/media/workingpapers/09-12-047.pdf; http://www.energy-bulletin.net/node/50353.

36. Sir Ralph Robins, 'Striving for perfection', Rolls-Royce, Derby, 2005.

37. Nagamori's comments in interview with author, Kyoto, 6 Oct. 2010. See *Financial Times*, 1 Nov. 2010.

38. Estimates from Nagamori.

39. The 2030 sales target is part of a long-held set of ambitions for Nagamori, confirmed to the author in 2010.

40. Rosenberg interview with author, London, 19 June 2003. See *Financial Times*, 22 Oct. 2003.

## 3 The spice of life

1. Philip Gibbs, 'Is glass liquid or solid?', Usenet Physics Frequently Asked Questions, 1996 (http://www.desy.de/user/projects/Physics/General/Glass/glass.html).
2. Descriptions of the glass industry in history are in Madeline Chinnici, *Innovations in Glass* (Corning, NY: Corning Museum of Glass, 1999); L. M. Angus-Butterworth, *The Manufacture of Glass* (London: Pitman, 1948); Richard Price (ed.), *The Corning Museum of Glass: A Guide to the Collections* (Corning, NY: Corning Museum of Glass, 2001).
3. David Landes, *The Wealth and Poverty of Nations: Why Are Some So Rich and Others So Poor?* (London: Little, Brown, 1998), p. 280.
4. Bisazza interview with the author, Dec. 2006, with extra information from the company in July 2010.
5. Galbraith, *The Affluent Society* (London: Hamish Hamilton, 1958).
6. Alta Macadam (ed.), *Blue Guide – Venice* (London: Ernest Benn, 1980), p. 103.
7. Whitney's career, Landes, *The Unbound Prometheus*, pp. 307–8. Whitney had a big role in making interchangeable parts a widely used technique – even though Landes thinks his role in initiating use of the ideas in modern times has been overemphasized.
8. Mokyr, *The Lever of Riches*, pp. 104–5.
9. 'The life of Henry Ford', from Henry Ford Museum (http://hfmgv.org/exhibits/hf/).
10. 'Model T Ford production', compiled by R. E. Houston, Ford Production Department, 3 Aug. 1927 (www.mtfca.com/encyclo/fdprod.htm).
11. The price dropped to $290 in 1923. For price data see Daniel Vaughan, '1914 Ford Model T news, pictures, and information' (http://www.conceptcarz.com/vehicle/z1676/ford-model-t.aspx).
12. Ford remark in Peter Drucker, *Management* (London: Pan, 1979), p. 196.
13. Ford defended his methods against allegations that he had 'de-skilled' the workplace. Ford said: 'We have put a higher skill into planning, management, and tool building, and the results of that skill are enjoyed by the man who is not skilled' (Henry Ford, *My Life and Work* (New York: Doubleday, 1922)).
14. In 1914, 13,000 workers at Ford made 260,720 cars using mass production techniques. The rest of the US car industry made roughly the same number of vehicles, but with nearly five times as many workers, who mainly used older, craft-based techniques.
15. Diebold, *Automation* (1952; New York: American Management Associations, 1983), p. 59. Diebold wrote: 'Many of the automatic and partially automatic factories so widely written about depend on inflexible production machinery of the type which is adaptable only to extremely long runs of product and useless for the more common medium of short runs . . . Only when the problem of automatic production of medium and short runs is solved will automatic control mechanisms be used to fullest advantage and on the widest scale.' Also, Peter Marsh, 'From mechanization to automation', adapted from *The Robot Age* (http://www.scribd.com/doc/30327610/2-4-a-From-Mechanization-to-Automation).
16. Peter Drucker, *Management: Tasks, Responsibilities, Practices* (New York: Harper & Row, 1973), p. 150.
17. Ibid., p. 151.
18. Krafcik used the expression for the first time in 'Triumph of the lean production system', *Sloan Management Review* (Oct. 1988).
19. James Womack, Daniel Jones and Daniel Roos, *The Machine That Changed the World* (New York: Simon & Schuster, 1990), p. 11.

20. One of the goals of lean production is to eliminate the need for large stocks of parts and finished goods, even though customers are being given greater choice of products – a target that with earlier systems of production would nearly always involve a build-up in inventories. Flexible mass production or high-volume customization is also aimed at minimizing complexity, a factor that is generally assumed to increase as product variety rises. How to cope with these different requirements – which were normally thought extremely tough to reconcile – was noted by James Abegglen and George Stalk in a book in 1985. 'Increasing complexity is the bane of a factory manager's life. With increasing complexity comes an increased number of parts, greater material handling and inventory, more diverse product flows, higher supervision requirements, an increase of errors and defects and smaller batches produced in shorter runs. However there are many reasons for increasing complexity. Product lines are expanded to meet changes in consumer demand or to exploit a market niche where prices are higher or at least firmer' (Abegglen and Stalk, *Kaisha, the Japanese Corporation* (New York: Basic Books, 1985)).

21. Details of Toyoda's career, William Mass and Andrew Robertson, 'From textiles to automobiles: mechanical and organizational innovation in the Toyoda enterprises, 1895–1933', *Business and Economic History* 25:2 (Winter 1996).

22. Jeffrey Liker, *The Toyota Way* (New York: McGraw-Hill, 2004), p. 16.

23. Details of the plant's layout, Vivian Baulch and Patricia Zacharias, 'The Rouge plant – the art of industry', *Detroit News*, 11 July 1997 (http://apps.detnews.com/apps/history/index.php?id=189).

24. For Ohno's thoughts in the US, Toyota, *The Toyota Production System: Leaner Manufacturing for a Greener Planet* (Tokyo: Toyota Motor Company, 1998), p. 6.

25. Brad Stratton, 'Gone but never forgotten', *Quality Progress* (W. Edwards Deming Institute)(Mar. 1994).

26. The figures are from International Organization of Motor Vehicle Manufacturers (OICA), 'World motor vehicle production, 2008' (http://oica.net/wp-content/uploads/world-ranking-2008.pdf).

27. *Financial Times*, 21 Jan. 2009.

28. In 2010, the company discovered faults in some of its cars' accelerator systems in the US, potentially endangering drivers and other road users. It was forced to pay the US government a total of $49 million to settle two cases where it failed to comply with rules over vehicle recalls (Bernard Simon and Jonathan Soble, 'Toyota fined $32m over recalls failings', *Financial Times*, 22 Dec. 2010). Worries about safety were behind some consumers avoiding buying Toyota cars. The high value of the yen also added to the company's problems, which led to weaker sales and profits. At the end of 2011, it seemed likely that early in 2012 it would lose its position as the biggest auto-maker to either a resurgent General Motors or Germany's Volkswagen (*FT*, 24 Oct. 2011).

29. OICA, 'World motor vehicle production, 2010' (http://oica.net/wp-content/uploads/ranking-2010.pdf). Toyota's own data indicate that in 2010, out of the total of 8.6 million, it produced 4.1 million in Japan and 4.5 million overseas. In 1995 it made 4.4 million in total, 1.2 million of them outside Japan.

30. Toyota is unwilling to say how many variants its production system makes possible, arguing that the issue is too complex. However, conversations with other car-makers by the author indicate that this estimate is plausible. In its UK plant in Oxford (where it produces the Mini compact car) in 2007–8 BMW of Germany made some 200,000 vehicles a year. These vehicles can be made in $10^{16}$ possible variants. BMW says that 'generally the chance of two cars in one year of production [being] completely the same is very low. This would probably only happen if a dealer of two customers deliberately ordered two completely identical cars in the same market' (note from BMW public relations official to the author, 31 Oct. 2007).

31. Mass personalization is relevant especially for products which need to be made different from others so as to fit in with an individual's specific physiology. For

instance, personalized pharmaceuticals that are made to work with the unique biological details of a specific man or woman could be among the 'personalized' products of the future.

32. The mass personalization techniques work in conjunction with the 'progressive' form of lenses that Essilor invented in 1959, which correct for both near- and far-vision defects.

33. Fontanet joined Essilor in 1991 and for most of his career at the company was chief executive, stepping down to take the chairman's role at the end of 2009. His remarks are based on interviews with the author in Paris on 24 March 2004 and 10 October 2011. See also *Financial Times*, 21 Nov. 2011.

34. Essilor's total number of products accounts for the 100 million unique lenses made in 2010 together with an estimated 20 million different lenses made to a 'standard' design. The latter figure is based on an estimate that each standard lens is replicated roughly 10 times in the course of a year.

35. Interview by author with Colin Larkin, plant manager at Basildon tractor factory, 30 Jan. 2012. Of the 21,000 tractors made at the factory in 2011, about 14,000 were different. With the output of the plant valued at $1.3 billion in 2011, the variation quotient for the factory comes out at $93,000.

36. The study was based on questions given to companies in different areas of manufacturing and in different countries in 2006–7. The raw calculation from the survey suggests the average variation score per company is about $30,000. However, based on adjustments to give more weighting to component makers, it is sensible to divide the $30,000 by 10 to give an average adjusted variation score of $3,000.

37. Alvin Toffler was ahead of most commentators in predicting how variability was becoming increasingly important in manufacturing. *Powershift*, Toffler's 1990 book, noted how 'computer-driven technologies are making it possible to turn out increasingly customized goods aimed at niche markets' (Alvin Toffler, *Powershift* (New York: Bantam, 1991), pp. 51–2). Kurt Vonnegut, in *Player Piano* (1952; New York: Dell, 1999), is one of the few novelists who have made a point of emphasizing in a popular book the varied nature of the products associated with modern manufacturing. He devotes a page to a list of products observed on a pile of industrial debris, from air conditioners and amplidynes to zymometers (pp. 335–6).

38. Other companies producing 3D printers, sometimes called 'additive manufacturing' machines, include the US 3D Systems, Britain's Renishaw, Arcam of Sweden and Germany's EOS.

39. Telephone interview by author with Terry Wohlers, 7 Dec. 2011.

40. Aggarwal interview with the author, Vijayanagar, 24 Feb. 2006.

41. The famous line appears in 'The time-piece', a poem in *The Task*, 1785.

### 4 Free association

1. Estimate by the author.

2. Allen had a key role in the 1950s at Lotus, the pioneering UK racing car company started in 1952 by Colin Chapman. Peter Ross, 'Lotus Engineering Company – the first year', 2002(http://www.simplesevens.org/history/FirstYear/FirstYear.htm).

3. Air Bearings was started in 1993 by Ron Henocq. Allen and Henocq had been partners at Westwind but fell out and parted company.

4. The 'value chain' or 'global value chain' is defined in Hubert Escaith and Satoshi Inomata, *Trade Patterns and Global Value Chains in East Asia: From Trade in Goods to Trade in Tasks* (Geneva and Tokyo: World Trade Organization and Institute of Developing Economies, 2011), p. 10. The book states: 'These various steps to obtain finished products can be associated through the notion of a "value chain", which refers to the entire sequence of productive (i.e. value-added) activities, from the conception

of a product to its manufacturing and commercialization. The possibility of slicing up and optimizing value chain activities among multiple companies and various geographical locations has even spawned a broader term – the "global value chain".

5. Hans Christian Andersen, 'The princess and the pea', in *Tales, Told for Children* (Copenhagen: C. A. Reitzel, 1835).

6. Michael Porter, *The Competitive Advantage of Nations* (London: Macmillan, 1998), pp. 41–2.

7. Dagenham's history, Michael MacSems, 'A brief history of Ford of Britain' (http://www. enfostuff.com/history/A_Brief_History_of_Ford_of_Britian.html). In 2000, Ford announced it was stopping car manufacturing at the plant, with the loss of 1,900 jobs, but kept the factory open for making engines.

8. General Motors was started in Flint, Michigan, in 1908 by William Durant. In the next five years, it acquired 25 companies, giving it the base to overtake Ford as the world's biggest automotive supplier. General Motors was among a large group of companies from the US to follow Ford's lead in building European factories.

9. UNCTAD, *The World Investment Report 2011* (Geneva: United Nations Conference on Trade and Development, 2011); UNCTAD, *Assessing the Impact of the Current Financial and Economic Crisis on Global FDI Flows* (Geneva: United Nations Conference on Trade and Development, 2009).

10. The growth in world trade would have been impossible without huge investment in shipping networks and in innovations such as the shipping container; Marc Levinson, *The Box: How the Shipping Container Made the World Smaller and the World Economy Bigger* (Princeton, NJ: Princeton University Press, 2006). See also International Chamber of Shipping and the International Shipping Federation, 'Value of volume of world trade by sea' (http://www.marisec.org/shippingfacts//worldtrade/index.php).

11. The differential varies depending on the type of industry and location and can in some cases be higher than 30–50 per cent.

12. Kasra Ferdows, 'New world manufacturing order', *Industrial Engineer* (Feb. 2003); also Kasra Ferdows, Michael Lewis and Jose Machuca, 'Rapid-fire fulfillment', *Harvard Business Review* (Nov. 2004).

13. Bob Sternfels, a manufacturing specialist at McKinsey, is among the first to have used the term 'hybrid' or 'hybridized' in connection with manufacturing to denote a system where the emphasis is split between operations in high-cost and low-cost countries. Sternfels's comments in Peter Marsh, 'The alloy approach: how industry in the West is learning again to compete', *Financial Times*, 12 Dec. 2006. Also Peter Marsh, 'Foreign makers find advantages on more familiar turf', *Financial Times*, 8 May 2006.

14. Swaminathan telephone interview with author, 31 May 2011.

15. Radjou's comments in Stefan Wagstyl, 'Replicators no more', *Financial Times*, 6 Jan. 2011. Also Arnoud de Meyer and Ann Vereeke, 'How to optimize information sharing in a factory network', *McKinsey Quarterly* (Sept. 2009).

16. Webb interview with author, Poole, 2 Aug. 2010.

17. Scotting interview with author, London, 20 July 2005. *Financial Times*, 15 Sept. 2005.

18. While Tata and Mittal might be expected to be fairly close due to their shared nationality and similar degree of success, the two have very different personalities. Relations between them are at best cordial. In 2011, Tata announced he would be retiring as chairman in December 2012 with his replacement being Cyrus Mistry, a reclusive construction tycoon.

19. In 2011, Tata Motors encountered difficulties in selling its small car in its main India market in India, with the company's marketing approach being one factor, according to critics. It saw more success in the 'big car' end to its business, represented by JLR.

20. Forster interview with author, London, 6 May 2011. Also *Financial Times*, 9 May 2011. Later in 2011, Forster announced he was leaving Tata, with the reasons not publicly explained.

21. Ogawa interview with author, Hitachinaka, 8 Oct. 2010. See also *Financial Times*, 26 Oct. 2010.
22. Noji interview with author, Tokyo, 8 Oct. 2010.
23. Whether Nokia persists with this manufacturing strategy is open to question, as a result of a series of management upheavals during 2011. The changes came after Nokia acted in September 2010 to replace its chief executive Olli-Pekka Kallasvuo with Stephen Elop from Microsoft. The company later announced it was cutting large numbers of jobs at three of its big non-Asian plants, in Finland, Hungary and Mexico. See 'Nokia to slash 4,000 jobs in shift to Asia', *Financial Times*, 9 Feb. 2012.
24. Hultner interview with author, London, 20 May 2008. See also Peter Marsh, 'China's new formula: manufacturers begin to move beyond low cost', *Financial Times*, 29 May 2008.
25. Cutler telephone interview with author, 10 Dec. 2011. Also *Financial Times*, 10 Jan.2011.
26. Stefan Wagstyl, 'Indian R&D unhindered by cost issue', *Financial Times*, 7 Jan. 2011.
27. In 2011, Dyson remained the 100 per cent owner of the company though he was no longer its chairman, taking on instead the role of chief engineer.
28. Dyson interview with the author, Malmesbury, 4 Dec. 2003. See transcript, *Financial Times*, 11 Dec. 2003.
29. In a telephone interview with the author on 14 September 2011, Dyson said he was happy with his version of a hybrid strategy. 'The model [of having design and manufacturing widely separated] works for us, though clearly it would be easier if they were both together', he said (*Financial Times*, 15 Sept. 2011).
30. Knight's career, Jackie Krentzman, 'The force behind the Nike empire', *Stanford Magazine* (Jan.–Feb. 1997).
31. Corsten telephone interview with author, 22 June 2011. Peter Marsh, 'Closed encounters with suppliers', *Financial Times*, 7 July 2011.
32. Teichert interview with author, Landau, 10 Feb. 2005. In an email to the author on 10 Feb. 2012, Teichert confirmed that Einhell's strategy had remained essentially the same since 2005.
33. Due to a problem in the way the parts were designed or made, the vehicles' accelerators no longer worked properly. The affair forced public apologies from Toyota's top executives and dented the company's reputation for reliability and safety, *Financial Times*, 4 Nov. 2010.
34. *Financial Times*, 11 Nov. 2010.
35. Von Faber-Castell interview with author and Richard Milne, Stein, 22 Oct. 2007. Also *Financial Times*, 2 Jan. 2008.
36. The Faber-Castell plant in São Carlos, Brazil, is one of the biggest pencil factories in the world, in around 2010 making some 2 billion pencils a year.
37. Initially, graphite was thought to be a form of lead – mined in northern England. For this reason, the UK's early pencil-makers used 'plumbago' to describe the core to their products. Even though this misunderstanding has long been corrected, the name 'pencil leads' has stuck.
38. The wood comes from California Cedar Products Company, a company in California with operations around the world. The origins of the businesses lies in in Berolzheimer und Illfelder, a pencil-maker started in Fürth, a town near Stein, in 1856 by Heinrich Berolzheimer, the great-great grandfather of Charles Berolzheimer, CCP's president in 2011. Heinrich had emigrated to the US in the 1880s, where he set up Eagle Pencil Company, with his descendants later moving into the wood part of the business, and leaving pencil-making behind. This was done through a grandson of Heinrich Berolzheimer – also called Charles – acquiring CCP in 1927.
39. Peter Marsh, 'High and dry', *Financial Times*, 13 Apr. 2011. The need for flexibility in supply chain operations is one focused on by many commentators in the 2009–11

period; for instance see Yogesh Malik, Alex Niemeyer and Brian Ruwadi, 'Building the supply chain of the future', *McKinsey Quarterly* (Jan. 2011).

40. Various quasi-mathematical formulas have been published that can help companies to work out which parts of the world are the right places for plants in specific sectors to be located. The author produced one such study that analysed 50 types of manufactured goods – ranging from heart implants to shoes – to illustrate how the different factors interrelate. (See Peter Marsh, 'How the FT's scoring system for location of manufacturing works', *Financial Times*, 24 June 2004.) Phil Hanson and other industrial experts at the Institute for Manufacturing at the University of Cambridge have devised a set of mathematical tools for deciding where to put the different elements of companies' value chains, depending on factors such as operating costs, who the customers are, resources such as availability of labour, risks including the possibilities of supply chain disruptions, speed of capability to alter arrangements in an emergency and the degree of innovative thinking available at the location or in the local supply network.

## 5 Niche thinking

1. Data are based on the author's estimates.
2. Modern thinking on how companies can exploit their advantages in narrow industries started in the 1990s. For 'sliver strategies', see Lowell Bryan et al., *Race for the World: Strategies to Build a Great Global Firm* (Boston: Harvard Business School Press, 1999). The authors wrote: 'Twenty years from now some $50 trillion [$50,000 billion] of globally integrated economic activity will permit an extraordinary degree of specialization. An economy of this size could easily be disaggregated into 5,000 global business arenas, each representing $10 billion of production. Or perhaps 50,000 "global microbusiness arenas", each of which would represent $1 billion of production. Or, more likely still, 5 million tightly defined "global nanostructures" representing $10 million of production each.' Also Peter Marsh, 'A little goes a long way – niche companies are using technological advances and the internet to win global customers', *Financial Times*, 4 Jan. 2001.
3. Shih's remarks in interview with author and Kathrin Hille, Taipei, 27 Sept. 2004; also *Financial Times*, 24 Nov. 2005.
4. Collins's comments cited in Hermann Simon, *Hidden Champions of the 21st Century: Success Strategies of Unknown World Market Leaders* (New York: Springer, 2009), p. 14.
5. Simon has put his views in two books, ibid. and *Hidden Champions: Lessons from 500 of the World's Best Unknown Companies* (Boston: Harvard Business School Press, 1996).
6. Corning's sales includes products other than LCD glass. In 2010 the company had sales of LCD glass of $3 billion in its wholly owned operations. It sold another $4.8 billion of this glass through its Samsung Corning Precision (SCP) joint venture with Samsung of South Korea, where both companies have a 50 per cent stake. However, the technology used in this venture mostly belongs to Corning. Taking into account the $7.8 billion combined sales of both businesses, Corning's LCD glass operations are normally regarded as accounting for about 60 per cent of the world's LCD business. Since the matter is sensitive, Corning does not divulge what it considers to be its share. However, the company's LCD glass activities are highly profitable. In 2010, this part of Corning's operations, including the contribution from SCP, contributed $3 billion of Corning's $3.6 billion net income.
7. Details of Corning's growth are in Margaret Graham and Alec Shuldiner, *Corning and the Craft of Innovation* (New York: Oxford University Press, 2001).
8. Day's comments in ibid., p. 33.
9. Flaws interview with author, London, 20 Mar. 2007.

10. Data for the LCD business mainly estimated by the author, aided by information from Corning.
11. Simon, *Hidden Champions of the 21st Century*, p. 20.
12. Willis interview with author, Elverson, 30 Sept. 2008. See also *Financial Times*, 11 Feb. 2009.
13. McMurtry interview with author, Wotton-under-Edge, 19 Oct. 2011.
14. Radice interview with author, Villa Cortese, 2 June 1997. See also *Financial Times*, 9 Sept. 1997. As of 2011, Radice was still in charge of his family company, along with Marisa Carnaghi, his wife.
15. From Simon, *Hidden Champions of the 21st Century*, p. 18. Simon's study is far from exhaustive but is probably the most complete survey of companies of this sort yet conducted.
16. Ibid., p. 30. The figures are based on a relatively small sample of 134 companies out of 1,316 that Simon and his research colleagues approached. The data should be used with care, but they underline the strong underlying growth capabilities of many niche companies. Also Bernd Venohr, *How Germany's Mid-Sized Companies Get Ahead and Stay Ahead in the Global Economy*, 2008 (http://www.berndvenohr.de/download/vortraege/GermanMidSizedGiants_080615.pdf). In 2011, Germany had 28 privately owned industrial goods manufacturers, many of them leaders in niche fields, with annual sales of $3 billion or more, according to estimates by the author (*Financial Times*, 30 Aug. 2011).
17. Krubasik remarks at German–British Forum conference, London, 23 Nov. 2010.
18. For a depiction of these conditions, including a vivid account of the development of a typical postwar German engineering success story, Hermann Kronseder, *My Life* (Neutrabling, Bavaria: Krones, 1993). Kronseder was the founder of Krones, a German company which is the world's biggest maker of bottling systems.
19. Raith interview with author, Herzogenaurach, 10 Feb. 2000. See also Peter Marsh, 'The families who engineer a German success story', *Financial Times*, 15 Apr. 2000. Raith retired in 1999 as chief executive of Schaeffler, then called by its former name INA, to be replaced with Jürgen Geissinger, who in 2011 was still running the company. INA was founded in 1946 by brothers Wilhelm and Georg Schaeffler, and was run by the two of them, and then, when Wilhelm died, by Georg on his own until his death in 1996, when Raith replaced him.
20. Stewart Fleming, 'Survivor in a stricken industry', *Financial Times*, 26 Sept. 1983.
21. Leibinger interview with author, Ditzingen, 19 June 1996. Also *Financial Times*, 23 Sept. 1996. In 2005 Leibinger retired as chief executive of Trumpf, being replaced by his daughter Nicola Leibinger-Kammüller, but continued as supervisory board chairman. In 2011, he was still in this position.
22. Leibinger interview with author, Ditzingen, 22 June 1998. *Financial Times*, 23 Sept. 1999.
23. Bostelmann interview with author, Chard, 13 Aug. 2010. *Financial Times*, 28 Sept. 2010.
24. Interview by author with Hitoshi Mizorogi, Disco chief executive, Tokyo, 4 Oct. 2010.
25. Umicore's history, René Brion and Jean-Louis Moreau, *Materials for a Better Life: Two Hundred Years of Entrepreneurship and Innovation in Metals and Materials* (Brussels: Umicore, 2005).
26. Heidsieck interview with author, Hanau, 26 Feb. 2002, *Financial Times*, 11 Apr. 2002. Heidsieck left Heraeus in 2003.
27. Barber interview with author, Amersham, 25 July 2003. Barber retired as Halma chairman in 2003, having stepped down as chief executive in 1995. In 2011, Halma's strategy still contained most of the elements mapped out by Barber. (Interview by author with Andrew Williams, Halma chief executive, Windsor, 4 Oct. 2011.)

28. In January 2012, Putzmeister was acquired by Sany, a big Chinese maker of construction machines, for $690 million (Chris Bryant, 'Sany set to buy German pump-maker', *Financial Times*, 30 Jan. 2012).
29. Gilbert Nolde (ed.), *All in a Day's Work: Seventy-Five Years of Caterpillar* (Peoria, IL: Caterpillar, 2000).
30. Virtual replacement of cable-actuated machinery by hydraulic equipment from the 1940s onwards, Clayton Christensen, *The Innovator's Dilemma: When New Technologies Cause Great Firms to Fail* (Boston: Harvard Business School Press, 1997), pp. 64–73.
31. The son of a Paris tax collector, Pascal's work in hydraulics led him to devise the forerunner of the modern barometer (James Burke, *Connections* (London: Macmillan, 1978), p. 74). Details of the link between Pascal and Bramah are provided in Wessels Living History Farm project, http://www.livinghistoryfarm.org/farminginthe40/machines_11.html. For applications of hydraulics in medieval times, Derek Birdsall and Carlo Cipolla, *The Technology of Man* (London: Wildwood House, 1980), p. 89.
32. For Maudslay's contribution to developments in interchangeable parts production, see chapter 3.
33. Information from Mike Baunton.
34. *Financial Times*, 20 Sept. 2007. Diether Klingelnberg stepped down as chief executive in 2004, handing over to his son Jan – the seventh generation of the Klingelnberg family to be in charge of the company.
35. Yasunori Kuba, *Master of Manufacturing Technology: The 70-Year History of Mazak* (Tokyo: ND Publications, 2009).
36. At http://www.mazak.co/englis/index.html (as of June 2011).
37. At http://www.hilti.co/holcom (as of June 2011).
38. At http://www.woodward.com (as of June 2011).
39. At http://www.tente.co/ (as of June 2011).
40. At http://www.blum.co/ (as of June 2011).
41. Evrell telephone interview with author, Dec. 2000, *Financial Times*, 4 Jan. 2001.
42. Munters' service division was acquired in October 2010 by Triton Partners, a German private equity business, on the basis that it could perform better split away from the product operations. At around the same time, the rest of Munters was purchased by Cidron Intressenter, a Swedish financial group.
43. Ludwig interview with author, London, 12 June 2007; see also *Financial Times*, 25 Oct. 2007. 'Having a service capability differentiates us from companies that sell lighting components but nothing else,' Ludwig said. Ludwig left the job of chief executive in 2010 and joined the company's supervisory board.
44. Rocca interview with author, Buenos Aires, 4 Oct. 2006; see also *Financial Times*, 17 Oct. 2006.

## 6 The environmental imperative

1. Author's estimate based on data from packaging industry. See also Coca-Cola, *2009/2010 Sustainability Review* (Atlanta: Coca-Cola, 2010).
2. Data based on author's estimates, using figures from Fridolin Krausmann. I am grateful to Krausmann for further analysis related to his original data. See Krausmann et al., *Growth in Global Materials Use, GDP and Population during the 20th Century* (Klagenfurt: Institute of Social Ecology, Alpen-Adria University, 2009). Also Iddo Warnick and Jesse Ausubel, 'National materials flows and the environment', *Annual Review of Energy and Environment* 20(1995): 463–92; A. M. Diederen, *Metal Minerals Scarcity: A Call for Managed Austerity and the Elements of Hope* (Rijswijk: TNO Defence, Security and Safety, 2009); Dennis Meadows, 'Perspectives on *Limits to Growth*: 37 years later', World Resources Forum, Davos, 2009; Martin Birtel, Stephan Lutter and Stefan Giljum, 'Global resource use – worldwide patterns of resource

extraction', World Resources Forum, St Gallen, 2008; Mike Ashby, 'Eco-selection: environmentally informed material choice', seminar notes, Cambridge University Engineering Department, 2005.

3. The two most plausible estimates for 2010 global carbon dioxide emissions, counting all human activities, are 33 billion tonnes from the Netherlands Environmental Assessment Agency (PBL), and 38.7 billion tonnes from the World Steel Association (WSA). The International Energy Agency (IEA) provides a lower estimate. (See Netherlands Environmental Assessment Agency, *Long-Term Trend in Global CO2 Emissions, 2011 Report* (The Hague: Netherlands Environmental Assessment Agency, 2011); International Energy Agency, *C02 Emissions from Fuel Combustion: 2010 Edition*, and *C02 Emissions from Fuel Combustion: Highlights, 2011 Edition*.) Of the 38.7 billion tonnes estimate from the WSA, almost 80 per cent is from combustion of carbon-containing fossil fuels, with the rest coming from other industrial and agricultural activities such as forest fires. Both the PBL and IEA data fail to account for some sources of carbon dioxide, from activities not involving fuel consumption, that the WSA figures cover. As a result, the WSA data are regarded by the author as more likely to be correct. The 39 billion tonnes figure for carbon dioxide emissions in 2010 that is used in this chapter is based on the WSA calculations, rounded to the nearest 1 billion tonnes. I am grateful to Henk Reimink of the WSA for help with the data. In 1990, according to PBL, carbon dioxide emissions from all human activities were 22.7 billion tonnes, an increase of 45 per cent on the 1970 level of 15.5 billion tonnes. Using PBL data, which take 33 billion tonnes as world carbon dioxide output in 2010, in that year China was the world's biggest carbon dioxide emitter, with a total of 8.9 billion tonnes, followed by the US with 5.32 billion tonnes. Then came the 27-nation European Union (4 billion tonnes), India (1.8 billion tonnes), Russia (1.7 billion tonnes) and Japan (1.2 tonnes). The largest carbon dioxide emitters in Europe outside Russia in 2010 were Germany (830 million tonnes) and Britain (500 million tonnes). Between 2003 and 2010, carbon dioxide emissions from China doubled, and in India they increased by 60 per cent.

4. International Energy Agency data indicate that producing goods in factories was in 2008–9 and 2009–10 responsible for roughly 30 per cent of total final energy demand and carbon dioxide emissions from man-made sources. The higher figure of about 90 per cent takes into account use of manufactured products: gas turbines for creating electricity, petrol engines for cars, electric motors and so on. Clearly another big factor influencing energy consumption patterns and carbon dioxide emissions is intensity of use. (International Energy Agency, *Key World Energy Statistics, 2010 Edition* (Paris: IEA, 2010); International Energy Agency, *Energy Technology Transitions for Industry: Strategies for the Next Industrial Revolution* (Paris: IEA, 2009); International Energy Agency, *C02 Emissions from Fuel Combustion: 2010 Edition* (Paris: IEA, 2010); International Energy Agency, *C02 Emissions from Fuel Combustion: Highlights, 2011 Edition* (Paris: IEA, 2011).)

5. Duncan Pollard (gen. ed.), *Living Planet Report 2010: Biodiversity, Biocapacity and Development* (Gland, Switzerland: World Wildlife Fund International, 2010).

6. Details of heavy industry in the ancient Roman Empire from Dartmouth Toxic Metals Superfund Research Program, http://www.dartmouth.ed/~toxmeta/toxic-metals/more-metals/copper-history.html.

7. Genesis 1: 28, King James Bible.

8. The verse is a translation of Li Bai's poem 'Tale of sorrowful song'. The verse was used by Gustav Mahler as the basis for 'Das Trinklied vom Jammer der Erde', a song featuring in his 1908 composition *Das Lied von der Erde* ('The song of the earth'). See Chicago Mahlerites, '*Das Lied von der Erde*: the literary changes' (http://www.mahlerarchives.net/DLvDE/DLvDE.htm; http://www.mahlerarchives.net/DLvDE/Das_Trinklied.htm).

9. From 'The parsonage', Book 8 of Wordsworth's poem *The Excursion*, first published in 1814; William Wordsworth, *The Complete Poetical Works* (London: Macmillan, 1888).

10. Ruskin's remarks are from Ruskin, *Unto This Last: Four Essays on the First Principles of Political Economy*, 1862. The relevant passage is: 'Whence it appears that many of the persons commonly considered wealthy, are in reality no more wealthy than the locks of their own strong boxes are, they being inherently and eternally incapable of wealth; and operating for the nation, in an economical point of view, either as pools of dead water, and eddies in a stream . . . or else, as mere accidental stays and impediments, acting not as wealth, but (for we ought to have a correspondent term) as "illth", causing various devastation and trouble around them in all directions.'

11. De Tocqueville, *Journeys to England and Ireland* (1835; Piscataway, NJ: Transaction, 1979). Passage cited in Alasdair Clayre (ed.), *Nature and Industrialization* (Oxford: Oxford University Press, 1977), pp. 117–18.

12. Aldo Leopold, 'Game and wild life conservation', *Condor* 34:2 (1932): 103–6.

13. Arnold Toynbee, *Mankind and Mother Earth* (Oxford: Oxford University Press, 1976), p. 17.

14. One of the most prominent of these studies was Sir Nicholas Stern, *Stern Review on the Economics of Climate Change* (London: HM Treasury, 2006).

15. Lovins telephone interview with author, 14 Aug. 2009.

16. Zeitz speech, London, 24 May 2011. Until 2011, Zeitz was Puma's chief executive, before stepping up to be chairman. He is also chief sustainability officer of PPR, the French group that owns Puma.

17. World Business Council for Sustainable Development, *Sustainable Consumption Facts and Trends: From a Business Perspective* (Geneva: WBCSD, 2008).

18. Kranendijk interview with author, London, 27 Mar. 2009.

19. Lowry interview with author, London, 7 Sept. 2009.

20. Watt interview with author, London, 14 Dec. 2010.

21. Cox telephone interview with author, 9 Apr. 2009.

22. Michael Braungart and William McDonough, *Cradle to Cradle: Remaking the Way We Make Things* (London: Vintage, 2008); also Peter Marsh, 'Green secrets to be shared with industry', *Financial Times*, 20 May 2010.

23. Braungart interview with author, London, 19 May 2009.

24. *The Potential for Substituting Manpower for Energy* was a report by Stahel and Genevieve Reday-Mulvey that described a vision of an 'economy in loops' which features reuse of materials and a minimalist use of energy. The report led to a book, Walter Stahel and Genevieve Reday-Mulvey, *Jobs for Tomorrow, the Potential for Substituting Manpower for Energy* (New York, Vantage Press, 1981). For more details: http://www.product-life.org/en/cradle-to-cradle.

25. Stahel interview with author, London, 2 July 2009.

26. Both sets of comments from Braungart in this paragraph are from interview with author, London, 3 Mar. 2010.

27. The sentence is from Michael Braungart, William McDonough and Andrew Bollinger, 'Cradle-to-cradle design: creating healthy emissions – a strategy for eco-effective product and system design', *Journal of Cleaner Production* 15 (2007).

28. Interview with author, 3 Mar. 2010.

29. Friedrich Schmidt-Bleek, *The Fossil Makers*, trans. Reuben Deumling (Carnoules, Provence: Factor 10 Institute, 1993).

30. Coca-Cola, *2009/2010 Sustainability Review*.

31. Press release on *PET's Carbon Footprint: To Recycle or Not to Recycle*, report on plastic bottle recycling, commissioned by SRI Consulting: http://www.sriconsulting.com/ Press_Releases/Plastic-Bottle-Recycling-Not-Always-Lowest-Carbon-Option_16605. html.

32. Coca-Cola, *Annual Report, 2010* (Atlanta: Coca-Cola, 2011).

33. Data from ArcelorMittal in email 7 Feb. 2012.
34. Ludwig's comments made to the author in a telephone interview, 27 Nov. 2011. In June 2008, the author talked to Ludwig and several other local residents on a visit to Cleveland. The complaints about the works are partly linked to the site being in a natural hollow, which prevents rapid dispersal of airborne pollutants. Nearly half a million people live within 10 kilometres of the facility. There is no evidence that the works has a pollution record any worse than other steel plants of a similar vintage. Between 2008 and 2011, ArcelorMittal says that 'in spite of a challenging economic environment' the Cleveland works has invested in several environmental projects designed to reduce its environmental impact, such as through capturing extra energy from recycled blast furnace gas, reducing the energy consumption of two large boilers on its site and installation of low-pollution burners at a hot strip mill reheat furnace' (email from the company, 4 Feb. 2012).
35. From 1975 to 2005, in steel mills in Western Europe and North America the average energy consumption per tonne of crude steel produced decreased on average by about 50 per cent, as a result of technological improvements. Over the same period, the amount of materials used to make 1 tonne of steel by the blast furnace route fell by 21 per cent, according to the World Steel Association ('Fact sheet: the three Rs of sustainable steel', Brussels, 2011).
36. Hauge's comments sent by email 4 Feb. 2012.
37. ArcelorMittal, *How Will We Achieve Safe Sustainable Steel? Corporate Responsibility Report 2008* (Luxembourg: ArcelorMittal, 2009), p. 32.
38. To make 1 tonne of recycled steel using electric arc furnaces requires 880 kilograms of scrap steel, 150 kilograms of coal and 43 kilograms of limestone (World Steel Association, 'Fact sheet: raw materials').
39. Calculations based on 39 billion tonnes of global carbon dioxide emissions in 2010 from human activities. Out of this, an estimated 13.4 billion tonnes were produced as a direct effect of manufacturing operations. Carbon dioxide emissions from steel plants in 2010 were 2.5 billion tonnes, with 2.3 billion tonnes due to blast furnace-based plants and 200 million tonnes from electric arc furnaces. Data based on IEA statistics. I am grateful to the WSA for help in compiling these estimates.
40. For the world, in 2011 the average amount of carbon dioxide produced when making 1 tonne of steel was roughly 2.3 tonnes for the blast furnace/basic oxygen process route, and 0.7 tonnes for the electric arc process. The latter figure includes the carbon dioxide emitted in electricity generation that is a key requirement for this process. For all steel plants, the world average counting both types of steel was about 1.8 tonnes of carbon dioxide per tonne of steel, according to the WSA.
41. Mittal telephone interview with author, 28 July 2010.
42. Eder's comments in interview with author, London, 1 June 2009.
43. Boston Consulting Group, *Steel's CO2 Balance: A Contribution to Climate Protection* (Chicago: Boston Consulting Group, 2010).
44. Wang telephone interview with author, 17 Mar. 2010.

## 7 China rising

1. The biggest steel-makers in the world in 2010 by output are in a 'league table' from *Metal Bulletin* magazine, http://www.metalbulletin.com/stub.aspx?stubid=12542. In 2010 Ansteel was the seventh biggest Chinese steel producer, with Hebei, Baosteel, Wuhan, Shagang, Shougang and Shandong above it.
2. IHS Global Insight dataset.
3. Data from World Steel Association.
4. Speech by Pascal Lamy, director-general of the World Trade Organization, July 2010 (http://www.wto.org/english/news_e/sppl_e/sppl162_e.htm).

5. See for instance James Kynge, *China Shakes the World* (London: Weidenfeld & Nicolson, 2006); Jimmy Hexter and Jonathan Woetzel, *Operation China: From Strategy to Execution* (Boston: Harvard Business School Press, 2007); Donald Sul, *Made in China* (Boston: Harvard Business School Press, 2005); Ted Fishman, *China Inc.: How the Rise of the Next Superpower Challenges America and the World* (New York: Scribner, 2005).

6. China has benefited from massive inward investment by foreign companies. World Bank and International Bank for Reconstruction and Development, *World Investment and Political Risk* (Washington DC: World Bank, 2011).

7. *The Economist*, 29 July 2010.

8. Dan DiMicco, chairman and chief executive of Nucor, the US steel-maker, is a fierce critic of China's trade policies. Giving evidence to a US House of Representatives committee in 2010, DiMicco said: 'Chinese practices like currency manipulation and illegal subsidies are protectionist. We [the US] must have the will to change the way we work with China. It is time to stop allowing their growth to come at our expense' (http://waysandmeans.house.gov/media/pdf/111/2010Sep15_DiMicco_Testimony.pdf).

9. Other concerns relate to allegations that China uses its growing economic and political muscle to collect technical secrets from competitors by illicit means. See Peter Marsh and Jamil Anderlini, 'Data out of the door', *Financial Times*, 2 Feb. 2011.

10. *Zou chu qu* is mentioned in Yang Zhizhong, 'A real opportunity for the West as China looks abroad', *Financial Times*, 6 Apr. 2011. Also 'Singapore as an energy hub for China, too', *Business Times Singapore*, 27 Oct. 2010.

11. Zhizhong, 'A real opportunity for the West'. Also Grisons Peak Bank, 'Growing Chinese outbound investments in Europe', 2011 (http://www.grisonspeak.com/index.php?page_id=feature_vol9).

12. Zhang interview with author, Anshan, 19 Apr. 2008. Zhang reiterated his thinking in another interview two years later: 'I would like Anshan to be a partner in other steel operations around the world, perhaps in the US, Europe or Australia. We need to be present in other markets [outside China] since this is a good way to test our products and processes to make sure they are up to the best levels of other countries' (interview with author, Tokyo, 4 Oct. 2011; see *Financial Times*, 5 Oct. 2011).

13. Zhang regards Mittal as a role model.

14. Negative sentiments on this score were voiced by Jeff Immelt, chief executive of General Electric, who complained to an audience of Italian executives that China was becoming increasingly protectionist. In a particularly barbed passage, Immelt said he was 'not sure that in the end they [the Chinese government] want any of us [foreign companies] to win, or any of us to be successful' (*Financial Times*, 2 July 2010). Immelt did not intend the remarks to be made public. He later played down his comments. Other business chiefs have voiced more even-handed views. Sandy Cutler, chief executive of Eaton, the US industrial conglomerate, said in 2010: 'There are some political pressures inside China to favour local companies when awarding [government] contracts but this is not the same as saying that the climate is acting to discourage companies based outside China' (*Financial Times*, 28 Dec. 2010).

15. Peter Marsh, 'ArcelorMittal holds discussions with Chinese group over link-up', *Financial Times*, 5 May 2008. The idea of a link was abandoned without any announcement over the following months.

16. Tim Geithner, the US Treasury Secretary, gave voice to these feelings in 2009: 'The undervalued renminbi helps China's export sector and means imports are more expensive in China than they otherwise would be. It undercuts the purchasing power of Chinese households. It encourages outsourcing of production and jobs from the United States. And it makes it more difficult for goods and services produced by American workers to compete with Chinese-made goods and services in China, the

United States, and third countries' (testimony to Senate Committee on Banking, Housing, and Urban Affairs, 16 Sept. 2009, http://banking.senate.gov/public/index. cfm?FuseAction=Files.View&FileStore_id=bfcd0ca0-823f-4d89-aa32-450b3564a2c7).

17. In late 2010, China's reserves came to $2,600 billion, more than any other country's, accounting for 30 per cent of the global total.

18. Johannpeter interview with author, Tokyo, 2 Oct. 2010; *Financial Times*, 4 Oct. 2010.

19. Danjczek interview with author, Tokyo, 3 Oct. 2010.

20. Zhang interview with author, Tokyo, 4 Oct. 2010; *Financial Times*, 5 Oct. 2010.

21. Mokyr, *The Lever of Riches*, p. 209.

22. Landes, *The Wealth and Poverty of Nations*, p. 343. In the same passage Landes explains further China's prevailing cultural characteristic: 'The sense of give-and-take, of standing on the shoulders of giants, of progress – all of these were weak or absent.'

23. Data from International Steel Statistics Bureau.

24. Jung Chang and Jon Halliday, *Mao: The Unknown Story* (London: Vintage, 2005), p. 448.

25. Yeung interview with author, Shajing, 23 Apr. 2008.

26. Styles interview with author, Zhongshan, 23 Apr. 2008; *Financial Times*, 13 Aug. 2008.

27. Wang's comments in John Reed, 'China's car market to triple by 2020', *Financial Times*, 13 Jan. 2011.

28. Daniel Schäfer, 'Chinese push into Germany's heart and soul', *Financial Times*, 11 Aug. 2010.

29. Whiley interview with author, London, 4 Apr. 2011; *Financial Times*, 26 Apr. 2011.

30. Fehrenbach's comments in Daniel Schäfer, 'Reflected glory', *Financial Times*, 19 Jan. 2011.

31. Wen interview with author, Hong Kong, 25 Apr. 2008; Peter Marsh, 'China's new formula: manufacturers begin to move beyond low cost', *Financial Times*, 28 May 2008.

32. Bostelmann interview with author, Chard, 13 Aug. 2010.

33. Lenovo eschews the term 'company headquarters', preferring to call its operational hubs 'centres of excellence'. It believes that a twenty-first-century global company should split power between a number of locations, making the term 'headquarters' inappropriate. Lenovo has three such hubs, with offices in Singapore complementing Morrisville and Beijing.

34. The table tennis table was evident at Lenovo's Morrisville office when the author visited on 9 Oct. 2008.

35. Apart from a four-year spell between 2005 and 2009 when he stepped aside, Liu was in overall charge of Lenovo's direction from 1984 to 2011, when he retired as chairman.

36. Liu's comments in Mure Dickie, 'China's high-tech hero: man in the news Liu Chuanzhi', *Financial Times*, 11 Dec. 2004.

37. Qiu interview with author, Beijing, 18 Apr. 2008.

38. These remarks from Liu were made some 16 months before he retired from the company. Kathrin Hille, 'The man who took his chance', *Financial Times*, 5 July 2010.

39. Patti Waldmeir and John Reed, 'China's can-do carmaker; man in the news Li Shufu', *Financial Times*, 27 Mar. 2010.

40. Day left Johnson Security in 2011.

41. Day telephone interview with author, 7 Apr. 2011.

42. Hessbrüggen comments in Daniel Schäfer, 'Family values galvanise toolmaker', *Financial Times*, 26 Apr. 2011.

43. Taylor telephone interview with author, 6 Apr. 2011; see *Financial Times*, 26 Apr. 2011.

44. Blumenberg retired from his job as the joint venture president at the end of 2011.

45. Blumenberg interview with author, Nanjing, 16 Apr. 2008; see also *Financial Times*, 28 Oct. 2008.

46. Brudermüller interview with author, Hong Kong, 25 Apr. 2008. At the time Brudermüller was head of BASF's Asia activities. He was promoted to vice-chairman in 2011.

**8 Crowd collusion**

1. Kosciuszko wrote these words shortly before his death in 1817. Website of American Association of the Friends of Kosciuszko at West Point, http://www.kosciuszkoatwestpoint.org/custom3.html.
2. World orthopaedic industry sales in 2010 were $39.7 billion, Stryker, *Fact Book, 2010–2011* (Kalamazoo: Stryker, 2011).
3. BioCrossroads, *Warsaw, Indiana: The Orthopedics Capital of the World* (Indianapolis: BioCrossroads, 2009); Timothy Aeppel, 'Sticks and stones may break bones, but Warsaw, Indiana, makes replacements', *Wall Street Journal*, 26 Oct. 2006(http://biocrossroads.com/Documents/2006-News/WSJ-10-26-06.aspx); Jessica DuLong, 'Welcome to Warsaw: Indiana's orthopedics capital of the world', *Today's Machining World* 2:5 (2006).
4. Europa InterCluster, *The Emerging of European World-Class Clusters* (Brussels: Europa InterCluster, 2010); Joseph Cortright, *Making Sense of Clusters: Regional Competitiveness and Economic Development* (Washington DC: Brookings Institution, 2006); Michael Porter, 'Clusters and the new economics of competition', *Harvard Business Review* 76:6 (Nov.–Dec. 1998): 77; Michael Porter, 'Location, competition, and economic development: local clusters in a global economy', *Economic Development Quarterly* 14:1 (Feb. 2000): 15–34. Porter, in *The Competitive Advantage of Nations*, provides a fuller analysis.
5. Claas van der Linde, 'Findings from the cluster meta-study', Institute for Strategy and Competitiveness, Harvard Business School, 2002.
6. For high-tech clusters in Silicon Valley and around Boston, Massachusetts, AnnaLee Saxenian, *Regional Advantage: Culture and Competition in Silicon Valley and Route 128* (Cambridge, MA: Harvard University Press, 1996). For a description of clusters in India, see National Innovation Foundation, http://www.nif.org.in/bd/list_industrial_clusters.
7. The top 100 Chinese industrial clusters, 'Update on industrial clusters in China', Industrial Cluster Series 6, Li & Fung Research Centre, Hong Kong, June 2010 (www.lifunggroup.com/eng/knowledge/research/LFIndustrial6.pdf).
8. Michael Enright, *The Greater Pearl River Delta* (Hong Kong: Enright, Scott & Associates, 2010).
9. Patrick Anderson, *The State of the Worldwide Orthopaedic Industry* (Kalamazoo, MI: Stryker, 2007); Dane Miller, 'Influence of patients on implant performance', Biomet, Warsaw, IN, 2007.
10. Gigerich's comments, 'Study offers insight into regional clusters', *Indianapolis Business Journal*, 18 June 2007.
11. Nancy Dunne, 'Shining future for the city of spare parts', *Financial Times*, 21 Oct. 2004.
12. Stetler interview with author, Pierceton, 6 Dec. 2007.
13. 'Warsaw firm thriving on children's orthopedics products', *Indianapolis Business Journal*, 14 Apr. 2008.
14. Stuart Rosenfeld, *Creating Smart Systems: A Guide to Cluster Strategies in Less Favoured Regions* (Carrboro, NC: Regional Technology Strategies, 2002), p. 13.
15. Jorge Siopack and Harry Jergesen, 'Total hip arthroplasty', *Western Journal of Medicine* 162 (1995): 243–9.
16. Pablo Gomez and Jose Morcuende, 'A historical and economic perspective on Sir John Charnley, Chas F. Thackray Limited, and the early arthroplasty industry', *Iowa Orthopaedic Journal* 25(2005): 30–7; B. M. Wroblewski, 'Professor Sir John Charnley (1911–1982)', *Rheumatology* 41:7 (2002): 824–5.
17. Yorkshire medical cluster, http://www.medilink.co.uk.
18. The original name for Danek was Biotechnology Inc. The company switched to Danek in 1990.

19. Confindustria Ceramica, *The Great Book of Sassuolo* (Bologna: Confindustria Ceramica, 2007), p. 137. Porter, *The Competitive Advantage of Nations*, also gives an account of the Sassuolo industry, p. 210.

20. Kenneth Warren, *World Steel: An Economic Geography* (Newton Abbott: David & Charles, 1975).

21. At http://www.cutlers-hallamshire.org.uk/html/history/.

22. Lord (Charles) Aberconway, *The Basic Industries of Great Britain* (London: Ernest Benn, 1927), ch. 3.

23. The Outokumpu site in Sheffield makes stainless steel, a specialized type of material used in products such as cutlery, surgical instruments and kitchenware. In 2012, the Finnish company became the biggest stainless steel producer in Europe with a $3.3 billion deal to buy the stainless steel operations of ThyssenKrupp, the German steelmaker.

24. 'Tell the world it's made in Sheffield,' pamphlet from Made in Sheffield organization; http://www.madeinsheffield.org.

25. In 2002, John Bramah, a descendant of Joseph, became Sheffield's Master Cutler, a ceremonial title awarded by the Company of Cutlers. Master Cutlers hold this title for a year and are expected to carry out duties linked to promoting local industry.

26. Peter Marsh, 'Survive the credit crisis the Alpine way', *Financial Times*, 29 Jan. 2009. The article introduces the Alpine Ring.

27. Stefan Köhler and Anne Otto, *The Role of New Firms for the Development of Clusters in Germany* (Saarbrücken: Institute of Employment Research, 2006); Khalid Nadvi and Gerhard Halder, *Local Clusters in Global Value Chains: Exploring Dynamic Linkages between Germany and Pakistan* (Brighton: Institute of Development Studies, University of Sussex, 2002); Gerhard Halder, 'Local upgrading strategies in response to global challenges: the surgical instrument cluster of Tuttlingen, Germany', in Hubert Schmitz (ed.), *Local Enterprises in the Global Economy: Issues of Governance and Upgrading* (Cheltenham: Edward Elgar, 2004); Surgical Mechanics' Guild, Baden-Württemberg, '18th century beginnings of surgical mechanics', 1989 (http://www.chirurgiemechanik. de/En/History/index.asp?).

28. Mumford, *Technics and Civilisation*. Also Carlo Cipolla, *Clocks and Culture, 1300– 1700* (London: Collins, 1967).

29. David Landes, *Revolution in Time: Clocks and the Making of the Modern World* (Cambridge, MA: Harvard University Press, 2000), p. 88. Other historical details, http://www.clocksonly.com/watch_history.html.

30. Analysis of locations of the Swiss watch and component makers by the author, 2009, based on Federation of the Swiss Watch Industry (FHS) data. Of 627 companies studied, 32 per cent were in and around Neuchâtel; 25 per cent in the Berne area; 15 per cent in the Jura, near Le Brassus; and 11 per cent in Geneva. Another 5 per cent were in Vaud. The rest of Switzerland accounted for 12 per cent. Parts of the Jura area are sometimes labelled 'Watch Valley', partly to attract tourists: for instance, http:// www.tour-smart.co.uk/destinations/switzerland/time-out-in-the-watch-valley/.

31. European Foundation for the Improvement of Living and Working Conditions, *The Automotive Cluster in Baden-Württemberg, Germany* (Dublin: Eurofound, 2004).

32. Paini interview with author, Pogno, 3 Mar. 2008.

33. Meloda interview with author, San Maurizio d'Opaglio, 14 Feb. 2001. Peter Marsh, 'Valve makers keep it in the cluster', *Financial Times*, 21 May 2001. The company name was changed to O&M in 2009.

34. Leibinger telephone interview with author, 16 May 2008. Karl Leibinger is a nephew of Berthold Leibinger, chairman of the supervisory board of Trumpf, the laser cutting machine maker.

35. Arve Industries represents businesses in the area, http://www.arve-industries.fr/ entreprises_adherentes-fr5_0.html.

36. Norbert Sparrow, 'Microtechnology in healthcare: Franche-Comté is ready for its close up', *European Medical Device Technology* (1 Sept. 2006). Also Les Hunt, 'Engineering in miniature', *DPA* (1 June 2008) (http://www.dpaonthenet.net/article/16189/Engineering-in-miniature.aspx).

37. Heinrich Christen, *Switzerland: The Medtech Country* (Zurich: Ernst & Young, 2008); Peter Biedermann et al., 'Switzerland – a hot spot for medical technology', excerpts from the survey 'The Swiss medical technology industry 2008', Medical Cluster, Bern, 2008.

38. The growth of medical equipment production in Switzerland is related to the AO Foundation, a Swiss medical institute set up in 1958 to promote the development of orthopaedic implants. The main person behind AO was Maurice Müller, a pioneering Swiss surgeon; see http://www.swissinfo.ch/eng/Home/Archive/Surgeon_of_the_century_leaves_enduring_legacy.html?cid=655292.

39. The two companies Hayek took charge of in 1983 were Allgemeine Schweizer Uhrenindustrie and Société Suisse pour l'Industrie Horlogère. The merged ASUAG-SSIH formed a new business, Swiss Corporation for Microelectronics and Watchmaking (SMH), which Hayek rechristened Swatch in 1998.

40. 'Nicolas Hayek: business consultant who saw that a cheap disposable novelty could help to save the Swiss watch industry', *The Times*, 30 June 2010; Ian Rodger, 'Europe's timely champion', *Financial Times*, 20 July 1992; 'The outsiders who saved Omega and the Swiss watch industry', Watches Corner website, 28 Aug. 2007.

41. Based on estimates by author. Federation of the Swiss Watch Industry, *The Swiss and World Watchmaking Industry in 2010* (Bienne: Federation of the Swiss Watch Industry, 2011).

42. In 2011, Swatch retained its central role in the Swiss watch industry. Nayla Hayek, Nicolas Hayek's daughter, and Nick, his son, were respectively chair and chief executive. In early 2011, Swatch was looking to expand its worldwide staff as a result of surging sales. Haig Simonian, 'Swatch looks to increase workforce', *Financial Times*, 11 Mar. 2011; Simonian, 'Shared horse hobby helps Swatch palace business', *FT*, 25 Mar. 2011; Simonian, 'Swatch hopes to call time on supply of components', *FT*, 12 Nov. 2011; Peter Marsh, 'Swatch decision throws a spanner in Swiss watch industry's works', *FT*, 10 Aug. 2005.

43. The Cambridge 'cluster' of technology-based businesses is often labelled the 'Cambridge phenomenon'. The term was coined in 1980 by Peta Levi in an opening sentence, 'A phenomenon of considerable significance to British industry is taking place in Cambridge': Peta Levi, 'Flourishing in the Cambridge parkland', *Financial Times*, 18 Nov. 1980. Also, http://www.cambridgephenomenon.com/phenomenon; Segal Quince Wicksteed, *The Cambridge Phenomenon: The Growth of High Technology Industry in a University Town* (Cambridge: Segal Quince Wicksteed, 1985); Bill Wicksteed, *The Cambridge Phenomenon Revisited: Parts One and Two* (Cambridge: Segal Quince Wicksteed, 2000); David Gill et al., *Funding Technology: Britain Forty Years On* (Cambridge: University of Cambridge Institute for Manufacturing, 2007); Peta Levi, 'Cambridge: the place where success breeds growth', *FT*, 30 Nov. 1982; Peter Marsh, 'Cambridge – eggheads and chips: the network of connections which has made the university city the fastest-growing centre in Europe for high-technology businesses', *FT*, 4 July 1987.

44. Herriot telephone interview with author, 6 Dec. 2012.

45. Eiloart obituary, see Rodney Dale, 'Tim Eiloart: entrepreneurial Cambridge spirit and early green champion', *Guardian*, 28 May 2009.

46. Rodney Dale, *From Ram Yard to Milton Hilton: A History of Cambridge Consultants* (Cambridge: Cambridge Consultants, 1983).

47. Spears interview with author, Birmingham, 4 Aug. 2011. Peter Marsh, 'Network pools resources to reap solid rewards', *Financial Times*, 29 Aug. 2011.

### 9 Future factories

1. Jain telephone interview with author, 25 Mar. 2011. Other remarks by Jain in this section are also from this interview.

2. Ross is among the US's most prominent purchasers of 'distressed assets'. He was founder and chairman of International Steel Group, the US company bought by Mittal in 2004. Thanks to his large stake in ISG, Ross made $267 million from the deal (*Financial Times*, 28 Oct. 2004; *FT*, 29 Oct. 2004).

3. Mikhail Roco, 'Nanotechnology research directions for societal needs in 2020', paper, 1 Dec. 2010 (http://www.nanotechproject.orgshprocess/assets/files/8350/roco_presentation.pdf). Also Mikhail Roco, Chad Mirkin and Mark Hersam, *Nanotechnology Research Directions for Societal Needs in 2020* (Berlin: Springer, 2010).

4. Richard Feynman, 'Plenty of room at the bottom', lecture at California Institute of Technology, 1959 (http://www.its.caltech.edu/~feynman/plenty.html).

5. The Taniguchi paper, 'On the basic concept of nanotechnology', was given at a Tokyo conference in 1974 organized by the Japan Society of Precision Engineering. It is cited in Jeremy Ramsden, 'What is nanotechnology?', *Nanotechnology Perceptions* 1 (2005): 3–17. Also, 'History and future of nanotechnology', Nanotechnology Research Foundation, 2008–9 (http://www.nanotechnologyresearchfoundation.org/nanohistory.html).

6. Eric Drexler, *Engines of Creation: The Coming Era of Nanotechnology* (New York: Anchor, 1986).

7. Gogotsi interview with author, Philadelphia, 30 Sept. 2008. Other remarks in the section also from this interview. Also Yury Gogotsi (ed.), *Carbon Nanomaterials* (Boca Raton, FL: Taylor & Francis, 2006).

8. Wagner interview with author, Regensburg, 5 Oct. 2007. Peter Marsh, 'The code for a successful start-up', *Financial Times*, 23 Jan. 2008. In 2010 Geneart was acquired by the US company Life Technologies, the product of a 2008 merger between Invitrogen and Applied Biosystems.

9. Clive Cookson, 'A new twist on life', *Financial Times*, 11 Aug. 2009.

10. In 2000 Venter played the pivotal scientific role in the worldwide effort to decode the human genome – the sequencing of the 3 billion chemical 'letters' of the human genetic code. Clive Cookson, 'The selfish geneticist', *Financial Times*, 30 Dec. 2000; Clive Cookson and David Firn, 'Breeding bugs that may help save the world', *FT*, 28 Sept. 2002. In 2005, Venter co-founded Synthetic Genomics.

11. Venter telephone interview with author, 12 Sept. 2007. Peter Marsh, 'Leading the evolution out of the fossil fuel age', *Financial Times*, 22 Oct. 2007.

12. National Research Council, *A New Biology for the 21st Century* (Washington DC: National Academies Press, 2009). Also Amy Harmon, 'Exploring differences in the new DNA age', *International Herald Tribune*, 10 Nov. 2007; Amy Harmon, 'It's all about me', *Montreal Gazette*, 3 June 2007.

13. Patrinos interview with author, Egham, 31 Jan. 2007. Patrinos joined Synthetic Genomics from a post as director of the Office of Biological and Environmental Research at the US Department of Energy, where he oversaw work on the human genome project.

14. Synthetic biology is likely to involve new regulatory requirements to safeguard against either real or imagined dangers: Michael Rodemeyer, *New Life, Old Bottles: Regulating First-Generation Products of Synthetic Biology* (Washington DC: Woodrow Wilson International Center for Scholars, 2009). See also Ian Sample, 'Genetics: man who played God? Artificial life raises scientific hopes – and fears', *Guardian*, 21 May 2010.

15. Cronin's comments in the *Observer*, 28 Aug. 2011.

16. In 2009 the London-based Institute of Materials, Minerals and Mining awarded Arvedi its Bessemer gold medal, named after the nineteenth-century British steel pioneer, for his work on the new steel process.

17. Arvedi interview with author, London, 29 Oct. 2009. Other remarks are from this interview.

18. Federico Mazzolari, 'Endless strip production', paper delivered at World Steel Association conference, Tokyo, 2010.

19. In 2011, the Siemens/Arvedi partnership was still struggling to find the first buyer for its ESP technology. A potential competitor emerged when Posco, the big South Korean steel-maker, said it was interested in commercializing its own version of 'endless' steel strip technology (*Financial Times*, 1 Dec. 2011).

20. 'Industry: titanium to the fore', *Time*, 11 Aug. 1952.

21. Dhariwal telephone interview with author, 3 Nov. 2011.

22. Geoffrey Owen, 'Material lessons for modern times', *Financial Times*, 1 Nov. 2011. Also Geoffrey Owen, *The Rise and Fall of Great Companies: Courtaulds and the Reshaping of the Man-Made Fibres Industry* (Oxford: Oxford University Press, 2010).

23. Tony Roberts, 'The carbon fibre industry worldwide 2011–2020: an evaluation of current markets and future supply and demand' (http://www.caroledesign.co.uk/nick/New%20files/Carbon_Fibre_2011-2020.pdf).

24. St Ville interview with author, London, 11 Dec. 2009. Peter Marsh, 'Downturn fails to deter Armor's design on funds', *Financial Times*, 11 Apr. 2009.

25. Peter Marsh, 'Manufacturing an experiment', *Financial Times*, 13 Apr. 2010.

26. Yemm interview with author, Edinburgh, 25 Aug. 2011.

27. Goldman telephone interview with author, 25 Mar. 2011.

28. For a profile of Fodor, see Ben Goertzel, http://www.goertzel.org/benzine/FodorProfile.htm, personal website.

29. Tim Lenoir and Eric Giannella, 'The emergence and diffusion of DNA microarray technology', *Journal of Biomedical Discovery and Collaboration* 1:11 (2006).

30. Hauser interview with author, Cambridge, 18 July 2008. Peter Marsh, 'Rewriting the rule book', *Financial Times*, 26 Sept. 2008.

31. Peter Marsh, 'Russian state pledges to invest £400m in UK plastic chips group', *Financial Times*, 18 Jan. 2011.

32. Simon Rabinovitch, 'China outlines strategic industries', *Financial Times*, 4 Aug. 2011.

## 10 The new industrial revolution

1. Joel Mokyr, *Twenty-Five Centuries of Technological Change: An Historical Survey* (London: Routledge, 2001).

2. Rosenberg interview with author, London, 19 June 2003.

3. The figure is adjusted for inflation. US National Science Foundation estimates put world R&D spending at $1,107 billion in 2007 and $525 million in 1996, using current year dollars (National Science Foundation, *Science and Engineering Indicators: 2010*, see www.nsf.gov/statistics/seind10/c4/c4h.htm; www.nsf.gov/statistics/seind10/c0/fig00-01.xls). On an inflation-adjusted basis, the change from 1996 to 2007 works out at a 25 per cent increase. The Battelle R&D consultancy puts 2010 global R&D spending at $1,150 billion (Battelle, *2011 Global R&D Funding Forecast*, Dec. 2010, http://www.battelle.org/aboutus/rd/2011.pdf). See also Unesco science statistics, http://stats.uis.unesco.org/unesco/tableviewe/document.aspx?FileId=252; R. D. Shelton and P. Folan, *The Race for World Leadership of Science and Technology: Status and Forecasts*, paper at Conference on Scientometrics and Informetrics, Rio de Janeiro, 2009 (http://itri2.or/Rpape/2009).

4. Royal Society, *Knowledge, Networks and Nations: Global Scientific Collaboration in the 21st Century* (London: Royal Society, 2011).

5. US Patent and Trademark Office, *Patent Counts by Country/State and Year: Utility Patents, 1963-2010* (Alexandria, VA: US Patent and Trademark Office, 2011).

6. Lipsey, Carlaw and Bekar, *Economic Transformations*; Jovanovic and Rousseau, 'General purpose technologies'; Timothy Bresnahan and Manuel Trajtenberg, 'General purpose technologies: engines of growth?', *Journal of Econometrics, Annals of Econometrics* 65:1 (1995): 83–108; Vernon Ruttan, *The Role of the Public Sector in Technology Development: Generalizations from General-Purpose Technologies* (Cambridge, MA: Center for International Development, Harvard University, 2001).

7. For a fuller discussion of open innovation see Henry Chesbrough, *Open Innovation: The New Imperative for Creating and Profiting from Technology* (Boston: Harvard Business School Press, 1996).

8. Mihail Roco and William Sims Bainbridge, *Converging Technologies for Improving Human Performance: Nanotechnology, Biotechnology, Information Technology and Cognitive Science* (Dordrecht: Kluwer Academic, 2003); Alfred Nordmann (rapporteur), *Converging Technologies – Shaping the Future of European Societies* (Brussels: European Commission, 2004); John Patton, 'A historical perspective on convergence technology', *Nature Biotechnology* 24 (2006): 280–1.

9. Royal Society, *Knowledge, Networks and Nations*.

10. Data are from National Science Foundation, *Asia's Rising Science and Technology Strength: Comparative Indicators for Asia, the European Union, and the United States* (Washington DC: National Science Foundation, 2007).

11. IHS Global Insight dataset.

12. Figures for China's manufacturing employment are notoriously hard to calculate due to the absence of accurate data sources. However, the most plausible estimates for recent years come from Koen de Backer of the OECD. De Backer puts the figure for 2008 at about 122 million (Koen De Backer, *Global Value Chains – Selected Policy Issues*, Workshop at Revisiting Trade in a Globalized World conference, Chengdu, China, Oct. 2011, p. 5). China's manufacturing employment for 2008 has been separately estimated at 100 million by Judith Bannister (Judith Bannister and George Cook, 'China's employment and compensation costs in manufacturing through 2008', *Monthly Labor Review* (Mar. 2011)). De Backer's figure is based on Chinese government data together with discussions with Chinese officials. The estimate for 2010 of 130 million has come from the author, aided by a telephone conversation with De Backer (26 Jan. 2012). The 328 million estimated total world manufacturing employment in 2010 comes from the author. This uses the 130 million figure for China and is otherwise based on discussions in May 2011 with Keith Edmonds of the Oxford Economics consultancy who kindly provided data for manufacturing employment for the world's most important countries in terms of economic output. In order of rankings of manufacturing employment in 2010, the next biggest countries after China are India (51 million), Indonesia (13.8 million), Brazil (12.7 million), US (11.5 million), Russia (11.3 million) and Japan (10.3 million).

13. World Trade Organization, 'World trade 2010, prospects for 2011', press release, 2011; WTO, *International Trade Statistics 2010* (Geneva: WTO, 2010); Tables A1a and A1b, 'World merchandise exports, production and gross domestic product, 1950–2009', in WTO, 'Appendix tables', in *International Trade Statistics 2010*; Central Intelligence Agency, *The World Factbook* (Washington DC: CIA, 2011).

14. Wayne Morrison, *China–US Trade Issues* (Washington DC: Congressional Research Service, 2011), is particularly useful as it gives a long run of China/US trade data to 1980. Also World Trade Organization, *International Trade Statistics 2010*.

15. All manufacturing output data are from IHS Global Insight dataset.

16. US Bureau of Labor Statistics, 'International comparisons of hourly compensation costs in manufacturing, 2009', news release, 8 Mar. 2011; US BLS, 'International comparisons of manufacturing productivity and unit labor cost trends, 2009', news release, 13 Oct. 2011; US BLS, *International Comparisons of Annual Labor Force Statistics* (Washington DC: US Bureau of Labor Statistics, 2011).

17. The efforts in Japan appeared especially successful to many in the US and Europe. This led in the 1970s and 1980s to a sustained bout of interest in the Japanese manufacturing 'miracle' – in particular how it had been achieved and how other countries could learn from it. See Chalmers Johnson, *MITI and the Japanese Miracle* (Stanford: Stanford University Press, 1982); Ezra Vogel, *Japan as Number One* (Cambridge, MA: Harvard University Press, 1979); Abegglen and Stalk, *Kaisha, the Japanese Corporation*.

18. Robert Scott, *Unfair China Trade Costs Local Jobs* (Washington DC: Economic Policy Institute, 2010); Robert Morley, 'The death of American manufacturing: globalization and outsourcing are hammering our icons of industry', *Trumpet* (Feb. 2006) (http://www.thetrumpet.co/?page=article&id=1955); Ian Fletcher, 'The manufacturing rebound is a myth', *Huffington Post*, 22 May 2011 (http://www.huffingtonpost.co/ian-fletcher/the-manufacturing-rebound_b_865166.html?); Christoph Bliss et al., *China's Shifting Competitive Equation: How Multinational Manufacturers Must Respond* (New York: Booz & Co., 2008); Arvind Kaushal, Thomas Mayor and Patricia Riedl, *Manufacturing's Wake-Up Call* (New York: Booz & Co., 2011). For other assessments: Peter Schott, *The Relative Sophistication of Chinese Exports*, National Bureau of Economic Research Working Paper w12173, 2008; Hung-gay Fung et al., *Impacts of Competitive Position on Export Propensity and Intensity: An Empirical Study of Manufacturing Firms in China* (Munich: Munich University Library, 2007). In Pan Yue and Simon Evenett, *Moving Up the Value Chain: Upgrading China's Manufacturing Sector* (Winnipeg: International Institute for Sustainable Development, 2010), the argument is proposed that China still has to develop high-value industrial technology of its own. Edward Steinfeld, director of the MIT Sloan China Management Project, says that on balance the effects of China's prowess in manufacturing are positive for the US and Europe. 'In essence, China today – a country at the peak of its modernisation revolution – is doing something it historically never really did before. It is playing our [the US and European] game,' Steinfeld says (Ting Shi, 'Why the West should not fear China', *South China Morning Post*, 11 Aug. 2010).

19. Morrison, *China–US Trade Issues*. In 2010 General Motors sold 2.35 million cars and trucks in China compared to 2.21 million in the US. In that year GM had seven joint ventures and two wholly owned foreign enterprises, with a total of 32, 000 employees in China.

20. The relevance to trade of these value chains is spelt out in Escaith and Inomata, *Trade Patterns*. See also Andreas Maurer, *Trade in Value-Added: Methodologies and Experiences*, presented at Revisiting Trade in a Globalized World conference, Chengdu, China, Oct. 2011; De Backer, *Global Value Chains*.

21. Robert Koopman, Zhi Wang and Shang-jin Wei, *How Much of Chinese Exports Is Really Made in China? Assessing Foreign and Domestic Value-Added in Gross Exports* (Washington DC: International Trade Commission, 2008); Ari van Assche, *What Is Behind Made in China?*, presented at Revisiting Trade in a Globalized World conference, Chengdu, China, 2011. In *Is China Export-Led?* (Hong Kong: UBS Investment Research, 2007), Jonathan Anderson argues that the 'value-added' component of China's exports is substantially higher than suggested by the headline figures, which are expressed in gross revenue terms.

22. Some of the classification issues are explained in Vera Norrman and Mary Beth Garneau, 'ISIC 46 (rev 4): wholesale trade and commission trade, except of motor vehicles and motorcycles', sector paper, 24th Voorburg Group Meeting, Vienna, 2010; Diana Hicks, 'Structural change and industrial classification', *Structural Change and Economic Dynamics* (Feb. 2011); Teresa Fort, 'Breaking up is hard to do: why firms fragment production across locations', research paper, University of Maryland, 2011.

23. Robert Yuskavage and Jennifer Ribarsky, 'Global manufacturing and measurement issues raised by the iPhone', Powerpoint presentation, Bureau of Economic Affairs, Washington DC, 2011.

24. Yuqing Xing and Neal Detert, *How the iPhone Widens the United States Trade Deficit with the People's Republic of China*, ADBI Working Paper 257 (Tokyo: Asian Development Bank Institute, 2010).

25. Working out value-added surpluses or deficits involves many difficult calculations based on data that companies are frequently not keen to provide since they involve commercial confidences. For instance, in the case of the iPhone, the calculated $48 million value-added US surplus with China for 2009 could be a substantial underestimate. The calculation fails to account for exports from the US to China of software and other intellectual property that is created by Apple in the US and is a substantial part of the value of the product. The software and intellectual property – as manifested by design and general engineering know-how – is not manifested in physical components. However, it is important in creating the notional factory transfer price for each iPhone of $179. Apple does not disclose the value of this know-how, or whether any of it is accounted for in the factory transfer price of the product that is derived from assembly activities in China. If the 'US know-how' value were to be part of the factory transfer price, then a much bigger part of the latter would be derived from the US than is indicated by the $121.5 million value of components that is taken into account in the value-added calculations. As a result, the value-added surplus taken by the US in relation to China for the iPhone would be higher than the calculated figure, and the US's deficits with the other countries involved in the assembly activity, including Japan, South Korea and Germany, would be correspondingly lower.

26. 'US know-how value' for the iPhone is accounted for by Apple as part of the company's activity in selling its products in the US. However, as the previous note indicated, at least part of the 'US know-how value' for the product may be considered by Apple as part of the costs of producing its iPhones in China. Where these costs are accounted for is not disclosed by Apple.

27. This is an inference that can be drawn from the Xin/Detert study above (note 24). Similar conclusions can be drawn from studies of the iPad (Kenneth Kraemer, Greg Linden, and Jason Dedrick, *Capturing Value in Global Networks: Apple's iPad and iPhone* (Irvine, CA: Personal Computing Industry Center, 2011), and Greg Linden, Kenneth Kraemer and Jason Dedrick, 'Who captures value in the Apple iPad?', unpublished working paper, 2011).

28. Greg Linden, Kenneth Kraemer and Jason Dedrick, 'Who captures value in a global innovation network? The case of Apple's iPod', *Communications of the ACM* (Association of Computing Machinery) 52:3 (Mar. 2009).

29. Data in the next three sections related to economic output, productivity and the manufacturing workforce are based on estimates by the author using S. N. Broadberry, *The Productivity Race: British Manufacturing in Perspective, 1850–1990* (Cambridge: Cambridge University Press, 1997); Bairoch, 'International industrialisation levels', figures quoted in Kennedy, *The Rise and Fall of the Great Powers*; World Trade Organization data; IHS Global Insight dataset; United Nations Statistics Division databases; Oxford Economics data; US Bureau of Labor Statistics data; De Backer, *Global Value Chains*; Stanley Lebergott, 'Labor force and employment', in Dorothy Brady, *Output, Employment, and Productivity in the United States after 1800* (Cambridge, MA: National Bureau of Economic Research, 1966); Shahid Alam, *A Short History of the Global Economy since 1800* (London: Institute for Policy Research and Development, 2003); Craig Lindsay, *A Century of Labour Market Change: 1900–2000* (London: Office of National Statistics, 2003); Leigh Shaw-Taylor et al., *The Creation of a 'Census' of Adult Male Employment for England and Wales for 1817*, research paper, Cambridge Group for the History of Population and Social Structure, University of Cambridge, 2010; Leigh Shaw-Taylor et al., 'The occupational structure of England c.1710 to c.1871', work in progress, 2010; Leigh Shaw-Taylor, 'The occupational structure of England and Wales, c.1750–1911', draft research paper, 2009; Geoffrey Robinson,

'Automation: too much anxiety or too little?', *New Scientist*, 8 June 1978. Details of the calculations are available on request: peter.marsh@ft.com.

30. US Bureau of Labor Statistics, consumer price index (CPI) database (http://www.bls.go/cp/data.htm).

31. Over the 100-year period from 1900 to 2000, manufacturing production rose by a factor of 48 (see Figure 1 in chapter 1) while the numbers working in the sector went up from 45 million to 278 million. According to estimates by the author, aided by data from Oxford Economics, manufacturing employment in 1980 was 186 million, in 1990 it was 244 million, in 2000 278 million and in 2010 328 million. The world population for these same years was, respectively, 4.4 billion, 5.3 billion, 6.1 billion and 6.8 billion (UN statistics). That makes the percentage of the world population working in manufacturing for 1980, 1990, 2000 and 2010 4.2 per cent, 4.6 per cent, 4.6 per cent and 4.8 per cent. On the assumption that for each of these years, the working population of the world is roughly half the total population, the proportion of the global workforce in manufacturing industry between 1980 and 2010 stayed within a fairly narrow range of abut 8.5 per cent to 10 per cent. Although it would appear by no means impossible to devise credible numbers for manufacturing employment for the 1900–80 period, valid estimates for these years have so far proved hard to reach. However, as a result of the strong growth in global manufacturing in the 1950s and 1960s, which was accompanied by only subdued increases in productivity, it might be surmised that manufacturing employment as a proportion of the population could have risen well above 5 per cent, perhaps to as high as 8 per cent, which might have put the proportion of the world's workforce in manufacturing in the 15–17 per cent range.

32. The percentage figures come from Bairoch, 'International industrialisation levels', figures quoted in Kennedy, *The Rise and Fall of the Great Powers*. Bairoch's data have been the subject of some critical comments by some economists who argue they should be treated with caution. However, as a guide to the shape of the world economy in the nineteenth century and earlier, Bairoch's estimates are extremely useful, and have been treated as such by several highly respected economic commentators such as Paul Kennedy, Nick Crafts and Robert Allen.

33. The calculations behind the productivity numbers are too voluminous to include in this book. However, as an indication of how these calculations have been done, output per worker in manufacturing in the rich countries in 2010, expressed in 2005 US dollars, was $93,529, as against $12,021 in the poor countries, making a productivity advantage of 7.8 times. In 2000 the comparable numbers were $76,406 and $8,457, giving an equivalent advantage of 9 times. In 1900, the comparable numbers were $5,495 and $796, an advantage of 6.9. Further details can be obtained by request from the author at peter.marsh@ft.com.

34. The data on manufacturing employment are based on information from Keith Edmonds of Oxford Economics, supplied in May 2011, with some adjustments and assumptions made by the author.

35. IHS Global Insight dataset; United Nations Statistics Division databases.

36. Such worries are far from new. Concerns about ebbing industrial strength were expressed in the UK for most of the twentieth century, and even in the nineteenth; see Sir Monty Finniston, *Engineering Our Future: Report of the Committee of Inquiry into the Engineering Profession* (London: HMSO, 1980); Correlli Barnett, *The Audit of War* (London: Macmillan, 1986); Wallis and Whitworth, *The American System of Manufactures*. For a more recent, thoughtful discussion of the UK's challenges, see Chris Benjamin, *The Lost Origins of Industrial Growth* (London: Institute for Public Policy Research, 2011). The concerns so expressed are part of a broad trend in which politicians and industrial experts in specific countries consider how other nations are doing better, with manufacturing being a frequent focus. In the 1960s, Europe suffered anxieties about the possibility that the US was outdoing the continent in industry and

technology. For instance, Jean-Jacques Servan-Schreiber, *The American Challenge* (New York: Avon, 1969), and his related *The World Challenge* (London: Collins, 1981). For an expression of unease in the US about the competitive threat from other countries, see Michael Dertouzos, Robert Lester and Robert Solow, *Made in America* (Cambridge, MA: MIT Press, 1989).

37. Specific concerns have come from the US steel industry, for instance from Dan DiMicco, the outspoken chairman and chief executive of Nucor, the big US steelmaker: DiMicco, *Steeling America's Future: A CEO's Call to Arms* (Charlotte, NC: Vox Populi, 2006). Also Mark Reutter, *Making Steel: Sparrows Point and the Rise and Ruin of American Industrial Might* (Champaign: University of Illinois Press, 2005). In early 2011, President Barack Obama appointed Jeff Immelt, General Electric chief executive, to advise him on the economy and jobs. Immelt responded by saying restoring the US's 'manufacturing might' should be the main goal for the country as it sought to lay the basis for a lasting recovery (*Financial Times*, 22 Jan. 2011). Useful analysis comes from Marc Levinson, *'Hollowing Out' in US Manufacturing: Analysis and Issues for Congress* (Washington DC: Congressional Research Service, 2011); and Marc Levinson, *Job Creation in the Manufacturing Revival* (Washington DC: Congressional Research Service, 2011).

38. Harold Sirkin, Michael Zinser and Douglas Hohner, *Made in America, Again: Why Manufacturing Will Return to the US* (Chicago: Boston Consulting Group, 2011).

39. The US and the UK in particular have seen a number of calls from business groups, often aided by supporting analysis from government bodies and research organizations, for more effort to be made to strengthen manufacturing. Some examples from the US: Council on Competitiveness, *Ignite 2.0: Voices of American University Presidents and National Lab Directors on Manufacturing Competitiveness* (Washington DC: Council on Competitiveness, 2011); Stephen Ezell and Robert Atkinson, *The Case for a National Manufacturing Strategy* (Washington DC: Information Technology and Innovation Foundation, 2011). An earlier similar set of ideas came from the National Council for Advanced Manufacturing, *Making Manufacturing a National Priority* (Washington DC: National Council for Advanced Manufacturing, 2007). In the UK, John Willman, *Innovation and Industry: A Manifesto for Manufacturing* (London: Policy Exchange, 2010). For a government view: Peter Mandelson, 'A new industrial activism', speech to Royal Society for the Encouragement of Arts, Manufactures and Commerce, London, 17 Dec. 2008; Department for Business, Enterprise and Regulatory Reform, *Manufacturing: New Challenges, New Opportunities* (London: BERR, 2008).

40. President Obama made insourcing of manufacturing the main item for a meeting of business leaders at the White House in January 2012, see 'Call to action to invest in America at White House "Insourcing American Jobs" forum', 11 Jan. 2012, Office of the Press Secretary, White House (http://www.whitehouse.go/the-press-offic/201/0/1/president-obama-issues-call-action-invest-america-white-house-insourcing).

# Bibliography

Abegglen, James and Stalk, George, *Kaisha, the Japanese Corporation*. New York: Basic Books, 1985.

Aberconway, Charles (Lord), *The Basic Industries of Great Britain*. London: Ernest Benn, 1927. At http://www.gracesguide.co.uk/The_Basic_Industries_of_Great_Britain_by_Aberconway.

Adriaanse, Albert et al., *Resource Flows: The Material Basis of Industrial Economies*. Washington DC: World Resources Institute, 1997.

Alam, M. Shahid, *A Short History of the Global Economy since 1800*. London: Institute for Policy Research and Development, 2003. At http://iprd.org.uk/wp-content/plugins/downloads-manager/upload/A%20Short%20History%20of%20the%20Global%20Economy%20Since%201800.pdf.

Alder, Ken, *Engineering the Revolution: Arms and Enlightenment in France, 1763–1815*. Princeton, NJ: Princeton University Press, 1997.

Alexander, William and Street, Arthur, *Metals in the Service of Man*. London: Penguin, 1979.

Allen, Robert, *Global Economic History: A Very Short Introduction*. Oxford: Oxford University Press, 2011.

American Society of Mechanical Engineers, 'The world's first industrial gas turbine set, GT Neuchâtel: A historic mechanical engineering landmark'. Neuchâtel, 1988. At http://files.asme.org/asmeorg/Communities/History/Landmarks/12281.pdf.

Amersham International, *Amersham: Our Heritage, 1874–2001*. Amersham: Amersham International, 2001.

Andersen, Hans Christian, 'The princess and the pea'. In *Tales, Told for Children*, Copenhagen: C. A. Reitzel, 1835.

Anderson, Jonathan, *Is China Export-Led?* Hong Kong: UBS Investment Research, 2007. At http://www.allroadsleadtochina.com/reports/prc_270907.pdf.

Anderson, Patrick, *The State of the Worldwide Orthopaedic Industry*. Kalamazoo, MI: Stryker, 2007.

Anderson, Ray, *Mid-Course Correction*. White River Junction, VT: Chelsea Green, 1998.

Angus-Butterworth, L. M., *The Manufacture of Glass*. London: Pitman, 1948.

ArcelorMittal, *How Will We Achieve Safe Sustainable Steel? Corporate Responsibility Report 2008*. Luxembourg: ArcelorMittal, 2009. At http://www.arcelormittal.com/rls/data/upl/720-3-2-CRReport2008.pdf.

ArcelorMittal, *Safe Sustainable Steel: Corporate Responsibility Report 2010*. Luxembourg: ArcelorMittal, 2011. At http://www.arcelormittal.com/rls/data/upl/720-3-4-Arcelor-Mittal_CR_Report_2010.pdf.

Arora, Ashish, Landau, Ralph and Rosenberg, Nathan (eds), *Chemicals and Long-Term Economic Growth: Insights from the Chemical Industry*. London: John Wiley, 1998.

Ashby, Mike, 'Eco-selection: environmentally informed material choice'. Seminar notes, Cambridge University Engineering Department, 2005. At http://www.ifm.eng.cam.ac.uk/sustainability/seminar/documents/051019ashby.pdf.

Ashton, T. S., *The Industrial Revolution, 1760–1830*. Oxford: Oxford University Press, 1948.

Ayres, R. U. and Warr, B., 'Accounting for growth: the role of physical work'. *Structural Change and Economic Dynamics* 16:2 (2005): 181–209.

Ayres, R. U., Ayres, L. W. and Warr, B., 'Exergy, power and work in the US economy, 1900–1998'. *Energy* 28:3 (2003): 219–73.

Babbage, Charles, *On the Economy of Machinery and Manufactures*. London, 1832. Website version at http://www.wissensnavigator.com/documents/CharlesBabbage.pdf.

Bairoch, P., 'International industrialisation levels from 1750 to 1980'. *Journal of European Economic History* 11 (1982).

Bannister, Judith and Cook, George, 'China's employment and compensation costs in manufacturing through 2008'. *Monthly Labor Review* (US Bureau of Labor Statistics) (Mar. 2011). At http://bls.gov/opub/mlr/2011/03/art4full.pdf.

Barker, T. C., *An Age of Glass*. London: Boxtree, 1994.

Barnett, Correlli, *The Audit of War*. London: Macmillan, 1986.

Barron, Iann and Curnow, Ray, *The Future with Microelectronics*. London: Frances Pinter, 1979.

Bashforth, G. Reginald, *The Manufacture of Iron and Steel*, vol. 2: *Steel Production*. London: Chapman & Hall, 1959.

Battelle, *2011 Global R&D Funding Forecast*, Dec. 2010. At http://www.battelle.org/aboutus/rd/2011.pdf.

Behrman, Daniel, *Solar Energy: The Awakening Science*. London: Routledge & Kegan Paul, 1979.

Bell, Daniel, *The Coming of Post-Industrial Society: A Venture in Social Forecasting*, with a new foreword by the author. New York: Basic Books, 1999.

Benjamin, Chris, *Strutting on Thin Air*. London, 2009.

Benjamin, Chris, *The Lost Origins of Industrial Growth*. London: Institute for Public Policy Research, 2011. At http://docs.jean-jaures.net/NL460/24.pdf.

Berg, Maxine, *The Machinery Question and the Making of the Political Economy 1815–1848*. Cambridge: Cambridge University Press, 1980.

Berg, Maxine, *The Age of Manufactures, 1700–1820: Industry, Innovation and Work in Britain*. London: Routledge, 1994.

Berg, Maxine (ed.), *Markets and Manufacture in Early Industrial Europe*. London: Routledge, 1991.

Bessemer, Henry, 'The manufacture of malleable iron and steel without fuel'. Paper delivered to the British Association, London, Aug. 1856. At http://www.banklands.com/Bessemer%27s%201856%20paper.htm. Also in *The Times*, 15 Aug. 1856, at http://www.theengineer.co.uk/journals/pdf/21800.pdf.

Bessemer, Henry, *Sir Henry Bessemer, F.R.S.: An Autobiography*, 1905. With a concluding chapter completed with the assistance of his son. Website version produced by Eric Hutton, 1996, at http://www.history.rochester.edu/ehp-book/shb/start.htm.

Best, Michael, *The New Competitive Advantage: The Renewal of American Industry*. Oxford: Oxford University Press, 2001.

Biedermann, Peter et al., 'Switzerland – a hot spot for medical technology'. Excerpts from the survey 'The Swiss medical technology industry 2008', Medical Cluster, Bern, 2008. At http://www.helbling.ch/hol/publications-1/swiss-medical-technology-industry-2008

BioCrossroads, *Warsaw, Indiana: The Orthopedics Capital of the World*. Indianapolis: BioCrossroads, 2009.

Birdsall, Derek and Cipolla, Carlo, *The Technology of Man*. London: Wildwood House, 1980.

Birtel, Martin, Lutter, Stephan and Giljum, Stefan, 'Global resource use: worldwide patterns of resource extraction'. World Resources Forum, St Gallen, 2008. At http://www.worldresourcesforum.org/issue.

Bliss, Christoph, Haddock, Ronald, Winkler, Conrad and Grichnik, Kaj, *China's Shifting Competitive Equation: How Multinational Manufacturers Must Respond*. New York: Booz & Co., 2008. At http://www.booz.com/media/uploads/Chinas_Shifting_Competitive_Equation.pdf.

Bodanis, David, *Electric Universe*. London: Abacus, 2006.

Boston Consulting Group, *Perspectives on Experience*, with foreword by Bruce Henderson. Boston: Boston Consulting Group, 1972.

Boston Consulting Group, *Steel's CO2 Balance: A Contribution to Climate Protection*. Chicago: Boston Consulting Group, 2010. At http://www.stahl-online.de/medien_lounge/Hintergrundmaterial/ReportCO2BilanzStahl_engl.pdf.

Bouquet, Tim and Ousey, Byron, *Cold Steel: Britain's Richest Man and the Multi-Billion-Dollar Battle for a Global Empire*. London: Little, Brown, 2008.

Braun, Ernest and MacDonald, Stuart, *Revolution in Miniature: The History and Impact of Semiconductor Electronics*. Cambridge: Cambridge University Press, 1978.

Braungart, Michael and McDonough, William, *Cradle to Cradle: Remaking the Way We Make Things*. London: Vintage, 2008.

Braungart, Michael, McDonough, William and Bollinger, Andrew, 'Cradle-to-cradle design: creating healthy emissions – a strategy for eco-effective product and system design'. *Journal of Cleaner Production* 15 (2007): 1337–48. At http://professorlonnie-gamble.com/uploads/EnergyCourse2011/19146867-Cradle-to-Cradle-Design.pdf.

Bresnahan, Timothy and Gordon, Robert, *The Economics of New Goods*. Chicago: University of Chicago Press, 1997.

Bresnahan, Timothy and Trajtenberg, Manuel, 'General purpose technologies: engines of growth?'. *Journal of Econometrics, Annals of Econometrics* 65:1 (1995): 83–108. Also National Bureau of Economic Research Working Paper 4148 (Oct. 1995). At www.nber.org/papers/w4148.

Briggs, Asa et al., *Technology and Economic Development*. London: Penguin, 1963. (Based on articles originally in *Scientific American*.)

Bringezu, Stefan, Schütz, Helmut and Moll, Stephan, 'Rationale for and interpretation of economy-wide materials flow analysis and derived indicators'. *Journal of Industrial Ecology* 7:2 (2003): 43–64.

Brion, René and Moreau, Jean-Louis, *Materials for a Better Life: Two Hundred Years of Entrepreneurship and Innovation in Metals and Materials*. Brussels: Umicore, 2005.

British Plastics Federation, *The World of Plastics*. London: British Plastics Federation, 1986.

Broadberry, S. N., *The Productivity Race: British Manufacturing in Perspective, 1850–1990*. Cambridge: Cambridge University Press, 1997.

Brown, T. J. et al., *World Mineral Production, 2003–2007*. Keyworth, Nottinghamshire: British Geological Survey, 2009. At http://www.bgs.ac.uk/mineralsUk/downloads/wmp_2003_2007.pdf.

Bruen, Robert, 'Overcoming greatness: the decline and recovery of British mathematics in the post-Newton era'. 1995. At http://www.lucasianchair.org/papers/newton-effect.html.

Bryan, Lowell, Fraser, Jane, Oppenheim, Jeremy and Rall, Wilhelm, *Race for the World: Strategies to Build a Great Global Firm*. Boston: Harvard Business School Press, 1999.

Bünte, Hans, *300 Years of Dillinger Steel Works*. Dillingen: Dillinger Hüttenwerke, 1985.

Burke, James, *Connections*. London: Macmillan, 1978.

Burn, Duncan (ed.), *The Structure of British Industry*. Cambridge: Cambridge University Press, 1958.

Bush, Vannevar, 'As we may think'. *The Atlantic*, July 1945. At http://www.theatlantic.com/magazine/archive/1945/07/as-we-may-think/3881/.

Cardwell, Donald, *Turning Points in Western Technology*. New York: Neale Watson, 1972.

Cardwell, Donald, *The Fontana History of Technology*. London: Fontana, 1994.

Carey, James, *Communication as Culture: Essays on Media and Society*. New York: Routledge, 2009.

Central Intelligence Agency, *The World Factbook*. Washington DC: CIA, 2011. At https://www.cia.gov/library/publications/the-world-factbook/rankorder/2078rank.html.

Chang, Jung and Halliday, Jon, *Mao: The Unknown Story*. London: Vintage, 2005.

Chesbrough, Henry, *Open Innovation: The New Imperative for Creating and Profiting from Technology*. Boston: Harvard Business School Press, 1996.

Chicago Mahlerites, '*Das Lied von der Erde*: the literary changes'. Mahler Archives. At http://www.mahlerarchives.net/DLvDE/DLvDE.htm; http://www.mahlerarchives.net/DLvDE/Das_Trinklied.htm.

Chinnici, Madeline, *Innovations in Glass*. Corning, NY: Corning Museum of Glass, 1999.

Christen, Heinrich, *Switzerland: The Medtech Country*. Zurich: Ernst & Young, 2008. At http://www.six-swiss-exchange.com/download/about/div_pub/swiss_med_tech_report_2008_en.pdf.

Christensen, Clayton, *The Innovator's Dilemma: When New Technologies Cause Great Firms to Fail*. Boston: Harvard Business School Press, 1997.

Christian, David, 'World history in context'. *Journal of World History* 14:4 (Dec. 2003). At http://www.historycooperative.org/cgi-bin/justtop.cgi?act=justtop&url=http://www.historycooperative.org/journals/jwh/14.4/christian.html.

Cipolla, Carlo, *Guns and Sails*. London: Collins, 1965.

Cipolla, Carlo, *Clocks and Culture, 1300–1700*. London: Collins, 1967.

Cipolla, Carlo, *Before the Industrial Revolution*. London: Methuen, 1976.

Clapham, John, *A Concise Economic History of Britain: From the Earliest Times to 1975*. Cambridge: Cambridge University Press, 1963.

Clayre, Alasdair (ed.), *Nature and Industrialization*. Oxford: Oxford University Press, 1977.

Coca-Cola, *2009/2010 Sustainability Review*. Atlanta: Coca-Cola, 2010.

Coca-Cola, *Annual Report, 2010*. Atlanta: Coca-Cola, 2011. At http://www.thecoca-cola-company.com/investors/pdfs/form_10K_2010.pdf.

ConfindustriaCeramica, *The Great Book of Sassuolo*. Bologna: ConfindustriaCeramica, 2007.

Cook, Andrew, *Thrice through the Fire: A History of the William Cook Company from 1985 to 1998*. Sheffield: William Cook, 1999.

Cortright, Joseph, *Making Sense of Clusters: Regional Competitiveness and Economic Development*. Washington DC: Brookings Institution, 2006. At http://www.brookings.edu/reports/2006/03cities_cortright.aspx.

Council on Competitiveness, *Ignite 2.0: Voices of American University Presidents and National Lab Directors on Manufacturing Competitiveness*. Washington DC: Council on Competitiveness, 2011. At http://www.compete.org/images/uploads/File/PDF%20Files/Ignite_2.0_.pdf.

Court, W. H. B., *A Concise Economic History of Britain: From 1750 to Recent Times*. Cambridge: Cambridge University Press, 1967.

Courtney, Arlene, 'Historical perspectives of energy consumption'. Course materials for Energy and Resources in Perspective, Western Oregon University, 2005. At http://www.wou.edu/las/physci/GS361/electricity%20generation/HistoricalPerspectives.htm.

Crafts, Nicholas, *Globalisation and Economic Growth: A Historical Perspective*. Revised version of Tore Browaldh Lecture, University of Gothenburg, 14 Jan. 2003. Oxford: Blackwell, 2004.

Cruikshank, Jeffrey and Sililia, David, *The Engine That Could: 75 Years of Value-Driven Change at Cummins Engine Company*. Boston: Harvard Business School Press, 1997.

Dale, Rodney, *From Ram Yard to Milton Hilton: A History of Cambridge Consultants*. Cambridge: Cambridge Consultants, 1983.

Davies, Keith, *The Sequence: Inside the Race for the Human Genome*. London: Orion, 2002.

Dawson, Keith, *The Industrial Revolution*. London: Pan, 1972.

De Backer, Koen, *Global Value Chains – Selected Policy Issues*. Workshop at Revisiting Trade in a Globalized World conference, Chengdu, China, Oct. 2011. At http://www.wto.org/english/res_e/statis_e/miwi_e/koen_de_backer_chengdu_oct11.pdf.

De Tocqueville, Alexis, *Journeys to England and Ireland*. Piscataway, NJ: Transaction, 1979. First published 1835.

Dedrick, Jason, Kraemer, Kenneth and Linden, Greg, 'Who profits from innovation in global value chains? A study of the iPod and notebook PCs'. *Industrial and Corporate Change* 19:1 (2010): 81–116. At http://icc.oxfordjournals.org/content/19/1/81.abstract.

Department for Business, Enterprise and Regulatory Reform, *Manufacturing: New Challenges, New Opportunities*. London: Department for Business, Enterprise and Regulatory Reform, 2008. At http://www.berr.gov.uk/files/file47660.pdf.

Department for Business, Innovation and Skills, *Learning from Some of Britain's Successful Sectors: An Historical Analysis of the Role of Government*. London: Department for Business, Innovation and Skills, 2010. At http://www.bis.gov.uk/assets/biscore/economics-and-statistics/docs/10-781-bis-economics-paper-06.

Dertouzos, Michael, Lester, Robert and Solow, Robert, *Made in America*. Cambridge, MA: MIT Press, 1989.

Diamond, Jared, *Guns, Germs and Steel*. London: Vintage, 1988.

Diebold, John, *Automation*, with a new introduction by the author. New York: American Management Associations, 1983.

Diederen, A. M., *Metal Minerals Scarcity: A Call for Managed Austerity and the Elements of Hope*. Rijswijk: TNO Defence, Security and Safety, 2009.

DiMicco, Dan, *Steeling America's Future: A CEO's Call to Arms*. Charlotte, NC: Vox Populi, 2006.

Drexler, Eric, *Engines of Creation: The Coming Era of Nanotechnology*. New York: Anchor, 1986. Website version at http://e-drexler.com/d/06/00/EOC/EOC_Table_of_Contents.html.

Drucker, Peter, *Management: Tasks, Responsibilities, Practices*. New York: Harper & Row, 1973. Website version at http://www.4shared.com/document/80DTNU8O/Management_-_Tasks_Responsibil.html.

Drucker, Peter, *Management*. London: Pan, 1979.

DuLong, Jessica, 'Welcome to Warsaw: Indiana's orthopedics capital of the world'. *Today's Machining World* 2:5 (2006). At http://www.todaysmachiningworld.com/welcome-to-warsaw-indiana%E2%80%99s-orthopedics-capital-of-the-world/.

E2V, *E2V: Celebrating 60 Years of Bright Ideas, 1947–2007*. Cambridge: Granta Books, 2007.

Enright, Michael, *The Greater Pearl River Delta*. Hong Kong: Enright, Scott & Associates, 2010.

ERA Foundation, *The Sustainability of the UK Economy in an Era of Declining Productive Capability*. Leatherhead: ERA Foundation, 2010.

Escaith, Hubert and Inomata, Satoshi, *Trade Patterns and Global Value Chains in East Asia: From Trade in Goods to Trade in Tasks*. Geneva and Tokyo: World Trade Organization and Institute of Developing Economies, 2011. At http://www.wto.org/english/res_e/booksp_e/stat_tradepat_globvalchains_e.pdf.

Europa InterCluster, *The Emerging of European World-Class Clusters*. Brussels: Europa InterCluster, 2010. At http://www.intercluster.eu/index.php?option=com_flexicontent&view=items&cid=1:frontpage&id=159:release-of-the-white-paper-on-the-emerging-of-world-class-clusters&Itemid=1.

European Foundation for the Improvement of Living and Working Conditions, *The Automotive Cluster in Baden-Württemberg, Germany*. Dublin: Eurofound, 2004. At http://www.eurofound.europa.eu/emcc/publications/2004/ef0493en1.pdf.

Evans, Steve et al., *Towards a Sustainable Industrial System*. Cambridge: Institute for Manufacturing, 2009.

Ezell, Stephen and Atkinson, Robert, *The Case for a National Manufacturing Strategy*. Washington DC: Information Technology and Innovation Foundation, 2011.

Federation of the Swiss Watch Industry, *The Swiss and World Watchmaking Industry in 2010*. Bienne: Federation of the Swiss Watch Industry, 2011. At http://www.fhs.ch/statistics/watchmaking_2010.pdf.

Fenau, Claude, *Non-Ferrous Metals*. Brussels: Umicore, 2002.

Ferdows, Kasra, 'New world manufacturing order'. *Industrial Engineer* (Feb. 2003).

Ferdows, Kasra, Lewis, Michael and Machuca, Jose, 'Rapid fire fulfilment'. *Harvard Business Review* (Nov. 2004).

Feynman, Richard, 'Plenty of room at the bottom'. Lecture at California Institute of Technology, 1959. At http://www.its.caltech.edu/~feynman/plenty.html.

Finniston, Monty (chair), *Engineering Our Future: Report of the Committee of Inquiry into the Engineering Profession*. London: HMSO, 1980.

Fishman, Ted, *China Inc.: How the Rise of the Next Superpower Challenges America and the World*. New York: Scribner, 2005.

Forbes, Nashaud and Wield, David, *From Followers to Leaders: Managing Technology and Innovation*. London: Routledge, 2004.

Ford, Henry, *My Life and Work*. New York: Doubleday, 1922. At http://www.gutenberg.org/ebooks/7213.

Forester, Tom (ed.), *The Microelectronics Revolution*. Oxford: Blackwell, 1980.

Fort, Teresa, 'Breaking up is hard to do: why firms fragment production across locations'. Research paper, University of Maryland, 2011.

Fung, Hung-gay, Yong-Gao, Gerald, Lu, Jiangyong and Mano, Haim, *Impacts of Competitive Position on Export Propensity and Intensity: An Empirical Study of Manufacturing Firms in China*. Munich: Munich University Library, 2007. At http://mpra.ub.uni-muenchen.de/5674/.

Galbraith, J. K., *The Affluent Society*. London: Hamish Hamilton, 1958.

Galbraith, J. K., *The New Industrial State*. London: Penguin Books, 1969.

Gantz, John and Reinsel, David, *Extracting Value from Chaos*. Framingham, MA: IDC, 2010. At http://idcdocserv.com/1142.

Gardner, Gary and Sampat, Payal, *Mind over Matter: Recasting the Role of Materials in Our Lives*. Washington DC: Worldwatch Institute, 1998.

Giedion, Siegfried, *Mechanization Takes Command*. London: Norton, 1969.

Gill, David, Minshall, Tim, Pickering, Craig and Rigby, Martin. *Funding Technology: Britain Forty Years On*. Cambridge: University of Cambridge Institute for Manufacturing, 2007. At http://www.etcapital.com/britain.pdf.

Gilmore, James and Pine, Joseph, *Markets of One*. Cambridge, MA: Harvard Business Review (book), 2000.

Gimpel, Jean, *The Medieval Machine: The Industrial Revolution of the Middle Ages*. Aldershot: Wildwood House, 1988.

Godet, Michel and Ruyssen, Olivier, *The Old World and the New Technologies*. Luxembourg: European Commission, 1981.

Gogotsi, Yury (ed.), *Carbon Nanomaterials*. Boca Raton, FL: Taylor & Francis, 2006.

Gomez, Pablo and Morcuende, Jose, 'A historical and economic perspective on Sir John Charnley, Chas F. Thackray Limited, and the early arthroplasty industry'. *Iowa Orthopaedic Journal* 25 (2005): 30–7. At http://www.ncbi.nlm.nih.gov/pmc/articles/PMC1888784/#__sec1.

Goodman, L. Landon, *Man and Automation*. London: Penguin, 1957.

Graham, Margaret and Shuldiner, Alec, *Corning and the Craft of Innovation*. New York: Oxford University Press, 2001.

Greenberger, Martin (ed.), *Computers and the World of the Future*. Cambridge, MA: MIT Press, 1962.

Habakkuk, H. J., *American and British Technology in the Nineteenth Century: The Search For Labour Saving Inventions*. Cambridge: Cambridge University Press, 1962.

Halder, Gerhard, 'Local upgrading strategies in response to global challenges: the surgical instrument cluster of Tuttlingen, Germany'. In Hubert Schmitz (ed.), *Local Enterprises in the Global Economy: Issues of Governance and Upgrading*. Cheltenham: Edward Elgar, 2004.

Handel, S., *The Electronic Revolution*. London: Penguin, 1967.

Hansen, Philip, *The History of the William Cook Company and the Cook Family, from the 18th Century to 1985*. Sheffield: William Cook, 1985.

Hanson, Dirk, *The New Alchemists*. New York: Avon, 1982.

Hatfield, H. Stafford, *Inventions and Their Uses in Science Today*. London: Penguin, 1940.

Hawker, Paul, Lovins, Amory and Lovins, L. Hunter, *Natural Capitalism: The Next Industrial Revolution*. London: Earthscan, 2000.

Hexter, Jimmy and Woetzel, Jonathan, *Operation China: From Strategy to Execution*. Boston: Harvard Business School Press, 2007.

Hey, David, 'The South Yorkshire steel industry and the Industrial Revolution'. *Northern History* 42:1 (Mar. 2005). At http://www.sheffieldindexers.com/Memories/South%20Yorkshire%20Steel%20Industry.pdf.

Hicks, Diana, 'Structural change and industrial classification'. *Structural Change and Economic Dynamics* (Feb. 2011). At http://works.bepress.com/diana_hicks/21.

Hobsbawm, E. J., *Industry and Empire*. London: Penguin, 1969.

Hollingdale, S. H. and Tootill, G. C., *Electronic Computers*. London: Penguin, 1975.

Hunter, Robert, 'The value of iron: [from] T'ub al-Cain to today [and] tomorrow', Metal Bulletin conference, Rotterdam, 2004.

Hunter, Robert, 'Riding the super cycle on a roller coaster, or reflections on the commodities boom'. Metal Bulletin conference, Monaco, 2008.

IHS Global Insight, 'Global manufacturing output data 1980–2010, with split between different countries/regions'. Dataset.

Inaba, Seiuemon, *Walking the Narrow Path: The Fanuc Story*. Oshino: Fanuc, 1991.

Institute for Manufacturing, *Making the Right Things in the Right Places: A Structure Approach to Developing and Exploiting 'Manufacturing Footprint' Strategy*. Cambridge: University of Cambridge Institute for Manufacturing, 2007.

Institute for Manufacturing, *Understanding China's Manufacturing Value Chain: Opportunities for UK Enterprises in China*. Cambridge: University of Cambridge Institute for Manufacturing, 2008.

International Chamber of Shipping and the International Shipping Federation, 'Value of volume of world trade by sea'. At http://www.marisec.org/shippingfacts//worldtrade/index.php.

International Energy Agency, *Energy Technology Transitions for Industry: Strategies for the Next Industrial Revolution*. Paris: IEA, 2009. At http://www.iea.org/publications/free_new_Desc.asp?PUBS_ID=2104.

International Energy Agency, *C02 Emissions from Fuel Combustion, 2010 edition*. Paris: IEA, 2010.

International Energy Agency, *Key World Energy Statistics, 2010 Edition*. Paris: IEA, 2010. At http://www.iea.org/textbase/nppdf/free/2010/key_stats_2010.pdf.

International Energy Agency, *C02 Emissions from Fuel Combustion: Highlights, 2011 Edition*. Paris: IEA, 2011. At http://www.iea.org/co2highlights/co2highlights.pdf.

International Energy Agency, *Technology Roadmap, Electric and Plug-In Hybrid Electric Vehicles*. Paris: IEA, 2011.

International Energy Agency, *World Energy Statistics 2011*, Paris: IEA, 2011. At http://www.iea.org/textbase/nppdf/free/2011/key_world_energy_stats.pdf.

# BIBLIOGRAPHY

Irvine, Gregory, *Japanese Cloisonné*. London: V&A Publications, 2006.

Jackson, Sue and Bertényi, Tamás, 'Recycling of plastics.' Cambridge: MIT Institute, 2006. At http://www-g.eng.cam.ac.uk/impee/topics/RecyclePlastics/files/Recycling%20 Plastic%20v3%20PDF%20WITH%20NOTES.pdf.

Jeremy, David, *Transatlantic Industrial Revolution*. Oxford: Blackwell, 1981.

Jeremy, David, *The Transfer of International Technology*. Aldershot: Edward Elgar, 1992.

Jewkes, John, Sawers, David and Stillerman, Richard, *The Sources of Invention*. London: Macmillan, 1958.

Johnson, Chalmers, *MITI and the Japanese Miracle*. Stanford, CA: Stanford University Press, 1982.

Jones, Eric, *The Record of Global Economic Development*. Northampton, MA: Edward Elgar, 2002.

Jovanovic, Boyan and Rousseau, Peter, 'General purpose technologies.' In Philippe Aghion and Steven Durlauf (eds), *Handbook of Economic Growth*, vol. 1B. London: Elsevier, 2005.

Kaushal, Arvind, Mayor, Thomas and Riedl, Patricia, *Manufacturing's Wake-Up Call*. New York: Booz & Co., 2011. At http://www.strategy-business.com/media/file/sb64_11306. pdf.

Kenjo, T. and Nagamori, S., *Permanent-Magnet and Brushless DC Motors*. Oxford: Oxford University Press, 1985.

Kennedy, Paul, *The Rise and Fall of the Great Powers: Economic Change and Military Conflict from 1500 to 2000*. London: Fontana, 1989.

Kipling, Rudyard, 'Cold iron', *The Delineator* (Sept. 1909). Republished in Rudyard Kipling, *Rewards and Fairies*, London: Macmillan, 1910. See http://www.kipling.org.uk/rg_ coldiron1.htm; http://www.kipling.org.uk/bookmart_fra.htm.

Klemm, Friedrich, *A History of Western Technology*. London: George Allen, 1959.

Kluge, Jürgen et al., *Shrink to Grow: Lessons from Innovation and Productivity in the Electronics Industry*. London: Macmillan, 1996.

Köhler, Stefan and Otto, Anne, *The Role of New Firms for the Development of Clusters in Germany*. Saarbrücken: Institute of Employment Research, 2006. At http://www-sre. wu-wien.ac.at/ersa/ersaconfs/ersa06/papers/275.pdf.

Koopman, Robert, Wang, Zhi and Wei, Shang-jin, *How Much of Chinese Exports Is Really Made in China? Assessing Foreign and Domestic Value-Added in Gross Exports*. Office of Economics Working Paper. Washington DC: International Trade Commission, 2008. At http://www.usitc.gov/publications/332/working_papers/ec200803b_revised.pdf.

Kraemer, Kenneth, Linden, Greg and Dedrick, Jason, *Capturing Value in Global Networks: Apple's iPad and iPhone*. Irvine, CA: Personal Computing Industry Center, 2011. At http://pcic.merage.uci.edu/papers/2011/Value_iPad_iPhone.pdf.

Krausmann, Fridolin (ed.), *The Global Sociometabolic Transition: Long-Term Historical Trends and Patterns in Global Material and Energy Use*. Working Paper 131. Klagenfurt: Institute of Social Ecology, Alpen-Adria University, 2011.

Krausmann, Fridolin et al., *Growth in Global Materials Use, GDP and Population during the 20th Century*. Klagenfurt: Institute of Social Ecology, Alpen-Adria University, 2009. Also in *Ecological Economics* 68:10 (2009): 2696–705.doi:10.1016/j.ecolecon.2009.05.007. At http://www.uni-klu.ac.at/socec/downloads/2009_KrausmannGingrichEisenmenger_ Growth_in_global_materials_use_EE68_8.pdf.

Krentzman, Jackie, 'The force behind the Nike empire', *Stanford Magazine* (Jan.–Feb. 1997). At http://www.stanfordalumni.org/news/magazine/1997/janfeb/articles/knight. html.

Kronseder, Hermann, *My Life*. Neutrabling, Bavaria: Krones, 1993.

Kuba, Yasunori, *Master of Manufacturing Technology: The 70-Year History of Mazak*. Tokyo: ND Publications, 2009.

Kynge, James, *China Shakes the World*. London: Weidenfeld & Nicolson, 2006.

Landels, J. G., *Engineering in the Ancient World*. London: Constable, 2000.

Landes, David, *The Unbound Prometheus: Technical Change and Industrial Development in Western Europe from 1750 to the Present*. Cambridge: Cambridge University Press, 1969.

Landes, David, *The Wealth and Poverty of Nations: Why Are Some So Rich and Others So Poor?* London: Little, Brown, 1998.

Landes, David, *Revolution in Time: Clocks and the Making of the Modern World*. Cambridge, MA: Harvard University Press, 2000.

Layton, Christopher, *European Advanced Technology: A Programme for Integration*. London: George Allen & Unwin, 1969.

Leadbeater, Charles, *Living on Thin Air: The New Economy*. London: Viking, 1999.

Lebergott, Stanley, 'Labor force and employment'. In Dorothy Brady, *Output, Employment, and Productivity in the United States after 1800*. Cambridge, MA: National Bureau of Economic Research, 1966. At www.nber.org/chapters/c1567.pdf.

Leggett, Jeremy (ed.), *The Solar Century: The Past, Present and World-Changing Future of Solar Energy*. London: Profile, 2009.

Lenoir, Tim and Giannella, Eric, 'The emergence and diffusion of DNA microarray technology'. *Journal of Biomedical Discovery and Collaboration* 1:11 (2006). doi:10.1186/1747-5333-1-11. At http://j-biomed-discovery.com/content/1/1/11.

Leopold, Aldo, 'Game and wild life conservation'. *Condor* 34:2 (1932): 103–6. Quoted at http://www.botanicalgardening.com/globalwarming.html.

Levinson, Marc, *The Box: How the Shipping Container Made the World Smaller and the World Economy Bigger*. Princeton, NJ: Princeton University Press, 2006.

Levinson, Marc, 'Hollowing Out' in US Manufacturing: Analysis and Issues for Congress. Washington DC: Congressional Research Service, 2011. At http://forbes.house.gov/ UploadedFiles/CRS_-_Hollowing_Out_in_U_S__Manufacturing.pdf.

Levinson, Marc, *Job Creation in the Manufacturing Revival*. Washington DC: Congressional Research Service, 2011. At http://www.fas.org/sgp/crs/misc/R41898.pdf.

Liker, Jeffrey, *The Toyota Way*. New York: McGraw-Hill, 2004.

Linden, Greg, Dedrick, Jason and Kraemer, Kenneth, *Innovation and Job Creation in a Global Economy: The Case of Apple's iPod*. Irvine, CA: Personal Computing Industry Center, 2009. At http://pcic.merage.uci.edu/papers/2009/InnovationAndJobCreation.pdf.

Linden, Greg, Kraemer, Kenneth and Dedrick, Jason, 'Who captures value in a global innovation network? The case of Apple's iPod'. *Communications of the ACM* (Association of Computing Machinery) 52:3 (Mar. 2009). At http://pcic.merage.uci.edu/papers/2008/ WhoCapturesValue.pdf.

Linden, Greg, Kraemer, Kenneth and Dedrick, Jason, 'Who Captures Value in the Apple iPad?' Unpublished working paper, 2011.

Lindsay, Craig, *A Century of Labour Market Change: 1900–2000*. London: Office of National Statistics, 2003.

Lipsey, Richard, Carlaw, Kenneth and Bekar, Clifford, *Economic Transformations: General Purpose Technologies and Long Term Economic Growth*. Oxford: Oxford University Press, 2005.

Lipson, E., *The History of the Woollen and Worsted Industries*. London: Cass, 1965.

Lovins, Amory et al., *Small Is Profitable: The Hidden Economic Benefits of Making Electrical Resources the Right Size*. Snowmass, CO: Rocky Mountain Institute, 2002. At http://www. smallisprofitable.org/ReadTheBook.html.

Lovins, L. Hunter, 'Rethinking production'. In *State of The World: Innovations for a Sustainable Economy*, Washington DC: Worldwatch Institute, 2008.

Macadam, Alta (ed.), *Blue Guide: Venice*. London: Ernest Benn, 1980.

Macaulay, David, *The New Way Things Work*. London: Dorling Kindersley, 1998.

Mackintosh, Ian, *Sunrise Europe: The Dynamics of Information Technology*. Oxford: Blackwell, 1986.

McNeil, Ian (ed.), *An Encyclopedia of the History of Technology*. London: Routledge, 1990.

Maddison, Angus, *Monitoring the World Economy, 1820–1992*. Paris: OECD, 1995.

Maddison, Angus, *Chinese Economic Performance in the Long Run*. Paris: OECD, 1998.

Maddison, Angus, *The World Economy: A Millennial Perspective*. Paris: OECD, 2001.

Maddison, Angus, *The World Economy: Historical Statistics*. Paris: OECD, 2003.

Mandelson, Peter, 'A new industrial activism'. Speech to Royal Society for the Encouragement of Arts, Manufactures and Commerce, London, 17 Dec. 2008. At http://webarchive.nationalarchives.gov.uk/+/http://www.berr.gov.uk/aboutus/ministerialteam/Speeches/page49416.html.

Marsden, Ben, *Watt's Perfect Engine*. Cambridge: Icon, 2002.

Marsh, Peter, *The Silicon Chip Book*. London: Abacus, 1981.

Marsh, Peter, *The Robot Age*. London: Abacus, 1982.

Mass, William and Robertson, Andrew, 'From textiles to automobiles: mechanical and organizational innovation in the Toyoda enterprises, 1895–1933' (1996 Newcomen Prize essay). *Business and Economic History* 25:2 (Winter 1996).

Matos, Grecia and Wagner, Lorie, *Consumption of Materials in the United States, 1900–1995*. Washington DC: US Geological Survey, 1998. At http://pubs.usgs.gov/annrev/ar-23-107/aerdocnew.pdf.

Matthews, Emily et al., *The Weight of Nations: Material Outflows from Industrial Economies*. Washington DC: World Resources Institute, 2000.

Matthias, Peter, *The First Industrial Nation: The Economic History of Britain 1700–1914*. London: Routledge, 1983.

Maurer, Andreas, *Trade in Value-Added: Methodologies and Experiences*. Presented at Revisiting Trade in a Globalized World conference, Chengdu, China, Oct. 2011. At http://www.wto.org/english/res_e/statis_e/miwi_e/maurer_chengdu_oct11.pdf.

Maynard, Andrew, 'Synthetic biology and nanotechnology', 26 Jan. 2008. At http://2020science.org/2008/01/26/synthetic-biology-and-nanotechnology/#ixzz1fjjTkOhd.

Mazzolari, Federico, 'Endless strip production'. Paper delivered at World Steel Association conference, Tokyo, 2010.

Meadows, Dennis, 'Perspectives on *Limits to Growth*: 37 years later'. World Resources Forum, Davos, 2009. At http://www.worldresourcesforum.org/files/meadows1.pdf.

Miller, Dane, 'Influence of patients on implant performance'. Biomet, Warsaw, IN, 2007.

Mitchell, James, The Bessemer Centenary Lecture, delivered at the Royal Institution, London, May 1956. At http://www.banklands.com/Sir Henry Bessemer.htm.

Mitchell, James (ed.), *The Illustrated Reference Book of Man and Machines*. Leicester: Windward, 1982.

Mitchell, William Norman (ed.), *The Marvels of Modern Industry: The Story of the Machine Age*. Chicago: University of Knowledge, 1940.

Mokyr, Joel, *The Lever of Riches*. Oxford: Oxford University Press, 1990.

Mokyr, Joel, *Twenty-Five Centuries of Technological Change: An Historical Survey*. London: Routledge, 2001.

Mokyr, Joel, *The Enlightened Economy: An Economic History of Britain 1700–1850*. New Haven, CT: Yale University Press, 2009.

Moore, James, *Capital Goods: The Supply-Side Revolution*. London: Redburn Partners, 2010.

Morrison, Wayne, *China–US Trade Issues*. Washington DC: Congressional Research Service, 2011. At http://www.fas.org/sgp/crs/row/RL33536.pdf.

Mumford, Lewis, *Technics and Civilisation*. London: Routledge & Kegan Paul, 1934.

Musson, A. E., *The Growth of British Industry*. London: Batsford, 1978.

Nadvi, Khalid and Halder, Gerhard, *Local Clusters in Global Value Chains: Exploring Dynamic Linkages between Germany and Pakistan*. Brighton: Institute of Development Studies, University of Sussex, 2002. At http://www.ids.ac.uk/files/Wp152.pdf.

National Council for Advanced Manufacturing, *Making Manufacturing a National Priority*. Washington DC: National Council for Advanced Manufacturing, 2007.

# BIBLIOGRAPHY

National Research Council, *A New Biology for the 21st Century*. Washington DC: National Academies Press, 2009. At http://www.nap.edu/openbook.php?record_id=12764&page=R1.

National Science Foundation, *Asia's Rising Science and Technology Strength: Comparative Indicators for Asia, the European Union, and the United States*. Washington DC: National Science Foundation, 2007. At http://www.nsf.gov/statistics/nsf07319/.

National Science Foundation, *Science and Engineering Indicators: 2010*. At www.nsf.gov/statistics/seind10/.

Netherlands Environmental Assessment Agency, *Long-Term Trend in Global CO2 Emissions; 2011 Report*. The Hague: Netherlands Environmental Assessment Agency, 2011. At http://www.pbl.nl/en/publications/2011/long-term-trend-in-global-co2-emissions-2011-report.

Nolde, Gilbert (ed.), *All in a Day's Work: Seventy-Five Years of Caterpillar*. Peoria, IL: Caterpillar, 2000.

Nordmann, Alfred (rapporteur), *Converging Technologies – Shaping the Future of European Societies*. Brussels: European Commission, 2004. At http://ec.europa.eu/research/conferences/2004/ntw/pdf/final_report_en.pdf.

Norrman, Vera and Garneau, Mary Beth, 'ISIC 46 (rev 4): wholesale trade and commission trade, except of motor vehicles and motorcycles'. Sector paper, 24th Voorburg Group Meeting, Vienna, 2010. At http://voorburggroup.org/Documents/2010%20Vienna/Papers/2010%20-%2071.pdf.

Oliver, John, *History of American Technology*. New York: Ronald Press, 1956.

Open University, 'Energy resources: an introduction to energy resources'. At http://openlearn.open.ac.uk/mod/oucontent/view.php?id=399545&section=1.

Owen, Geoffrey, *From Empire to Europe: The Decline and Revival of British Industry since the Second World War*. London: HarperCollins, 1999.

Owen, Geoffrey, *The Rise and Fall of Great Companies: Courtaulds and the Reshaping of the Man-Made Fibres Industry*. Oxford: Oxford University Press, 2010.

Parsons, Charles, *The Steam Turbine*. The Rede Lecture, 1911. Cambridge: Cambridge University Press, 1911. At http://www.history.rochester.edu/steam/parsons/index.html.

Patton, John, 'A historical perspective on convergence technology'. *Nature Biotechnology* 24(2006): 280–1. doi:10.1038/nbt0306-280. At http://www.nature.com/nbt/journal/v24/n3/full/nbt0306-280.html.

Pisano, Gary and Hayes, Robert (eds), *Manufacturing Renaissance*. Boston: Harvard Business Review (book), 1995.

Pollard, Duncan (gen. ed.), *Living Planet Report 2010: Biodiversity, Biocapacity and Development*. Gland, Switzerland: World Wildlife Fund International, 2010.http://wwf.panda.org/about_our_earth/all_publications/living_planet_report/.

Porter, Michael, 'Clusters and the new economics of competition'. *Harvard Business Review* 76:6 (Nov.–Dec. 1998): 77. At http://hbr.org/1998/11/clusters-and-the-new-economics-of-competition/ar/1.

Porter, Michael, *The Competitive Advantage of Nations*. London: Macmillan, 1998.

Porter, Michael, 'Location, competition, and economic development: local clusters in a global economy'. *Economic Development Quarterly* 14:1 (Feb. 2000): 15–34. At http://edq.sagepub.com/content/14/1/15.full.pdf+html.

Price, Richard (ed.), *The Corning Museum of Glass: A Guide to the Collections*. Corning, NY: Corning Museum of Glass, 2001.

Rada, J., *The Impact of Microelectronics*. Geneva: International Labour Office, 1980.

Ramsden, Jeremy, 'What is nanotechnology?' *Nanotechnology Perceptions* 1 (2005): 3–17. At http://pages.unibas.ch/colbas/ntp/N03RA05.pdf.

Reid, T. R., *Microchip: The Story of a Revolution and the Men Who Made It*. London: Pan, 1985.

Reutter, Mark, *Making Steel: Sparrows Point and the Rise and Ruin of American Industrial Might*. Champaign: University of Illinois Press, 2005.

Robb, Drew, 'Combined cycle gas turbines: breaking the 60 per cent efficiency barrier'. *Power Engineering International* (1 Mar. 2010). At http://www.powerengineeringint. com/articles/print/volume-18/issue-3/features/ccgt-breaking-the-60-per-cent-efficiency-barrier.html.

Roberts, Tony, 'The carbon fibre industry worldwide 2011–2020: an evaluation of current markets and future supply and demand'. At http://www.caroledesign.co.uk/nick/ New%20files/Carbon_Fibre_2011-2020.pdf.

Robins, Ralph, 'Striving for perfection'. Rolls-Royce Centenary Lecture. Rolls-Royce, Derby, 2005. At http://www.rolls-royce.com/Images/rrlecture_tcm92-5494.pdf.

Roco, Mikhail, 'Nanotechnology research directions for societal needs in 2020'. Paper, 1 Dec. 2010. At http://www.nanotechproject.org/process/assets/files/8350/roco_ presentation.pdf.

Roco, Mihail and Bainbridge, William Sims (eds), *Converging Technologies for Improving Human Performance: Nanotechnology, Biotechnology, Information Technology and Cognitive Science*. Dordrecht: Kluwer Academic, 2003. At http://www.wtec.org/ ConvergingTechnologies/Report/NBIC_report.pdf.

Roco, Mikhail, Mirkin, Chad and Hersam, Mark, *Nanotechnology Research Directions for Societal Needs in 2020*. Berlin: Springer, 2010. At http://www.wtec.org/nano2/ Nanotechnology_Research_Directions_to_2020.

Rodemeyer, Michael, *New Life, Old Bottles: Regulating First-Generation Products of Synthetic Biology*. Washington DC: Woodrow Wilson International Center for Scholars, 2009. At http://www.synbioproject.org/library/publications/archive/synbio2/.

Rodengen, Jeffrey, *The Legend of Nucor Corporation*. Fort Lauderdale: Write Stuff Enterprises, 1995.

Rogich, Donald and Matos, Grecia, *The Global Flows of Metals and Minerals*. Washington DC: US Geological Survey, 2008. At http://pubs.usgs.gov/of/2008/1355/.

Rogich, Donald, Amy, Cassara, Iddo, Wernick and Marta, Miranda, *Material Flows in the United States: A Physical Accounting of the US Industrial Economy*. Washington DC: World Resources Institute, 2008.

Rosenberg, Nathan, *Perspectives on Technology*, Cambridge: Cambridge University Press, 1976.

Rosenberg, Nathan and Birdzel, L. E., *How The West Grew Rich: The Economic Transformation of the Industrial World*. London: Taurus, 1986.

Rosenfeld, Stuart, *Creating Smart Systems: A Guide to Cluster Strategies in Less Favoured Regions*. Carrboro, NC: Regional Technology Strategies, 2002.

Rosenfeld, Stuart, *A Governor's Guide to Cluster-Based Economic Development*. Washington DC: National Governors Association, 2002. At http://hdrnet.org/298/1/AM02CLUSTER. pdf.

Royal Society, *Knowledge, Networks and Nations: Global Scientific Collaboration in the 21st Century*. London: Royal Society, 2011.

Ruskin, John, *Unto This Last: Four Essays on the First Principles of Political Economy*. First published 1862. Charlottesville: University of Virginia Library Electronic Text Center, 2001. At http://etext.virginia.edu/etcbin/toccer-new2?id=RusLast.xml&images=images/ modeng&data=/texts/english/modeng/parsed&tag=public&part=all.

Ruttan, Vernon, *The Role of the Public Sector in Technology Development: Generalizations from General-Purpose Technologies*. Cambridge, MA: Center for International Development, Harvard University, 2001. At www.cid.harvard.edu/archive/biotech/ papers/discussion11_ruttan.pdf.

Saxenian, AnnaLee, *Regional Advantage: Culture and Competition in Silicon Valley and Route 128*. Cambridge, MA: Harvard University Press, 1996.

Schieber, Jürgen, 'Earth: our habitable planet'. Chapters for geology course, Indiana University, 2007. At http://www.indiana.edu/~geol105/.

# BIBLIOGRAPHY

Schmidt-Bleek, Friedrich, *The Fossil Makers*, trans. Reuben Deumling. Carnoules, Provence: Factor 10 Institute, 1993. At http://www.factor10-institute.org/files/the_fossil_makers/FossilMakers_Intro.pdf.

Schmitz, Hubert (ed.), *Local Enterprises in the Global Economy: Issues of Governance and Upgrading*. Northampton, MA: Edward Elgar, 2004.

Schonberger, Richard, *World Class Manufacturing: The Next Decade*, New York: Simon & Schuster, 1996.

Schott, Peter, *The Relative Sophistication of Chinese Exports*. National Bureau of Economic Research Working Paper w12173, 2006. (Alsoin *Economic Policy* (Jan. 2008).) At http://ssrn.com/abstract=897027.

Schumacher, E. F., *Small is Beautiful: A Study of Economics As Though People Mattered*. London: Vintage, 1993.

Schwartz, Peter, Leyden, Peter and Hyatt, Joel, *The Long Boom*. London: Orion, 2000.

Science and Technology Policy Research and Information Centre, *Taiwan Research Report 2010*. Taipei: STPI, 2010. At www.stpi.narl.org.tw/STPI/English/images/Taiwan%20Research%20Report.pdf.

*Scientific American*, 237:3 (1977). *Microelectronics* issue, with introduction by Robert Noyce.

Scott, Robert, *Unfair China Trade Costs Local Jobs*. Briefing paper. Washington DC: Economic Policy Institute, 2010. At http://www.americanmanufacturing.org/files/91b2eeeffce66c1a10_v5m6beqhi.pdf.

Segal Quince Wicksteed, *The Cambridge Phenomenon: The Growth of High Technology Industry in a University Town*. Cambridge: Segal Quince Wicksteed, 1985.

Servan-Schreiber, Jean-Jacques, *The American Challenge*. New York: Avon, 1969.

Servan-Schreiber, Jean-Jacques, *The World Challenge*. London: Collins, 1981.

Shaw-Taylor, Leigh, 'The occupational structure of England and Wales, c.1750–1911'. Draft research paper prepared for the INCHOS workshop, Cambridge, 29–31 July 2009. At www.geog.cam.ac.uk/research/projects/occupations/britain19c/papers/paper5.pdf.

Shaw-Taylor, Leigh et al., *The Creation of a 'Census' of Adult Male Employment for England and Wales for 1817*. Research paper, Cambridge Group for the History of Population and Social Structure, University of Cambridge, 2010. At www.geog.cam.ac.uk/research/projects/occupations/britain19c/papers/paper2.pdf.

Shaw-Taylor, Leigh et al., 'The occupational structure of England c. 1710 to c. 1871'. Work in progress, 2010. At www.geog.cam.ac.uk/research/projects/occupations/britain19c/papers/paper3.pdf.

Shell, *Technology Futures*. London: Shell, 2004.

Shell, *Shell Energy Scenarios to 2050*. The Hague: Shell, 2008. At http://www.shell.com/home/content/aboutshell/our_strategy/shell_global_scenarios/shell_energy_scenarios_2050/.

Shelton, R. D. and Foland, P. *The Race for World Leadership of Science and Technology: Status and Forecasts*. Paper at Conference on Scientometrics and Informetrics, Rio de Janeiro, 2009. At http://itri2.org/Rpaper/.

Sherwood Taylor, F., *A History of Industrial Chemistry*. London: Heinemann, 1957.

Siemens, 'Materials for the environment – world's largest gas turbine'. 2007. At http://www.siemens.com/innovation/en/publikationen/publications_pof/pof_fall_2007/materials_for_the_environment/world_s_largest_gas_turbine.htm.

Simon, Hermann, *Hidden Champions: Lessons from 500 of the World's Best Unknown Companies*. Boston: Harvard Business School Press, 1996.

Simon, Hermann, *Hidden Champions of the 21st Century: Success Strategies of Unknown World Market Leaders*. New York: Springer, 2009.

Siopack, Jorge and Jergesen, Harry, 'Total hip arthroplasty', *Western Journal of Medicine* 162 (1995): 243–9. At http://www.ncbi.nlm.nih.gov/pmc/articles/PMC1022709/pdf/westjmed00055-0049.pdf.

Sirkin, Harold, Zinser, Michael and Hohner, Douglas, *Made in America, Again: Why Manufacturing Will Return to the US*. Chicago: Boston Consulting Group, 2011. At http://www.bcg.com/documents/file84471.pdf.

Sleigh, Jonathan, Boatwright, Brian, Irwin, Peter and Stanyon, Roger, *The Manpower Implications of Microelectronic Technology*. London: HMSO, 1979.

Smiles, Samuel. *Industrial Biography: Iron Workers and Tool Makers*. London: Murray, 1863. Website version at http://www.worldwideschool.org/library/books/hst/biography/IndustrialBiography/toc.html.

Smith, Adam, *An Inquiry into the Nature and Causes of the Wealth of Nations*. London, 1776. Website versions at http://www.ebbemunk.dk/smith/toc2.html; http://www.econlib.org/library/Smith/smWN.html.

Sparrow, Norbert, 'Microtechnology in healthcare: Franche Comté is ready for its close up'. *European Medical Device Manufacturer* (1 Sept. 2006). At http://www.emdt.co.uk/article/microtechnology-healthcare-franche-comteacute-ready-its-close.

Spitz, Peter, *Petrochemicals: The Rise of an Industry*. New York: John Wiley, 1988.

Stahel, Walter and Reday-Mulvey, Genevieve, *Jobs for Tomorrow, the Potential for Substituting Manpower for Energy*. New York: Vantage Press, 1981.

Steinbock, Dan, *The Nokia Revolution: The Story of an Extraordinary Company That Transformed an Industry*. New York: Amacom, 1988.

Stern, Nicholas, *Stern Review on the Economics of Climate Change*. London: HM Treasury, 2006. At http://webarchive.nationalarchives.gov.uk/+/http:/www.hm-treasury.gov.uk/sternreview_index.htm.

Strix, *Strix Group: The First Fifty Years*. Isle of Man: Strix, 2001.

Stryker, *Fact Book, 2010–2011*. Kalamazoo, MI: Stryker, 2011. At http://phx.corporate-ir.net/External.File?item=UGFyZW50SUQ9NDE4MjY4fENoaWxkSUQ9NDQ2MzAyfF R5cGU9MQ==&t=1.

Sul, Donald, *Made in China*. Boston: Harvard Business School Press, 2005.

Sullivan, Daniel, Sznopek, John and Wagner, Lorie, *20th Century US Mineral Prices Decline in Constant Dollars*. US Geological Survey Open-File Report 00-389, 2000. At http://pubs.usgs.gov/of/2000/of00-389/.

Surgical Mechanics' Guild, Baden-Württemberg, '18th century beginnings of surgical mechanics'. At http://www.chirurgiemechanik.de/En/History/index.asp?A_highmain=2&A_highsub=0&A_highsubsub=0.

Szirmai, Adam, 'Industrialisation as an engine of growth in developing countries, 1995–2005'. Paper for publication in *Structural Change and Economic Dynamics*, 2011.

Sznopek, John L., *Drivers of US Mineral Demand*. US Geological Survey Open-File Report 2006-1025, 2006. At http://pubs.usgs.gov/of/2006/1025/2006-1025.pdf.

Tanford, Charles and Reynolds, Jacqueline, *Nature's Robots: A History of Proteins*. Oxford: Oxford University Press, 2003.

Thompson, E. P., *The Making of the English Working Class*. London: Penguin, 1968.

Thomson, George, *The Foreseeable Future*. Cambridge: Cambridge University Press, 1957.

Toffler, Alvin, *Future Shock*. New York: Bantam, 1970

Toffler, Alvin, *The Third Wave*. London: Pan, 1981.

Toffler, Alvin, *Powershift*. New York: Bantam, 1991.

Toynbee, Arnold, *Mankind and Mother Earth*. Oxford: Oxford University Press, 1976.

Toyota, *The Toyota Production System: Leaner Manufacturing for a Greener Planet*. Tokyo: Toyota Motor Company, 1998.

Tudge, Colin, *So Shall We Reap*. London: Penguin, 2004.

UNCTAD, *Assessing the Impact of the Current Financial and Economic Crisis on Global FDI Flows*. Geneva: United Nations Conference on Trade and Development, 2009. At http://www.unctad.org/en/docs/webdiaeia20091_en.pdf.

UNCTAD, *The World Investment Report 2011*. Geneva: United Nations Conference on Trade and Development, 2011. At http://www.unctad.org/en/docs/wir2011_embargoed_en.pdf.

US Bureau of Labor Statistics, *International Comparisons of Annual Labor Force Statistics*. Washington DC: US Bureau of Labor Statistics, 2011. At http://www.bls.gov/fls/flscomparelf/lfcompendium.pdf.

US Bureau of Labor Statistics, 'International comparisons of hourly compensation costs in manufacturing, 2009'. News release, 8 Mar. 2011. At http://www.bls.gov/news.release/pdf/ichcc.pdf.

US Bureau of Labor Statistics, 'International comparisons of manufacturing productivity and unit labor cost trends, 2009'. News release, 13 Oct. 2011. At http://www.bls.gov/news.release/pdf/prod4.pdf.

US Patent and Trademark Office, *Patent Counts by Country/State and Year: Utility Patents, 1963–2010*. Alexandria, VA: US Patent and Trademark Office, 2011. At www.uspto.gov/web/offices/ac/ido/oeip/taf/cst_utl.pdf.

Usher, Abbott Payson, *A History of Medieval Inventions*. New York: Dover, 1988.

Van Assche, Ari, *What Is Behind Made in China?* Presented at Revisiting Trade in a Globalized World conference, Chengdu, China, Oct. 2011. At http://www.wto.org/english/res_e/statis_e/miwi_e/van_assche_chengdu_oct11.pdf.

Van der Linde, Claas, 'Findings from the cluster meta-study'. Institute for Strategy and Competitiveness, Harvard Business School, 2002. At http://www.isc.hbs.edu/MetaStudy2002Prz.pdf.

Venohr, Bernd, *How Germany's Mid-Sized Companies Get Ahead and Stay Ahead in the Global Economy*. 2008. At http://www.berndvenohr.de/download/vortraege/GermanMidSizedGiants_080615.pdf.

Verne, Jules, *Journey to the Centre of the Earth*. Oxford: Oxford University Press, 2008. (First published 1864.) Website version at http://www.online-literature.com/verne/journey_center_earth/.

Vogel, Ezra, *Japan as Number One*. Cambridge, MA: Harvard University Press, 1979.

von Buchstab, Viktor, 'Fifty years of CAD history'. *Design Engineering* (Oct. 2005). At http://www.bizlink.com/designengineering/oct2005/50_years_cad.pdf.

Vonnegut, Kurt, *Player Piano*. New York: Dell, 1999. First published 1952.

Wagner, Donald, 'Early iron in China, Korea, and Japan'. Paper to annual meeting, Association for Asian Studies, Los Angeles, 25–28 March 1993. At http://www.staff.hum.ku.dk/dbwagner/KoreanFe/KoreanFe.html.

Wagner, Donald, *The Traditional Chinese Iron Industry and Its Modern Fate*. Copenhagen: Nordic Institute of Asian Studies, 1997. At http://www.staff.hum.ku.dk/dbwagner/Fate/Fate.html.

Wallis, George and Whitworth, Joseph, *The American System of Manufactures*, ed. and introd. Nathan Rosenberg. Edinburgh: Edinburgh University Press, 1969. (First published 1854.)

Warnick, Iddo and Ausubel, Jesse, 'National materials flows and the environment'. *Annual Review of Energy and Environment* 20 (1995): 463–92. At http://phe.rockefeller.edu/NatMats/.

Warr, Benjamin and Ayres, Robert, *Dematerialisation vs. Growth: Is It Possible to Have Our Cake and Eat It?* Working paper, Centre for the Management of Environmental and Social Responsibility, INSEAD, Fontainebleau, 2004. At http://www.insead.edu/facultyresearch/research/doc.cfm?did=1340.

Warr, Benjamin and Ayres, Robert, *Economic Growth, Technological Progress and Energy Use in the US over the Last Century*. Working paper, INSEAD Business in Society Centre, Fontainebleau, 2006. At http://www.insead.edu/facultyresearch/research/doc.cfm?did=2156.

Warren, Kenneth, *World Steel: An Economic Geography*. Newton Abbott: David & Charles, 1975.

Weston, John and Otter, N. E. (pseud.), *Otter: The First Forty Years*. Buxton: Otter Controls, 1986.

Westra, M. T., *Energy, Powering Your World*. Rijnhuizen: Institute for Plasma Physics, 2005. At http://www2.efda.org/multimedia/downloads/booklets_and_articles/EPYW_english.pdf.

White, Lynn, *Medieval Religion and Technology*. Berkeley: University of California Press, 1978.

Wickett, Justin, 'Coal in human history'. 2008. At http://www.duke.edu/~jyw2/Coal_in_Human_History.pdf.

Wicksteed, Bill (principal author), *The Cambridge Phenomenon Revisited: Parts One and Two*. Cambridge: Segal Quince Wicksteed, 2000.

Wiener, Martin, *English Culture and the Decline of Industrial Spirit, 1850–1980*. Cambridge: Cambridge University Press, 1981.

Wilburn, David, Goonan, Thomas and Bleiwas, Donald, *Technological Advancement: A Factor in Increasing Resource Use*. US Geological Survey Open-File Report 01-197, 2001. At http://pubs.usgs.gov/of/2001/of01-197/.

William, Trevor (ed.), *A History of Technology*, vol. 6: *The Twentieth Century, Part 1*. Oxford: Oxford University Press, 1978.

Willman, John, *Innovation and Industry: A Manifesto for Manufacturing*. London: Policy Exchange, 2010.

Woetzel, Jonathan, *Capitalist China: Strategies for a Revolutionized Economy*. Hoboken, NJ: John Wiley, 2003.

Womack, James and Jones, Daniel, *Lean Thinking*. New York: Simon & Schuster, 1996.

Womack, James, Jones, Daniel and Roos, Daniel, *The Machine That Changed the World*. New York: Simon & Schuster, 1990.

Wordsworth, William, *The Complete Poetical Works*. London: Macmillan, 1888. Website version of *The Excursion*, Book 8, at http://www.bartleby.com/145/ww405.html.

World Bank and International Bank for Reconstruction and Development, *World Investment and Political Risk, 2010*. Washington DC: World Bank, 2011. At http://www.miga.org/documents/WIPR10ebook.pdf.

World Business Council for Sustainable Development, *Sustainable Consumption Facts and Trends: From a Business Perspective*. Geneva: WBCSD, 2008. At http://www.wbcsd.org/pages/edocument/edocumentdetails.aspx?id=142&nosearchcontextkey=true.

World Steel Association, 'Fact sheet: raw materials'. World Steel Association, Brussels, 2011. At http://www.worldsteel.org/publications/fact-sheets.html.

World Steel Association, 'Fact sheet: the three Rs of sustainable steel (reduce, reuse and recycle)'. World Steel Association, Brussels, 2011. At http://www.steel.org/en/Sustainability/~/media/Files/SMDI/Sustainability/3rs.ashx.

World Trade Organization, 'Appendix tables'. In *International Trade Statistics 2010*. Geneva: WTO, 2010. At http://www.wto.org/english/res_e/statis_e/its2010_e/its10_appendix_e.htm.

World Trade Organization, *International Trade Statistics 2010*. At http://www.wto.org/english/res_e/statis_e/its2010_e/its10_toc_e.htm.

World Trade Organization, 'Table A1: World merchandise exports, production and gross domestic product, 1950–2010'. In 'Appendix: historical tables', in *International Trade Statistics 2011*. At http://www.wto.org/english/res_e/statis_e/its2011_e/its11_appendix_e.pdf.

Xing, Yuqing and Detert, Neal, *How the iPhone Widens the United States Trade Deficit with the People's Republic of China*. ADBI Working Paper 257. Tokyo: Asian Development Bank Institute, 2010. At http://www.adbi.org/files/2010.12.14.wp257.iphone.widens.us.trade.deficit.prc.pdf.

Yelle, Louis, 'Adding life cycles to learning curves'. *Long Range Planning* 16:6 (Dec. 1983).

Yue, Pan and Evenett, Simon, *Moving Up the Value Chain: Upgrading China's Manufacturing Sector*. Winnipeg: International Institute for Sustainable Development, 2010. At www.iisd.org/pdf/2010/sts_3_moving_up_the_value_chain.pdf.

Yuskavage, Robert and Ribarsky, Jennifer, 'Global manufacturing and measurement issues raised by the iPhone'. Powerpoint presentation, Bureau of Economic Affairs, Washington DC, 2011. At www.bea.gov/about/ppt/1_Global%20Manufacturing.ppt.

Zeng, Ming and Williamson, Peter. *Dragons at Your Door: How Chinese Cost Innovation Is Disrupting Global Competition.* Boston: Harvard Business School Press, 2007.

Ziman, John (ed.), *Technological Innovation as an Evolutionary Process.* Cambridge: Cambridge University Press, 2000.

Zink, John, 'Steam turbines power an industry: a condensed history of steam turbines'. *Power Engineering* (1 Aug. 1996). At http://www.power-eng.com/articles/print/volume-100/issue-8/features/steam-turbines-power-an-industry.html.

# Index

Note: Page numbers in **bold** refer to Figures